GREATER

NOWHERES

◆   ◆   ◆

GREATER
NOWHERES

◆　　◆　　◆

Dave Finkelstein
and
Jack London

◆　◆　◆

THE LYONS PRESS
Guilford, Connecticut

An imprint of The Globe Pequot Press

First Lyons Press edition, 2005

Copyright © 1988 by David Finkelstein and John L. London
Foreword copyright © 1988 by Philip Caputo
Maps and illustrations copyright © 1987 by Helen L. Burton
Introduction © 2004 by David Finkelstein

First Fireside edition, 1990

Designed by Caroline Cunningham

The Lyons Press is an imprint of The Globe Pequot Press

10 9 8 7 6 5 4 3 2 1

Printed in the United States of America

ISBN 1-59228-396-9

Library of Congress Cataloging-in-Publication Data is available on file.

Grateful acknowledgment is made for permission to reprint excerpts from:

"Honolulu" by William Somerset Maugham. Copyright 1921 by William Somerset
Maugham. From the book *The Trembling of a Leaf.* Reprinted by permission of
Doubleday, a division of Bantam, Doubleday, Dell Publishing Group, Inc.

A Town Like Alice by Nevil Shute. Copyright © 1950 by Nevil Shute. Reprinted by
permission of William Morrow & Co, Inc.

Kangaroo by D. H. Lawrence. Copyright © 1923 by Thomas Seltzer Inc. Copyright
renewed 1950 by Frieda Lawrence. All rights reserved. Reprinted by permission of
Viking Penguin Inc.

"Sunday Morning" from *The Collected Poems of Wallace Stevens*, by Wallace
Stevens. Copyright © 1923 and renewed 1951 by Wallace Stevens. Reprinted by
permission of Alfred A. Knopf, Inc.

"Aborigines" by Shiva Naipaul. Originally published in *The New Republic*, 1985.
Reprinted by permission.

To my mother, and Evelyn, without whose support and encouragement this book would not have been written (Dave)

For my wife, Elaine, and my daughters, Mary, Stephanie, and Janine (Jack)

The wise traveller travels only in imagination
. . . Those are the best journeys, the journeys
that you take at your own fireside, for then you
lose none of your illusions.

W. Somerset Maugham
(Jack's epigraph)

And this brings me to what I wanted to tell you
when I started this letter, Noel, and I hope it
won't be too much of a shock. I'm going on to
Australia from here.

Don't think me absolutely crazy for doing
this.

Nevil Shute
(Dave's epigraph)

Contents

Acknowledgments
(and Absolutions)

Anthony Burgess has observed that book writing "engenders tobacco-addiction, an over-reliance on caffeine and dexedrine, piles, dyspepsia, chronic anxiety, [and] sexual impotence." If the two of us have been spared these afflictions, we owe it to the many friends who saw us through the project, easing the way with encouragement, advice, and often material assistance.

Gary Soucie and Marty Hill at *Audubon* magazine bear full responsibility for having sent us out into the Australian bush in the first place, while Ken Danforth at *National Geographic* was guilty of having initially planted the idea of a book in our unreceptive minds. Jeanne Drewsen, a literary agent who professed to be our friend even as she sought to cast us in the role of authors, single-handedly molded the idea into a project. Now that the book is done, we forgive them all, as we also forgive Peter Friedman for having first suggested, some twenty-five years ago, that we take up writing as a way of life.

Chris O'Hanlon, however, deserves our unequivocal gratitude, for he tried to discourage us from the very outset. A brilliant young Australian writer we met in Sydney before embarking on our journey into the bush, Chris later consented to read through a draft of this work (when he might have been doing his own) and offered many invaluable suggestions. Novelist Lee Tulloch and photographer Tony Amos, who befriended us in Australia (and who shortly thereafter moved to New York), have been similarly helpful in commenting on individual chapters of the book. Four other Sydneysiders, Rea Francis, Zeke Solomon, Flora Parker Bloomfield, and Professor Harry Messel, also contributed to the project by sharing with us their extensive knowledge of things Australian, though without the extraordinary efforts of Rick Kot, an editor with the touch of the alchemist, all the knowledge in the world wouldn't have been much use to us.

As for material assistance, we are indebted to Qantas Airways in general, and to Howard Goldberg and Pat Dunch, in particular, for spotting us as impecunious writers the moment we stepped through the door and for responding so generously to our needs by flying us to Sydney and several other Australian cities from which we embarked on our journey into the bush. Air Queensland's Paul Phelan and Bob Dennis took over for them in Cairns, arranging for us to travel around the Torres Strait islands on board "Air Queenie's" own flights and, in the case of some of the smaller atolls, Sunbird Air.

We are beholden to Ted Wright and Sonia Smirnow for graciously providing us "a home away from home" at the Regent Hotel in Sydney and to Neil Coulthard and Mike Meade for doing likewise at the Princes Hotel in Perth. Herschel Hurst, Mike Seale, and David Harbour of the Australian Information Service provided all sorts of vital assistance, as did Bill Baker and Peggy Bendel of the Australian Tourist Commission, Dion Bromilow and Barry Stinson of the Western Australian Tourism Commission, and Geoff Doyle of the Queensland Tourist and Travel Corporation.

Finally, we must thank the thousands upon thousands of wonderful Australians we met, in the towns as well as in the bush, who contributed to our efforts through their extraordinary warmth, humor, and openheartedness. In this book we introduce you to but a fraction of them, and only hope that it can convey some idea of the land and the great characters who live there. And though she appears only peripherally in these pages, we must single out for special thanks Dame Mary Durack, who through her person as much as through her poetically written chronicles of her country's frontier history, moved us greatly and by so doing helped us to understand the Australian bush. The eloquent granddaughter of an impoverished Irish pioneer, to us she represents the best of everything that is Australia.

Foreword

by
Philip Caputo

Reading about travel, as one of the epigraphs to this book suggests, can be preferable to traveling itself. It is often better than being there. This is especially true of adventurous travel, as opposed to touring. The armchair explorer, snug in his living room, does not have to endure the heat, cold, mud, dust, insects, fevers, and occasional dangers faced by the foolish handful who are compelled to journey to the few remote and wild places remaining on this overcrowded and overcharted planet.

For that reason, if no other, lovers of travel literature should find *Greater Nowheres* a cause for rejoicing; it is such a marvelous evocation of the Australian Outback that it will spare them the discomforts, as well as the considerable expense, of going to that desolate part of the world. Had this book existed two years ago, I might have resisted the authors' summons to join them on the last leg of their long and sometimes difficult trek. Curled up on my couch, I would not have breathed bulldust for nearly two months, nor ridden day after bone-jarring day over rocky, potholed trails that left me feeling as if I'd spent eight hours inside a cement mixer. I would have experienced, but only vicariously, the cold and fear of bathing in a tidal river while my friends kept watch on the bank for the protruding eyes of a saltwater crocodile intent on transforming me into a human Big Mac. And, speaking of eating, I would have avoided the gustatory delight of chomping into a campfire sandwich as seasoned with flies as a deli bagel is with sesame seeds. Such inconveniences and hazards are the price the adventurous traveler pays for the privilege of seeing things for himself; but when, for the price of a book, you can avoid the former while enjoying the latter, why bother?

It is not my intention to exaggerate the rigors of the trip, but the risks and difficulties of going into the Outback should not be under-estimated any more than they should be overstated. To give the American reader some idea of what the Australian interior is like, imagine the part of the United States lying between the Appalachians and the Rockies as one enormous wasteland, with hardly a distinguishing natural feature in it, and so few people that its entire population could fit into a city the size of Denver. Some corners of this vast wilderness, which covers about two-thirds of the continent's three million square miles, have yet to be properly mapped. There are few roads, most of them unpaved; great distances separate towns, cattle stations, rivers, and water holes; the temperature in the summer often exceeds 120 degrees Fahrenheit, and the terrain is so flat and undifferentiated that a ride of even two or three hundred miles can end with the traveler feeling as though he has gone in a circle. More than once, we felt our maps and compass were useless in a landscape in which where we were looked exactly like where we had been.

Exploring such a place is absolutely not an enterprise for amateurs, gifted or otherwise. Dave Finkelstein and Jack London, both seasoned travelers and experienced outdoorsmen, had gone through Western Australia on their own, though their plans for Queensland and the Northern Territory, where I joined them, were even more ambitious and daring: they were going off the track, directly into the heart of the wilderness. We did so in a four-wheel-drive landcruiser equipped with a long-range fuel tank, spare jerry cans of gasoline and water, three batteries, extra heavy-duty shock absorbers, two spare tires, spare parts, repair tools, tow cables, a chest full of rations, a compass, a CB radio, an ax, machetes, and a Winchester rifle. Yet, even when pre-pared for every imaginable contingency, going "beyond the Black Stump," as the Aussies call it, is not without its perils. Fording a river, you might be swept away by one of the ferocious flash floods common during the Wet; if you break an axle or rupture a fuel tank during the Dry, you may be faced with the prospect of waiting for someone to rescue you, or of walking a long, long way to the nearest town or cattle station. The second course is discouraged by those who know the bush; you probably will die of thirst or sunstroke, if you are not first bitten by a poisonous snake or attacked by one of the wild bulls or wild boar that roam the interior in large herds.

"Doing a perish" is the Australian phrase for dying in the Outback, to distinguish that form of demise from garden-variety deaths. While we were there, we heard several macabre tales that may have been intended to warn us. I am not sure. Although Aussies have a great sense of humor, which is as essential out there as water, they also possess a morbid streak that delights in telling stories of the grim fates the bush metes out to the unlucky or unwise. One such account was given us by the bunkhouse cook at Kilamaroe, a remote cattle station. Several years back, the cook said, the manager of a neighboring ranch, his two young sons, and a party of ringers (Australian cowboys) were bringing in a herd for branding. The manager started to ride across a river to round up some strays, but he and his horse were carried off by the current and drowned. Toward nightfall, the cowboys found his body, washed up on a bank some distance downstream. While they rode back to the station house to fetch a vehicle in which to evacuate the corpse, the sons kept vigil over it all night, lighting bonfires to keep at bay the wild boar that had caught its scent and were grunting in the scrub nearby. The image stuck in my mind. I thought of my own two boys, raised in the comforts of the American middle class, when I pictured those young men, huddled in the darkness, lighting bonfires so their dead father would not be devoured by feral pigs.

It was not the sort of picture the Australian Tourist Commission likes to paint, but *Greater Nowheres* is not about tourist Australia, its sand-girt coasts decorated with cuties in skimpy bathing suits, its bays a playground for yachtsmen and surfers. This book is a mosaic of people, some hardy pioneers, some escapists, some just plain lunatics, who have forsaken modern civilization to live in one of the most unforgiving places on earth. The aforementioned tourist Australia is the one inhabited by the overwhelming majority of the country's 16 million people. They have most of the attitudes and ambitions of their urban and suburban counterparts in the United States, but the characters in *Greater Nowheres* are unusual, if not unique. Collectively, they embody the Australian national image, or, rather, the illusion the nation likes to have of itself as a land of self-reliant frontiersmen, squinting with agate eyes into a dust-hazed sun. Americans should recognize this fantasy. The New York lawyer who wears cowboy boots to the office is mirrored by the Sydney barrister who secretly fancies himself another Crocodile Dundee, the outback movie hero portrayed by Paul Hogan (who acquired his physique in a gym, not by wrestling salties).

Reality falls short of the illusion. Where doesn't it? There are a few true-to-life Crocodile Dundees in the bush, one of whom London describes in a chapter of this book, but most of the people who live there are rather unheroic, or heroic in a way that would not look well on the screen. Most, for one thing, do not possess leading-man figures. Some Aussies did fit the image, rangy and rawhide tough, but the most common physiological trait was the beer belly. Though these men may spend weeks in the saddle, eating nothing but hardtack and beef jerky, their guts bulge because they drink colossal, indeed astronomical, amounts of beer. It quenches the thirst and, when consumed in sufficient quantities, creates a mellow alcoholic fog through which the Outback does not appear as horrible as it does when viewed with sober eyes.

To generalize a bit, outback dwellers fall into two broad categories: those who are bush-born and bush-bred, working the sheep and cattle stations pioneered by their ancestors in the last century; and those who are recent settlers, former city and townspeople seeking financial and personal independence in the wide open spaces. You will meet plenty of both in *Greater Nowheres,* and I'm confident you'll find them as fascinating and varied a lot of humanity as the writers did. The depressing uniformity in outlook and opinion that characterizes much of contemporary life, thanks in part to the homogenizing effect of modern communications, is absent in the Outback. Cruel as it is in other respects, it is congenial to the development of idiosyncrasies. There are, of course, plenty of solid, laconic cattlemen, but eccentrics, screwballs, rainbow-chasers, scammers, schemers, and dreamers also flourish in that arid emptiness. God knows, nothing else does.

This is not to say that the inhabitants don't have anything in common with one another. One refrain was heard over and over from the new settlers, whenever they were asked why they had turned their backs on civilization to subject themselves to so much hardship and loneliness. A century ago, they might have answered, "To tame the wilderness," but because conquest is no longer a moral imperative among white men, these modern frontiersmen and women responded in a less stirring fashion: "We wanted to get out of the rat race." These words were repeated so frequently that one began to wonder if they were being uttered under instructions from some mysterious higher authority, the Ministry of Motivations. At first, one can accept escape from the so-called rat race as a valid reason for living in primitive conditions, fancying the respondents as outback Thoreaus, sacrificing comfort to win self-sufficiency in their waterless Waldens. But only after probing more deeply into their backgrounds did we discover that whatever race these people had been running, they had definitely been in the rear. To be sure, there were encounters with Australian ex-Yuppies, fast rats who'd chosen to pull off the fast lane; the rest, however, had been living in the margins of Australian society. They were unskilled laborers, laid-off service industry employees, and, yes, a few people on the run from court summonses and bad debts. They were, in short, the outcasts of the postindustrial world, for whom the Outback is less a land of opportunity than it is a place of exile. They aren't looking for their main chance, but their last chance. That is in the great Australian tradition, by the way; the country was founded as a penal colony and settled by ex-convicts.

That brings me to one of the major impressions I gained from my trip into the Australian bush. I had pictured the Outback, not only as a frontier, but as one where I would find the spirit of the Old West still alive and well. There were a couple of moments when indeed I felt as if a time machine had transported me to west Texas, circa 1875, but all resemblance ended there. To an American, the word "frontier" implies a territory in transition from an unsettled to a civilized state. In that sense, the interior of Australia is not a frontier, or, to twist the idea around, it is a permanent one. Judging from the histories I've read, an Aussie from 1888 could visit the Outback of today and feel right at home. Probably, he would feel the same in 2088. Barring quantum leaps in irrigation and agricultural technology, or some dramatic climatic change, prosperous farms and bright new cities springing up in the Outback are as unimaginable as orange groves in Antarctica. The land is too severe. It resists taming, not with an active ferocity, like a jungle or mountain range, but with a supine defiance. It is, in its indifference, unappeasably hostile. If its personality could be subjected to psychoanalysis, it would have to be classified as "passive-aggressive." It merely lies there, level, monotonous, endless, its impassive face grayish-brown in color, its voice the sear wind that seems to hiss into the ear of settler or sojourner, "Submit, *submit.*"

Submission, seen in its most extreme form among the aboriginals, is the toll the Outback charges for survival. It yields little, offers nothing; and that tyrannical stinginess perhaps accounts for the inertia of many outback dwellers. The spirit of the Old West—or what I'd imagined to be the spirit of the Old West—is lacking in them. This is not to say that they are in any way dispirited or defeated; rather, they have

xvii

had to make compromises with their uncompromising environment on a scale far greater than that required of American pioneers, who, entering a rich and generous continent, could ride their westering wagons to jubilant cries of "manifest destiny!" because they knew that bountiful game, good water, and fertile soil awaited them beyond the horizon. Today's Australian pioneer may have a sense of his destiny, but it is not so manifest, for what lies beyond his horizon is more scrub, bleeding off into deserts of sand and spinifex, the deserts giving way to yet more scrub, and the scrub to desert once again.

The mere sight of that austere landscape creates a melancholy, and a sense of temporal dislocation. The Outback does not belong to the here and now. It seems, simultaneously, to be a part of the earth that has not evolved since the dawn of creation, and a prefiguration of the earth as it will be in the distant future, when the sun becomes a red giant and all the seas and rivers run dry. This atmosphere of timelessness may partially explain the aboriginal concept of "the dreamtime," a mythical state in which past, present, and future are one. It may also explain the odd lassitude that characterizes some white Australians, leading jury-rigged, improvised lives, always putting things off, contenting themselves with just scraping by. "Aw, dontchya worry, mate, she'll be right," was a phrase heard repeatedly in the bush. Sometimes it was an expression of quiet confidence, other times one of carelessness, an Anglo-Saxon version of *mañana*.

The question arises, what drove the authors, two presumably successful, middle-aged American men, to go to such an unappealing place? The authors describe their motives in the following pages. Dave Finkelstein and Jack London proved to be oddly compatible traveling companions, with London's Irish romanticism counterpointing Finkelstein's Talmudic rationalism. Together we stalked saltwater crocs with our cameras, hunted wild boar, took part in a novel cattle roundup in which helicopters replaced horses, slept under a sky bigger than the one Texans boast about, and experienced the pleasure of vagabonding with only what we could carry, and wide open country before us. I don't wish to sound as if we were seeking male-menopausal merit badges on some over-forty boy scout trek. To correct any such misimpression, there was a point when I questioned my sanity in making the trip. We were in the utterly wild Northern Territory, the outer back of the Outback, and I was lying in a swag, knocked flat by a 105-degree fever brought on by infected insect bites. The nearest town, a squalid aboriginal settlement over a hundred miles away by dirt track, had no doctor or clinic. There was half-serious talk among my companions of asking the owners of the cattle station where we were camped to radio Australia's Flying Doctor Service and have me evacuated by plane. I managed to rally and avoid that ignominy, but I think the point is clear: the Outback is not for the average tourist. If you're the sort whose idea of fun is climbing Mount Kilimanjaro or poling up the Amazon, then it is the place for you. Otherwise, stay home, pour yourself a drink, and with Dave Finkelstein and Jack London as your guides, take an imaginative journey into Australia's "greater nowheres." As I said in the beginning, it's better than being there.

Introduction to the 2005 Edition of *Greater Nowheres*

Exactly two decades have elapsed since the two middle-aged ne'er-do-wells who authored *Greater Nowheres* traveled to Australia and spent the better part of a year venturing to the farthest reaches of that country's most inhospitable wilderness areas. Ostensibly, our purpose had been to learn something about Australia's most fearsome predator, the man-eating saltwater crocodile—at the time of our trip Paul Hogan's outrageously funny movie, *Crocodile Dundee*, had yet to hit the theaters—but before long we became far more fascinated, captivated would be the more appropriate word, by the strange breed of men and women who, for whatever reason, had chosen to make their lives in such an utterly hostile environment. *Greater Nowheres* is the story of those extraordinary people.

The publication of the current edition of this book—for which the authors are indebted to the impeccable taste and (hopefully) infallible literary judgment of none other than the editorial director of The Lyons Press, Jay Cassell—has led me to wonder how the Australian Outback has changed in the past twenty years, and how the *dinki-di* Aussies who inhabit that part of the planet have fared in maintaining their much-cherished isolation against encroachments from the outside world.

Certainly, from the writer's point of view, it's hard these days to find any destination, however remote, that hasn't been inundated by an almost pestilential flood of mass tourism. "[S]olitary explorations are a thing of the vanishing past," laments novelist Nicholas Delbanco in a

xxi

recent *Harper's Magazine* article on travel writing. "Those who once were travelers are tourists now; those who set out for points un-known...have been supplanted by the gang who follows where a tour guide leads."

Since the original edition of *Greater Nowheres* appeared in 1988, I've continued to spend considerable time in Australia, but not in the bush. Of late, a favorite hang-out of mine has been Bribie Island, just a few miles north of Brisbane on the Sunshine Coast of Queensland. Bribie boasts its fair share of the wickedly venomous creatures common throughout Australia—tiger snakes, funnel-web spiders, and others too numerous to mention—and in the night mating dingoes howl like wolves at our backdoor. Still, Bribie is not the bush. On the contrary, it's a very cultured community, whose concerns, like those of the vast majority of urban-dwelling Australians, are far removed from issues confronting the Outback. For answers to my questions about what changes had occurred in the bush in the years since *Greater Nowheres* was first published, I've had to turn elsewhere.

In this regard, the Fates were kind, for just a few weeks before sitting down to write this foreword, out of the blue I received a long and newsy letter from a wonderful Aussie character who had played a prominent role in the *Greater Nowheres* narrative—John Barlow, the Bushranger (whom readers will meet in "The Gulf of Carpentaria"). A variety of jobs, ranging from horse-breaker and horse-breeder to business consultant and local government manager, had caused him to relocate so many times in the intervening years that we had lost touch with one another and not corresponded for almost a decade. Now, along with his own personal news, John's letter had this to report:

> Very little has changed in northern Australia during the twenty years since you traveled the rough bush tracks in search of the tales—both tall and true—that formed the foundation of *Greater Nowheres*. The spectacular beauty of a sunset viewed from Broome on the Kimberley Coast of Western Australia is no less spectacular today that it was back then. The Northern Territory's Top End remains much the same. Isolation still pervades the vast cattle stations of the Gulf of Carpentaria, lessened slightly, perhaps, only by the availability of more sophisticated communication systems. And Cape York Peninsula continues to display its rugged personality, albeit to an increasing number of tourists.
>
> While I myself have not returned to that part of Australia as often as I would have liked in the past couple of years, I have kept track of many

of the folks whose stories are recounted in *Greater Nowheres*. Some, like me, have left the North to take up challenges in other regions of Australia. Others will never leave—a lonely grave marker the only reminder of their passing. Those who remain, however, continue to display the adventurous, pioneering spirit that years ago opened up this rugged part of the country.

To be sure, advances in telecommunications technology have made these remote regions considerably less isolated than they were when you were here. The stockman working on a vast cattle property in Queensland's Gulf of Carpentaria or the Northern Territory can now return to the homestead at the end of a punishing day in the saddle and relax in front of the television set. The mother of a sick child on a cattle station on the Cape York Peninsula can now pick up a telephone and call a doctor at any hour. The manager of a remote grazing property in the Kimberley region of Western Australia can now access information about cattle prices or the weather by connecting his laptop computer to the Internet. Similarly, the child who once received long-distance education by using high-frequency radio to access the School of the Air now uses an interactive satellite television connection to achieve the same result.

Even the drivers of the massive, eight-trailer 'road trains,' the trucks used to deliver supplies to isolated properties and transport cattle to market, are now able to access their offices by satellite telephone. Instead of having meshwork of sealed roads and rough-as-guts bush tracks to themselves, though, they now must share them with a new wave of vehicle-borne 'adventurer,' each of who believes that he or she is blazing a new trail of discovery.

Following routes that were once merely tracks cut along the lines of least resistance through the bush, the modern-day 'adventurer' is able to access areas, which, as recently as twenty years ago when you were here, were open only to the most intrepid of travelers. Many of those bush tracks have now become sealed highways. Others, if not sealed, are nonetheless well-surfaced and well-signposted, accessible even to the increasing number of 'gray nomads'—traveling pensioners—towing a caravan behind the family sedan.

These folks know, of course, that Australia remains a relatively safe traveling environment. But as a few unfortunate ones have discovered, to their eternal dismay, northern Australia still has an abundant population of very large, very voracious saltwater crocodiles in its rivers, waterholes, and on some of its coastal beaches. And while they haven't eaten too many travelers in recent years, they have attacked enough of them to make swimming in some settings a risky, if not downright dangerous, proposition. Of course, if their campsite is on the coast, rather than beside an inland river or a billabong, there's always the deadly box jellyfish to add excitement and challenge to their travel experience— None of that has changed.

Needless to say, however, not everything is the same as it was when you were here. Many of those Nowheres covered in *Greater Nowheres* have now actually become Somewheres. Several of the remote, well-hidden campsites you used when traveling through the bush, have now become popular oases, clearly marked on colorful tourist maps. And in many spots where one was once able to establish a rough but comfortable camp beside a quiet, scenic waterhole at the end of each day, five-star resorts now provide luxury accommodations, catering to the culinary desires of the most demanding tourist.

But some Nowheres do still exist and are there to be found by any genuinely free spirit willing to hook a caravan behind his four-wheel-drive and dream, say, of finding that isolated campsite beside an as yet undiscovered waterhole teeming with huge fish, where no neighbor will object to the sound of his generator (but where, as noted, he now can also get a half-decent television signal and even be within cellphone range so he can call the grandkids back at home). Not quite the same dreams that motivated the original graziers who settled the country, or those of subsequent generations who followed in their footsteps, perhaps, but dreams nonetheless.

As for the more 'permanent residents,' many of the faces may have changed since you were here, but the strength of character of the people living and working in the bush country of northern Australia essentially remains the same. They exude the same pioneering spirit of their predecessors, and express the same high hopes as those you encountered two decades ago. They have the same sense of adventure and the same sense of humor. And last but not least, they display the same generous measure of hospitality.

So there you have it—*Greater Nowheres* lives on—not only in its literary incarnation (thanks to The Lyons Press), but in reality as well.

DAVID FINKELSTEIN
NEW YORK CITY
DECEMBER 2004

GREATER

NOWHERES

◆   ◆   ◆

1

Introduction

Daisy Bates in the Eastern Goldfields

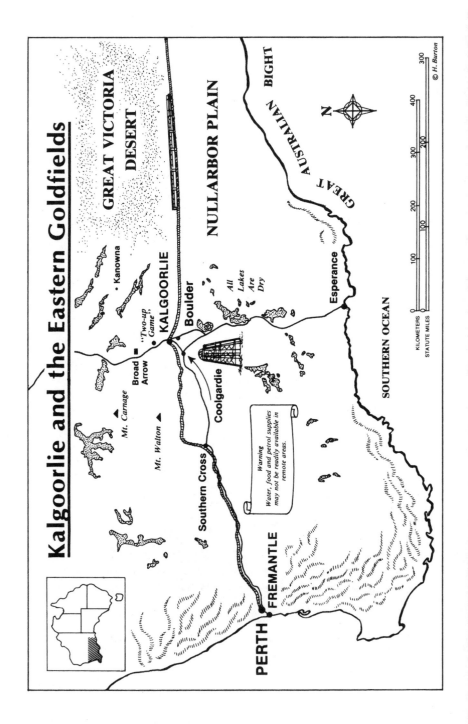

Kalgoorlie and the Eastern Goldfields

GREAT VICTORIA DESERT

NULLARBOR PLAIN

GREAT AUSTRALIAN BIGHT

• Kanowna

"Two-up Game", • Kalgoorlie

KALGOORLIE

Boulder

All Lakes Are Dry

Esperance

SOUTHERN OCEAN

Broad ■
Arrow

▲ Mt. Carnage

▲ Mt. Walton

Coolgardie

Warning
Water, food and petrol supplies may not be readily available in remote areas.

◄ Southern Cross

PERTH

FREMANTLE

N

KILOMETERS   100   200   300   400
STATUTE MILES   100   200   300

© H. Burton

1

"Passengers will please remain seated when the plane comes to a halt at the international arrivals terminal," announced the flight director of the Qantas 747 shortly after we had touched down at Sydney's Kingsford-Smith Airport and were taxiing toward the gate. "Government regulations require that all aircraft arriving from overseas be sprayed to prevent the introduction of harmful insects into Australia." Sitting in the bulkhead jumpseat with a microphone in his hand, he smiled and added amiably: "They reckon we've got enough of our own."

Through the window we could see the ground crew as they maneuvered the docking ramp into place, and when the door of the aircraft opened, two uniformed men—khaki shirts, epaulets, shorts, and white knee socks, the works—boarded the plane. Each took a position at the head of an aisle, looking very serious indeed. Jack was later to insist that, in addition to the two aerosol cans each was wielding, the officials were also outfitted in gas masks and white coveralls, but I managed to convince him that twenty-three hours in the air had left him so disoriented that he could just as likely have spotted a pair of sulphur-crested cockatoos we'd been reading about in an especially vivid article in the Qantas in-flight magazine.

But however they were dressed, there could be no disagreement that the two officials went about their business with military precision. Simultaneously raising their aerosol cans toward the ceiling, they marched down the aisles with outstretched arms, dispensing a

3

fine mist of aromatic insecticide throughout the cabin as if bestowing a benediction on arriving passengers, many of whom insisted on coughing despite the flight director's assurance that the spray consisted of pyrethrin, a nontoxic derivative of the chrysanthemum. During our short layover in Honolulu we'd been met with the traditional gift of leis, and we couldn't help but find a salvo of bug spray a bit unnerving.

"Welcome to Australia," said a smiling, suntanned hostess as we trailed the fumigators off the plane and made our way through Health Inspection to the Customs area. A number of overseas flights had arrived simultaneously, and hundreds of exhausted, luggage-laden tourists were strung out in long lines behind Immigration Control, doggedly waiting to have visas inspected and passports stamped.

We took our place behind a young couple from California, casually attired in beach sportswear and sandals, who, like most vacationers to Australia, planned to visit Sydney, Melbourne, and the Great Barrier Reef on a three-week tour. Time permitting, they also hoped to squeeze in a flight to Alice Springs, which would enable them to spend a day climbing Ayers Rock. Except for that Ayers Rock excursion, their uncomplicated itinerary held considerable appeal to me, and as the queue inched forward I began to question my judgment in having committed myself to the sort of rough-and-ready adventure that had brought Jack and me to Australia. Here I was, prepared to spend the better part of a year engaged in some romantic, hastily conceived four-wheel-drive expedition to what we'd been repeatedly warned was one of the most desolate areas on the face of the planet. Why had I done such a thing? My first impulse was to blame it all on Jack, but there was more to it than that.

Neither of us had come to Australia to fulfill anything like a heroic destiny. Jack and I were both middle-aged dropouts driven, at this point of our lives, more by fancy than by fate. I had abandoned a career, first as a lawyer, then as a China specialist for a large New York foundation. Unlike my friends, who enjoyed marriage so much they had tried it many times, I had remained single, and having been spared the necessity of paying alimony and child support, I was living a relatively carefree existence. Many people assumed I was independently wealthy (and a few even voiced the suspicion that I was working for the CIA), but in fact, I was just independently poor, and that was good enough for me.

Since leaving the foundation, where I first learned the art of spending other people's money, I had passed the time as a free-lance layabout (to borrow a phrase from Tom Stoppard), bumming around the world on one journalistic assignment or another, always in search of new vistas, new places to fish, new ways to look at life—and continually inspired by all that turned up.

Not many years before, Jack, too, had become temporarily single again. After he and his wife had divorced, he resigned his position at a small New England college, where he taught English literature, and went to work as a commercial fisherman off Montauk. One winter he drifted south, to the Florida Keys, and there he continued to support himself by fishing and then by restoring old houses.

Jack and I had met as students and now we saw each other often when he passed through New York on the way from Key West to Boston to see his daughters. (Jack's own father had abandoned his family, and Jack was determined not to do likewise.) We had a lot in common since neither of us had the slightest interest in the traditional measures of success, which prompted some of our more highly ambitious friends to regard us both as misfits in a work-oriented society. Eventually, we began to think that perhaps they were right.

Australia had the reputation of being a country full of misfits, jolly ones at that, and in the past few years Jack and I often talked about going there. An untamed land, the last frontier, people unrestrained by social conventions, and all that sort of thing. Australians may have been archconservatives politically, but the country was said to be the last place on earth where people clung to the notion that you could be an individual, do what you pleased even if it meant living to harsh excess.

That was especially true out in the bush, or so it was said. Although eighty-five percent of the population lived in Australia's coastal cities, the last place any Aussie wanted to be, the last thing he wanted to do, was to be cooped up in an office for eight hours a day, five days a week. Some people referred to Australia as "a summer camp for adults"; others regarded it as "the largest uncaged lunatic asylum in the world." It sounded like our kind of place.

Jack had yet another motive for wanting to go. As a boy of thirteen, in an attempt to run away from home, he and his friend, Joe Lee, had tried to sail from Boston to Australia in an eighteen-foot dory they had rigged as a schooner. They only got as far as Cape Cod, but that aborted voyage and the romantic visions it inspired had remained with him ever since. During the intervening thirty-odd years Jack had come to view a journey into the Australian bush as more than simply an extended trek; it had become a quest, an expedition of the spirit, which would provide him challenges he had never before confronted. One night, not long after we returned from a marlin fishing trip to Cuba, Jack called me from Florida and regaled me with promises of still greater adventure awaiting us on the frontiers of Australia. "Time is passing us by," he said. "In a couple of years we'll be hitting fifty. We better go now or we'll never get there at all."

He left the logistics to me. "You're the professional schnorrer," he said, which I interpreted to mean that he wanted to go to Australia, but only at a discount. That was understandable. Jack was a romantic. If the exigencies of the modern world necessitated flying Qantas to his Heart of Darkness, at least the tickets should be free. And as far as he was concerned, the least I could do was get them.

It was easier than I expected. A chance meeting with the editor of *Audubon* magazine provided me with the opportunity to convince that guileless man that his publication was woefully lacking in its coverage of Australian wildlife. Rising to the bait, he suggested an in-depth report on the saltwater crocodile, which was living under the shadow of some awfully bad press. The reptile had long been held responsible for "the most devastating animal attack on human beings in recorded history," an incident in which it reportedly had annihilated over a thousand Japanese infantrymen trapped by British troops in a swamp near the Bay of Bengal on a single night in 1945.

Crocodylus porosus had gained the reputation of being "the most ferocious man-eater on earth, killing approximately 2,000 people a year," and the northern part of Australia, which was the only country where the saltwater crocodile was fully protected, had become one of its last remaining habitats. So it stood to reason that most of its current victims would have to be Australians living in the bush along the northern fringes of the country. With an assignment from one prestigious magazine in our pocket, that assured at least one free ticket from the airlines.

To be on the safe side, I called an editor at *Field & Stream*, titillated him with stories about barramundi, an Australian gamefish about which I knew nothing (though I heard that it swam in crocodile-infested waters), and pulled a second assignment out of the hat. Score: two stories, two free tickets.

"We'll deal with those two duped editors later," said Jack.

He neglected to add "and one gulled government." Somewhere along the way, we had convinced the Australian Information Service that we were the ideal candidates for their journalist exchange program—they evidently hadn't realized that the other Jack London had been dead for over half a century.

We were off.

1

Everybody who goes to Australia is impressed by Sydney—affluent, cosmopolitan, glamorous Sydney. Everybody talks about the city's sun-drenched beauty, its leisurely laid-back pace. "At its most congenial, Sydney is Gauguin's Pacific, reset but not significantly corrupted by urban technology," wrote one visitor from the north. It was true. Heavy Georgian government buildings and modern skyscrapers of glass and concrete exist side by side, juxtaposed against stately Victorian and Colonial homes set dramatically on sandstone cliffs amidst lush semitropical vegetation.

Jack and I had complimentary rooms high atop the Regent Hotel (which is reputed to be the finest in the world and probably is), and from them we looked out over the fjordlike harbor all the way to the steep white bluffs of the Sydney Heads, where it funnels out into a cobalt blue Pacific Ocean. Throughout the day and into the evening the harbor teemed with a festive armada of yachts and sailboats, scudding before the wind with colorful billowing spinnakers, seemingly oblivious to the container ships, luxury liners, and gray Australian Navy warships moving in and out of the heavily trafficked port.

Off to the left was the Harbour Bridge, a half-century old landmark of British Empire. A single-arch span known as "the coathanger," it looked a lot like the Goethals Bridge (linking Staten Island to New Jersey), and Sydneysiders never tired of telling you that Paul Hogan, of *Crocodile Dundee* fame, had once worked there as a bridge painter. Off to the right was the renowned Opera House, "a sculptured cluster of spinnaker-like curves," which people considered a reflection of the Australian free spirit. If so, it was only skin deep because the stage was so small ballet dancers complained of not having enough room to maneuver on it.

We often took ferries from Circular Quay, the main wharf for Sydney's water-borne commuter traffic, to visit friends who lived in the harbor-side suburbs of Manly, Mosman, and Kirribill. From the water the city became a theatrical backdrop and the entire scene, full of vibrant light and color, gave us a powerful sense of exhilaration.

One brilliantly sunny Saturday afternoon we were invited to a public relations party celebrating the opening of the Bora Bora Club Med in Tahiti. Sydney was one continual round of parties, where business never seemed to intrude, and this particular party was held on Shark Island, a rectangular-shaped green hill in the harbor that was reached by ferry from Rose Bay. There were about 150 guests, most of whom were editors and "journos" representing virtually every newspaper and magazine in Sydney. Food and drink, especially drink, were abundant. A troupe of lithe, brown-skinned Tahitian dancers had been brought in for the show, and between numbers the women in the troupe shed one costume for another in full view of the audience, as if to deny that the missionaries had ever made an impact on Polynesian culture. But apparently this was nothing new around Sydney because no one seemed to take much notice of them.

"I want to meet the chaps who are going into the bush," said a tall blond woman, strolling over to us with a drink in her hand. She was dressed in a stylish outfit that wouldn't have been out of place in Saint-Tropez. Her name was Lee and she had just resigned as features editor of *Vogue* (Australia) to become editor-in-chief of *Harper's Bazaar* (Australia). She introduced us to her new husband, Tony, a shy young man with a boyish face and a punk hairstyle, who told us he was a model, a surf bum, and an aspiring photographer.

"No Sydneysider in his right mind would go anywhere near the bush," said Tony. "You're better off staying on the Boomerang Coast," he added, referring to that curved strip of coastline extending along the eastern seaboard, from Brisbane in the north to Adelaide in the south. "That's where everybody lives." (Approximately the size of the United States, Australia has a population of only 16 million, 14 million of whom live along the Boomerang Coast.)

"You won't find much beyond the Black Stump, mate," agreed Chris O'Hanlon, a writer friend of Lee's with shoulder-length hair and the face of an Irish pug. "It's a place where men are men and the sheep are nervous." An American publisher had once given Chris a contract to write a book about his travels by road around Australia but he had ended up giving the advance back. "It was an expensive, fruitless journey," he said. "The land was beyond comprehension."

O'Hanlon was not exaggerating, for more than any other continent in the world, excepting perhaps Antarctica, Australia is a hostile place, and not even New South Wales, its most densely populated and industrialized state, can escape the consequences. In the seaside suburbs north of Sydney, between Manly and Palm Beach, for instance, mountainous rogue waves, some over forty-five feet high, occasionally thunder in off the Pacific during a storm to sweep unsuspecting victims into the sea.

Although Sydney itself isn't subject to that sort of thing, its harbor is a spawning ground for many species of sharks. Bathers on city beaches are protected by vertical nets, which break up the sharks' preying patterns, or by nets that encircle the beach and provide a more or less sharkproof swimming area. As an added precaution, helicopters fly regular patrols over the harbor, keeping a lookout from above. When we arrived in early January, the story was going around of a dog that had slipped off the deck of a sailboat during a weekend race and had been instantly taken by a large hammerhead. We heard, too, that occasionally ocean currents would carry poisonous sea snakes, common on the Great Barrier Reef, as far south as Sydney.

And danger did not lurk only in the waters. The city itself was habitat to any number of deadly snakes and insects. On a visit to some friends at their ranch-style home in the suburb of Cremorne, we noticed posted on the door of their refrigerator a card containing two "emergency phone numbers"—one the local ambulance service, the other the Commonwealth Serum Laboratories. Above the telephone numbers was a color illustration of a large, hairy spider, its antennae outstretched and its fangs poised, and below the numbers were instructions on how to treat a bite victim while awaiting assistance.

"The Sydney funnel-web spider," it warned, "is one of the world's deadliest spiders. It is often found in swimming pools and bathtubs. Children can die within fifteen minutes of its lethal bite."

Constantly surrounded by such hazards, Sydneysiders hardly gave them a thought. With fatalistic indifference to the implacability of nature—a hallmark, perhaps, of the Australian character—our friends in Sydney viewed these perils not as something striking or dramatic, as outsiders might, but simply as part of everyday life, to be taken in stride. While they considered it foolhardy to live along the San Andreas fault—that was being ostrichlike in the face of impending but certain disaster—their own city they believed was the safest place in the world. And they roared with laughter when a visiting friend of theirs from England admitted to being so terrified by what he had heard about Sydney that, even on the twentieth floor of the Hilton, he checked under his bed every night for snakes.

We, at least, were sophisticated enough to know that there were no snakes at the Regent, but we still took a good look around before jumping into the pool at our friends' house in Cremorne. And for good reason—they had discovered a funnel-web spider there only the day before. Sydney, it seemed, *was* a dangerous place, but no worries, mate, the time had come to leave behind the manifest perils of the city for the unknown ones of the bush.

2

Early the next morning, after a light breakfast at our hotel, Dave and I assembled our baggage and headed for the Sydney railway terminal. A full-scale restoration project was under way on the dome-covered Central Station, an impressive Victorian edifice constructed of sandstone, steel, and glass. Jostling past surfboard-toting teenagers and women pushing prams, we made our way across the crowded concourse to the Country Platform, where we found the Indian-Pacific. The train, so named because it runs from ocean to ocean, spans the Australian continent, linking Sydney to distant Perth, 2,475 miles away. Except for the absence of the Amtrak arrow, it looked from the outside like any passenger train you'd see in America—a snub-nosed diesel locomotive pulling baggage cars and a few double- and single-berth sleepers in addition to the dining and lounge cars. The Indian-Pacific, however, was billed as one of the last great passenger-carrying trains in the world. It inaugurated service in February 1970, and according to most railroad aficionados only the renowned Blue Train, operating between Johannesburg and Cape Town, manages to provide its patrons with the equivalent creature comforts. Shortly before we left the States, in fact, we had read a glowing piece in *Gourmet* magazine, in which Richard Condon (author of *Prizzi's Honor*) described the culinary delights—he called the food "splendiferous"—and stimulating experiences awaiting the transcontinental traveler who chose to take this "luxury cruise train."

Before the conversion to electric diesels in the early 1950s, travelers must have found the trip interminable. Antiquated steam-driven locomotives were forced to make frequent stops on the long run across the desolate Nullarbor Plain to take on fuel and water from huge tenders. Since freight trains had priority, those carrying passengers were often shunted off onto one of the many sidings on the single track line, and further delays were encountered during the stops for changeovers necessitated by three different gauges of track on the route. To pass time while they waited passengers entertained themselves by singing songs around the piano, which became standard equipment in the lounge cars.

I myself was no stranger to long train trips. As a child during those frequent periods when my parents were either separating or reconciling, I found myself aboard either the Super Chief or the 20th Century Limited so often that I seriously considered a career as a conductor or a porter. I was too young to recall much about those journeys except that we always stopped in the Chicago terminal, which had a diner where I was allowed to order bacon and egg breakfasts, a curious detail to lodge itself in the mind of a five-year-old. Even though most of the grand old trains had long since passed into oblivion, I convinced Dave that we should take the Indian-Pacific to Perth, pointing out that this was a rare opportunity for us to savor such a journey.

As we made our way west from Sydney, the rolling green countryside of the Blue Mountains just outside the city gave way to the flat, dun-colored landscape of western New South Wales. This was sheep country, a sharp contrast to the lush grasslands and fertile farming areas closer to the coast, not to mention the mountain ski resorts in the Australian "Alps" and the tranquil inlets of the Hawkesbury River region just north of Sydney.

By afternoon of the second day, we had crossed into South Australia, the only state not originally settled by convicts. Comprising an area larger than Texas, Arkansas, and Louisiana combined, South Australia boasted a population smaller than Houston's. Though Adelaide, the capital, is surrounded by some of Australia's finest vineyards—in the 1840s German immigrants had made their way to the rich Barossa Valley, bringing their customs and wine-making skills to the new land—the city of churches was now reputed to be a rather staid place.

While the southeastern corner of South Australia was fertile and hilly, the northern part of the state quickly turned flat and arid. We learned that the residents in the opal mining town of Coober Pedy, which sat on the edge of the Simpson Desert, lived in underground caves to escape the extreme heat. The region as a whole seemed barely capable of supporting the sheep and cattle that were being raised on a few far-flung stations. Off in the distance were the Flinders Ranges, a dark blue blur on the horizon. Closer by, flocks of white cockatoos and colorful rosellas sitting in paddocks broke into flight as the train passed. At about five in the evening we pulled into Port Pirie, north of Adelaide on Spencer Gulf, reputed to have the largest concentration of great white sharks in the world. A young woman had just been fatally attacked while swimming at a beach on the Gulf and the headlines of the local tabloid read: MOTHER EATEN AS CHILDREN WATCH.

An hour or so after departing Port Pirie dinner was announced and we hastily made our way to the dining car. The Indian-Pacific featured two seatings for every meal and we had opted for the second, assuming it would allow for a more leisurely meal, but our first breakfast disabused us of that notion. "I'll take that for you, sir, and here's your porridge," said the waiter, snatching the bowl from in front of Dave, who was too nonplussed to rescue the three prunes he had been looking forward to eating. As it turned out both seatings were hurriedly served in forty-five minutes flat, after which the dining car was cleared as quickly as if martial law had been declared. But we readily adapted, and by lunchtime we were wolfing down the undistinguished food and guzzling our beverages as hastily as all the other passengers.

Although Dave and I had each taken a compartment to ourselves, we soon discovered they weren't places one wanted to spend a great deal of time. It seemed that there was a design defect in the single-berth car we were in, so that whenever a toilet in one of the compartments was used, the ventilation system picked up the odor and recirculated it throughout all the other compartments. The first time it happened, we both rushed from our rooms out into the corridor, gagging and wondering what was going on. With a handkerchief pressed to his face Dave found the steward at his station at the far end of the car, standing by the open door. "Right this way, gents," he said, knowing immediately why we were there. "I'll give ya the all clear in a few minutes." It seemed that Richard Condon, like the hero of his *Manchurian Candidate*, had suffered a bit of brainwashing himself, and by journey's end both Dave and I agreed that we had a score to settle with him.

With our compartments proving uninhabitable, we decided to take refuge in the lounge car, which, according to the photos in a brochure we had been sent, was always crowded with shapely young women drinking around the piano bar. They seemed as carefree as if they were in a cabaret, and their smiling faces couldn't help but convince us that the three-day and three-night journey from Sydney to Perth would pass quickly.

No matter how many times we wandered hopefully into the lounge, however, the only companionship we ever found there was pensioners—some knitting, some dozing, some playing cards—who admitted blithely that the only reason they had chosen the train for this long trip was to avail themselves of the half-price discount they were entitled to as senior citizens.

The one exception in the crowd was Michael Driscoll, a distinguished-looking middle-aged man who was accompanying his oldest daughter to Perth, where she would be starting college. They had boarded the train at the mining town of Broken Hill, the nearest stop to his small sheep farm in South Australia. With his prematurely gray hair, and a bit of a brogue, he could have passed for an Irish bard, and to some extent, he qualified as one. With self-effacing modesty, he told us about the theater group he had organized in his isolated little town of less than two hundred people, mentioning that they had recently performed Shakespeare's *Richard III* and, ironically enough, Synge's *Riders to the Sea.*

After a sleepless night in my berth I rose on cramped elbows and looked out the window to see low red sand hills that rose like stark islands in an otherwise flat and featureless gray-green sea of saltbush and spinifex. We were on the Nullarbor Plain, once the limestone bottom of a great sea, now a vast, sun-baked plateau of inhospitable desert totally devoid of trees, as its very name suggests. Each day during a seemingly interminable summer on the Nullarbor, the sun climbs in the cloudless sky, charring the dull rust-colored earth and blackening jagged rocks until the ground looks as though it is littered with cinders. The heat rising from the desert floor merges with the prevailing east wind, which drives it like a firestorm across the heart of the country.

The Nullarbor extends for a distance of eight hundred miles, and our train crawled through it ponderously. For three hundred of those miles the track was dead straight, without even the hint of a curve. Geologists might marvel at the fact that this huge hunk of earth is "undisturbed Mesozoic" and has undergone few, if any, changes since rising from the sea some 100 million years ago, but that didn't make looking at it any easier. Unlike the unfamiliar country I'd encountered on previous trips which actually drew my eye, here I found myself looking away from the numbing, oppressive landscape for physical relief.

Early on our second afternoon out we stopped outside a little railroad town named Hughes, just east of the border between South and Western Australia, pulling off on a siding to let a freight train pass. As we stepped out of our car, we were instantly blinded by a glare of white light that to our unaccustomed eyes approached the intensity of a nuclear flash. The sun was directly overhead, and a blast of swirling heat struck us with the force of a shock wave.

We walked along the rock-strewn tracks toward the locomotive,

13

kicking up clouds of red dust, and although there was practically no humidity we both began to perspire freely. I watched with detached fascination as glistening beads of sweat appeared on my exposed arms. There was something intimidating if not hostile about the Nullarbor, and despite the proximity of the train and the safety it afforded, standing there on the shimmering desert floor I felt soft and frail.

Undoubtedly it was the disturbing awareness of my own vulnerability that suddenly prompted me to recall a haunting occurrence I witnessed one summer, some years earlier, on the rugged Maine coast. A young woman was swept off the rocks by a wave and pulled out to sea by the current. As a strong swimmer my first impulse was to dive in and rescue her, but I realized how futile a gesture that would have been, as did the lobster fishermen standing on the cliff beside me. The waves were breaking against the jagged rocks below and the icy water was too cold to survive in for more than a minute or two. I stood there helplessly, unable to do anything but watch her slip beneath the water's surface.

It was difficult to imagine that around the turn of the century, Daisy Bates, the "Great White Queen of the Never Never," spent much of her adult life in an equally hostile environment, enduring heat, starvation, and even attacks of blindness (called sandy blight) to minister to the aboriginals of the Nullarbor. Born into a family of Irish gentry, she emigrated to Australia as a young woman, and from 1913 to 1947 (by which time she was already in her late eighties) lived alone in a tent in what she described as a "world of silence and moving shadows." Frequently glimpsed by passengers on the Trans-Australian Express, the little Victorian lady would be driving her camel buggy through the desert, holding a parasol over her head and dressed in a sober, high-collared blouse, black ankle-length skirt, high-heeled boots buttoned to the calf, wide-brimmed hat, and white cotton gloves.

"It takes some time for the beauty of the open places to reach one's soul," she wrote to one of her friends, "but once there, hills, sea, river, wood, all are as nothing beside the beauty of the flat land that goes on and on in infinite open space from sunrise to the glorious sunset."

Along the eleven-hundred-mile route that stretched from Port Pirie to Kalgoorlie were thirteen settlements just like Hughes, all of which owed their existence solely to the railroad. Most of them were named after long-forgotten prime ministers, and they were now inhabited only by the work gangs (and their families) who maintained the tracks and serviced the forty-odd trains a week that passed through. Once there were fifty-two such towns, but the number of crews had been drastically reduced when the old jarrah-wood ties were replaced by concrete sleepers, designed to endure the Nullarbor's extreme climate much longer.

As we passed through the little hamlets, where earlier residents had planted a few pathetic trees around their weather-beaten bungalows, we caught only occasional glimpses of their inhabitants. Urban Australians were often contemptuous of people living in the bush, referring to them as drifters and dropouts. But our first exposure to the bush convinced us that their dismissiveness scarcely did justice to the hardened breed of people capable of existing under such severe conditions. We wanted to learn who they were and what had brought them to places like the Nullarbor. There had to be romance in these lives, romance or at least a streak of "fine madness," and we were determined to discover it.

3

The Nullarbor was a perfect place to catch up on Australian history, a subject about which both Jack and I were almost totally ignorant. All we knew were the basics: that in the beginning there was Gondwanaland, a "supercontinent" consisting of what is now Australia, Antarctica, India, Africa, and South America, which when it disintegrated left Australia in isolation; that "terra australis incognita" was a term used by European geographers in the Middle Ages to denote the as yet "undiscovered" land mass to the south (which their mythological maps pictured as rivaling in size the huge continent of Asia that lay opposite it in the Northern Hemisphere); that, in fact, the aborigines, a tribe from Asia escaping an ice age, had discovered it long before, anywhere from forty thousand to seventy thousand years earlier; and that the Europeans, having searched for it for hundreds of years, eventually stumbled upon it, mainly through miscalculation and shipwreck, in the seventeenth century.

When the early Dutch explorers finally found Australia—the first to have set foot on Australian soil is thought to have done so around 1606—they named it New Holland, undoubtedly to honor that place on the far side of the globe for which they were so homesick. But they soon realized that their discovery bore little resemblance to its namesake. "This land is a barren and arid plain, where no fruit trees grow, nor is there any growth fit for the use of man," wrote Jan Carstensz, commander of the sailing ships *Arnhem* and *Pera.* "Many places are overgrown with brushwood and stunted wild trees. It has little fresh water, and the little there is has to be collected in pits dug for the purpose.

"There is a complete absence of coves and inlets, with the exception of a few bays unsheltered from the ocean winds. Extending into the interior flow many salt rivers across which natives haul their wives and children, dragging them on poles and boughs of trees."

New Holland was, in the words of historian Geoffrey Blainey, a "cul-de-sac, a dead end," its proximity to the East Indies its only link to the outside world. Even if the Dutch navigators had explored every bay and inlet of Australia's coastline, says Blainey, "they would probably have found nothing to induce them to promote trading posts."

After mapping the hideously inhospitable north, south, and west coasts, the Dutch had seen enough. Their interest in the place ceased altogether, and they left New Holland to fester in its own bad reputation. Symbolically, Willem de Vlamingh, the explorer/navigator who named the Swan River (along whose banks now stands Perth), fired derogatory salutes as he sailed away—"a signal of farewell to the miserable South Land," he wrote in his log.

The first Englishman happened upon Australia in 1688. William Dampier, a buccaneer by profession, was also an artist, an ornithologist, and a Royal Navy commander. Like de Vlamingh before him, he left the place a disillusioned man.

"The land is of dry and dusty soil, destitute of water," Dampier wrote of his visit to the northwest coast. "The inhabitants of this country are the miserablest people in the world. The Hodmadods [Hottentots] of Monomatapa, though a nasty people, yet for wealth are gentlemen to these, who have no houses and skin garments, sheep, poultry and fruits of the earth as the Hodmadods have. Their eyelids are always half-closed to keep the flies out of their eyes; they being so troublesome here that no fanning will keep them from coming to one's face; and without the assistance of both hands to keep them off, they will creep into one's nostrils and mouth, too, if the lips are not shut very close."

Poor Dampier. Apprenticed in his youth to a Weymouth fisherman who often sailed in the icy waters off Newfoundland, he had vowed to restrict his future voyaging to warmer climes. There he was in the tropics, despising not only the land but its people as well. Yet much to his credit, Dampier concluded his account with what may well be one of the world's great understatements. "If it were not for that sort of pleasure which results from the discovery even of the barrenest spot on the globe," he wrote, "this coast of New Holland would not have charmed me much." Subsequently cashiered from the Royal Navy, he died a penniless man.

Almost a century went by before Captain Cook, that extraordinary navigator, rediscovered Australia. As the first European to set foot on its eastern shore, he claimed the continent for Great Britain in 1770. Cook dropped anchor at Botany Bay, a few miles south of where Sydney now stands, and, unsure as to whether this east coast belonged to the same land the Dutch had seen to the west, he christened it New South Wales. It, too, bore little resemblance to its namesake, though it was more inviting than the country Dampier had encountered. Consider Alan Moorehead's description of it:

> The part of the coast on which Cook was now making his first landing is not quite typical of all this dryness. The bush here comes down to the shore and the transparent sea-water froths and sparkles like champagne as it tumbles in long rollers on to beaches of yellow sand. In the estuaries one escapes from the restlessness of the sea into backwaters full of reeds where ducks and wading birds abound, and beyond these the hills, thickly covered with bush, rise up from the sea plain . . . It is very beautiful and it has that kind of rugged expansiveness that makes the traveller feel alive and free.

Ironically, Cook and his crew had sailed into Botany Bay at the wettest time of year and were seeing what was normally arid land at its very best. Yet they mistakenly concluded that they had come upon it at its worst, at its drabbest and driest. "This optimism," says Blainey, "was crucial in Australian history. If they had really understood the infertile soil and the extreme heat, their report would have rejected Botany Bay [as a penal colony]. And no British settlement of the Australian continent would have been founded in 1788."

Cook himself may have been sanguine but his brilliant shipboard scientist, Joseph Banks, was more pessimistic. "In the whole length of the coast which we sailed along," noted Banks, "there was a very unusual sameness to be observed in the face of the country. Barren it may justly be called, and in a very high degree, at least as far as we saw. A soil so barren and at the same time entirely devoid of the help derived from cultivation could not be supposed to yield much to the support of man." Curiously, it was Banks, an otherwise humane man, who suggested that Australia might be the place to settle convicts sentenced to transportation to the colonies.

The then-reigning monarch, George III, was not overly excited by what had been claimed in his name. Had he not lost the American colonies around that time—particularly Georgia, which until then had been the regular dumping ground for Britain's undesirables—and had his squalid city prisons and river-berthed convict hulks not become so dangerously overcrowded, Australia might have been left to fester yet another hundred and fifty years. But this was not to be. On His Majesty's orders, the first fleet of convict ships set sail for Botany Bay in 1787. Only later was it realized that George III had given the command just as he was declining into his first bout of insanity.

4

Late in the evening of our second day out, the train pulled into Kalgoorlie, an old and, thanks to the rising price of gold, recently resurrected gold-mining town on the western edge of the Nullarbor. Back in Sydney, almost two thousand miles away, people talked about Kalgoorlie, if not with quite the sense of romanticism Americans once spoke of Dodge City, with a sort of grudging admiration. It was a historic place, with a raffish reputation. Most Australians had never been to Kalgoorlie, but they regarded it as the quintessential one-horse western town. Plenty of boozing, brawling, and semilegal bordellos. You could smell gold fever in the air, if not the actual gold in the ground.

It sounded intriguing, and if nothing else, it broke up the three-day train ride. We got off the train and checked into a nondescript motel not far from the station. The night was hot, and deathly still.

Walking out onto Hannan Street the following morning, we found ourselves reaching for our sunglasses with the frantic motion of a sheriff going for his holstered six-gun. The light was dazzling, almost painfully so. But as we'd learned in our forays outside the train, even the best glasses couldn't do much against that Southern Hemisphere sun.

Screwing our faces into a more or less permanent squint, we ambled up the street, as wide still as it had been in gold rush days, when camel teams and bullock carts needed all the room they could get just to turn around. With the space now being used by angle-parked vehicles instead of camels, both sides of the nearly treeless thoroughfare—Hannan Street was Kalgoorlie's main drag—were studded with dust-encrusted Land Rovers, beat-up old vans, and an occasional shiny new Mercedes. A row of gaunt, scarecrowlike telephone poles, overburdened with drooping wires and looking strangely out of place, ran the length of the street, not on one side but smack in the middle, where they served as a sort of honorary (and easily ignored) median divider.

At the first opportunity, Jack pulled me into a pub, where we stood for a moment adjusting our eyes to the relative gloom and wiping the sweat from our faces before heading to the bar. Jack asked for two beers.

"Will that be middies, schooners, ponies, pots, or pints?" asked the bartender, spotting us as tyros unschooled in the terminology of serious drinking.

"Middies'll be fine," said Jack, watching to see which of the many-sized glasses lined up behind the counter the bartender would grab. (The nomenclature differs from state to state, but in Western Australia, a "pony" is five ounces; a "middy," ten; a "schooner," fifteen; and a "pot," twenty. If you ask simply for a "glass" of beer, you get seven ounces and if you ask for a "handle," a slang term, you get whatever glass comes with a handle in that particular pub. A jug contains the equivalent of about six middies, and once you get away from draft beer, a "tinny" is the equivalent of our can, and a "stubby" is the same as one of our six-pack bottles. Whew!)

"This is country that likes killin' people," said the leathery-faced, boozy-eyed old-timer standing next to us at the bar. He seemed to be mumbling to himself more than he was talking to us, but he had a point. Though it was still early in the morning, the temperature outside had already reached 110 degrees in the shade. And Hannan's pub, awash with spilled beer from overfilled middies and pint mugs, was already so noisy and crowded with customers—many of them bearded, rough-looking characters, wearing sweat-stained T-shirts and sporting tattoos, with only a few more respectably dressed business types—it looked as if the place had simply never bothered to close the night before. Standing cheek to jowl in the smoke-filled room, everyone seemed to be a participant in one animated conversation or another.

Hannan's was a typical Australian pub, an institution characterized by charitable observers as the scene of "raucous bonhomie," part watering hole and refuge from the heat, part social club, where the male bonding, or "mateship," crucial to the country's early settlement (and the key to an understanding of its history) survived to this day. Cynics regarded the pub simply as a place where "pitiful people piss their wages against the wall," and women often condemned it as a hangout where husbands hid from their wives most of their waking hours. Jack and I were to spend much of our time in pubs, if only because they were generally the center of a town's activity, where one met the locals and listened to them yarn. "Beer drinking," boasted one Australian journalist, "is our greatest national pastime. Beer has long been the prime lubricant in our social intercourse and the sacred throat-anointing fluid that accompanies the ritual of mateship. To sink a few cold ones with the blokes is both an escape and a confirmation of belonging."

Being of Irish stock himself (at least on his mother's side), Jack felt very much at home at Hannan's. Beer in hand, he smiled contentedly, leaned against the bar, and breathed deeply, as if to inhale the hop-flavored atmosphere of conviviality surrounding him.

"Look around you, Dave," he observed. "It's in the genes." He was right. We could have been at a bar somewhere in South Boston. But while it might have been in *his* genes, it certainly wasn't in mine, and I prevailed on him to drink up so we could move on.

Kalgoorlie—the name apparently was a rendering of an aboriginal word for a species of silky pear that grew in the region and was used by the aborigines as food—had been established as a township a few years after Paddy Hannan discovered gold in the area in 1893. It now boasted a population of only about 20,000, all living within a three-mile radius of the town hall, but Hannan Street alone seemed to have enough pubs to service all of Australia. The Criterion Hotel, the Exchange Hotel, the Federal Hotel, the Palace Hotel, the Star and Garter Hotel—most were two-storied reddish-yellow sandstone structures, early 1900s frontier architecture, with balustraded balconies, red-brick parapets, and overhanging corrugated-iron roofs.

A closer-than-casual look at the second story of the Criterion, however, revealed that behind its beautiful wood and wrought-iron veranda was a false front. In other words, it and many other of the establishments in town were no longer in the business of providing lodgings. True, places like the Palace and the Old Australia did still maintain a few upstairs rooms to accommodate the occasional traveling salesman or tourist who preferred the atmosphere there to the more modern motels on the outskirts of town. But it was a far cry from the old days, when the town was so prosperous it boasted a staggering total of ninety-two hotels! When the Palace opened in 1897, for instance, it offered "cuisine special, viands perfect, and bars handsomely fitted and stocked . . . and provided with one comfort long neglected—lounge chairs, seductive and comfortable, to soothe the jaded magnate." Nowadays the Palace was little more than a licensed pub, and even at that early hour of the morning, it was as crowded as Hannan's, as were all the hotels. In years gone by, a lot of prospectors had died of thirst around the area that was later to become Kalgoorlie. Clearly, the townsfolk had decided that it would never happen again.

At the intersection of Maritana and Hannan streets was a traffic light, the only one in town. In fact, according to the map, it was the only one within three hundred miles of Kalgoorlie. We took a left on Maritana simply because Hannan Street seemed just about ready to end. A couple of blocks farther along, past the pink-stone post office with its four-sided clock tower, past the plate-glass windows of a pizza parlor, a couple of coffee shops, and various other storefronts, including the fossicker shop, the main street simply gave way to the Nullarbor, with only the slightest hint of a struggle. On the eastern edge of town, surrounded by tailing dumps and straddling the entrance shafts to "the richest square mile of gold-bearing ground in the world," stood the worn, derricklike headframes of the mines. Kalgoorlie, or more precisely, the twin towns of Kalgoorlie/Boulder, had been built on the ancient seabed of Yilgarnia, unchanged geologically for 700 million years. "Its solitude," wrote a local historian, "may well have remained virtually undisturbed but for the gold in its rocks."

Around the turn of the century some huge nuggets had been found here, nuggets whose names—Map of England, Little Darling, Golden Eagle, Bobby Dazzler, Never Can Tell, Little Hero, Dad 'N' Bob— suggested their shapes or conveyed the elation of their discoverers. Herbert Hoover, a young man in his twenties at the time, had been a mine manager in Kalgoorlie during its heyday. Now the mineworks were a scene of semi-industrial decrepitude, set off at the northern end by a strange-looking hill, a slag heap about six hundred feet high known to the residents of that desolate flatland as Mt. Charlotte. Beyond lay an emptiness so vast, a horizon so distant, and an uninterrupted expanse of sky so vividly blue, we almost had to avert our eyes in agoraphobic disbelief.

Walking along Maritana Street, we crossed a railroad bridge and continued in a northwesterly direction toward yet another pub, making frequent detours to inspect the side streets along the way. (For the benefit of thirsty strangers, every pub in town was clearly marked on a map handed out by the local tourist office.) Several stately old homes, with spring-watered lawns and well-tended gardens, graced some of the neighborhoods. Despite their elegant bullnose verandas (the word "bullnose" describing the curved shape of the roofs), for the most part the houses were rather shabby and unkempt—blistered, peeling, white weatherboard structures, many of which sat on their original quarter-acre blocks. The lots were bounded in front by sagging picket fences, which needed painting (and shoring up) as urgently as the houses behind them. Rusty, corrugated-iron roofs, once so practical because they could be put in wagons and carted off for use on other temporary structures at new mining sites, now only added to the general sense of impermanence and decay. Kalgoorlie, according to the local historian quoted above, was "a town in which most people seem happily unaware that the outward appearance of the family residence is a status symbol of modern living."

Each yard was spacious enough to have accommodated a horse and carriage, which in earlier days had evidently been stabled behind the house. The stables, of course, had long since given way to carports (and the horses and wagons to Toyotas), but these makeshift garages still shared space with the old-fashioned "dunny," an outhouse that generally stood in solitary splendor under the shade of some broad-canopied tree in the back of the yard. Though even the run-down places more often than not had toilet facilities inside the house (sometimes, as we were to see later, even in quaint little rooms that boasted finely patterned stamped-metal walls), their outdoor dunnies remained nonetheless very much intact. As one elderly Kalgoorlie lady said, as she proudly escorted us on a tour of her house, "the dunny looks like the sentry box at Buckingham Palace . . . but it's much more useful."

Just before we reached the pub on Maritana Street, we came upon, of all things, a "Tex-Mex restaurant" named Margarita's. It was closed, but someone who looked young and idealistic enough to have been the owner was sitting at a table inside, apparently doing inventory. He was counting chili peppers.

We knocked on the door, hoping for a chat and a respite from the heat. A puckish-looking fellow in his early thirties answered and introduced himself in a thick Aussie accent. It sounded something like "Dive Hy"—we hadn't yet heard the old vaudeville joke that a bison was something Australians wash their hands in—but we discovered when he wrote it down for us that his name was really Dave Hay. He invited us in for a cold beer and we were happy to accept.

"What in the world brought you to Kalgoorlie to run a Tex-Mex restaurant?" asked Jack (who himself had once owned a restaurant in Boston) as we took our places at a pepper-covered table.

"Well, it was just a case of 'go East, young man.' I came up here as an architect from Perth. The town didn't have an architect, or a Mexican restaurant. So you see an opportunity . . . ," said Dave, making a sweeping gesture with his arm as if the opportunity were obvious, "and you grab it."

"But it probably didn't have an Ethiopian restaurant, either," I suggested.

"Yeah," he chuckled, absentmindedly separating the chilis into small piles. "But Mexican's a lively sort of restaurant and that's what I reckoned Kalgoorlie needed. Maybe I've sort of toned down the heat, just to make it more amenable to Australian tastes. That's why we have a range of . . . bland sorts of things. Besides, Mexican's cheap.

"Here in Kalgoorlie people are willing to take a bit of an each way bet on their tucker. Kalgoorlie's a gambling sort of town, and I'm a gambler myself. To you fellas it must seem like the middle of nowhere but, believe me, there are a lot greater nowheres than this in Australia. There are millionaires living in Kalgoorlie. They don't have to live here, but they do. I won't be spending my life here, that's for sure. But then, that's what it's been all about since people started prospecting here. It's the sort of place that gives you a start, a chance. You can take a punt here, and you can win . . . or lose."

"Strikes me it might be a lonely place for a single man," I said.

"No, it isn't," he replied, a lascivious smile crossing his face. "There are always a certain amount of females around town—schoolteachers, nurses, professional sorts. They're sort of normal human beings. But then you get the locals. All they know is getting pissed and trying to get a root. Real scrubbers they are. The smaller the town the worse it is. They come in here looking for jobs as waitresses, sporting homemade tattoos on their arms . . . and elsewhere. I imagine they're homemade. I hope they're not professionally done."

"What's your biggest problem living in Kalgoorlie?" asked Jack, opening another stubby.

"Dishwashers," he replied, without a moment's hesitation, "you can't get 'em. My latest one's named Dog. Alf, my old dishwasher, was leaving. 'Look, I'll get you another dishwasher,' he said. His idea of getting another dishwasher? He went into the pub across the road and yelled: 'Hey, anybody want a job as a dishwasher?' In comes this bloke, Dog, a bikey. His Harley-Davidson is crook and that's why he needs the job. The patrons looked at him and they said: 'That's not your cook, is it?' I said: 'No, no, he's only the dishwasher.'

"He's got two earrings through each nipple. He's got 'Love' and 'Hate' and tattoos all over his body. 'Dog, you like tattoos, do you?' I wouldn't have said that to him initially, but he's a harmless sort, at least when he's sober. 'I reckon they're good, people look at 'em,' he said. It's the same with his bloody Mohawk haircut. He reckons it pulls women. Maybe it does, exactly the sort he's after.

"Australia may not be a third-world country," Dave went on, pausing momentarily to search for a chili pepper that had fallen on the floor, "but Australians are a third-world people, especially in places like Kalgoorlie. Limited opportunities, limited education, limited aspirations. People haven't got much out of life and life's not going to give them very much. Australia's a boring place. There's not much to do. Well, people don't know what to do, so what they do is drink. This town is full of people like that. I've even become a bit of an ocker myself since leaving Perth. It's a bad sort of thing when people are so proud of being so limited."

"Do you think things are changing?" I asked.

"I suppose," he reflected. "Maybe things are improving. Take restaurants. About ten years ago someone in Perth invented garlic bread, which was unheard-of then. It was the biggest innovation of all time, at least as far as Perth was concerned. That guy made a million bucks simply on the strength of his garlic bread. Now, every restaurant has it. So I guess there *has* been a sort of progress."

5

The little railroad settlements we'd passed through on the Nullarbor had nothing in the way of accommodations for visitors, and Kalgoorlie was the first stop where we could conceivably get to know locals and explore the nearby ghost towns. Early one morning, with no plans for the afternoon, we walked into a dingy coffee shop on Hannan Street. We were the only customers, and since the air conditioning wasn't helping much to lower the temperature, we took places at a green plastic booth directly under a ceiling fan. A sign on the wall read: PLEASE NOTIFY STAFF IF YOU MOVE TO ANOTHER SEAT, an odd request given the fact that there were only eleven tables in the entire establishment. My stomach was rumbling from too much Swan beer the night before, and it really began to churn in earnest when Dave abruptly announced: "I've got a thought. Let's go and see the mayor."

Before I could reply, the waitress, who looked too young to be out of high school, finally finished her conversation with the cook and came over to our table. We ordered a simple breakfast, forgoing her recommendation of one of the Australian delicacies on the menu—a cold (tinned) spaghetti sandwich or baked beans on toast.

"What do you want to see the mayor for?" I asked, as she sauntered away. After all those years of living in Boston, the last thing I wanted to do was waste time listening to a politician. "The mayor isn't going to give you the keys to the city, or to the whorehouses, either." Over the past few days we'd heard a great deal about the notorious ladies of Kalgoorlie, and Dave was trying to find a way to approach them other than as a client.

"The fellow we met last night at the pub said he was quite a character, but you were drinking so much, you probably don't remember."

"You ought to give temperance lectures at the Salvation Army," I growled in return. Dave was usually bright and alert early in the day, when he scored most of his points in our ongoing verbal duel. I preferred to start slowly, simply to make a balanced contest of it, and by midafternoon things would even out. Just to be sporting, I often delayed finishing him off, usually waiting till evening to move in for the kill. My favorite arena was a pub, where I felt like an old club fighter at home in familiar surroundings.

"I've always said that alcohol seems to balance you. Now you have chips on both shoulders." Dave was laughing. "Let's go see the mayor, and you can take it out on him." Aside from prospecting and drinking, we'd discovered there wasn't a great deal to do in Kalgoorlie, so I agreed to go along, washing my last piece of toast down with a final slug of lukewarm coffee.

Outside Kalgoorlie's town hall, a stately old buff-colored Victorian structure built in 1908, sat a statue of Paddy Hannan holding a water bag, which served as a drinking fountain for passersby. A diminutive Irish immigrant up from the goldfields of Ballarat and Bendigo, northwest of Melbourne, Paddy struck a rich reef in 1893, kicking off a gold rush that brought Kalgoorlie into existence. Poor Paddy. Even immortalized in bronze, and almost a hundred years after his death, he still couldn't escape the fiery Australian sun. But now, adding insult to injury, his statue was periodically set upon by vandals, who stole his water bag, and profaned by drunks, who used it as a urinal.

The doors of the town hall opened onto a wide hardwood staircase that led to the second floor. A receptionist told us that the mayor probably had time to see us, even if we didn't have an appointment, and a few minutes later a secretary ushered us into Mayor Finlayson's office. It would have been impossible to tell from observing the lavishly appointed chamber that the Australian dollar had recently plummeted on the world currency market. The high ceilings, rich hard-wood-paneled walls, and sumptuous furnishings were reminders that Kalgoorlie had always been a wealthy town, where money, if not water, flowed freely. Over a thousand tons of gold have been extracted from the "Golden Mile" alone, and even today it is still considered one of the richest gold-bearing reefs in the world.

The "Goldfield Guru," as one of his constituents had called him the night before at Hannan's, rose from behind his desk to greet us. A tall, gaunt fellow in his late fifties with the determined look of a man with a mission, he offered us two luxuriously upholstered Edwardian chairs, and after the usual exchange of pleasantries, I asked him about the town's future. I'd by now begun to grow curious about a place whose existence depended almost entirely on gold, an exhaustible resource.

"I think our future's very exciting," replied Mayor Finlayson, look-ing as pleased as a poker player who'd been dealt a pat hand. "The Asia-Pacific Conference projected that within this area, population will increase by four hundred million in the next fifteen years. Those people will need beef, sheep, wool, and grain, and we have the ability to produce all those things. Kalgoorlie is in the center of that region, and it has the centrifugal force to bring everything into it."

My sense of geography apparently had been muddled by the Nullar-bor crossing. Kalgoorlie didn't seem to be in the center of anything, except the desert. The Pacific region that His Honor referred to was thousands of miles away, across one of the most forbidding stretches of country on earth. And the land around the goldfields was far too arid even for grazing cattle, not to mention growing grain or other kinds of farming.

"How do you propose to get around the problem of insufficient water?" I asked him.

"Again, the emphasis is on technology. Technology is coming to the fore," he replied. As he spoke I noticed that, oblivious to the stately surroundings, a fly had alighted on His Honor's forehead. "We are seeing that we can use salt water in mining, where it was not possible before."

"But I didn't think you could water crops with it, and the average rainfall here is less than eight inches a year. That's hardly enough to make Kalgoorlie the garden spot of the Pacific."

"True, the population of Australia will be limited by the amount of fresh water we have," said Mayor Finlayson, setting the intruding insect to wing with a sweep of his hand. "But in time, technology will have the solution to this as well. We'll bring down water from the Ord River and create an inland sea. We must divert water from the far northwest, and it must come down in canals." He had begun to assume the evangelical fervor of a preacher at a tent revival.

"I've proposed we use nuclear explosives to bring about the sort of thing I'm talking about," he said in a booming voice, pointing his finger toward the heavens for emphasis, or perhaps to invoke divine guidance. "We've got to convince people that using nuclear devices for peaceful purposes is a very commonsense thing to do.

"This country has no national service. We need it. I think we ought to be directing some of our youth into the type of national project I'm talking about. They'd live in air-conditioned barracks in out-camps, with food flown in by caterers. The canal would be built by young people operating big machinery, and it would be challenging. At the same time it would be character building. Instead of paying them not to work, like we do now, we would pay them to be part of a national project."

It was a novel notion. A series of nuclear explosions would certainly put Kalgoorlie on the map. And if young people in Australia were anything like their counterparts in the States, they'd jump at the opportunity to get off the dole, leave unappealing places like Perth and Sydney, and live in character-building out-camps in the middle of the Gibson Desert.

"Granted, my scientific background is nonexistent," I said, changing the subject because all his talk about nuclear explosions was making my headache worse, "but with the heat and low humidity of the desert, wouldn't the evaporation rate in a canal over fifteen hundred miles long be extraordinary?"

"You're quite right," Mayor Finlayson conceded. "That's one of the problems that concern us. We will never be able to store the water. But we are laying the foundation today for the next seventy-five years. Perhaps that's pessimistic, maybe I should be saying a hundred and seventy-five years."

Gazing out the window toward the desert as if he could already see the town mushrooming like a nuclear dust cloud, he remarked, "Nothing can stop us—this area will continue to grow. So long as we don't lose the drive, the enthusiasm, and the initiative. The future of this region is up to us, we either take it or leave it," he said, raising his voice and pounding his right fist into his left palm for emphasis.

He paused for a moment as if waiting for the applause to subside. "And I tell you we're determined to take it," he added, so inspired by his own rhetoric that he'd apparently forgotten we couldn't vote for him.

I snapped him back to the present, stirring the pot a little by asking him about his problems with Boulder, the town adjacent to Kalgoorlie. The locals had told us that His Honor was involved in a bitter dispute with Boulder's Shire Council.

"I always say I have no trouble at all getting along with people who agree with me," he said with a trace of a smile on his face. "But if they're wrong over in Boulder, I've got to tell them so. We must not have people in our midst who prevent progress." Any hint of a smile vanished and His Honor became visibly annoyed as he contemplated his obstructionist adversaries.

Up to that point Dave had been silent, but now he saw an opening to get into a subject that had been concerning him. "Do the whorehouses on Hay Street have a place in your vision of Kalgoorlie's future?" he asked.

"Indeed they do," replied Mayor Finlayson indignantly, "they've always been there. They're accepted as part of the wild life of Kalgoorlie. I see no reason for it to change, so long as they conduct themselves in the exemplary way they have for the last seventy-five years."

"But, Your Honor," I protested, "isn't prostitution illegal?"

"Of course it's illegal, so we have to get around that somehow. How do you get around something that is illegal, and yet is prominently displayed?" He paused for a moment, pondering a solution to his dilemma, then continued. "To accomplish this, you require a number of things. You need the tolerance of the community, you need good judgment by the madams, and you need the balance of the police and local authorities. You must have a combination of all three of those."

"How would a madam demonstrate her good judgment?" I asked, intrigued by the possibilities of Kalgoorlie's carnal co-op.

"It's the way in which they present themselves," His Honor replied. "If you met those madams, you would not take them for anything other than efficient housewives. I admire the way they go about things in conducting their houses. There is no display, and they always conduct themselves in an exemplary manner."

"Do you know any personally?" asked Dave.

"I meet them from time to time and I'm always pleased to, because I have respect for them and the way they go about the work that they do," said Mayor Finlayson. "I recognize, too, that they make a valuable financial contribution to our community."

"How would I go about meeting one?" asked Dave, titillated by the prospect of chatting with a sporting lady, and perhaps making his own small contribution to the community.

"I'm afraid it's a business on which I'm not an authority. But if you take yourself down to Hay Street any night you have some spare time and money, I'm certain you'll have no difficulty getting an introduction."

With such a meeting virtually assured we bid our farewells to Mayor Finlayson and stepped back out onto Kalgoorlie's deserted main street, trying to imagine it teeming with millions of commuters. Our glimpse of bush politics had intrigued us, tempted as we were by the prospect of meeting housewifely madams. There was a style we appreciated in Mayor Finlayson, a style we heard was shared by the president of Boulder Shire, Digger Dawes, who had a reputation even in far-off Sydney for being a political maverick and for having one of the fastest wits in the west.

6

The tourist bureau had provided us with a car, and we drove southeast along a wide road, past houses and small businesses that quickly gave way to the open-cut and vertical shaft mines of the Golden Mile. With only the Eastern Goldfields Technical College standing between them as a demarcation at "the half way," Boulder merged so imperceptibly with Kalgoorlie that the twin towns were practically indistinguishable. Though they had once been fiercely individual communities—an early proposal that Boulder become a suburb of Kalgoorlie was overwhelmingly defeated in an election—nowadays that individualism was reflected only in the antagonism between their two political leaders.

Although Kalgoorlie stood closer to the goldfields surrounding Paddy Hannan's original find, it was three miles from the more productive mines along the so-called Great Boulder strip, which were directly adjacent to Boulder itself. In the early days horse-drawn carriages carried fares back and forth along this route. The cab drivers solicited business by hollering, "Right away to the Boulder," which was the closest point they could get to the Great Boulder Lease, the mine from which the town took its name.

A number of Boulder's wide thoroughfares, including Hamilton and Lane streets, were named after prominent mine managers, and the town sprang up within sight of the mine's towering slime heaps and within earshot of its stamping batteries. Before the turn of the century, miners camped in makeshift shelters on their leases, close to the condensing plants from which they obtained water. In those days, water was more valuable in the goldfields than whiskey, and on washing day the clothes even had to be separated according to their dirt value.

At the shire council building, the sprightly eighty-year-old Digger Dawes met us in the waiting room and led us a winding route through a labyrinth of corridors to his office. In sharp contrast to Mayor Finlayson's spacious quarters, Digger's cubbyhole had barely enough space for the two chairs he brought in for us and placed in front of his desk.

"So you'd like a bit of a chat, would ya? Well, I'm warnin' ya, if ya get me started, ya might not be able ta stop me," cautioned Digger. "Go fer yer bloody life," he urged with a leprechaunlike grin on his face.

"With a name like Digger I take it you were once a prospector," said Dave.

"Take anything ya like, but you'd be wrong." He chuckled. "I got the name because when I was a small boy, I used ta dig in the ground lookin' fer gold. Used ta find it too. Never great chunks. Just little bits. I was just a bloody schoolboy lookin' for a few bob to buy a book. My father was a prospector down from Victoria. He was poor all his bloody life, and us kids, we were poor. We had the ass hangin' out of our pants and had to fend for ourselves. It was good trainin' to learn how to be self-reliant.

"If some bastard had a paddy full of turnips, you'd knock off a few, and you'd pinch the grapes out of the bloody mine manager's yard. Ya bought the cheapest bloody vegetables, and ya had soup and maggoty meat when ya could get it. Ya'd just knock the maggots off. It didn't do ya any harm. It made ya appreciate the good things in life, and taught ya to be independent. Most people were like that in those days.

"I worked on the dry blowers for a while, and then got a job as a blacksmith's striker. If ya asked somebody to do that now, they'd say, 'Oh, fuck that.' Ya give a bloke a shovel today, and ya'd think ya put a bloody bedpan in his hands. He'd say, 'Where's the backhoe?'

"After that I got a job at the power station. Forty bloody tons a day we took out of the wood trains and lumped down in front of the boilers. I can tell ya that was bloody 'ard work too. The size of those bloody logs the dings used ta cut out in the wood line. Fuckin' dings, I don't know how they lifted 'em."

30

"Dings?" said Dave.

"Dingbats, Italians. Ya've got a lot of 'em in America," Digger explained, "except ya call 'em dagos. I don't know what the bloody difference is. Stand in the garden for twenty-four hours and see a dago by." Like an old vaudeville comic, Digger couldn't resist even a bad joke, and laughed appreciatively.

"You've got a way with words," I observed.

"You bet I have," concurred Digger, laughing like a little boy who'd just tossed a firecracker. "I've been usin' 'em all my life. One thing I learned early on was to speak. I'm not afraid of anybody. There's nobody better than me. That's the great leveler. It used to be the Australian attitude. There's no one better than me, and no one worse.

"But we're losing it fast, with this government. People become bloody numbers, and there isn't anything left of democracy. It becomes rat shit, and it's been gradually shredded away. The Westminster Statutes, the basis of our laws, are being shattered. That's what's stuffed this country up, with these bastards that are in power today with their bloody socialistic programs. They've taken away the incentive for people to get off their ass to work for the betterment of themselves. They're the greatest bunch of no-hoping bastards ever put into bloody power."

Digger stopped his diatribe only when he noticed a distracted Dave was looking at a framed document on the wall.

"That's my Justice of the Peace certificate," he volunteered, "a bloody piece of paper ya can wipe yer coite on."

"Coite?" Dave repeated. "What's that?"

"Your asshole." Digger laughed. "Where've ya been all yer life?"

"Where did that expression come from?" I asked naively.

"Buggered if I know," replied Digger, with an impish grin on his face.

"What do you mean when you say democracy is rat shit?" queried Dave, obviously uncomfortable with the direction the conversation was taking.

"Gnawed away," said Digger. He glanced up at the photograph of Queen Elizabeth hanging beside his Justice of the Peace certificate. "You people don't have royalty, do ya?" he asked, his grin widening. "You'd give your right knacker to have that, wouldn't ya?"

"Knacker?" said Dave, leading with his chin again.

"One of yer balls," quipped Digger with glee. "Where did ya go to bloody school, mate?"

"The mayor over in Kalgoorlie—" Dave began, again attempting to raise the tone of the discussion.

"He's a useless cunt, and ya can quote me on that," snapped Digger, cutting him off. "If ya read the local paper today, he's sticking his nose into our business again. He says we've got a shoddy bloody airport. Of course it's not an international bloody airport, and it never will be, but we've got the greatest bloody jet service of any outback bloody town. See, we're at the dead end, in the dead heart, there's nothing left further on. It costs money to put an airplane down, and lift it up again."

"When you disagree with Mayor Finlayson at a council meeting, do you temper your language a bit?" asked Dave.

"I haven't called 'im a useless cunt yet, if that's what ya mean. But it's gettin' to the stage where I might. I don't criticize 'im publicly, but he criticizes me, repeatedly. Our council is always bloody wrong, and he's always bloody right," roared Digger, warming to the subject. "But I still get 'im at the bloody meetings. I fuckin' knock 'is ears back there, and that suits me just fine."

He laughed aloud, glanced at his watch and continued, "I've gut a fuckin' sheila comin' in ta see me in a little while. She used ta have an important job here. Yeah, nice tits, too," he added as an afterthought.

"You still have an eye for the ladies," observed Dave.

"Not at my age. I hafta settle for this." Digger laughed, showing us a large pad on his desk with a bosomy nude on it. "This is my Doodle Dolly," announced Digger. "Put out by one of the bloody companies here. When ya get ta be my age, you'll need one too."

Dave smiled, which prompted Digger to remark, "You look as happy as the boy who shot his father."

"Happy as what?"

"The boy who shot his father," repeated Digger. "Where have ya buggers been hiding all yer lives? I bet ya don't even know what knockers are."

"I bet we do," said Dave, thinking he'd finally scored a point.

"Well you're wrong again," Digger taunted. "That's what we call the whorehouses, and it has nothin' to do with mammaries. The knockers have been here ever since I can remember. Nothin' wrong with that. It's been going on for centuries.

"One thing I've learned over the years," Digger confided conspiratorially, "is never denigrate women. They're fifty percent of the population, and that's how I get back on the council time after time.

I butter 'em up. I don't say, 'Look at yer ass, it's six feet wide.' I say, 'Jesus, you're lookin' younger every day.' "

There was a knock on the door and Digger's secretary poked her head in the room to tell him his next appointment was waiting.

"The fuckin' sheila I'm expectin' is out there so I guess I better see her," he said after his secretary left. "If you two 'ave any more trouble understanding English, just let me know and I'll be glad to help ya out."

Digger accompanied us out to the waiting room. A matronly-looking woman sitting on the couch rose when she saw him. Digger beamed his most disarming smile, walked over and put his arm around her. She was slightly overweight and towered over him. As we walked out the front door, we heard him say, "How are ya, darlin'? You're lookin' just gorgeous today."

As we made our way back to the car, dodging a lone pickup truck that came careening down the dusty street, I couldn't help but be struck by the candor of both Digger and Mayor Finlayson. Though Digger was irrepressible and Finlayson a bit pompous, both possessed qualities that Kalgoorlie/Boulder voters, and Australians in general, seemed to admire unqualifiedly—pugnacity, irreverence, and unconventionality. Certainly, both men followed in a long political tradition. In writing about William Patrick Crick, a popular politician at the turn of the century, for instance, one historian lamented: "The violence of his tongue and the irresponsibility of his behavior involved him in countless brawls, many of them physical. Early in his public life, he distinguished himself at a debating society by throwing a glass of water into the face of the chairman, Judge Windeyer, with whom he was in disagreement. He was uncontrollable in debate and uninhibited in invective."

On the other hand, there was an innate fairness that underlay their politics. Digger's conviction that "there's nobody better than me and there's no one worse" summed it all up. Notwithstanding his frequent references to "dagos," "dingbats," and "boongs," terms that in another person's mouth would have sounded cruel and bigoted, it was clear that Digger's rough frontier sense of democracy allowed every man a "fair go." His was an attitude we were to encounter frequently during our travels throughout the country, where in the bush it was not unusual for station owners to socialize with stockmen and in the towns for professional men to fraternize with workingmen in pubs. Despite a long history of brutality and indifference, at best, toward its aboriginal population, Australia as a whole was characterized by a magnanimity derived from what one observer described as "a deep belief in the essential sameness and ordinariness of mankind."

7

Back in Kalgoorlie we decided to pay a visit to a pub we hadn't yet frequented, the Piccadilly Hotel, a dilapidated old building near the railway station. Working behind the bar were its two proprietors, the O'Shaughnessy brothers, large men who talked of nothing else but cricket and "Australian rules" football. The pub was not particularly busy, but the O'Shaughnessys managed to keep themselves in almost perpetual motion, sidestepping from tap to customer to cash register as if they were practicing lateral field running for the pub team. Mrs. O'Shaughnessy, the wife of one of the brothers, was also helping out behind the bar. A petite, attractive, dark-haired woman in her mid-thirties, she would from time to time flit over to the "bottle shop," a small takeout counter facing out on the dreary hallway, to sell beer by the case to people too busy to come in and drink it by the pint.

The Piccadilly was the favored home-away-from-home for transcontinental trainmen laying over in Kalgoorlie between crew changes. A number of them were now slouched over the bar, sour-faced and obviously in no mood to be sociable but in no mood, either, to retire to the solitude of their rooms upstairs. Their heads nodded as imperceptibly as bidders at an auction whenever they wanted another beer, and Mrs. O'Shaughnessy was as adroit as any auctioneer in picking up their signals. "It'll be steak and chips for tea this evening, gentlemen," she announced, as she responded to one such signal with yet another frothing pint. The two trainmen mumbled some sort of agreement, as unintelligible as it was unenthusiastic, without even bothering to look up.

Perched on a nearby barstool was a desiccated, vinegary-looking woman, who stood up every now and then only to pull a couple of darts out of the dartboard by the door for a few desultory throws. Drinking rum, puffing cigarettes, and munching peanuts, she kept complaining to whichever O'Shaughnessy would listen that the nuts were "as stale as an Afghan's toenails." The best that could be said for her simile, which made us wince, was that it had historical underpinnings. Afghans and their camel teams had played a major role in the development of Kalgoorlie, carrying precious water to prospectors during the gold rush and later helping to build a railroad through the desert. They were considered to be reliable because, as Muslims, they were the only people in Australia who didn't drink booze. Australians still commonly referred to one branch of the railroad—from Tarcoola in South Australia to Alice Springs in the Northern Territory—as "the 'Ghan."

As I stepped to the bar to replenish our pints, I made the mistake of exchanging a "g'day" greeting with her and following it up with a "pretty hot out there" type of remark. Such inanities are never allowed to go unpunished.

"I've been in Kalgoorlie since 1950," she said, in a voice so harsh she almost seemed to be snarling. "Came with two kids and a dog. My husband was drinkin', right here at the Piccadilly, and he didn't 'ear the siren when the train came in." She interrupted her monologue to tell me proudly that she was sixty-six years old. It was easy to believe her.

I ordered another beer and, like a college boy at a mixer, looked around the pub for an avenue of escape. Oblivious, the woman droned on.

"My oath, I love the plyce. Wouldn't go anywhere else. I'm shit-scared of flyin' so I'd certainly never go abroad. Why should I—there's so much to do around 'ere."

"What do you do besides play darts?" I asked politely.

"Why, nothin'," she replied, surprised, even perplexed, by the question. Then, blessedly, she sank into silence, staring at her near-empty glass of rum as if wondering who had drunk it.

On the other side of the room, Jack was talking with a young, well-dressed fellow, who motioned for me to join them. "Let me shout you Yanks to a beer," he said.

His name was Rod, and in the course of conversation it came out that he was a Kalgoorlie lawyer. Well, not quite. He was originally from Perth but for some reason he had gone to high school in Kalgoorlie. After law school he had decided to return to Kalgoorlie to open a practice. But he was no country bumpkin; if anything, the image he projected—in the way he dressed and in his manner of speech—was that of a city slicker enjoying the ostentatious ease of living in a country town.

"Has anybody told you about old Tom Hartrey?" he asked, a wry grin crossing his face at the opportunity to treat us to this nugget of Kalgoorlie folklore. "Tom Hartrey was a lawyer in town. Practiced until he was eighty-seven." Good straight men, we shook our heads and waited for the rest.

"Well, these four fellas went up north hunting," he continued, "and during the trip, one of them got shot—dead. It was strictly an accident. But his three mates were worried, so instead of burying him on the spot, they threw him in the boot of the car and drove back to Kalgoorlie to see their lawyer, Tom.

"Well, you know the roads out here. It took them five days to get back to Kalgoorlie. It was summertime, and when they got into town, they drove right over to old Tom's and told him.

" 'Where did ya bury him?' Tom asked.

" 'We didn't. We got 'im in the boot,' they said.

" 'He'd be a bit off by now, wouldn't he?' said Tom.

" 'Naw, we gutted 'im first,' they said."

We groaned. Our newfound friend, Rod, chuckled. "That's Kalgoorlie," he said.

There was an awkward lull in the conversation, as there tends to be after most such stories, and everyone took another few swigs of beer. When Rod started up again, it was to mention that one of his clients was the well-known madam of the Hay Street whorehouses.

"She's a decent woman, she is," he insisted. "In her fifties now. Gives money to good causes. In her will she even left her body to medical science. A few months later, though, she remembered she had a lot of platinum in her teeth and she asked me to rewrite it. She's got a young kid at some fancy private school—he's got no idea his mother's a famous madam.

"First time I met her I was just a student. Quite a few years ago. I won the lottery one weekend on the bus coming home after a football game. It was a two-hour trip but it always took us four. We used to drink so much there was no end to our pissing. The bus driver was always stopping to let us out.

"When we got back into town, the driver took us to Hay Street and I went in. The rest of the team always waited outside in the bus."

Rod was a short fellow, and while not exactly slightly built, he wasn't heavyset either. He had a youngish, almost scholarly-looking face, and it was hard to imagine him as a member of a football team, particularly in Australia, where the game was played without helmets or padding.

"There was a time clock by the bed. Like an egg timer. Can you imagine, I was dickin' against the clock. And it went off before I did. But the lady had a sense of charity. She gave me an extra minute. It was like a 'time out' in football.

"No chance of disease there," he added. "The girls are examined every couple of weeks by a doctor, and they check out their clientele like hawks. If a bloke looks suspicious, they either throw him out or soak him in Dettol Dip. That'll kill bloody well anything."

The thought suddenly occurred to me that we, too, should meet the madam of the Hay Street whorehouses. After all, they were a historic institution in Kalgoorlie.

Rod assured us that the madam was "easily accessible," then chortled at his choice of words. This would be the time to get her, he advised, chortling again. It was now a little after five o'clock, and the brothel doors wouldn't open for business till seven. We shouted Rod to a round, exchanged a few pleasantries while we drank up. Jack had little inclination to conduct serious research, so he stayed on at the Piccadilly while I went off on my own. "You'll get nothing there without a fistful of fifties," he quipped as I headed out the door.

Hay Street was the only street in town that, suddenly and unaccountably, changed names in the middle. At one intersection it simply became Brookman, perhaps because the police, whose headquarters was about four blocks up from the whorehouses, would have been embarrassed by a Hay Street address, which the Australian public associated with Kalgoorlie's houses of ill repute. But the police had nothing to fear by way of comparison, for while the station house was a bright, modern building, the whorehouses, whose vestibulelike frontages lined both sides of the street further down, looked like the shabby stalls of a Southeast Asian market after all the vegetables had been sold. Several stalls, in fact, had been gutted by fire and were lying idle. A year earlier one of the madam's new recruits had been shot by a jealous boyfriend, who also incinerated the place and then shot himself. "Just a domestic row," she told reporters at the time, "not brothel-related."

But why were two patrol cars parked in front of the madam's residence? What were the police doing at brothel headquarters instead of at their own? Putting these questions aside, I strode boldly up to the open door and pulled out my bona fides. A sign under the bell said RING FOR SERVICE, but that proved unnecessary, for I was welcomed by a lovely young blonde in her early twenties who was straddling a stool on the unenclosed porch at the entrance, apparently waiting for the seven o'clock signal for business to begin. Wearing tight tan pants and a white blouse that fit snugly over her large but far from matronly bosom, she gave the appearance of having just stepped out of a *Playboy* centerfold, yet with her innocence still intact.

"Hi, my name's Candy." There was an enchanting lilt to her voice and a surprising gentleness to her manner. I had been clutching my credentials as if they were a talisman against the devil, but now I handed them to her. They included a letter from the Western Australian Tourist Commission requesting that I be extended "every courtesy" and be given "all possible assistance." I told Candy I wanted to meet the madam.

"I like your shirt," she said. It was a T-shirt from the Galapagos and what she was admiring, presumably, was an artist's rendering of two frigate birds.

"Where's it from?"

"Ecuador," I replied.

"Where's that?"

"South America," I answered.

"Oh, sorry," she said.

Finding nothing more to say, Candy slid off the stool, and with an artless sensuality glided down the long corridor leading to the salon, taking the letters with her. A few minutes later she returned with a slovenly-looking woman who identified herself as the housekeeper and who was wielding a mop as if to prove it.

"The madam can't see you," she barked, handing me back the letter. "She's tied up."

"Tied up," I exclaimed. "But she doesn't open for business till seven."

"She entertains the demons around this time," said the housekeeper, as if the information was a matter of public record, "and she can't be disturbed."

"The what?" I asked.

"The demons—the police," she explained. And without further ado, she marched off, mop in hand, like a character out of a Chekhov play.

Candy seemed to sense my disappointment.

"Would you like to come back and see me at seven?" she asked, but before I even had time to consider the offer, she began reciting the price list. "The cheapest is $30—just for sex. Forty dollars for French and sex. It's $60 for half an hour, $120 an hour. The hourly rate includes everything, French and sex." She paused, then appended an explicit caveat in a way that made her sound positively virtuous: "But I don't do Greek—anal. Just a kiss and a cuddle and we get right down to it." Nothing was said about Dettol Dip or dickin' against the clock.

"No, thanks," I demurred, and concerned about hurting her feelings, added: "Not this time, anyway."

I needn't have worried. As if to show that there we were still friends, she flashed a warm smile. "Have a very pleasant evening. Remember, my name's Candy. Yeah."

With the exception of one or two clerics in town, who from time to time fulminated against the evils of harlotry from the pulpit and in the local newspaper, everyone in Kalgoorlie was remarkably tolerant of the madam and her Hay Street whorehouses. Perhaps it was a legacy handed down from gold rush days—the legendary "whore with the heart of gold" sort of thing. Or perhaps it reflected a more general attitude toward prostitution, pervasive throughout Australia. After all, even Sydney had its "gentlemen's clubs," where a number of large, prestigious corporations were openly known to maintain credit accounts.

One morning shortly after my abortive visit to interview the madam, Jack and I were invited to tea by two lovely old spinster sisters, who except for a brief sojourn in Melbourne had spent their entire lives in Kalgoorlie. Now in their eighties, the two women lived together in an old house on a quiet side street, reminiscing about their childhood years, when they often accompanied their father, a famous goldfields physician, as he made his rounds by horse and carriage.

The Laver sisters, as they were affectionately known, thought Kalgoorlie "lucky" to have the madam and her girls in town.

"We don't call them whores," cautioned Elizabeth. "To us they're 'the girls.'"

"Yes, we treat them with respect," her sister agreed. "They're just doing a job. You know, we've never had much rape out here in the goldfields."

8

Before we left the eastern goldfields we wanted to see Coolgardie, which had been established even before Kalgoorlie. Back in the 1890s a traveler who had made the same trip by coach that we were now making by car described it as follows: "The ride is not an inspiring one . . . undulating, sparsely wooded country that is scorched and dismal." Little had changed in the intervening span of years—we drove through a desertlike landscape described on the map as "scattered scrub," "abandoned mines," and "lakes," the latter a heartless misnomer for what in reality were dried-out, sunbaked salt pans, which might have seen water twenty years ago, if that. The interminable gray-green scrub was only occasionally interrupted by a few stunted gums.

Though the goldfields had once boasted "lots of stands of substantial trees—mulga, mulga pine, gimlet, and the straggling forests of salmon gum," over the years all had been cut down for firewood to fuel the mines and to purify water. Before 1903, when a remarkable three-hundred-mile pipeline was completed, sufficient quantities of fresh water could only be obtained by desalinating brackish bore water with wood-fired condensers. Working first with horse and dray and then, when the nearby timber was exhausted, with narrow-gauge railway lines that extended into the bush for hundreds of miles in every direction, the firewood companies "denuded the earth and contributed greatly to the frequent and fearful dust storms that often afflicted the region."

It had never occurred to anyone living in Coolgardie during the gold rush that the ore would run out, and a great town rose out of the desert. Before the coming of the railroad, thousands made the trek north across the arid wastelands from Southern Cross on bicycles and wagons, or pushing wheelbarrows piled high with all their worldly possessions. In 1894 the telegraph arrived, and two years later the railroad, electric lights, and telephones. By the turn of the century the population had soared to over 15,000.

The boom showed no signs of abating. Magnificent buildings were erected on the assumption that Coolgardie would remain the permanent capital of the goldfields, and it quickly became the third largest town in Western Australia; only Perth and Fremantle were bigger. During its heyday, the town boasted a large government hospital with fourteen doctors, six banks, seven newspapers, one state school and three private schools, twenty-three hotels, and three breweries. A miniature zoo had been laid out, and there were even plans to build a theater. It also had a mosque, which was the site of one of the rare instances of major crime to occur in the area—an Afghan camel driver, Goulam Mahomet, shot and killed a fellow countryman while the latter was kneeling in prayer. Unlike the American west, where gunfights and murders were commonplace, the Australian goldfields were practically free of violence. In recalling his Australian mining days Herbert Hoover once remarked: "They had one great virtue in their joys; when they did get solace from the desert in drink, they never seemed to think of shooting up the town; and anyway, they had nothing to shoot with. They ran to sentiment.

They'd put their arms around each other's shoulders and sing of mother."

Today, Coolgardie is virtually a ghost town, surrounded by sunscorched country that looks as if it had witnessed a desperate struggle. In their feverish search for gold, prospectors had gouged deep holes into the earth before abandoning those "shows" and rushing off to search elsewhere when the elusive metal petered out. Behind them, they left desolation pockmarked with gaping pits and strewn with piles of rubble and abandoned mining machinery.

A few people now hung on in Coolgardie, still managing to eke out an existence. May and Frank Waghorn had once raked through old rubbish tips searching for antique bottles when they weren't behind the counter of their Curio Shop and Museum. But like so many before them, they were about to pull out and go elsewhere. Those that remained inevitably congregated at the Denver City, a grand old Victorian structure on Bayley Street, and the only hotel left from the boom days. Still operating as a pub, it also serviced the occasional tourist.

As we walked along Bayley Street I tried to imagine it as one oldtimer had vividly recalled it: "It is still not difficult to realize that sixty years ago this wide street echoed the voices of crowding pedestrians, the rattle of polished sulkies and the click of fine horses, the grind of heavy drays, and the almost silent ponderous plod of loaded cameldteams."

We wandered into the old graveyard at the edge of town. Typhoid had claimed the lives of more than two thousand settlers between 1894 and 1899, and many had been buried there. With an almost macabre delight, diggers had occasionally prospected for gold in cemeteries, like the one in the ghost town of Kanowna, where nothing remained but the street signs and the railway platform. But that hadn't been the case in Coolgardie, where we found one tombstone epitaph that read: "Phyllis 5 years. It is well with the child."

Mike Charlton was one Coolgardie resident who had only recently moved to the town. A few years earlier he had left his job as an accountant in Perth and struck out for the Western Australian goldfields. We met him at the Denver City that lazy Sunday afternoon, and he invited us home with him. We lounged around his backyard, drinking beer under an immense Japanese pepper tree that obviously had been planted long ago. Some nameless person had carried that seed across the desert, and it had endured the arid climate and even flourished. Now its delicate green foliage shaded us from the fiery midday sun.

There was a haunting serenity about his place. The only discernible sound was the soft rustling of lacy leaves in the great tree overhead as a desert breeze wafted through it. Occasionally, the cawing of a crow pierced the stillness. That melancholy outcry was like a lamentation, and made Coolgardie seem all the more desolate.

A magnificent major mitchell perched in a black cage just outside the porch door. Mike had captured the cockatoo far out in the bush before it had learned to fly. The brilliant pink and gray plumage of that exotic creature provided a striking contrast to its stark surroundings.

"A few years back I ran across a book called *Glint of Gold* in my dad's library," began Mike, as he handed me another beer. "It was about the old days in the goldfields and blokes just walking along pickin' up bucketfuls of the stuff. Crikey Moses, I thought, they couldn't have picked up the lot.

"So one weekend my brother and me came up here for a bit of a look, but we never even saw color. We stuck at it, though, an' I learned about prospectin'. Gold was only about $30 an ounce back then, and ya had to find a few ounces to make good money."

To me, Mike was an unlikely-looking prospector. I'd been weaned on old films like *The Treasure of the Sierra Madre* and he wasn't the grizzled, rough character I had come to expect. Mike was a tall, thin, ascetic-looking fellow in his early thirties, who looked as if he'd be more at home on a college campus. He lived in an old house in back of an abandoned bakery with his wife, Judy, and their two young children. He'd bought both properties a few years before for "a song."

"When metal detectors first came out, I didn't think they worked," Mike continued, "but a mate of mine took his to Cue, and came back with five ounces for a weekend. We bought one and went out to Meekatharra and spent a couple a' weeks there, but didn't do any good.

"So back we went to Perth to get an idea of how the machine worked. We had the instruction book and we could read. But it wasn't quite that simple," said Mike knowingly, as he recalled the experience. "So I got another mate of mine to show me how to use the detector. After that we came to Coolgardie, and I haven't looked back since.

"I started using the detector in 1979. I remember because gold went up then to around $800 an ounce. It freaked me right out. I never understood before then, even when I read the books, what possessed those old-timers to grab a water bag and charge off hundreds of miles into the bush to risk their lives. That's gold fever.

"The second day after I got here, I went out over that hill," said Mike, pointing to a low red mound less than half a mile away, "and picked up a three-ounce nugget. That was worth over a month's wages. I figured someone must've lost it a long time ago because I reckoned that to find gold like that ya had to go beyond the Black Stump, away from civilization. So Judy and I talked it over and we decided I should give my job away and go at it full-time.

"By Jesus, when you start finding gold, there's nothing in this world like it. First one pops up here! Another there! And another one! It's like walkin' around pickin' up hundred-dollar bills. You just didn't want to stop."

Mike's growing enthusiasm as he recalled the experience became infectious, and at one point I got so caught up by it I was ready to grab a water bag and race off into the desert myself for a life of adventure. I found myself thinking back to my twenties, when I had almost emigrated to Australia with my wife and three daughters, and it occurred to me that, had the marriage not failed, I might actually have ended up doing what Mike was doing now.

"We were the first in this area," Mike continued, "but as time went on, you'd look out across the flats and see campfires all through the scrub. There were people everywhere, looking for gold. But they thinned out after a spell because Coolgardie is a rough place to use a detector. Lots of tin cans, nails, and other things that drive people crazy. I've heard of blokes shootin' detectors or wrappin' 'em around trees.

"My father's a solicitor, and at the time he thought I was pretty irresponsible. But after that day I picked up a sixty-seven-ounce nugget and got over $40,000 for it, I guess he decided that maybe I wasn't doin' too bad."

"You make it sound pretty easy," said Dave. "Why haven't a lot of other fellas gone out and made their fortunes?" If I had any illusions about searching for gold, one glance at Dave snapped me back to reality. Mike had emphasized that in the Australian bush one was totally dependent on his mate. And there sat mine, slouching in a rocking chair, bush hat on his head and fly net over his face, looking like a displaced bee keeper.

"You've gutta have a knack for this," answered Mike. "Besides, I've spent a lot of time poring over books, searching through old records, and studying maps at the Historical Society in Perth. It took years, but I *learned* where to find the gold."

Mike's six-year-old daughter came out of the house carrying some cold cans of beer. The sun, filtering through the leaves of the pepper tree, glinted off her white dress and light blond hair. Mike watched her as she approached, giving her the tender look a doting father reserves for his favorite child. Melanie smiled shyly, basking in the attention. Her face radiated delight as she handed her father the beer and sat down on the bench beside him.

"There's more to prospectin' than just goin' out and pickin' up gold," he continued. "You've gutta feel as comfortable out in the bush as you would sittin' here. If you're out under a gum it's like sittin' under this old tree. You've gutta feel as if you belong. There's nothin' out there that'll kill ya. Snakes go the other way.

"The real danger is bein' careless about water, and it's somethin' ya can't take lightly. Even people that spend a lot of time in the bush can dehydrate without knowin' it. Ya can be on your back before ya know it. I passed out once myself. Fortunately, I was with my brother.

"There's only one thing out there that scares me now," he added, his tanned face darkening at the thought. "Bloody Alsatian dogs that've crossed with dingoes. A mate of mine was drivin' along a track, when down the other way came these three Alsatian dingoes. The bloody dogs started snarlin', tryin' to get into his vehicle at him. He hadda run 'em over. When I go out there now, I always carry a shotgun. I never used to bother, but I do now."

Mike led us over to the corrugated-iron bakery shed. Inside sat a 1930 Chrysler convertible and an old Chevy, both in extraordinary condition, extremely dry climate keeping them almost entirely free of rust. Old bottles and other curios lay around the shed, stacked in wooden crates. It was an antique collector's treasure trove.

"There's things in the bush you'd never expect to find," he said. "Once I stumbled across an old wood-train line that ran a couple of hundred miles into the scrub. No record on the maps of it ever being there. In the old days the government used to tax the trains for each foot of track they laid. This one had been done on the sly.

"I followed it all the way to the end. The tracks were pulled up a long time ago, and every few miles along the old sleeper bed was an abandoned camp, with thousands of old bottles just lying around. They must have pulled out in a big hurry because they left their furniture and didn't even bother to take pots and pans off the stoves. I dragged those automobiles outta there with my four-wheel-drive."

Melanie stuck her pretty blond head through the open door and announced, "Mummy wants you should all cum in for tea."

"Ya see, I've really got all I want," Mike began, as we walked into his house. "I wouldn't swap this for anythin'. It's a life that's been kind to me. I wouldn't recommend it for everybody, but it suits me. I could sit on my backside now and never have to work again. I'm happy here, and I just want to enjoy life. If ya want to work all day, the rewards are there. Still heaps of gold out there for blokes that want to look for it. They'll never find the lot.

"I didn't see the sense of saving up till I'm sixty-five to get a gold watch. I can buy one now. I've seen 'em coming through in their cars, people who've saved all their lives to get a proper holiday. I've thought, what the hell, I'm doing it right now."

After a pleasant tea in their old-fashioned kitchen we left Mike and Judy's place, and headed back to Kalgoorlie, but not before dropping by the old Coolgardie train station to have a look around. Since the railway had long ago stopped running there, now it was little more than a dusty, cobwebbed museum. Outside the station was a vintage steam engine, but I was more interested in the moldy display case that hung on a wall inside. In words and old photographs it related the story of Modesto Varischetti, an Italian immigrant who in 1907 was trapped a thousand feet underground in a tiny air pocket of a flooded mine shaft and who was finally saved only by the determined efforts of his mates. Divers with helmets, suits, and air lines were dispatched from Fremantle, hundreds of miles away, but it took a Welsh miner, who himself had been a diver, to find Varischetti and keep him alive with food and water until the mine was pumped out nine days later.

Everyone in the goldfields seemed to know the Varischetti story, and Mike Charlton had referred to it in a discussion about mateship. Mateship is a quality deeply ingrained in the Australian character, and though it was still early in the journey, I was already beginning to appreciate the conditions that had led to people's placing such an emphasis on it, particularly in the Outback.

Australians and Americans often regard themselves as sharing common values stemming from a comparable frontier heritage. Yet however similar their histories, the geography of the two countries gave rise to marked differences in national character. In the relatively benign American wilderness, where abundant fish and game ensured the survival of even the most inexperienced settler, self-reliance and individualism might have been virtues. But such notions were less appropriate in the Australian bush, where water itself was often impossible to come by and where even today road maps caution against traveling alone in uninhabited areas, which pose a constant threat to life. Out of this kind of adversity evolved mateship, the quintessential Australian virtue, assurance that one's fellows would see him through whatever hardships the land might inflict.

2

North to Broome

Lugger at Broome

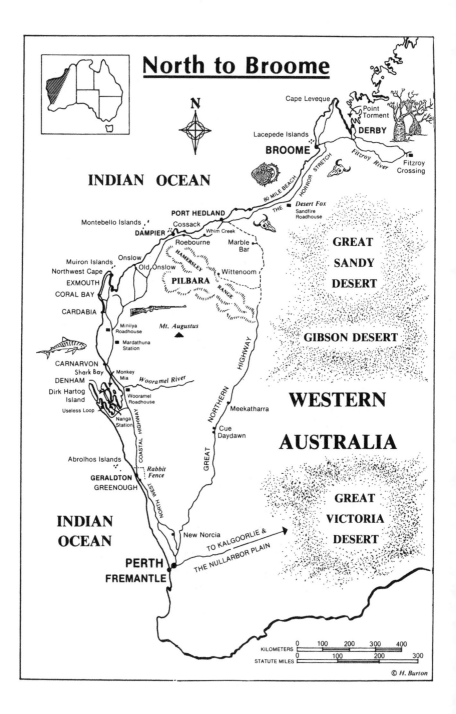

North to Broome

N

INDIAN OCEAN

Cape Leveque
Point Torment
DERBY
Lacepede Islands
BROOME
Fitzroy River
Fitzroy Crossing

80 MILE BEACH
THE
HORROR STRETCH

Desert Fox
Sandfire Roadhouse

PORT HEDLAND
Montebello Islands
Cossack
DAMPIER
Whim Creek
Roebourne
Marble Bar
HAMERSLEY
Muiron Islands
Onslow
Northwest Cape
Old Onslow
EXMOUTH
PILBARA
Wittenoom
CORAL BAY
RANGE
CARDABIA

GREAT SANDY DESERT

Minilya Roadhouse
Mt. Augustus
Mardathuna Station

GIBSON DESERT

CARNARVON
Shark Bay
Monkey Mia
DENHAM
Wooramel River
Dirk Hartog Island
Wooramel Roadhouse
Useless Loop
Nanga Station

WESTERN

HIGHWAY
GREAT NORTHERN

Meekatharra

AUSTRALIA

Abrolhos Islands
COASTAL HIGHWAY
Cue
Daydawn
Rabbit Fence
GERALDTON
GREENOUGH
NORTH WEST

GREAT VICTORIA DESERT

INDIAN OCEAN

New Norcia
TO KALGOORLIE &
THE NULLARBOR PLAIN

PERTH
FREMANTLE

KILOMETERS 0 100 200 300 400
STATUTE MILES 0 100 200 300

© H. Burton

1

The day before we left Kalgoorlie an Antarctic cold front pushed across the Southern Ocean and the Great Australian Bight, bringing brisk weather to Esperance on the coast and moderating even the desert heat far inland. On a refreshingly cool, starry evening, Jack and I walked to the Kalgoorlie station at the edge of town and waited on the platform for the westbound Indian-Pacific, which would take us to Perth.

The train broke the stillness of the night, pulling into town around 11 P.M., and we clambered aboard. Locating our compartments, we threw our bags on the berths and, ever hopeful, made yet another foray to the lounge car. But except for a waiter thumbing through a newspaper, the car was deserted, and rather than interrupt his reading, we decided to turn in for the night. The following morning the train arrived in Perth, the capital of Western Australia, a state four times the size of Texas with less than one-tenth the population. Perth was the point of departure for the first leg of our "serious journey" north.

Known alternately as "the sunniest of Australian capitals" and "the most isolated capital in the world," Perth stands on the north bank of the Swan River, twelve miles from the Indian Ocean and seventeen hundred miles from Adelaide in South Australia. (The road between the two cities was paved only in 1976.) Though not as cosmopolitan as Sydney—the arrival of the Concorde in Perth caused such excitement that offices were emptied when workers rushed to the rooftops to watch its approach—it's an immaculate city, free of the industrial blight and grime one usually associates with urban environments. The tinted glass and burnished metal of recently built skyscrapers gleamed in the morning sun as we made our way along tree-lined St. George's Terrace, past century-old white stone buildings, sparkling new shopping arcades with red brick Tudoresque facades, and the lush green park of Government House Gardens. Even on weekdays, windsurfers and pleasure craft of every description dotted the river, and along its banks people sat on the grass enjoying Perth's relaxed atmosphere.

But despite the leisurely pace of the city, new construction was booming, and a number of old buildings were being refurbished in what, after all, was the capital of Western Australia, the "last frontier." The fire station on Murray Street, a heavy Edwardian sandstone edifice enlivened with iron-lace decorations, had been painstakingly restored, its "rusticated stonework" exterior a rough-hewed imitation of the natural stone itself. His Majesty's Theater, a more opulent Edwardian structure whose balconies, pilasters, and pediments gave it the appearance of a huge white wedding cake, still served as a local playhouse.

We stopped at the Mayfair Pub for a drink and there got into a conversation with a well-dressed fellow standing at the bar, a Perth businessman who referred to the pub as "my outer office." As a dinki-di Western Australian, our drinking companion revered Alan Bond, who to him embodied what Perth was all about—namely, a place to make money and then to use it in the pure pursuit of pleasure. Bondy, as the renowned entrepreneur/millionaire yachtsman was called in those parts, was a self-made man who had started as a Fremantle sign painter. He had come a long way from those days, but his huge red rendition of a dingo still stood over the Dingo Flour Company, on the road between Perth and Fremantle, like a huge monument to his humble beginnings.

Bondy, his admirers liked to point out, had always taken "the hard jobs, the high jobs," and with the money thus earned he bought property in the Perth area and developed it. He was brash, aggressive, and relentless, and those same characteristics that led to his becoming a multimillionaire also enabled him, finally, in 1983, to beat the Americans at their own game and wrest the treasured America's Cup from the New York Yacht Club.

Bondy's shrewdness was legendary, and people likened him to a boardroom Napoleon or a corporate Ned Kelly, the notorious nineteenth-century Australian outlaw who had since become a folk hero. And if he was ruthless, that trait was redeemed in the eyes of his admirers by his charm. "He's the only person I know who could get his hand up a stewardess's dress before the plane even got off the ground," said our companion at the bar.

During the ten days or so we spent in Perth, often in the company of friends from the South Perth Yacht Club, we cruised up the Swan River to visit the vineyards on its banks or sailed downriver to the town of Fremantle, which had somehow managed to retain its turn-of-the-century seaport atmosphere despite the frenzy of activity that engulfed the place as it prepared for the 1987 America's Cup races. (To many people in Western Australia, winning the Cup in 1983 was a more important historical event than having won World War I.) We spent one sparkling clear day unsuccessfully trolling offshore for marlin on a sportsfisherman out of Fremantle, anchoring at sunset off nearby Rottnest Island, a much-publicized wildlife sanctuary that according to our host was even more popular among locals as the ideal spot for "dirty weekends." And night after night we ate freshly caught Indian Ocean crayfish and prawns at a small but superb restaurant called the Fishy Affair on James Street, enjoying after-dinner coffee at one of several outdoor cafés in Northbridge, the city's modest "Latin Quarter." Perth certainly had its attractions.

But Jack and I were committed to our journey into the bush, and early on we had resolved to spend no more than two weeks in Perth, making whatever arrangements were necessary and then proceeding on the trek north. Why north? Because the northern part of W.A., or to put it another way, the northwestern corner of Australia, was reputed to be one of the wildest places on the continent. That was particularly true of the region beyond Broome, a vast, sparsely populated frontier area along the tropical coast of Western Australia known as the Kimberleys. Habitat to the man-eating *Crocodylus porosus* and home to ex–crocodile hunters and an odd assortment of other such "bushies" (the term urban-dwelling Australians applied to anyone living "beyond the Black Stump"), the Kimberleys were so remote that, as Western Australians liked to point out, some of its rugged wilderness had never felt the foot of man.

Before we left town we contacted Peter Eaton, an estate agent known to a lawyer friend of ours in Sydney. Peter, we'd been told, specialized in the sale of large station properties in the Western Australian bush and would probably be able to give us some useful advice about our proposed trip.

When we phoned, Peter told us that he'd be leaving the following day for New Norcia, the site of an old Benedictine monastery where he had recently become involved in a hotel project. Since we ourselves were ready to leave Perth, we arranged to meet the next morning at his home in City Beach, a suburb overlooking the Indian Ocean. The plan was to follow him up to New Norcia, seventy-five miles to the north, in the four-wheel-drive Toyota the Western Australian Tourist Commission had provided us.

When we pulled up to his modest ranch-style house at 6 A.M. the following morning, Peter was already waiting, a tall, thin, intense man in his mid-fifties who seemed possessed by a boundless but nervous energy. Standing in the driveway, he lectured us on the dangers of going into the bush unprepared and offered to lend us some of his own equipment, which we were more than happy to have. Then, after introducing us to his wife, Margaret, who served us a quick cup of coffee, he hustled us out of the house, jumped into his car, and led us out of the city.

We followed Peter's battered Volvo onto a highway running through the fertile valley around Perth, where the Avon River flows down from the Darling Range to join the Swan, which in turn meanders through lush farmland and vineyards before emptying into the sea at Fremantle. The road passed through wheat fields and paddocks that, now, at the height of summer, were slightly sunburnt and brown, but were said to be in winter months "as green and smooth as billiard tables." The drive took about two hours, and we reached the sprawling dust-covered outpost of New Norcia (which the Aussies pronounced something like "new nausea") by midmorning.

2

On January 8, 1846, a party of European missionaries landed at Fremantle. They knelt in the burning sand, thanked God for their safe arrival, and immediately divided into three parties. The first sailed for Sydney, while the remaining two set off into the virgin bush of Western Australia to establish aboriginal missions, one heading south, the other north. The Sydney-bound group of monks drowned when they were shipwrecked, and the party that went south also met with failure when the natives refused to be converted by men so obviously unable to provide for themselves in the bush.

Only the third band—two monks, two lay missionaries, and an Irish catechist—accomplished their goal, though several members of the group died in the process. After an arduous trek over the Darling Range, they came to an area called the Victoria Plains, which was thick with scrub and thorny vegetation. They chose a site for their settlement on a freshwater lake at a place called Noondagoonda, where they built a "priests' hut." But a year later, after discovering that the land they had chosen had already been leased to some pastoralists (and after all their crops had been destroyed by wild horses), they moved to another location several miles away. There, under the leadership of Dom Salvado, they established a mission, calling it Nova Nursia after the Italian town where St. Benedict was born.

Dave and I followed Peter Eaton's Volvo up the narrow dirt road past the Benedictine monastery, a cluster of small Moorish-looking buildings huddled around a cathedral, and turned left into the dusty parking lot of the New Norcia Hotel. Peter was already out of his car waiting for us as we pulled in beside him, and he immediately launched into a discourse on his investment strategy. Our curiosity had been greatly aroused, as there was clearly little here worth developing, least of all the ramshackle hotel itself.

"The idea in this world is to con people," Peter Eaton confided to us with a knowing wink, as we joined him on the driveway. He had a lean and hungry look about him that could, at least in part, be attributed to his nervous energy. His furtive green eyes never seemed to fix on anything, darting constantly about like those of a hawk searching for something to swoop down upon. "Those monks have no idea what they've got here," the "here" being conveyed with a wide sweep of his arm that took in the full breadth of the rambling, rather Gothic structure in front of us.

"You see," he continued, "they've always been against tourists, but now I think they're beginning to realize they can't exist without 'em. That's why I was able to negotiate such a good lease. People are going to flock here. I can already see the tour buses out front. We're sittin' on a real gold mine."

Even though New Norcia was only about a hundred miles from Perth, it was on a secondary road that was lightly traveled. Sitting atop the crest of a hill, and surrounded by dead trees, the decrepit edifice he now led us toward looked as if it belonged on the set of a low-budget horror film. The hotel, which had the unenviable record of operating at a deficit since it had first been built almost a century ago, had just been taken over by a man with a financial obsession.

For years Peter Eaton had doggedly attempted to follow the course set by daring entrepreneurs like Alan Bond and Robert Holmes à Court, and was striving to become a multimillionaire. But unlike their well-publicized successes, those of Peter and the group of financial wizards with whom he was involved were the products of an unfailing talent for choosing projects that were monetary disasters. In addition to the New Norcia Hotel, they were currently saddled with a piece of property with the improbable name of Mt. Augustus.

That "investment" was an enormous rock, situated in one of the most remote and climatically inhospitable regions of W.A., where temperatures regularly exceeded 135 degrees. Mt. Augustus had nothing to recommend it except its size. For years Eaton and his colleagues had tried unsuccessfully to promote it as the largest monolith in the world, and consequently, as a greater attraction than the famous Ayers Rock in the center of the continent. But since it had such primitive facilities and could be reached only by chartered plane or four-wheel-drive vehicles, tour operators invariably failed to share their enthusiasm for the venture.

But headway had been made with their New Norcia project as the monks at the nearby Benedictine monastery, owners of the New Norcia Hotel, had allowed the Eaton group to operate it on a trial basis to determine its potential. Even though it had continued to lose more money for them, they had just leased the place for twenty years, and had grandiose plans for a massive refurbishing of the sixteen-room building. But they had "a bit of a problem," as Peter phrased it. "At least for the moment, we're working on limited capital."

Directly in front of the hotel was a tennis court surrounded by a wire fence. Termites had chewed away the wooden posts that supported it, and the wire was lying in tangled heaps on the ground. The court's surface was pockmarked with holes resembling miniature bomb craters, and all that remained of its net was a few tattered pieces of string blowing in the wind. "We'll resurface that," said Peter, "then do a bit more landscaping."

"Have you done some already?" I asked. There were no signs of any new plantings, and the entire grounds had gone to seed.

"Oh, yes," replied Peter, astonished at my failure to appreciate the improvements that had already been made. "We planted four thousand trees here, but most of them got eaten out by sheep. I conned the men in the Tree Department to come and plant them one weekend.

You see, the road that leads in here's all wrong. We're gonna reroute it and line it with big tall gum trees. Try and imagine what this place would look like at night with the moon shining on it," he mused. "What a landscape! I can see shadows growing longer and creeping up the hill."

He led us into the dingy lobby of the hotel, but the publican, Walt Dugan, was not in his office.

"He's probably in the bar having breakfast," offered Peter, as he led us down a gloomy hallway where the plaster was cracking on the walls and the paint was bubbling on the plaster.

Sitting on a stool at the bar drinking a glass of beer was Walt, a florid man with a mawlike double chin. His rotund belly hung over his belt and rested on his lap, and when he rose to shake hands he had to turn to the side as he couldn't reach us with his stomach in the way.

"Would ya like some brekie?" Walt asked. "Our brekie here's unreal, a real feature. I kin have my wife Cheryl whip ya up somethin', she's in the kitchen cleanin' up." He spoke with the rapidity of a machine gun, and raked us with a burst of words.

We gratefully declined and opted for a tour of the hotel. As we walked up the wide stairs from the lobby to the second floor, Walt stopped on the landing and, turning to us with a meaningful stare, asked, "You two are Americans, what does this remind ya of?"

"They're a lot like the stairs you once pushed me down, Jack," said Dave, nonplussed by our host's odd expression.

"No, no, I don't mean that," said Walt, surprised that neither of us had any notion what he was alluding to. "Doesn't it remind you of those Georgia mansions you see in the old movies of the Deep South? Youse blokes would know better than me, but this is somethin' outta *Gone With the Wind*. Sometimes I say to Cheryl when she's comin' downstairs from cleanin' up the rooms, 'Come on, lover, just imagine you're in Tara.' We call each other 'lover' when no one's around, that's how close we are."

Walt used the heavily enameled banister to haul himself up the stairs, and when we came to a room off the darkened hallway on the second floor he abruptly halted.

"This is the Bridal Suite," he explained. As if about to show us something titillating, he opened the door and smiled lasciviously, forcing his jowls further around the sides of his face, extending an open hand in an invitation for us to enter.

"Sometimes when the hotel is empty, Cheryl and I stay here. It's real romantic."

The room was like countless others in any seedy hotel. It was furnished with a sagging double bed that had a great hollow belly in the center of it. Against one wall was a chest of drawers with cigarette burns on the top, and a badly scratched armoire stood beside it. A drab institutional green paint and a few garish paintings on the walls provided the finishing touches.

"A very attractive painting," remarked Dave, pointing to a still life on a wall that had captured his fancy. A woeful attempt at depicting a bowl of fruit, it was executed in dark grays and greens that suggested a plate of spoiled vegetables.

"Isn't it magnificent?" Peter agreed. "You won't believe it, but I bought twenty-four of them exactly like that for a dollar a piece at a Travelodge that was remodeling. We've got one in every room."

Shambling over to the window, Walt brushed the dusty orange curtain aside with a hand covered with thick black hair. Turning to us and again grinning from jowl to jowl, he remarked, "What a view! Isn't that a feature? It's just unreal."

Through the grime-coated glass I could make out beyond the driveway a field of dead brown grass where, once upon a time, another optimistic soul had attempted to cultivate a golf green. It had now reverted to an enormous sand trap and was, as Walt had appraised it, unreal.

"How many guests can the hotel accommodate?" I asked, hoping to salvage something from the experience.

"There's sixteen rooms, but we can sleep over forty people," replied Peter. We'll be able to handle more when we build the new staff quarters."

"That must make for some interesting sleeping arrangements," Dave observed.

"Australians don't mind sharing if they can experience a bit of their history," offered Peter. "They want some of the old world charm, so they gutta go back to the past."

"Where's the bathroom?" asked Dave, opening the door of the armoire as if he expected to find it there.

"Just down the hall," replied Walt. "None of the rooms have them but people on holiday don't want that sort of thing."

"How many people stay here on average?" I asked.

"We've been averaging about two and a half guests a night," answered Peter, "but now that word's gettin' around we're open, things are pickin' up."

"It's unreal," said Walt.

As Peter and Walt led us back down the stairs they became caught up in their excitement and spoke to each other animatedly about elaborate future plans. I suggested to Dave that New Norcia might be a good, sound investment for him—the sort of blue chip holding he could put away and not have to worry about.

"Not a bad idea," he agreed. "The management really inspires confidence."

The only notable aspect of the dining room was its antique sideboard, to which Walt immediately called our attention. "That would be years and years old," he assured us. Then, gesturing toward a blank wall, he said, "We wanna take this outta here and have windows goin' right across."

"Imagine it with the grass growing," chimed in Peter.

"Yes, yes, it's unreal," added Walt, commencing a volley of words: "You get a few dandelions growing, and then the wild flowers. You'd have a mass of green with yellow dotted across it. Whatta feature!"

"Wouldn't it be a bit of a problem putting windows there?" I asked. "That looks like a weight-bearing wall."

"Well, a lot would have to go into it," Peter admitted.

"Massive sealed beams," proposed Walt, presumably meaning "steel." "It would be very expensive, but it can be done."

"We'll have musicians to entertain the dinner guests," the undaunted Peter declared, and to give us a bit of a preview, pushed a cassette tape of oddly funereal music into a cheap portable radio sitting on the sideboard.

Walking over to a window he gazed reverentially out on the landscape and outlined further his great plans, punctuated by frequent "that'll be a feature" and "it'll be unreal" from Walt.

For a fleeting moment it occurred to me that perhaps we were being conned. But the thought was immediately dismissed as wishful thinking—that was too much to hope for. At this point in our trip I had already met enough earnest Australians to know that this pair was serious. The country seemed to inspire a headlong, if heedless, entrepreneurial spirit. Business success was the ultimate objective in this frontier country where opportunity seemed so widely available.

When Peter finished his monologue Walt herded us through a rear door in the dining room to the courtyard, where he showed us an unevenly shaped plot that would soon hold a beer garden. As we stood in the center of the barbecue-pit-to-be, Peter treated us to a bit of a history lesson. "In the last century," he began, "Bishop Solgado, the bloke who started this all off, heard that a big brushfire was bearing down on the place and couldn't be stopped. He sent someone to the cathedral and told him to bring back a painting of the Virgin Mary. Bishop Solgado held it up in front of the fire and put it out. The people in the village built a shrine here to honor him. What I'm trying to do here is beautify, what'da ya call it . . . beautification, ya know, ya turn 'em into a saint."

"Could you possibly mean beatification?" asked Dave, who was always ready to assist people with words they couldn't pronounce.

"Ya, that's it. You see, we need a saint in Australia. There's never been one before, and we want it to be right here. That's my idea," Peter announced proudly, as he led us across the courtyard toward the stable.

The stable was a tall, single-story building with a large grape arbor on one side. Walt lumbered over to the arbor and plopped himself down in a chair under it. He pulled a dirty handkerchief from his pocket and mopped the perspiration that was running down his face and neck.

"These were the original staff quarters," he said. "Me 'n me wife come over 'ere when we wanna sorta relax. I put the light on there, and reach up an' get some vino, while Cheryl grills up somethin' for me on the barbie." Walt demonstrated his grape-picking technique by snatching a cluster off the vine and shoving a fistful of grapes into his mouth. " 'Ave some," he advised, "they're unreal."

Peter plucked a single red grape from the vine. He held it up against the sky with a forefinger and thumb, examining it in the light as if it were a rare gem. "Do you know what this is?" he asked.

"It's a grape," Dave replied with great conviction.

I knew immediately that he was mistaken. I didn't know exactly what it was either, but it obviously wasn't a grape.

"Outwardly it is, but it really isn't," revealed Peter, confirming my suspicions. "It's the seed inside that's the important thing. It's like this place in a way. What you see here now isn't what it's really like. You've got to be able to look beyond things."

"It's unreal," said Walt, shaking his head from side to side in admiration of Peter's power of divination. "Come on, we'll show ya the kitchen, that's where it all happens. It's a real feature."

A haggard-looking Cheryl stood in the kitchen scrubbing pots and pans, hardly an appropriate chore for a woman who was encouraged to consider herself another Scarlett O'Hara. Peter introduced us to her and to Bridget, a shapely redheaded woman in her mid-thirties who was peeling onions and had tears streaming down her face.

"Bridget's an expert on restoring old art masterpieces, and can tell if they're fakes or the real thing," Peter boasted. "She came over from England to help the monks repair some of their paintings, but she had a bit of a falling out with the abbot. Now she's our chef."

"Peter convinced me that peeling onions and restoring paintings are one and the same occupation," said Bridget, with more than a hint of irony. "These aren't actually onions, you know."

"Can you really identify a forged work of art?" asked Dave, still dubious about the monastery's claim that it had Raphaels in its collection.

"My ability to spot fakes isn't restricted to art," said Bridget, brushing the tears from her eyes with her forearm.

"You're gonna hafta do somethin' about this water," said Cheryl to Peter, harshly. "It's just filthy. S'not even fit to scrub pots with."

"No worries, Cheryl, she'll be right soon. I was just tellin' the boys about the problem," Peter lied. "Come on, fellas, I'll show you what I was talking about." He quickly made his escape by leading us out the back door and into the courtyard, leaving Walt behind to cover his retreat.

"Now it's water. You wouldn't believe the problems I have to put up with," said Peter, showing a bit of annoyance for the first time. "See, we had no water, so we conned the government into building a thirty-foot dam and catchment area. It's beautiful rainwater that runs into it, but the dam is made out of clay. It's the sort of clay that once it's in the water, it stays in suspension forever."

"You mean you serve that as drinking water to guests, and you use it to cook with?" asked Dave, making a feeble effort at generating some righteous indignation.

"Yeah, I wouldn't drink the bloody water here, but the beer's fair dinkum," Peter said with a devilish wink. "We just spent fifteen thousand dollars on a purification plant, but it hasn't helped much. I've been trying to con the health inspector. He's threatened to close us down. He's getting very pushy."

Walt joined us again, apparently having successfully put down the palace revolt.

"How in the world are you going to go ahead with any of your plans without a water supply?" I asked him. "Didn't you say the stuff underground was salty?"

"No worries," Walt assured us. "Once we get rolling, we'll get a deceleration plant to get rid of the salt."

"Do you mean desalinization?" queried Dave, himself confused by the high-tech terminology.

"Yeah, that's it. Ya know about them, do ya? Cost a fair bit of money, that would, but it'd be worth it. Right down here, all natural-growing trees and shrubs. The first twelve to eighteen months would be the worst, but just imagine what it would look like after that."

"It'll be unreal," I suggested, for once beating Walt to the punch.

"A real feature," added Dave.

3

After an eerie lunch with the abbot and monks of the Benedictine monastery, which in keeping with regulations was eaten in enforced silence, we headed back to the highway to continue the journey north. "When we get the hotel tarted up," we heard Peter shouting as we drove away, "it'll be worth a squillion dollars."

Although we were now crossing the narrow sliver of rolling coastal plain that extends from the southwest corner of W.A. a few hundred miles north, the land seemed to become less and less fertile. We drove past scraggly fields of strange native trees, like quandong, jam, banksia, and blackboy (which has a long flower spike protruding from its grasslike leaves and is thought to look like an aboriginal throwing a spear); past the deserted farming hamlet of Greenough (circa 1860), whose old stone buildings, some windowless and gaping, others beautifully restored by the National Trust (the equivalent of our National Heritage Foundation) were all that remained after drought, disease, and floods caused its early demise; past broad meadows of high, windswept grass, where sheep no longer grazed; past an occasional solitary river gum whose gnarled trunk, bent over by the force of the incessant winds, grew horizontally to the ground, stooped and twisted like an arthritic old man; past empty shells of churches that had long since lost their congregations.

We stopped at a small store on the main street of Geraldton, a small, sleepy town that attracted sun-seeking tourists in the winter months and commercial crayfishermen the year round. (The "rock lobster" they caught was in great demand, most of it air freighted from Perth to the United States.) There we picked up some ice for the "esky," and stocked it with bread, cheese, and other provisions to supplement the canned goods that Peter Eaton's forbearing wife, Margaret, had insisted we take along as "emergency rations only."

The fertile coastal plain came to an end a few miles north of town and we descended into a vast, treeless plain, glaring with heat. Off to the left was the treacherous Batavia Coast, where the Dutch ships

Batavia and *Zuytdorp* ran aground in 1629 and 1712, respectively. In fact, there were said to be over 320 shipwrecks along this part of Western Australia. Offshore, barely visible above sea level, were the low-lying Abrolhos Islands, their name a corruption of the Portuguese phrase for "Keep your eyes open," a warning the Dutch, to their regret, had not taken seriously enough. A bloody mutiny had followed the wreck of the *Batavia,* and as a result the Abrolhos Islands had gone down in history as the scene of Australia's first executions. The Dutch commodore, Pelsaert, also punished two of the mutineers by marooning them on the mainland, a fact that was now being used by residents of the region to explain "the strikingly European features of many local aborigines."

As the road veered slightly off to the right and away from the Indian Ocean, we could see in the distance, extending inland from the coast as far as our eyes could make out, the straggling remains of an old "rabbit-proof fence." Since the gray rabbit had been introduced (for sport) in the early days of settlement, it had multiplied to plague proportions, competing for pasture with money-earning stock, and leading sheep farmers to devise all sorts of ways for destroying it (e.g., seeding potatoes and carrots with detonators). During the Depression years, rabbits provided food and clothing for the poor—rabbit skins were called "the poor man's mink"—but in the 1950s the virus myxomatosis was used to decimate the population. The fence, which had never been of much use anyhow, was now totally obsolete.

Beyond lay the bush, that wide expanse of country that formed so large a part of Australia's mythology.

Most urban Australians define the bush as anything that isn't in the city, and the definition given by the *Australian Encyclopedia* seems to lend credence to that all-embracing view:

> Bush—a term probably derived from the Dutch **bosch,** which Australia appears to have acquired from South Africa, and which is widely applied to areas that are unoccupied or only sparsely settled. It also refers to particular types of forest as well as to areas where (as a writer in the Sydney *Bulletin* pointed out years ago) "there is practically no bush or trees or assorted shrubbery, though there may be scrubbery here and there."

While most Australians actually know very little about the bush, the bushless bush, that is, they tend to be defensive about the myth that has sprung up around it—the myth that Australia is a pioneering nation struggling to bring a vast, intractable continent under control, and that Australians, if no longer the lean, suntanned characters of yesteryear, still share the spirit of such seminomadic Aussie folk heroes as the Man from Snowy River or the Wild Colonial Boy. A well-known Australian social commentator, for instance, indignant when a British travel writer once tried to explain Sydney in terms of the "wasteland" lurking behind its suburbs, argued that Australians found nothing menacing about the bush at all. He did neglect to mention that to the average Australian, a "bush picnic" meant nothing more than a day's excursion to a park on the outskirts of town. Australians, in short, were "not a nation of bushmen, but a nation of city dwellers."

As if portending something ominous, a large rectangular road sign warned travelers NO WATER FOR NEXT 180 KM, and at that we decided to pull over on the shoulder and look around. Ahead lay an empty wasteland that stretched to the horizon and went on for hundreds and hundreds of miles beyond that. We were now, for the first time, completely on our own, for unlike those day trips we had made out of Kalgoorlie, this leg of the journey held no promise of a return to town each night and no comforting assurances of help in case of emergencies.

There was something curiously frightening about that thought. I had traveled to practically every remote spot on the face of the earth and yet, somehow, this was wilderness like I had never encountered, wilderness that seemed more desolate than the steppes of Central Asia and more threatening even than the mountain strongholds of Afghanistan's Hindu Kush. We were only a few miles outside Geraldton, and already I could sense an extraordinary solitude, almost a hostility. I suspected that Jack felt it, too.

Western Australians seemed to take some sort of perverse pride in the extreme conditions of their state, for W.A. had been blessed with a particularly depressing, almost terrifying landscape. D. H. Lawrence had hardly left Perth, on a visit to the house of friends sixteen miles from town, when he was struck by this aspect of the "Australian underdark." A few weeks later, having fled to the safety of civilization in the outskirts of Sydney, he described his feelings in his novel *Kangaroo*. The protagonist, a poet disenchanted with Europe, had journeyed to Western Australia, and was sorry he had:

> The vast, uninhabited land frightened him. It seemed so hoary and
> lost, so unapproachable. The sky was pure, crystal pure and blue, of
> a lovely pale blue colour; the air was wonderful, new and un-

breathed; and there were great distances. But the bush, the grey, charred bush. It scared him . . . It was so phantom-like, so ghostly, with its tall pale trees and many dead trees, like corpses, partly charred by bush fires; and then the foliage so dark, like grey-green iron. And then it was so deathly still. Even the few birds seemed to be swamped in silence. Waiting, waiting—the bush seemed to be hoarily waiting. And he could not penetrate into its secret. He couldn't get at it. Nobody could get at it. What was it waiting for?

We checked the tires on our four-wheel-drive Toyota. It was a four-door pickup truck with an open cargo bed, so we also made a show of tightening up the tarpaulin that was covering the equipment we had packed beneath it—a second spare tire (the first was bolted under the chassis), a machete, a shovel, jerry cans containing extra fuel and water, a battery-operated pump, and an inflatable bog bag in case the car got mired in mud. We were also carrying a host of other emergency items whose purpose I could only guess at and which I hoped Jack was able to use. (Some came with the truck as standard bush equipment, the rest had been lent to us by Peter Eaton.) If our vehicle broke down, I knew next to nothing about automobile mechanics, and Jack only slightly more.

I pulled the water bottle out of the esky and took a long swig before handing it to Jack. Then, slouched against the side of the Toyota, we stared out into space at the flat, eroded plain of scrub, covered with saltbush and desiccated grass, that lay before us. A few long minutes elapsed without a word passing between us before we climbed back toward the cab and headed off into it, our truck soon swallowed up by the surrounding bush, and our spirits with it.

The farther north we drove toward the Tropic of Capricorn, the more arid and harsh the landscape became. Ahead of us lay a two-pronged peninsula that jutted out into the Indian Ocean in a northwesterly direction, pointing feebly toward Java, over fifteen hundred miles away.

Shark Bay, Hopeless Reach, Disappointment Bight, Useless Loop—in characterizing the landmarks of this region the early explorers seemed to wish to anathematize it. The Shark Bay turnoff from the North West Coastal Highway, itself only a thin ribbon of tar cutting through endless miles of empty scrubland, was singularly uninviting, but because we had heard there was an isolated settlement on the eastern prong of the peninsula we took it nonetheless. Across from the

Overlander Roadhouse, a lonely rest stop for the infrequent triple-trailer "roadtrains" that hurtled south carrying cargoes of bleating sheep, we turned left and west to Shark Bay.

Driving directly into the low afternoon sun, we were nearly blinded by the sparkle of broken glass that littered virtually every inch of dust for miles on end along both shoulders of the narrow road. Mystified by the presence of so much debris in so remote a place, we stopped to investigate, and realized we were looking at the accumulated remains of thousands upon thousands of broken beer bottles (and a few that had escaped unbroken) thrown there from the earliest days of settlement right down to the present. Decades of exposure to the sun had melted the shards into all sorts of weird, contorted shapes, and brought out various shades of purple in some of the older fragments, giving the roadside an almost grotesque beauty.

The broken bottles represented a way of life, almost a tradition, in Western Australia, for in that enormous state people were inclined to measure distance not in terms of miles or hours traveled, but in terms of beers consumed. Nanga Station, for instance, which the Royal Automobile Club of W.A. described as "the only sheep station in Australia with a liquor license," was by our rather conventional way of reckoning about forty miles up the peninsula, or a little over an hour's drive away. But the only other customer at the Overlander Roadhouse, a weary-looking fellow who had just come down from Shark Bay and was stocking up on beer for the trip home to Geraldton, set us straight on that. "Nanga's a four-stubby trip," he said, making it quite clear that any other method of calculation was unthinkable.

After thirty minutes of driving, we saw the turnoff for Useless Loop. Although I had always associated them with Siberia, salt mines apparently were also indigenous to Western Australia. In fact, according to what we had been told, there wasn't anything else *but* salt mines at Useless Loop. Situated near the western tip of the peninsula, the area was said to be a veritable Gulag Archipelago, though one to which exile was self-imposed. Totally devoid of trees, the mines were surrounded by nothing but a white blanket of heat-reflecting salt. The temperature at the mine, we heard later, climbed to 136 degrees in the shade that day; in the trailer, with the air conditioners working full tilt, it measured 104. When we came to the Useless Loop turnoff, we declined to take it.

Close to sundown we arrived at Nanga, a run-down sheep station that served as a tourist resort and sometime fishing lodge. We had little choice but to stop for the night and introduce ourselves to the owner, who was eating his dinner in a room that was both kitchen and reception area. The only other guests were a group of ten or so miners from Useless Loop on weekend R & R.

Our accommodations consisted of a bare room illuminated by a single light bulb hanging from the ceiling. There was no furniture except for rusty cots with torn, stained mattresses pushed against insect-splattered walls. From their pungent odor I suspected that the shearers, if not the sheep, had been sleeping on them.

The group of Useless Loopers, which included the wife and children of the foreman, had just finished a family-style "barbie" they had prepared on a barbecue pit in front of the homestead—if Australia could claim a cuisine of its own, it would feature grilled hunks of lean, range-fed beef and lamb—and they were now sitting outside their cell-like quarters. Except for the foreman and his family, they were all drunk, and they were in the process of getting even drunker.

"Money's what got us 'ere," said the youngest of the group, after we'd accepted their invitation to join them. A wiry, light-complexioned fellow in his late twenties, he was a "Scouse," from Liverpool, and he was proud of the fact that he had left England for Australia when he was only fifteen years old. "We kin save $6,000 in a few months."

"What do you do with it?" I asked.

"Spend it," he replied. "Just bought 'er a hat." He nodded in the direction of the foreman's little daughter. "Thirty-five dollars—so what. Do whatever I please. Fly down to Perth and blow it in a couple of days.

"I've worked on the seismic in every desert in Oz lookin' for oil. Luv it out there. A'course, I argue with meself a lot. Have a fallin' out at least three times a day. But it's a relaxed way a'life. Look at this place. Where else can you find blokes drinkin' with the foreman on their day off?"

Jack wasn't about to let that one ride. "Everywhere," he answered. "You don't have to be an Australian to go out drinking with your foreman."

The Scouse fell silent, as if pondering the betrayal of Australian egalitarianism, and a slightly older, heavier-set fellow, sprawled on a reclining chair to the Scouse's right, took up the conversation.

"What got me up 'ere was a broken marriage," he said, in a subdued but bitter monotone. "I came home one afternoon and found my wife in bed with another man. So I bashed her one and left. I'm glad I did it. But that way it was desertion. My wife nicked everything—the kids, the car, the house. I came up 'ere to get away from all that. I can't afford Perth, women, or nothin' while I'm payin' maintenance."

He took a long pull on his stubby and then he, too, fell silent.

"We 'ave a good life here," said the foreman, as if his position demanded he make some sort of positive declaration.

"Yeah, we don't work 'ard," added the Scouse, "the machines do. And the piss is cheap. Only fifty-eight cents for a middie."

I half expected Jack to tell him that it was a long way to come for a cheap beer, but he was too busy swatting mosquitoes to take up the challenge.

Next morning, after a breakfast of burnt toast and instant coffee, we spent a few hours driving around the sheep station property with Ted Sears. Nanga had changed hands several times in the past few years, and Ted was its most recent owner. He was a handsome man in his early forties, wearing a faded blue shirt and torn jeans. There was a lot of gray in the thick growth of stubble on his unshaven face. I sat in the front seat of the badly dented four-wheel-drive truck, while Jack bounced around in the back as we lurched over the roadless, rocky terrain.

"Nanga used ta be owned by a syndicate," Ted explained. "They had big plans for the place but ended up doin' nothin'. When I took over—I got divorced four years ago and decided to opt out and leave Perth—the place was in ruins. Dead sheep were everywhere and there were so many fleas in the homestead we had to shovel 'em out in the carpets."

Except for having taken a shovel to the fleas, it didn't seem that Ted had yet been able to do much by way of improving the situation. Sheep carcasses littered the area around the artesian bore, the floor of the shearing shed had rotted through, and the fencing around the paddocks was badly in need of repair.

Each time we got out of the truck, we were enveloped by swarms of flies. Landing on our faces, they probed our eyes and climbed into our nostrils, extracting moisture wherever they could find it.

"Are the flies always this bad?" asked Jack, waving his hand back and forth across his face in a metronomelike movement known Down Under as "the great Australian salute." Even asking the question proved to be hazardous, for in the fleeting moment it took him to utter those few words, he ingested one of them.

"The first hundred ya swallow are the hardest," said Ted, smiling. "And after a lifetime in the bush ya can even get ta like 'em. It's the sandflies that drive you mad. They bite, an' for a couple of weeks in the winter ya can't even leave the homestead.

"Still, it's a lot better than the city. Perth's got too many people. Everyone's in a hurry. Work, work, work. No one has any time. Up here it's more casual."

Ted's statement had a hollow ring to it, a tone we both noticed.

"If your marriage hadn't failed," asked Jack, "would you be up here now?"

"No," he admitted, without the slightest hesitation. "My ex-wife's a city girl. She'd never 'ave come to a place like this."

4

Leaving Nanga the following day we continued up the peninsula, where we had only two possible destinations. One was Denham (also known as Shark Bay), the fishing village where the Useless Loopers often went to spend the day "on the piss." The other was Monkey Mia, a beach on the lee side of the peninsula where a much-publicized school of dolphins frolicked with bathers in a foot or two of water. We had some vague plans to hop a fishing boat at Denham and bum a ride across Shark Bay to Dirk Hartog Island, where a former Lord Mayor of Perth was reported to be living in mysterious seclusion. But since it was Sunday and stifling hot, and since a connection in Perth had suggested we call in at Monkey Mia and say hello to the couple who ran the caravan park, we decided to head to the beach.

Jostling over the bumpy road, we kept our eyes peeled for something resembling an Australian ape, but it was only later we learned that the name Monkey Mia did not refer to primates. The *Monkey* was a schooner that had visited Shark Bay in 1834, and Mia is said to derive either from the name of a ship reported lost in the area prior to that time or from the aboriginal term for ship. The winding track to the caravan park led us over some low sand dunes and ended abruptly on a long strip of white beach. The scrub stopped at the edge of the sand, and the entire area was treeless.

Having lived for years in the Florida Keys, Jack reckoned he had seen enough salt water, so he lay down in the front seat of the Toyota and dozed off. I walked into the tepid, knee-deep water and sat down, hoping at least to cool off. Within a few minutes, the promised dolphins appeared. One swam up, soon joined by two others, and I was circled several times. I stroked each one in turn, on the sides of their bellies, not on the top of their sensitive heads, as the sign on the beach warned. But they preferred food to friendship, and since I had no fish to offer, they quickly lost interest and swam over to a couple who were wading some yards away. Faring no better there, they soon turned tail and headed back out to deeper water.

It was late in the afternoon when we stopped by to see Wilf and Hazel Mason, bringing regards from Seaton, our mutual acquaintance in Perth. Hazel was away for the week, but Wilf, a man in his mid-fifties who still bore traces of the farmer he once was, invited us in for a drink. He had been out snapper fishing all day, and it was time for a beer.

"Hazel thinks it was a rush of madness to the brain that brought us out here," said Wilf, handing us a stubby. "Our children had grown up and we were looking for something to do that we could do together.

"We weren't lookin' to make a fortune. We were lookin' for a way of life. My old dad always said that his ambition was simply to have a little place on the side of the road and be a friend to man. We're just carrying that tradition on here.

"People think of this as hard country," he continued, settling back in his worn rattan chair with a look of contentment on his face, "but you learn to love a place if you're livin' close to it. Flies can be a damn nuisance, a'course. But you've got to realize that this is their environment, too. We have snakes come through the park and that gets people all upset. But we're living on the edge of the bush. You've got to expect that sorta thing. Hazel gets a bit negative when the field mice come into the house, but other than that it's a great spot to be in. I wouldn't take a million dollars for this place. We meet people and we keep busy. What more can you ask for in life?

"People tell me I'm a bloody fool," said Wilf, chuckling. "I help a bloke repair his trailer and when he asks how much, I say, that's alright, mate, do a turn for someone else some day. Is that so stupid?

"When we first came up here, an inspector from Perth made us clear all the people outta the caravan park. According to him, the place needed work before it could be registered. So the people stayin' here all left. But next mornin' every one of 'em came back, carrying tools, shovels, everythin'. And they said, right, what's gotta be done, and they went ta work. Two days later, when the park was opened again, they all came chargin' back like a great armada, with horns blowin' and whistles goin'. That's the spirit here—if people are in trouble, nine times out of ten an Australian will help 'em out. Surely, he must." Though he invited us to stay the night at Monkey Mia, even Wilf had to admit that Denham was the more interesting place. It wasn't far away, but we thought it best to get there and settle in before dark. The sand on the beach was still hot, and I could feel it burning through the soles of my sandals as Wilf walked us back to the truck.

"I'm glad old Seaton told you to stop by," said Wilf. "Seaton skippered a research boat that used to come into Shark Bay. That's how we met him.

"I'll tell ya a funny story. When he first came in he asked Hazel where he could get the sheets washed. So Hazel said, 'Oh, look, I'll put 'em through our machine, that's no problem.' And he said, 'Oh, good, luvey, that's great.' You know Seaton.

"This went on, oh, for a couple of years, maybe three times a year. So one day Seaton trundles up with a bundle of sheets and gives 'em to me. I said, 'Righto, Hazel's not here. I'll do 'em for ya.' He didn't want to leave 'em, but I said, 'No, no, I've got 'em now.'

"As I'm puttin' 'em in the wash, out falls this piece of paper, and he's got a note written on it: 'How about we meet between these sometime, honey?'

"The next night, the old bugger comes back to pick up his sheets. 'Oh, good, righto, what do I owe ya?' he says. 'The bill's right there on top,' I said. So he opens it up and I'd written: 'Not tonight, honey, you're not my type.' He's quite a character, that Seaton."

I had left Nanga a little depressed. While I myself was something of a dropout, I didn't feel much kinship for Ted Sears, perhaps because I found it hard to imagine myself leaving a beautiful city like Perth to settle on a grotty sheep station. Or perhaps it was because, rightly or wrongly, I felt a sadness in Ted, for like the Useless Loopers who frequented Nanga on their days off, he seemed to have fled to the bush in the wake of failure, not in the pursuit of a long-standing dream. Jack had obviously been affected similarly, and said little on the way to Monkey Mia.

But reflecting on what Wilf Mason had told us eventually lifted both our spirits. If I couldn't accept his claims about learning to love a place just by living close to it, there was a rare kindness, a warmth, in Wilf one seldom encountered. His very presence in those stark surroundings was reassuring, partly because he was such an affable human being and partly because he had retired to the bush, not retreated to it, and his zest for life was still very much intact.

Denham did, indeed, prove to have more to occupy our attention than Monkey Mia. A tiny fishing village, it rested snugly on the shore of Shark Bay, a shallow body of water named by the buccaneer William Dampier, who sighted large numbers of sharks when he first anchored there in 1699. In his search for drinking water, Dampier left the *Roebuck*, his "worn-out crone of a galleon," and went ashore on the spot where Denham now stands. He was unable to find any water, but his party did sight a kangaroo (or perhaps a wallaby), which was shot and eaten. In his *A Voyage to New Holland*, Dampier provided the first description in English of the now familiar marsupial: "We saw a sort of racoon. An animal with very short forelegs, but which goes jumping on its hind legs. It is very good meat."

Only a few houses stood on Denham's main street, which ran along the water's edge and terminated at the Seaside Caravan Park. A few newer homes and a small police station were scattered on a rise behind the town. Nearby, enclosed by a wire fence, was the "town tennis court," a rectangle of cracked and buckled cement turned brown-red over the years by the constantly swirling dust.

An old wooden jetty, with narrow rails and a hand car for hauling fish, ice, and other goods, extended a hundred yards or so out into the bay, and a few aging fishing boats were tied alongside. Across the street from the jetty was the general store, which also served as the post office, and a walk nearby led back to a run-down hotel, the town's only pub. Some of the two-hundred-odd residents of Denham, half of them Malay, half white, had for years been trying to get the town fathers to build a promenade along the shore and to plant a few trees there, both to beautify the place and break the stiff wind that came in off Shark Bay. Coconut palms had indeed been planted a number of years earlier, but cyclones had carried them away. For the present, at least, the waterfront was as bare and treeless as the Nullarbor, and the tropical sun seemed even more intense as it glared off the water.

The houses facing the bay had been built during the heyday of the pearling industry (pearling in Western Australia had its beginnings in Shark Bay) by the grandfathers of the people now living in them. Arthur Bassett's Scottish grandfather, for instance, was a windjammer captain trading out of Fremantle, who sailed to distant places such as Russia and China. He had settled in Denham around the turn of the century, using jarrah timber from the forests south of Perth to build a house a few yards from the water's edge. He had sent the timber up by steamship—in those days one called in every three months with mail and supplies—but he himself had brought the rattan furniture directly from Shanghai. Although it needed a coat of paint, the house otherwise remained in remarkable condition, especially considering that it had withstood any number of cyclones. And the rattan furniture was still in use.

Arthur was a sixty-year-old former pearler with one bad eye, and like his mother before him he had spent his entire life in Denham. Outside his home was a sign that read SHELL AND BOTTLE MUSEUM. The "museum" consisted of a small room on one side of the house, where Arthur kept on display hundreds of shells and a number of old bottles he had collected from some of the abandoned pearling camps on the offshore islands. "I don't get any money out of this, really," he told us, with his arm around his six-year-old half-Malay grandson. "But you meet nice people who come in to see them."

Further down the road lived Jim Poland, a brown-skinned man in his late fifties, whose grandparents were a combination of Malay and aborigine. As a boy Jim had learned to fish with a spear, but now was a commercial snapper fisherman using more conventional methods. (The "schnapper," as it is spelled in Australia, come from deeper water to spawn in Shark Bay, which perhaps explains the presence of all the sharks.) Poland told us that he occasionally still used a spear, to kill a sea turtle or a manatee—which the Aussies call a dugong—for dinner. Although that sort of hunting was illegal, he explained to us with a gleam in his eye that the law did make allowances for "native people," and he did, after all, have some aboriginal blood running in his veins.

To reach Denham, we had had to drive in from the coastal highway over a long stretch of dirt track, a track that was scheduled to be covered with bitumen (in Australia pronounced "bitch/umen") within the year. Arthur Bassett and the other older residents of Denham were worried about the impact the new road would have on the town's insular way of life. For them it meant a bay full of noisy speedboats, water skiers in tow, cutting up fishermen's nets and ruining the fisheries. It meant, too, an increased population and an influx of transients.

Hard as it was to imagine Denham as the target of a wholesale tourist invasion, Arthur Bassett's fears for the future were probably justified. For the Western Australian government, faced with diminishing international interest in the exploitation of its mineral re-

71

sources and a livestock industry devastated by drought, had recently embarked on a major campaign to develop tourism, promoting travel even to the most remote regions of the state.

The campaign had been moderately successful in drawing visitors from other parts of Australia (as well as from America and Europe) to the Perth/Fremantle area, particularly around the time of the America's Cup races, but it appeared to have touched an even more responsive chord among Western Australians themselves. With trailers in tow, hordes of them had taken to the road, especially during the winter months, ranging up and down the coastal highway like latter-day nomads, ever on the lookout for new destinations, new wilderness to "explore." The only thing that had kept Shark Bay relatively undiscovered was the fact that many travelers were reluctant to take their trailers (or caravans, as they were known in Australia) over the rough dirt track necessary to get there, which explained why Arthur Bassett was so concerned about the new road.

"We live a free and happy life here," said Arthur. "There's no rush or tear. Your time's your own and you just drift along as you feel like it. Now we're going to have the bikies and that sort coming in," he continued ruefully. "They'll have access to the town without ever having had to battle to get here."

But whether he was willing to acknowledge it or not, life in Denham had already begun to change. Sitting on the antique rosewood table his grandmother had brought over from England was a video machine. Even without the road, the modern world was intruding.

6

Noel Stafford was one of Denham's newer residents, and I met him in the laundry room of his Seaside Caravan Park early one evening while I was trying to unravel the mystery of how to operate a washing machine, a complicated and bizarre contraption that could only have been built in England by someone with a Rube Goldberg bent of mind. Until that moment I had prided myself on being an authority on all kinds of laundry equipment, for during the 1920s my grandaunt had arrived in Boston from Ireland and had opened a small shop on Beacon Hill, which she auspiciously dubbed the Monarch Hand Laundry.

As a fanciful child I imagined it was some sort of regal establishment where personages even greater than kings, Boston's Yankee nobility, brought their laundry to be hand-scrubbed by Irish washer-women. It was only later that I discovered that my aunt would have washed clothes for anyone who came into her establishment, provided they were willing to pay for the service.

When I was ten, Auntie decided she'd washed enough dirty Yankee laundry and she retired. My mother acceded to the Monarch throne and reigned there until she died in 1954, after which the venerable institution closed its doors forever. But until I was in my early teens, as heir apparent I lived in a kingdom of soapsuds and bleach. When I grew older, I actually did open my own laundromat, determined to carry on the noble family tradition. My birthright was forever denied me, though, because the golden age of laundries had long since passed.

Though there were three generations of detergent pulsating through my veins, despite my laundry lineage I was not equipped to deal with the complexities of operating Noel's machine.

"It's really not a bad washer, once you get the hang of it," Noel assured me on seeing my confusion. He patiently showed me how to take my dripping wet garments out of the tub and put them into the water extractor. "Now just add twenty cents, and she'll be right," he instructed, as he groped his way across the suddenly darkened room toward the door to turn on the lights, which were connected to a time switch that shut them off automatically every five minutes.

Later that evening we ran into Noel and his wife, Liz, at the Old Pearler Restaurant, a building constructed entirely from blocks of compacted shells. We'd spent all our evenings there since coming to Shark Bay, for besides the pub, it was the only place in town open after dark. The Staffords were drinking a bottle of wine and invited us to join them. A refined-looking couple in their early fifties, they had come up from Perth a few years earlier and bought the caravan park.

When they learned we were traveling around and getting a first-hand look at the Australian bush, Noel said, "I thought most Americans preferred to sit in armchairs reading about adventures or watching them on the telly."

"What do you mean?" I asked, surprised by his comment.

"We don't get many Yanks up here," he explained. "A few came through a while back from *Sports Illustrated*, but they were hardly sporting or adventurous people. They hired me to take them out to locations for bathing suit photos. We were chuffing out along this old station track and I thought everything was alright. But Christ, they nearly died they were so terrified. From then on, we had to haul them in the Mitsubishi with the soft springs and air conditioning. They had to be pampered like schoolchildren. You never heard such a pack of whingers. We usually don't have to deal with that sort of nonsense here," added Noel. "We have enough problems with dole-bludgers." Dole-bludgers was the Australian expression for people who lived off welfare.

7

We'd promised ourselves not to leave Denham without visiting Sir Thomas Wardle, the former Lord Mayor of Perth, who now lived in seclusion on Dirk Hartog, an offshore island that was the westernmost point of land in Australia. Brimming over with chutzpah, Dave telephoned Sir Thomas directly and wangled an invitation for us to spend a few days with him at his home. We threw a few things together, left the rest of our baggage at the caravan park, and raced down to the jetty.

Shortly after we'd arrived in town we'd been befriended by John Nye and Dave Hunt, his English partner in the Old Pearler, and had spent most of our evenings sitting around their restaurant socializing with them and their wives. John and Dave took it upon themselves to become our patrons, and it was through their arrangements that Naughty Don Rogers, Toyota dealer extraordinaire, had agreed to ferry us the twenty-three miles across Shark Bay to Dirk Hartog on his sportfishing boat.

When we arrived at the jetty, Naughty Don and his worthy crew of three were already waiting, tinnies in hand and engines running. We jumped aboard with our gear, which consisted mostly of a case of beer for Naughty Don's cooler and some Scotch whiskey and wine for Sir Thomas.

It was with some misgivings that we stepped on board the boat and placed ourselves at its skipper's mercy, for Naughty Don Rogers was the notorious wild man of Perth television. The loud and abrasive maniac in the commercials made used-car salesmen in the States seem like dignified and sedate gentlemen of commerce. During his one-minute television tirades, Don ranted, screamed, and even smashed cars with sledgehammers.

But the Don we met that morning was shy, soft-spoken, and a bit of an introverted fellow. In his early forties, Don was thinly built, but he carried an enormous beer belly on his slight frame. He did, in fact, have a beer in his hand, which he gulped in huge swallows. During the run over Don forced us to drink large quantities of beer with him, and ordered us to share the sandwiches he had brought along for the crew. We had little choice but to obey.

The high-pitched whine of the turbo-charged twin diesels made conversation difficult and drinking easy. I relaxed and enjoyed the long trip across the bay. Even Dave was feeling better. His badly jangled nerves were gradually returning to their normal state of extreme excitement now that he'd convinced me to abort plans for an expedition over the Canning Stock Route, a treacherous overland passage we'd heard about, at least for the time being. The sight of me on the bridge talking convivially with Naughty Don inspired him to refer to me as Nasty Jack for days thereafter.

As we neared the lee of Dirk Hartog I was reminded of one of the high coral islands in the Bahamas. The spot we approached was fringed by a white sand beach, and the water lapping its shore was flat calm and crystal clear. A hundred yards or so above the beach sat a low stone building whose exterior resembled the facade of a budget motel. It was coated with a textured gray-white stucco material, but most of the lumpy rocks showed through. Seven red doors were spaced evenly along the front of the long one-story structure, and between them were thick wire trellises supporting the pink and scarlet bougainvillaea that climbed to the roof. The white sand that ran up from the beach to the concrete walk in front of the building was dotted with thick clumps of spinifex and a few sharp-pointed silver-green yucca plants. Off to the left of the building leaned the yard's only trees, two sorry-looking date palms that were gradually losing their struggle against the elements.

As we came closer to shore, a solitary figure emerged from one of the doorways, waved, and began walking down the beach toward us. Naughty Don brought us in as close as possible, until the props began to kick up bottom. Rolling up our pant legs and pulling off our shoes and socks, Dave and I slipped over the side into the warm, shallow water and waded ashore.

"Don't do any bloody fuckin' thing I wouldn't do, mates," Don hollered loudly over the revving of the engines, lapsing for a moment into his on-camera alter ego.

Sir Thomas Wardle greeted us with a firm handshake and a wry smile as we stepped ashore. He was a tall, lean man and he wore a white cricket hat to keep the noon sun off his tanned patrician face.

With a gracious "Welcome to Dirk Hartog," he led us up the beach to the homestead, where his wife, Hulda, a well-preserved woman in her early sixties, was waiting. She wore a blue and white sun dress and her red hair, graying at the temples, was tucked under a wide-brimmed hat that protected her fair skin and pale blue eyes from the sun. We sat in the living room whose beamed ceiling and rough, white stuccoed walls reminded me of a Mexican-style hacienda in the American southwest, and while we took tea, Sir Thomas told us about their island.

Dirk Hartog was named after the Dutch sailor Dirck Hatich, master of the vessel *Eendracht*, who discovered the desolate isle on October 25, 1616. Blown off course on the way to Java, he was the first known European to have set foot on the west coast of Australia. (Ten years earlier Willem Jansz had made landfall near Cape York, on the other side of the continent.) Anchoring off the wind-blown north shore, which must have been a feat in itself, Hatich lowered a boat and with several crewmen rowed ashore. There they commemorated their landing with a pewter plate, which they hammered flat and inscribed with the details of their visit. They nailed the plate to a post and continued on to Java. The original plate later turned up in Holland's Rijksmuseum, when in 1902 a workman found it in the cellar and brought it the attention of the museum staff.

Dirk Hartog Island, fifty-two miles long and averaging four to six miles in width, once supported a Chinese pearlers' camp of about two hundred souls located near the site of the present homestead, but the rude shanty town had burned down years earlier, along with the original homestead building. Sir Thomas and his wife were the island's only inhabitants. After his financial empire crumbled, the island was one of the few possessions Sir Thomas had managed to hold on to, since he had kept it in his son's name.

Sir Thomas Wardle's rise from obscurity to fame and fortune had been a dramatic episode well chronicled in the Australian media. As a young man he'd worked as an itinerant farm hand, and when the war broke out he served as a sergeant in New Guinea and Malaya before being discharged in 1946. Starting with a single store in the 1950s, he parlayed his "Tom the Cheap" operation into a $78 million-a-year retail empire of 245 grocery and discount stores from Dubbo to Darwin.

"I knew there had to be a better method of retailing than the traditional Australian way," he explained, "so I decided to set up a self-service store. It wasn't a new idea, but I refused to set minimum prices. I discounted prices so some of the large manufacturers like Rothman's Tobacco and Eastern States Soaps refused to sell to me." But Tom the Cheap had a talent for surmounting such obstacles. When the Australian chocolate industry refused his business, he flew his private jet to England, organized his own supplies, and sold chocolate in his stores for a penny a pound profit. He arranged to have razor blades manufactured in Germany, and even sold tractors built on the Chinese mainland. His methods threw the Australian retail industry into chaos, and in his originality he was compared to Henry Ford.

Naturally Tom (who preferred that name to Sir Thomas) became the darling of the consumer public, especially budget-conscious housewives, whom he also liked to employ as store managers, knowing that they were ambitious and would work for cheaper wages than men. Tom became such a popular figure in the tabloid press that his friends persuaded him to run for mayor of Perth. In 1967 he won a landslide victory over five other candidates. For almost six years he was Lord Mayor of the city, besides being president of the W.A. National Trust and holding a host of other honorary appointments.

If Tom's rise to wealth and power had been rapid, his collapse was meteoric. In the mid-1970s the Australian economy suffered a severe recession, and Tom found himself in dire financial straits.

"Word got around," he told us bitterly, "get your money out of Tom the Cheap now or you won't get it at all. They started coming in from everywhere. I couldn't pay—all my money was tied up in property. I started selling things off for far less than they were worth. I sold commercial properties, the jet, all the stores. I even tried to sell the lease on Dirk Hartog, but nobody wanted it."

His creditors recovered only twenty-five cents on every dollar owed them; in the end, all Tom himself had left was a home in Perth, Dirk Hartog Island, and a great deal of public resentment. Though he remained comfortable by ordinary standards, Tom had fallen back to the point where he'd started from and ongoing litigation still pursued him. In the Alan Bond, Rupert Murdoch, and Robert Holmes à Court tradition, Tom was yet another successful entrepreneur, a model to be emulated. But a capricious public relishes a morality tale of failure even more than it craves a parable of success, and the fall of a lord provided the tabloids with sensational copy. Tom had soared to dizzying heights, mingling with the gods, but stripped of his wealth and power, he'd come crashing down to earth where most mortals belong.

We chatted with Tom and Hulda until midafternoon when the sun descended from its zenith and the outdoors became bearable again.

At Tom's suggestion that we go for a drive to check the stock tanks, which were about fifteen miles from the homestead, we piled into two battered four-wheel-drive vehicles and bounced off into the bush.

The mechanical condition of the vehicle I drove was desperate, but somewhat better than that of the one ahead of me carrying Tom and Dave. Mine sputtered and balked on the sandy track, a result of Tom's attempts to maintain the jeeps himself, since there was no one else to do it. Admittedly he knew very little about mechanics. He insisted on taking two vehicles on this trip because he'd recently broken down about twenty miles from the homestead. He'd spent hours on foot before managing to catch and ride back a partially wild stock horse.

As we rounded a bend in the road we saw a windmill whirling rapidly and clanking in the gale-like wind as it pumped up bore water to the tank. When we approached, sheep and the few wild angora goats drinking at the trough scattered in all directions. Tom examined the line from the windmill that fed it. "Last year I found three hundred dead sheep here," he said. "I had a manager taking care of the place who was supposed to ride out here every three days, but he hadn't bothered to. There was a break in the line and the water was running into the sand. If anyone had seen those dead sheep they'd've thought this was a worthless place and that I was neglecting my stock."

"It wasn't your fault, though," Dave offered.

"But you see, the fact is, it was," said Tom, reflectively. "If you want things right, unless you've got a lot of money you've got to do them yourself. I'm ashamed of the condition of this place. You just can't plant things in the rank sand and hope they'll grow. I tried that with coconut trees when I first came here, but they all died. Anything that's worthwhile has to be taken care of."

We drove on a few miles to the north toward the towering red sand dunes shimmering hazily in the late afternoon sun. At their base, the howling wind off the Indian Ocean was driving swirls of sand, and with a precision that would have made any craftsman envious, had already sculpted innumerable tiny ridges and furrows across the dunes' surface. Like the crests and troughs of diminutive waves, they raged on a miniature sea.

The wind hurtled stinging grains of sand into our faces as Tom led the way up the highest dune. Standing on its crest, we could see the ocean buffeting the windward side of the island, and deceptively tranquil Shark Bay edging its lee shore. Dirk Hartog Island, however seductive its solitude, was a forlorn and barren place.

We gratefully returned to the comforts of the homestead where

Hulda showed us our rooms. During dinner, Tom related some of the difficulties of operating an island sheep station. Supplies had to be sent over from the mainland by barge, and the wool had to be shipped back in the same way. During the sheep shearing season, while the shearers were on the island for as long as three weeks, it fell to Hulda to cook for them.

"When I first came here, it was all new to me," she mused. "Until this young chap in a cowboy hat, who was in charge of the lot, came in and told me, 'We'll 'ave breakfast at seven, mornin' tea at half past nine, dinner at twelve, afternoon tea at three, and supper at six, thanks very much, ma'am.' I thanked him very much too," said Hulda, laughing aloud.

"It nearly killed me. There was eleven of them, and could they eat. I had to cook for them five times a day and I only had a little caravan gas stove. I was really juggling everything around, trying to keep things hot and cooking at the same time. Steaming on the top, baking in the middle, but it wasn't funny." She shrieked with laughter, slapping her thigh as she recalled the experience.

We sat swapping yarns in the dining room overlooking Shark Bay, and toward dusk an old wooden fishing boat with a low cabin putt-putted into the cove out front and anchored up.

"That'd be Boonka Boonka," said Tom. "His real name's Bill McCarrey. But he's called Boonka Boonka because when he was in the navy during the war, he was a gunner on an artillery battery that made that sound. Bill's a commercial fisherman who spends most of his time looking for fish but never catching them. His eyesight's not too good. He won the lotto a while back, and every so often he's goes off to Thailand on holiday. No one has any idea how much he won. He keeps it pretty dark, but I think it was around $40,000."

"He's a most unusual chap," added Hulda. "His brother's under secretary for the treasury in W.A., which is a mighty important job. But Bill just wants to be a fisherman."

"How do you explain that?" Dave asked, his sense of balance gone askew by the thought of two brothers, one a successful secretary of the treasury, the other an unsuccessful fisherman.

"Just the way he drifted, I suppose," replied Tom. "I find the most interesting people I've met in Australia are people who've been pitchforked around. They never planned it, but suddenly success came along. It'd be difficult to say, wouldn't it, which of the two is better off—Boonka Boonka or his brother Charles. They're as different as chalk and cheese."

"He anchors out there every night, and when we see his cabin light, it gives us the feeling of not being so alone," Hulda said. "When I'm not here, Bill comes up in the evening with fish he's caught and has dinner with Tom. Sometimes they stay up half the night talking."

"He's not the hermit that he thinks he is," Tom observed. "He sees our lights here too. He comes ashore every morning and asks for a bit of rainwater. But it's true, I reckon. This is a lonely place if Hulda's away and he's not out there."

"Last year, early in the spring, before I went away," said Hulda, "we were planting things in the garden. Tom was putting seeds in and Bill came up and said, 'I've got a few cabbages I'd like to put in there if there's a bit a' room.'"

"When I told him I didn't mind," related Tom, "he put some seeds into the ground. Then he said something or other about cabbages and kings and pigs with wings. He's not always right in the head. The war, you know."

We stayed up well into the evening sipping Scotch whiskey with our hosts, who kept insisting it was too early to go to bed, and pointing out that they hadn't had any company in months. "We can sleep all we want after you've gone," Hulda said. But we knew the time had arrived when the lights in Boonka Boonka's cabin went out.

We had decided earlier that, despite Tom's invitation to stay longer, we would leave for the mainland that afternoon. We contacted Naughty Don and asked him to pick us up. In the middle of the afternoon, when his boat loomed on the horizon, we retrieved our gear from the rooms and, accompanied by Tom and Hulda, walked down to the water. There we bid our farewells, and when Don got close enough to shore, we waded out to him.

As we pulled away toward the mainland, the lord and lady of Dirk Hartog Island stood waving to us for a final time until finally they joined hands, turned away, and walked back up the beach to the homestead.

As I watched the island recede in the distance, it struck me that Tom Wardle may indeed have been as tragic a figure as some in Denham had claimed. His retreat to Dirk Hartog seemed an atonement for his failures, a notion of guilt and penance I could well understand, having been raised an Irish Catholic. Tom had resigned himself to spending the rest of his days on a remote island, trying to turn a run-down sheep station into a profitable operation. Perhaps the effort itself kept him going.

I had condemned myself to such an existence years before, when, driven by depression and self-pity after my marriage failed, I had taken work as a fisherman off the Long Island coast. The physical demands of setting and hauling nets from dawn till dusk, day after day, then sitting around late into the evening talking to the rest of the crew kept me so exhausted I seldom found time to reflect on my unhappiness.

Hulda, who didn't share Tom's commitment to the station, often returned for long periods to the sociable life of Perth, leaving Tom and Boonka Boonka to themselves, the island, and their late-night dialogues. I would have loved to have been party to the nocturnal discussions between those two unlikely friends—a lord turned hermit and a fisherman conversant with Lewis Carroll's *Through the Looking Glass*, speaking of cabbages and kings.

8

We hadn't expected to find much in Denham but had been pleasantly surprised. Now, after our stay in the Shark Bay area, we were actually reluctant to go. On the day we had planned to leave, we loafed around town for most of the morning, chatting with people who seemed like old friends—Naughty Don, Jim Poland, Arthur Bassett, and others— and who like us were just hanging around the jetty or making their unhurried way to the general store to mail a letter, pick up a parcel, or buy a cup of coffee.

We had our own morning coffee at the Old Pearler, which John Nye and Dave Hunt had purchased only a few months before. With the help of their wives they were serving three meals a day, including a huge breakfast for fishermen off the boats. This was all quite new for Denham, because the restaurant had been closed for years and even when it was open, it had served only dinners, and those sporadically.

Dave Hunt and his wife were East End Londoners who had been making their way around the world when they met John Nye and his wife at a bank in Melbourne. It didn't take long for the two couples, who were in their early thirties, to decide to join forces. After John "gave away" his office job and sold the house, the four of them hit the road in a caravan and headed out to Western Australia, eventually making their way to Denham.

After Jack went off to sweat out a few sets of tennis with John, I stepped outside, sat down at a shaded table, and began to write a few letters home. While sealing an envelope, I looked up to see a tough-looking little kid, a very little boy, toddling along the trafficless street that paralleled the water. Glancing in my direction, he gave me a suspicious once-over and then, apparently deciding that I was a stranger worth investigating, crossed over and ambled into the yard.

His dirty blond hair clashed with his swarthy skin, and dark, deep-set eyes hinted at aboriginal parentage way back down the line. He was holding a kitchen knife, not threateningly, like a weapon, but almost companionably, as if it were a peculiar substitute for a teddy bear. A dark T-shirt, as soiled and stained as the skin on his knees, hugged his already well-developed chest and shoulders, but below that he was wearing only a diaper, which was unraveling in so many places it could easily have been mistaken for a tattered pair of shorts. He squatted down in front of me and, sitting on his heels, started to saw away at some twigs on the ground, as if waiting for me to open the conversation.

"What's your name?" I asked.

"Alan," he said. "Alan Poland."

"How old are you?"

"Three," he answered. He looked nervously in either direction, and I wondered if he had snuck out from under his mother's eye.

Then he had a few proprietary questions for me—what was I doing there, where did I come from, who in town did I know.

"Which one of the Polands is your father?" I asked him, when my turn came around again.

"My father's the fuckin' black poofter," he replied. His answer wasn't exactly the response I had anticipated but it did demonstrate that the kid was precocious, and a true son of Australia. Barely out of infancy, he had already mastered the one acceptable form of expressing affection between men in the bush.

"If we call someone a 'useless bugger,' " an Australian had explained to me when I was first learning the language, "you can be sure we like him. If we call him a 'useless prick,' we're still friends, but we may be a little bit annoyed. When we call him a 'useless cunt,' then we're really angry."

Since "poofter" was the Australian equivalent of "fag" (differing only in that it was sometimes used in an affectionate way among friends), the little boy was probably trying to tell me that he really liked his old man, even though he might not be able to identify him by name.

*　　*　　*

By the time we pushed on, it was already late in the afternoon. Dave and John had insisted on treating us to a late send-off lunch, serving us the biggest and, we had to admit, the best hamburgers we'd ever eaten. This only intensified our regret at having to leave what we figured would be the last good restaurant we'd be seeing for some time and to say good-bye to two fellows—dropouts of a sort, though they were working fourteen hours a day to make a go of their new business—with whom we had become good friends in the short time we were there.

We realized all too soberly that we were leaving behind not only creature comforts, but, more important, a degree of companionship we couldn't realistically expect to find in the pubs that lay ahead of us. In Denham we had found people who enjoyed sitting around the dinner table late into the evening, talking about all sorts of things, sharing ideas and feelings on any number of subjects, serious and frivolous alike. The atmosphere in the Old Pearler, as the locals also knew, was conducive to that.

The patrons one met at the pubs were altogether different, or at least they seemed that way to me. They stood slouched at the bar, facing only their own drinks or their own weather-beaten images in the mirror on the wall. They might make chitchat with the publican and barmaid, or exchange occasional wisecracks with whoever was standing next to them, but they kept their feelings, their disappointments and their longings, pretty much to themselves. The very design of a pub seemed to ensure that. A pub was a place where people accustomed to solitude could socialize without having to be truly sociable, where they could cluster for a while, like larvae in a eucalyptus tree, without ever having to come out of their protective cocoons.

But Denham was an exception. According to what we heard, the publican there was a particularly irascible, unpleasant sort of man, and the townsfolk generally didn't like to patronize his pub. Luckily for them, the Old Pearler provided a refreshing alternative.

Jack and I were longtime friends and had done a lot of traveling together, but other people's company had always been important to us, and our suspicion that, once we left Shark Bay, there wasn't going to be much of that around left each of us wary. Were we really going to enjoy traveling through such monotonous country with only each other as companions? And we were more than a little worried about the effects that kind of quasi-isolation would have on our friendship, about the strains it might create. For we were beginning to realize that what one explorer had written in 1898 was to some extent still true:

In the Australian bush the traveller . . . has no spice of adventure
to spur him on; no beautiful scenery, broad lakes, or winding rivers
to make life pleasant for him. The unbroken monotony of an arid,
uninteresting country has to be faced. Nature everywhere demands
his toil. Unless he has within him impulses that give him courage to
go on, he will soon return; for he will find nothing in his surroundings to act as an incentive to tempt him further.

We drove out of Denham in silence, each of us lost in his own
thoughts, pondering those unsettling questions of impulses and incentive.

9

The sun was already beginning to set by the time we reached the main
road. We drove thirty miles north through totally barren, sandy countryside to the next roadhouse along the way—the B.P. Wooramel
Roadhouse and Caravan Stop—and pulled in around 8:30 P.M., just as
it was getting dark.

The "Brand Highway to Carnarvon Tourist Promotion Committee,"
which had more words in its title than members in its organization,
published a strip map for tourists describing the Wooramel Roadhouse as follows:

"Excellent takeaway foods, small dining facilities at present, but an
outdoor area has been provided—the stonework by their 14 year old
son. Cold drinks and snacks. Well appointed 1 bedroom Motel unit.
Just 22 km to Hamlin Bay. Ask Peta and Peter about the nearby old
Gladstone Port and Bibra Landing."

For the traveler who might have wanted to call ahead to reserve that
one motel room, the map listed the phone number simply as 1 R.
Wooramel was clearly not an overpopulated place.

Two sallow faces—Peta's and Peter's, I assumed—looked out from
behind the window of a small, dimly lit office at the sound of our
arrival, as if surprised to be receiving customers. Peter, a middle-aged
man, rose from behind a desk in the office, walked through into the
adjoining room, and stepped out the door. He thought we were in
need of diesel fuel and when we told him, no, we actually wanted a
place for the night, he seemed somewhat nonplussed. The facility, he
explained, was not really a caravan park of the kind we had in mind,
for it had no park and no on-site caravan accommodations. It was just
a roadhouse, a rest stop for fuel, sandwiches, and soft drinks, with an
empty lot in back. The lot he pointed to was indistinguishable from

the adjacent scrub, but it did at least provide a place where motorists with their own trailers in tow could pull in off the road and hook up to the generator-furnished power supply.

Peter invited us inside to discuss the problem with his wife, and between the two of them they came up with the idea of letting us stay in an unused trailer that was parked in the back. A "gift" from Peta's sister, it had apparently been abandoned there some months before. With that settled, we ordered steak sandwiches, and Peta went into the kitchen (which was completely bare except for a refrigerator and a portable burner against one wall) to prepare them. Meanwhile, Peter pulled over the only two chairs in the place and set us up at a small Formica table near the door.

We gobbled down our sandwiches the instant we were served. We weren't particularly hungry but the bleakness of the fluorescent lights and the drone of the air conditioner didn't create an atmosphere conducive to lingering. And we wanted to get out of our hosts' hair as quickly as possible.

The unused caravan, its partially deflated tires ballooning in the sand, was sitting forlornly where it had been abandoned, unprotected from the elements and slowly disintegrating. The door was stuck but gave way after a few hard yanks, revealing a decrepit interior that was covered in a thick layer of red dust and had the stale, dry odor of a long-sealed attic. The windows, too, were jammed shut, and I was reminded of David Carnegie's words, written when he was exploring Western Australia in 1896: "It was unpleasant enough to be roasted by day, but to be afterwards baked by night was still more so!"

Our worst misgivings about leaving Denham seemed all too well confirmed, and we dejectedly threw our sleeping bags on the dust-covered bunks and tried to sleep. Each time one of us turned over, though, the entire caravan shook, as if it had been hit by a strong gust of wind. Yet outside not a breeze was blowing—the night was hot and still. Thirty miles was a long way from Shark Bay, in more ways than one. I considered cursing Jack for getting me into this but I didn't have the energy. If this was the bush, I thought as I drifted off into a fitful sleep, I wanted none of it.

10

The Wooramel Roadhouse and Caravan Park, we learned the next morning at breakfast, was for sale. In fact Peter and Peta Birch wanted out so desperately that all they hoped to realize from a "distress sale" was what it cost them to build the facility in 1978. They didn't expect any compensation for the misery and frustration they'd experienced, accepting that those were not salable commodities, at least not in their line of work. Considering preinflationary prices and current construction costs, the park was an exceptional value.

There was no business or traffic on the lonely 125-mile stretch of coastal highway that extended from the Overlander Roadhouse to Carnarvon, so nothing distracted our hosts that dusty March morning. Nor had there been any the night before. The sun had only been up for forty-five minutes or so, but already the air conditioners were whirring loudly. Outside, around the fuel pumps, gusts of wind were beginning to stir up swirling red dust-devils and sand spouts—what the Australians called willie-willies.

As Dave and I ate our grilled tomato and cheese sandwiches, Peter related that both he and Peta were descended from families that had settled in W.A. in the early 1800s. "I reckon there's a bit of pioneering spirit still left in us," he said, "the pair of us sort of come back from a bit of a line up. Peta's family played a big part in opening up coastal shipping and in developing the pearling industry in Shark Bay.

"When we first started here, the state was still booming, and there was a demand for a facility like ours. This was where all the things were happening. Mining was going very well, oil was discovered off the Northwest Shelf, and there was a big natural gas field they were going to exploit near here.

"Everything had to come by on this road. None of the other road-houses had caravan parks, so we felt that we'd provide something that was a necessity to the traveling public. We did a study on it for a year, all the time trying to find land, which was very difficult to locate. That may sound strange, but most of it is pastoral property leased from the crown. There's very little freehold, and the other problem was water.

"This will give you an idea of what it looked like at first," said Peter, showing us first a photograph of some parched scrubland, and then one of the desolate highway. "There was nothing happening on it then."

"There we are clearing the land," he continued, handing us another photo. As he spoke, Peter occasionally managed a pained smile, but Peta, who sat silently beside him, seemed to be beyond the comfort of humor. She bore the pall of unhappiness visibly evident on her face. As her husband spoke, Peta looked dejectedly at the table, and gently rubbed the joints of her inflamed arthritic fingers.

"That's our eldest daughter with a shovel. She just finished a nursing course in Perth," he added, with more than a little pride in his voice. "That's Peta behind her, and that's our dog, Cindy. She's the one that left the mark in the concrete. It cost us in the vicinity of $160,000 to build the facility, but it would cost much more now. Here's our roadhouse arriving on the back of a lorry. It arrived on Sunday and we were in business Wednesday. This last one's a snapshot of some of the trees we planted," said Peter as he handed it to me. The out-of-focus photograph showed a row of small saplings, pathetic in their frailty, running along the caravan park's boundary line.

"Where are they now?" I asked. "What happened to them?" Nothing demarcated the line now but a bit of wire fence.

"We had a plague of rabbits," replied Peter. "I planted over a hundred gum trees in one day and that same night the rabbits came and destroyed all but one. You'd have to have seen it to believe it. All the trees and the scrub disappeared around us.

"The wind would bring the dust, and in the afternoon when it was blowing quite strongly, people couldn't find their own driveways. It was just shocking. If we did get a customer inside here, he couldn't even get back out to his car. That went on every day for months and months.

"The drought began in 1974 and continued through 1979. That was the worst year of all because of the winds. We had no rain that winter and it was absolutely devastating. During the winter of 1980 there was substantial rain and all the rivers flooded. We were out of business for more than a month and that was during the peak period, when tourists are traveling. It gave us a bit of rest, but it wasn't good for the pocket."

Peter had narrated his tale in a matter-of-fact tone that belied its Old Testament elements, but I could only marvel at how a wrathful God was keeping busy in W.A.

"What about insurance? Didn't the government help you?" asked Dave, who, until I convinced him otherwise, believed that enlightened governments were the ultimate salvation of mankind.

"No, insurance companies won't cover you for that sort of thing," replied Peter, sadly. "Perhaps I shouldn't say it, but I'm very resentful of all the bureaucracies that made this such a difficult project for us to complete. They were totally negative towards everything we tried to do. They kept losing our correspondence, and we were continually on the phone trying to sort out problems.

"We had a little block of land, and they threw in rules and regulations that would be applicable to building a Hilton. I don't know how

I managed to get through it all. If it hadn't been for the support Peta and the kids gave me," Peter added, shaking his head slowly, "but what I put them through . . ."

"But you've been through the worst of it," I interrupted, feeling the need to offer some consoling words. "After all that hard work, why sell now?"

"There's a saying that 'It's better to travel than arrive,' " Peter replied, "and I've found out that's true. When we came here, we were active, young forty-year-olds. Soon we're going to be burned-out fifty-year-olds. It's not just the harshness of the climate that's taken its toll on us. It's more like the Chinese water treatment. Drip, drip, drip, and eventually, you realize you've had enough. You can't continue motivating. I feel as if I'm starting to vegetate. I'm losing my memory. I'm becoming sort of backward. We've got to get way. See something new instead of just looking at that." Peter pointed out the window at the stunted scrub and dust that extended to the distant horizon.

"The thing that really brought everything home to me was a little problem we had here fifteen or sixteen months ago. Water levels dropped because we hadn't had a river for a couple of years. It was stinking hot, and I was drilling for water. I was up on top of the A-frame when the ladder gave out. Over I went, landing on my face and smashing myself up. I got up with my glasses driven through my face, a great hole in my leg, and bruised ribs.

"I couldn't stand up all the next day, and as I was lying in bed, I got thinking about things. Peta and I have worked our lives away. All we've done for twenty-odd years of our married life is slave our hearts out. Now was the time to be sensible and start getting the place lifted up. Making it a bit better so we could sell it.

"Ever since then it's on my mind constantly. I'm sick and tired of putting myself and my family in these adverse situations. We've only done one thing all our lives. I reckon it's high time we tried something different."

First, Peter Eaton with his New Norcia and Mt. Augustus, now Peter Birch with his Wooramel Roadhouse. It would have been easy to attribute improbable enterprises to an odd quirk shared by people named Peter, but no, there was Ted Sears at Nanga Station, too. More likely, it was some irrational impulse in the Western Australian psyche itself, bred in the bone. Following in the tradition of the early gold prospectors driven by dreams of striking it rich, the modern-day bush entrepreneurs had turned their backs on urban life—consumed by visions of building tourist empires far out in the wilderness. The Bondy-goes-bush syndrome, the desire to emulate Alan Bond and others like him by purchasing property and developing it, led the Birches and many others to buy up vast tracts of worthless land and invest in dubious ventures.

Peter Birch's ambitions and expectations were modest compared to those of the high-rolling entrepreneurs in Perth, yet he liked to think he was equally possessed of the "pioneering spirit." Peter believed that dogged determination and hard work always brought their rewards, but after years of frustrating and fruitless labor he had been forced to accept the fact that, at least at Wooramel, the old values didn't apply.

We had left Denham in gloomy silence, and now Wooramel, too. Dispirited by the hopelessness of Peter's and Peta's predicament, we threw our swags in the backseat of the Toyota and headed off up the empty road toward Carnarvon, past endless miles of drought-stricken paddocks.

11

We had intended to spend only as much time in Carnarvon (population: 6,000) as was necessary to say "g'day" to Des Clancy, a friend of a friend of ours from Perth. An ex–Papua New Guinea *kiap*, or patrol officer, Clancy was now "regional manager" of the area known as the Gascoyne, and from what we had heard he knew the district as intimately as he once had known the villages of New Guinea's Eastern Highlands. Dealing with the economic problems of the region's plantation and station owners may have been a bit more prosaic than mediating disputes between warring tribes of headhunters and cannibals, but as a good Aussie civil servant he was the kind of person who enjoyed himself no matter where he was posted. Over a cup of coffee in his office, he suggested we meet one or two people in and around town before moving on, and he made a few phone calls on our behalf to pave the way.

Carnarvon, said the town's tourist brochure, was "the sun's winter home and the tropical gateway to the North." That was the good news greeting people who ventured north of the 26th parallel. It was left to the less conspicuous brochures lying around the anteroom of Des Clancy's office to furnish the bad news. A pamphlet put out by the Health Department of Western Australia, for instance, bore the title,

Mozzies Are Bad News. "Mosquitoes that spread dangerous diseases are common in Australia, and are not all confined to tropical areas," it cautioned, in a sentence wonderfully sensitive to the realities of regional politics but perfectly clear as to where the bulk of the bad mozzies could be found. "They can carry viruses or parasites that cause Australian encephalitis, epidemic polyarthritis, malaria, dengue fever, yellow fever, and heart worm." The latter, at least, was fatal only to dogs.

The pamphlet *Let's Talk about Alcohol,* which cited a fairly recent Senate committee report entitled *Australia—An Intoxicated Society?,* revealed the statistic that about one out of every ten Australians was an alcoholic, or to quote the precise phrase used in the pamphlet, was "regularly drinking excessive amounts." Not one out of every ten adults, but one out of every ten people! And that was the *national* average. (America's alcoholism rate, by contrast, is four percent.) In the tropics, north of the 26th, the percentage was considerably higher. As a result, said the pamphlet, Australians suffered from an inordinate number of alcohol-related diseases, including beriberi, peripheral neuropathy, and chronic brain syndrome, not to mention the more common afflictions generally associated with overindulgence such as alcohol psychosis and cirrhosis of the liver.

Carnarvon itself was a small, sprawling, otherwise nondescript version of Kalgoorlie, with none of the latter's frontier charm. "The most that can be said about the town," observed one Australian wag who had passed through the area a few years before, "is that it's either the northernmost community of the South, or the southernmost community of the North." A couple of banks, a few small shops, and one supermarket comprised the main street, and a hodgepodge of weatherboard bungalows, which had replaced the mud-brick houses of an earlier time, spread out in blocklike lots from there. Whatever its merits in the old days, when Carnarvon was a thriving seaport shipping wool to the world, it was now a town without character, little more than a supply center for the surrounding district.

The Gascoyne was a relatively fertile area. Compared to places like Useless Loop and Wooramel, it was a veritable Garden of Eden, thanks to irrigation by the Gascoyne River, which was said to have water in it much of the time. We had to take that latter piece of information on faith because, on our visit, there was no water to be seen.

In many respects the Gascoyne was typical of rivers in the northwest, most of which were dry, sandy creek beds punctuated by an occasional pool of stagnant green water. But for the stands of smooth white river gums lining their banks, these water courses were indistinguishable from the surrounding scrubland. When enough rain fell to "bring the rivers down," however, the creek beds became raging torrents, overflowing banks and sweeping dead vegetation high up into the trees. Months later, when the river had once again turned to sand, clumps of debris remained hanging in the branches like giant birds' nests, the only indication that a flood had indeed torn through the area some time before.

What distinguished the Gascoyne was that, even when it appeared to have dried up, it flowed ceaselessly beneath the sand, a fact known to the region's first settlers. Early explorers had hoped to discover a river of major proportions feeding the Gascoyne at its source—a river they imagined must be draining the mountains and tablelands of the entire Australian interior—and the mid-1800s witnessed a number of unsuccessful inland expeditions in search of it. In 1874 a bushman named John Forrest launched what amounted to be the last such expedition, expecting to find the "river of dreams" north of the 26th parallel, along the tropic of Capricorn. All he found was "an arid plain with little but spinifex to relieve the monotony, with rare waterholes oceans of desert apart." The Gascoyne River was, in fact, fed by underground springs.

12

One of the people Des Clancy encouraged us to meet was Bruce Teede, the owner of a plantation on the outskirts of Carnarvon. To get to his place we drove back out of town, retracing our route past a few auto dealerships, a farm machinery showroom, a transport company office, and a few caravan parks, all of which advertised themselves as the "shadiest spot in the north." Carnarvon might boast about being "the place the sun went for winter," but the townsfolk seemed eager to announce that there were enough trees in town to get out from under it.

Teede was a short, tough-looking man in his mid-fifties, with a reddish face creased by years of exposure to the tropical sun. Starting as a toolmaker, he had "given away" that trade long before to become a whaler and then a 'roo shooter. Now, as he sat in his backyard in a T-shirt and shorts, a cold stubby in his hand and some empties on the table in front of him, he seemed comfortably settled into the life of a farmer, raising fruits and vegetables on his modest, twenty-two-acre property and running a small "pet meat factory," where kangaroo carcasses were ground into food for the dogs and cats of Perth.

"I used to shoot even when I was workin' at the whalin' station," he explained. "But the market for skins went crash a while back. That's when they started breedin' like rats." He seemed to go out of his way to justify 'roo shooting and to stress that it wasn't inhumane at all. Like Americans, most urban Australians encounter kangaroos only in zoos and view them, if not with as much affection as the cuddly koala, as a "national mammal" nonetheless, and therefore as an animal to be protected. Australians who live in the bush, however, regard them simply as pests.

"Any sheepman'll tell ya kangaroos gotta be culled or there's goin' to be no water or feed for stock. Professional shooters kill 'em clean—shoot 'em only through the head. If a carcass comes in here hit anywhere from sneezer to breezer, we don't want it."

Teede mentioned that his son would be going out 'roo shooting the following night. He'd be working a property further north along the coast and since we were heading in that direction anyway, we were invited to go along for the ride. We agreed to meet Guy Teede late the following afternoon at a small turnoff from the main road near Coral Bay, about two hundred miles away, and thanking his father for his hospitality and the heavy stalk of bananas he had cut off one of his trees, set off for a sheep station north of Carnarvon, where Des Clancy had arranged for us to spend the night.

13

"The dirt track into our place seems as if it'll never end," Dudley Maslen had warned me while giving directions over the phone to his Mardathuna Station. "But I can promise you that it eventually does."

By the time we reached its end the road to Mardathuna did seem like the longest twenty-six miles I had ever driven. The tedium of the landscape was certainly part of the problem. "In this sort of country," wrote the Australian author Henry Lawson, "a stranger might travel for miles without seeming to have moved, for all the difference there is in the scenery." But there was more to it than that, something I still can't explain.

Actually, the first stretch wasn't all that bad, for after almost a thousand miles on W.A. roads, we had become more or less accustomed to the swirling cloud of red dust that enveloped us whenever we turned off the bitumen in search of who-knew-what. But the last (and longest) section was a morass of deep ruts—cut into the track by vehicles struggling to hold the high ground and not bog in the mud—which the sun had hardened into clay casts after only a few days without rain. Sometimes paralleling, sometimes crisscrossing, the ruts had a hypnotic effect and I found myself involuntarily tracing them, trying to imagine and even anticipate the sudden maneuvers that had caused them.

After about an hour and a half of bouncing around in the cab of our four-wheel-drive through nothing but arid scrubland, we came around a bend and there, off to our left, almost like a vision, was a sprawling white homestead, complete with mown lawns, manicured hedges, palm trees, and flower gardens. It was such an anomalous, such a welcome sight, that we ignored the last few yards of road in front of us and slammed directly into a gaping pothole oozing with thick red mud.

A motherly-looking woman in her mid-thirties, Chris Maslen stood slightly over five feet in her sandals. Her light brown hair was tied at the nape of her neck and she had the full bosom of a woman who had borne children. Like the little girl in her arms, whose nickname Buggie was short for Bug-eye, she had a high forehead and large smiling eyes, and as she stepped forward to greet us, we knew she had had a major hand in making the homestead the beautiful place it was.

Wearing a pair of greasy work pants and a dark blue sweat-stained shirt, with the sleeves rolled up above his forearms, Dudley looked like the Australian stockman he was, though in boxing trunks he might have passed for an Irish heavyweight just past his prime. His tanned face seemed fixed in a permanent squint and deep furrows fanned out from the corners of his eyes. He spoke in a resonant voice that seemed to emanate from deep in his chest.

Besides the baby, the Maslens had three other children—Burke, Ben, and Polly—all between the ages of six and eleven. Skipping out of their homestead classroom, where they were the only students and their mother the only teacher, they came to greet us like schoolkids who knew the truant officer was temporarily off duty.

Polly's upper lip was disfigured, split when a horse had kicked her in the face. Ben's right index finger was missing, severed when he had too inquisitively inserted it into the machine that cut the sheets of corrugated iron used around the property. Station life was evidently full of hazards.

"Any more kids besides these?" I asked, as we walked up to the house.

"No, and no more coming," said Dudley, almost as if he was making a declaration. "Just bought myself a video machine. From now on it'll be other forms of amusement."

The homestead itself was spacious and comfortable, more like an antebellum southern mansion than a rough frontier outpost. It consisted of a cluster of whitewashed brick buildings, which included the large main residence and an annex housing both the kids' well-equipped schoolroom and several elegantly furnished guest rooms.

Between the main house and the annex was a swimming pool, where the older kids and the adults could cool off. But however inviting it looked to me, it went unused during the short time we were there. Perhaps no one considered 110 degrees hot enough for swimming.

Next to the annex was a large, windowless "cool house." An invention of the early Australian pioneers, the cool house—also known as the "Coolgardie safe"—was constructed of two layers of thick wire mesh packed with spinifex. It was kept saturated with water, which ran over the roof and dripped down between the grass walls. Evaporation did the rest, lowering the inside temperature by fifteen or twenty degrees. The homestead had two cool houses, one for the beer (before it went into the fridge) and one for the baby, who took her midday naps in its damp, dark interior. It looked to me like the type of place a snake might slither into for a nap, too, but no one seemed to worry much about that, least of all the baby.

Our rooms in the annex had wide French doors opening onto a veranda, which looked out across a gently sloping lawn to the desolate bush beyond. Before dinner that evening, I stood in the doorway listening to the whirring of the ceiling fan and trying to comprehend the vastness of that scene. Mardathuna Station encompassed three thousand square miles of terrain—an area nearly three times the size of Rhode Island—almost 2 million acres of bare, brown earth on which Dudley Maslen ran 75,000 sheep. It had been in his family for over three generations.

I was reminded of what Dame Mary Durack had told us back in Perth about the bush and the hold it could have on people. Her seventy-year-old brother, Reg, was a Greek scholar who had once thought of becoming a doctor. But he had forsaken that ambition, choosing instead the hard life of the bush because, as the aborigines put it, when he was a boy "his soul had been sung to the land."

94

Dinner was served at a long hardwood table in the main dining room. Mardathuna had two dining rooms, which was apparently the case in many old homesteads. Generally, the family ate in one, the staff—jackeroos, jilleroos, drovers, shearers, housekeepers, whatever—ate in the other. Some stations even had two kitchens, with an old "gin" cook (a gin was an aboriginal woman) toiling in one and the woman of the house, presumably the station owner's wife, working in the other.

The table had been set with an embroidered tablecloth, obviously a family heirloom, and china that Chris had taken out of a heavy jarrah-wood credenza especially for the occasion. Dudley apologized for the toughness of the mutton, but I was too busy luxuriating in our comfortable circumstances to care. The food was plain but hearty, the kind you'd expect to find on an Australian station, and there was plenty of it. The two boys, Burke and Ben, ate with us, giggling to one another from time to time but otherwise restrained and well-mannered under their father's watchful eye and in the presence of two strange "Yanks." When Dudley offered us an after-dinner drink, they asked to be excused and ran off to do their homework, checking first to make sure we'd be there the following morning. Their father was responsible for breakfast, they told us, and everyone, family and station hands alike, met in the kitchen around six o'clock to devour what sounded like a gargantuan meal.

Heading back to our rooms that evening, I noticed a framed poem hanging on a corridor wall. It was entitled "Water Mellon Creek" and signed only with the initials "L.A." The author, according to Dudley, was a stranger who had once camped out on the property. Her versification was no more inspired than her spelling, but two stanzas caught my eye:

> We wandered out cros't the big red land,
> When the noon day sun rode high,
> Past the stock yards and the stunted trees,
> Where we heard soft breezes sigh.
> What is it draws man to admire,
> Sights coarse and harsh as this?
> Why is it when our eyes move higher,
> Our hearts are filled with bliss?

For Chris Maslen the answer to the latter question was simple—station life did not fill her heart with bliss. Nor was her soul sung to the land. For one thing, it was no easy task being both mother *and* grade-school teacher to her children. That was apparent as I watched her the next morning in the schoolroom, admonishing Burke that his lessons were getting "more and more untidy," telling Ben that his school diary still contained "too many first-year sentences," and praising Polly, the youngest, for getting yet another gold star.

"It doesn't matter to them at all, except when they get sick of you," she said during a "smoko," the Aussie term for coffee break or, in the case of the kids, their much-awaited recess. "But I find it exhausting, and sometimes I lose my sense of humor." She wasn't complaining, just matter-of-factly describing station life, to which she was wearily resigned. Chris did admit that she often wished she was living back in the city, where she had grown up, the daughter of a wealthy Perth businessman.

"From the kids' point of view, the bush is fantastic," she said. "They grow up getting a lot of commonsense, which I think will suit them no matter what they do in life. But for me there's very little letup, and very little stimulation. I can't do anything just for myself. It's all station, looking after the crew and the family.

"It's not living, it's just existing. I don't even have time to sit down and browse through a magazine without feeling guilty. And you can't run away. There's nowhere to run to. You've just got to make it work."

Chris had, in fact, already begun to think of running away, at least in a manner of speaking. In the not-too-distant future she planned to move back to the city, even in the face of considerable misgivings.

"Dudley and I have spoken about it quite a bit because the cost of boarding school fees would be very high. We'll probably get a house in Perth. I'll stay there and Dudley will commute. But that has a lot of drawbacks, too. Sometimes you think you're making a change for the better, but in fact you're just swapping one set of problems for another. Once I leave here . . ." She didn't complete her thought and tried again. "These old homesteads . . ." Another false start. "There's a lot that won't be done. It'll be sad. I don't know . . . we'll just see what happens."

Dudley and I walked down to the hangar, a couple of hundred yards from the house, past the workshop where three young men were peering into the partially dismantled engine of an old bulldozer. Dudley shouted a few words of encouragement to them, and promised to put the engine together if they hadn't been able to assemble it by the time we returned. He had recently made a new axle for the bulldozer, tooling it himself on the metal lathe in the workshop.

Sweating profusely in the heat of the corrugated-iron hangar, he topped up the tank of the single-engine, twin-seater Cessna with a hose and hand pump attached to a forty-four-gallon drum of aviation fuel. Then he pushed the light aircraft out of the hangar and onto the dirt strip.

At nine in the morning, the sun was already beating down fiercely, but Dudley moved imperturbably around the plane, checking it out as casually (but no less thoroughly) as if he had just saddled up a horse and was now inspecting the tightness of the girth strap. We squeezed into our seats and taxied to one end of the short airstrip. The engine whined as Dudley pulled back on the stick, and we were off, leaving a swirl of red dust behind us.

When the plane climbed to eighty feet it leveled off, maintaining that altitude for several minutes while Dudley scanned the broad vista below us. Suddenly, he banked sharply to the left, and the plane swooped down to within ten feet of the ground, pulling out of the dive at what seemed to be the last possible moment. He must have executed that maneuver countless times in the past, because as the plane was plummeting earthward he simply looked at me and calmly explained that he was going down to check out a windmill-operated bore. A sheep had drowned in the nearby water trough a few days before, and he wanted to be sure that everything was now back to normal.

Two tight turns around the windmill were enough for Dudley to determine that everything was alright, and we climbed again, this time skimming over the desertlike terrain at an altitude of about forty feet. Dudley had more than eleven thousand hours' flying experience, but rounding up cattle and sheep by plane was nonetheless a hazardous business. Six of his friends had been killed doing it and someone had recently pointed out that at thirty-seven he was one of the oldest "surviving mustering pilots in W.A." I was happy to discover that mustering wasn't on the agenda that day.

"You handle this thing like a motorbike," I hollered over the sound of the droning engine. With all the hours spent in the enclosed cockpit of the plane, Dudley had suffered damage to his hearing and he had to lean toward me to catch what I was saying.

"Yeah," he replied, "a plane is like a shirt—you put it on and wear it."

I asked Dudley about a pipeline we flew over, a thin white strip of polythene tubing that looked strangely out of place stretching across the open plain.

"My grandfather started laying the pipeline with camels," explained Dudley, "and that was all steel. I would have laid, or relaid, over half of that, maybe twenty-five miles." There were forty-five miles of it crosscutting the station.

"There's a sense of menace in this country," I said, as we flew over an especially desolate area. "Do you ever feel that?"

"It's very hard for people who haven't been born into it to understand it," he replied. "I feel I belong to this country more than it belongs to me. I'd rather be out here than doing anything else. Before I got married I spent two years living in the bush. Lived in camps with the black fellas. I was in the saddle every day, shearing sheep and running cattle. It's a life I love."

As we turned and began to make our way back to the homestead, Dudley noticed a flock of sheep below.

"That mob shouldn't be out of the paddock," he said. "I guess we'll be doing some mustering after all." He pushed the stick forward and the plane went into a steep dive. My stomach rose into my throat.

Although the main mob of sheep was out in the open, Dudley headed for a few loners grazing under a tree and almost hidden from view. The tree was about twenty feet high, and we were aiming right at it. Its lowest branches hung about ten feet above the ground and as we approached I assumed he'd pull up and over them.

But instead he swooped beneath them, as if he were flying under an open umbrella. The wing missed the trunk of the tree, the wheels came within inches of the sheep, who fled into the open, and I felt my head to see if it was still there as the plane emerged from below the branches. Jack would have hated this. Not long before, we had flown together in a small plane over the jagged mountains and dense jungles of Papua New Guinea, where for the first time Jack had experienced what he described as "existential dread."

Dudley angled to the right and headed toward another tree, which was even lower than the first. But to my great relief, at the last moment he veered off.

"I'll drop you at the homestead and pick up Jack," said Dudley. "When I bring him back, I'll get those others out."

"Wonderful idea," I agreed.

14

Guy Teede, the 'roo shooter, was waiting at the appointed fork in the road a hundred-odd miles north of Mardathuna Station when we arrived an hour behind schedule the following day. "G'day," he greeted us, rising from the back of his truck, where he had been stroking his dog's head. "I was gettin' a bit worried about youse two. Thought ya mighta got bushed." Guy's face was friendly and open, and tanned as brown as meerschaum. He had long blond sunburnt hair, which he kept brushing aside as the hot wind kept blowing it in his blue-green eyes. Despite his gentle manner, Guy Teede gave the impression of being very capable for a fellow who was only twenty-four years old.

"Sorry we're late," I said. "We didn't think it'd take so long to get here. It didn't look that far on the map."

"Nothin' looks far in W.A. till ya hafta drive it. We'd best move on, though. We've a fair distance ta go yet, an' we wanna reach camp an' get settled in before dark."

The road to the north, as monotonous as the one to the south, was dotted on either side by spinifex and saltbush. Along the shoulder, occasional patches of parched scrub somehow clung to life, despite the fact it hadn't rained in months. A blanket of powdery red dust, raised by thermal winds blowing in from the center of the continent, covered all of the vegetation. Occasionally we'd catch glimpses of vividly colored lorikeets, taking flight from the side of the road when our passing vehicle startled them.

About forty miles farther along the bitumen Guy turned off on the winding dirt track to his right. We followed in his trail, our vision obscured by the huge red plumes raised by his truck, until about thirty miles on, we reached his camp, an old corrugated-iron shack in a dusty open paddock. A small "veranda" jutted out from its front, and three long-unridden stock horses that were using it as a shelter from the sun galloped off as we pulled up. At one time in the late 1930s the camp had been used by ringers during musters, and until a few years previously a 'roo hunter named Lance Banting, obviously a man who craved isolation, lived there.

"He was a bit of a character," Guy related. "Had his wife an' two kids 'ere. Kept a few chooks an' a couple of pet goats in the yard. Even tried to grow some veggies, but the chooks kept gettin' in 'em. Lance made good money shootin' 'roos here. Went out every night an' got sixty or so. After a while a drought come an' it rained somewhere else. The 'roos moved off an' he followed 'em."

A gust of wind blew across the paddock, stirring up a few red-dust willie-willies and sending tangled clumps of dead saltbush skittering across the yard. Nearby, the old Southern Cross windmill creaked as it turned, pumping up bore water into the watering tank for the stock, which was nowhere to be seen. On the other side of the yard, facing the veranda, was a refrigerated trailer. We walked over to it, our feet stirring up a cloud of powdery dust as if it were sifted flour. It rose up to our waists and hung suspended in the air. Alongside the trailer was a small generator that Guy primed with diesel fuel and turned with a hand crank. It balked and sputtered a few times before it finally started.

"Gotta cool it down fer tamarra," he explained.

We brought our gear into the camp and unrolled our swags on the iron-spring cots inside. Of the two rooms in the darkened shack, one served as kitchen, the other as a bedroom. Guy connected a wire from the generator to the light bulb that hung from the kitchen ceiling, illuminating a rough-hewn table and benches, which cast dim shadows on the dusty concrete floor. Off to one side, against a rusting corrugated-iron wall, stood an ancient kerosene refrigerator with an alcohol stove beside it. Attached to the opposite wall was an old oak telephone with a crank handle, which had once been used by ringers to call the Cardabia station homestead for supplies.

The shack had no windows, and with the sun beating down on the iron roof, it was very hot inside. I opened both doors to let the air pass through. Guy lit the stove, put the billy on to boil, and started to slice some onions for dinner. The billy was an old powdered milk tin with a triangular bend on its rim that served as a spout. A piece of wire was attached to either side so it could be suspended over a campfire.

"This one hasn't been used much cause it's not black enough," Guy said, when he noticed me scrutinizing it. "They reckon the blacker they are on the outside, an' the rustier inside, the better the tea tastes."

"What's our plan tonight?" Dave asked, joining us in the shack after shoveling horse manure off the veranda.

"We'll want ta finish our meal an' get a start while there's still daylight," said Guy, as he turned the steaks and sausages on the skillet. He gave it a shake and added the onions. "We don't wanna miss the golden hour."

"What's the golden hour?" I asked, surprised by the poetic imagery.

"That's the hour just before the sun goes down. 'Roo shooters call it the golden hour 'cause at dusk the 'roos are just comin' out of the thicket and ya don't need a light to see 'em.

"We'll head out across the flats towards those mountains we saw to the east, an' get down alongside the creek that runs through the middle of the property. There should be 'roos in there tryin' to get outta the wind. If we do a few there, I'll follow the creek as far as I can.

Maybe we'll see the shooter that works the next property. Sometimes ya can see his light ten miles away, like a big sweep on the horizon. We might try to catch him up, an' jus' say g'day. "We should be able to shoot thirty-five or so 'roos tonight if we're lucky. They're mostly scattered now. But you'd better get inta somethin' warm," he said, looking critically at our light clothes. "It gets bloody cold out there afta dark."

Guy walked outside to where he kept his swag and gear on the veranda and in a few minutes returned, having changed from shorts and thong sandals to dark blue coveralls, boots, and a knitted navy mate's hat. With his .222 caliber rifle and a box of triple-two shells, he could easily have passed for a commando about to slip behind enemy lines on night patrol. We grabbed our windbreakers and headed for his truck.

The battered four-wheel-drive had over 350,000 kilometers on it, and it looked as though it had gone through every battle in World War II. Dave took a seat beside Guy, I crowded in next to him, and we sped off down a rutted track. Night fell quickly, and though we were north of the tropic of Capricorn, the temperature dropped almost as fast.

The extreme fluctuation of temperatures in the Outback—in a single twenty-four-hour period the mercury might soar to 135 degrees during the day and plummet to below freezing at night—was caused by radiational cooling. No clouds in the sky filtered the intense rays of the sun, nor prevented the heat from escaping into the atmosphere once the sun had set. Even with jackets and sweatshirts on, we were cold.

Somehow Guy managed to follow an old trail that neither Dave nor I could even see. Once he passed a pile of rubble and remarked, "Someone's just dumped that."

"You told us you hadn't been here for three months," Dave protested. "How do you know?"

"If ya saw a bloody new buildin' goin' up in New York, ya'd recognize it, wouldn't ya?" replied Guy, effectively ending the argument.

Each time we came to an enclosed paddock, I got out and opened the gate, while Dave beamed the 200-watt spotlight mounted on the roof in a 180-degree arc, searching for 'roos. I shouted out when I finally spotted two amber-red eyes glimmering in the shaft of light as it swept the expanse off to our left, at the fourth paddock we entered.

"It's only a fox," Guy said, peering into the distance. He reached up and directed the beam on three pairs of luminous green eyes. "And over there—those are sheep. Maybe we'll see some feral cats, they've got greeny eyes too."

The sheep turned away from the light, ambling off into the bush, and we continued along, Dave pivoting the spotlight back and forth on either side of the track.

"Hold it! There's 'roos," said Guy, suddenly. Neither Dave nor I could see anything. Guy grabbed the handle from Dave and directed the beacon back across the field.

"There they are. Here, hold the light steady," Guy instructed Dave. We could now barely make out two kangaroos about a hundred yards away, blending in almost imperceptibly with the bush. Guy shut off the engine and reached down to pick up his rifle. He pointed it out the open window, using the door as a brace to steady his aim, and drew a bead on one of the 'roos through the telescopic sight. The animal was standing straight up on its hind legs as Guy slowly squeezed the trigger. The crack of the report shattered the stillness of the night and as the bullet slammed into the 'roo's head, it toppled over like a bowling pin.

"God damn!" I muttered in admiration of his marksmanship, as the other 'roo started to hop away. Guy directed the beam of light to a spot in front of it and it stopped in its tracks. Then he beamed the spotlight directly on the 'roo. Oblivious to the danger, it was on all fours munching on some shoots of vegetation. Guy whistled, and it stood up on its hind legs. He aimed for a small dot just below the animal's ear. Again the rifle cracked, and the 'roo went over on its side.

Moments later the two sixty-odd-pound animals were hanging on hooks from either side of the truck, their heads and paws discarded and their severed tails set aside, not for pet food but for aborigines, who relished them.

"I hope ya didn' think that was bloody terrible," said Guy, apologetically. "Was it as bad as ya thought it was gonna be?" He seemed concerned that our assessment of him had been diminished and that we now regarded him as some sort of savage. We assured him we understood. Shooting 'roos might have been profitable, but it was also necessary to control the population. Despite their value as one of Australia's most familiar symbols, kangaroos have proliferated to the point where most stockmen consider them vermin, and official estimates regarding their total number run anywhere from five to twenty million animals.

"Any sheepman will tell ya they've gotta be culled or there's not gonna be water an' feed for their stock," Guy went on, despite our assurances. "This land's sparse enough as is, an' somethin's gotta be done or the 'roos 'ud overrun it. Isn't it better to make use of the remains rather than leaving 'em out here, rotting, for the dingoes to eat?"

We drove on into the night, and Guy shot more 'roos as we came on them. He had his own code of ethics about the shooting. Although the law allowed it, he wouldn't take young 'roos, or females with joeys in the pouch. Even at great distance and in the dark, he could usually identify those by the bulges in their stomachs.

At one stop the light beamed on a huge 'roo feeding close to a white gum.

"That's a big male, a 'boomer' we call 'em. He's a beaut, that one! Got chunks outta 'is ears where 'e's been fightin' over does. He's worth a quid 'r two." Guy sighted the animal in his scope, killing the boomer with a single shot at about eighty yards.

"That's one reason I don't take the dog with me," said Guy. As we stood over the fallen 'roo, he pointed to the animal's hind feet. "A boomer like that could kill a dog or a man too. He'd hold 'im with 'is front paws an' rip 'im open with those nails on the back feet."

After he hung the huge carcass on the back of the truck, Guy approached us with a big smile on his face. "I reckon the best thing about goin' out 'roo shootin' is when you pull up at night, light a fire, an' boil the billy."

He gathered pieces of snakewood off the ground and, arranging them in a pyramid-shaped pile, struck a match to them. The kindling was so dry the fire was blazing in a matter of seconds. Both Dave and I were shivering, and we huddled close to it for warmth. Guy filled the billy with water from a container in the back of the truck and added some tea he spooned out of a lidded tin can.

"It's not Earl Grey," he joked, grinning, "but she'll be right."

There wasn't a hint of a cloud in the sky overhead and the galaxies and stars seemed much closer and more visible than they did in the Northern Hemisphere. Guy filled our mugs, and we sipped scalding hot tea, warming our hands on the tin containers. He pointed out the Southern Cross and other constellations I had never seen. He knew them all, well enough to set a course by them should he ever get lost in the bush.

"Do you ever get lonely out here?" I asked.

"Oh yeah, shit yeah," Guy answered. "Sometimes I come up with a mate of mine. He's a mad shooter, 'e is. But otherwise I come up by meself. Not the sort of thing ya want to do if you're scared of the dark, goin' out in the scrub by yourself. I only stay out for three or four nights at a go. That's easy enough. Not like some of the old-timers that were out for six months or what. That's what they did for a livin'. They carried everythin' they owned in their truck. The rifle, saucepans an' cups an' whatever was in their camp. Talk about bein' lonely . . ." His words trailed off.

When we finished our tea, Guy threw a couple of shovelfuls of sand on the fire and we moved on. There was no heater or windows in the truck and we crowded against one another for warmth, but when the wintry wind gusted, it penetrated our light clothing. Guy shot four more 'roos that were bunched together in a clearing. After the first one went down, the others just stood there, as if they were waiting their turn. He knocked them over one at a time, and then just drove over and picked them up. "We haven't seen you miss a single one," I said. "You're a helluva shot."

"No, I'm jus' about average. Dad's better than what I am. I've jus' 'ad a good night, is all. When ya come out 'roo shootin', ya've gotta be nice 'n' relaxed. If ya've 'ad a bloody real shit of a day, an' yer in a bad mood an' it's stinkin' hot, an' yer bloody sweatin', nothin' seems to go right for ya. Yer all tensed up an' ya might fire a couple of shots an' miss. You've always gotta be in the right sorta mood. Otherwise ya tend to squeeze the trigger a bit too hard. If I get to feelin' that way, most times I'll just pull up an' 'ave a cuppa, or jus' lay down on the ground an' 'ave a sleep."

We moved around in the bush until about two o'clock in the morning. Guy shot a few more 'roos, surprising me when he missed one completely. He stopped and boiled the billy again, and when he realized Dave and I were cold and tired, he headed back to camp. As we passed a dry creek, the hunter's moon illuminated a thatch of white ghost gums on the bank. The wind soughed through their branches, and I was reminded of a bleak winter landscape far away in distant New England. Back in camp, indifferent to our state of being covered from head to foot with red dust, we crawled into our bedrolls and immediately fell asleep.

Shortly after dawn Dave and I woke to the smell of frying bacon. We rolled up our swags and joined Guy in the kitchen. He had just finished making the Australian specialty "jaffle sandwiches" out of bread and tinned spaghetti. "There's plenty of tucker if ya'd like to stay on for another night or two," he offered.

We thanked him, but explained we had to get back on the road. "Nothin' looks far in W.A. until ya hafta drive it," I reminded him, "and we really have a long way to go."

We chatted for a bit and then went outside. The young sun was already beginning to dissipate the chilly morning air, and the first few bush flies were already buzzing around our faces. I stood in the brilliant sunlight trying to get warm, feeling like a scaly, dust-encrusted lizard.

Dave took the dishes over to the stock tank and washed them, while I walked over to the refrigerated trailer with Guy. A scale was suspended outside the door, and I helped him weigh the 'roos before he hung them up inside. He'd shot only twenty-three the night before, but if we hadn't been with him, he'd have stayed out until dawn and done much better. No worries, he assured me, he planned to go out shooting for another night or two. Then he'd call his father on the radio to come up in the refrigerated truck and haul the lot back to the pet food factory in Carnarvon.

We had a bit of a wash at the stock tank, and tried to get some of that red dust off. But it didn't do much good. The wind had picked up and was whipping around raising more of it. Fine particles of dust tingled in my nostrils, and I couldn't clear my throat.

Even in the early morning light, which usually showed things to their best advantage, the camp had a forlorn aspect to it. It was hard to imagine how Lance Banting or anyone else had ever lived there.

We stowed the gear in our truck and said our good-byes to Guy. As we drove off, he stood with his dog in the middle of the yard, waving. When we reached the crest of the hill a mile or so down the track, I looked back and saw the two figures motionless in the yard, dust swirling around them until they became indistinguishable from their surroundings, as heedless of time as the land itself.

15

My heart stopped pounding when we picked up the bitumen again. Even though I'd kept insisting to Dave that we weren't lost, I really had my doubts. After leaving Guy Teede we had continued north until we came to a turnoff to the east, a rough, poorly marked track running through what the map described as "scrubby range" before it rejoined the North West Coastal Highway some sixty miles away. After a moment's pause to debate the pros and cons of taking the shortcut or playing it safe by sticking to the bitumen, we turned right and took the track.

The pockmarked road wound endlessly through the scrub, intersecting at times with other trails bound for who-knew-where. With the sun behind us, we knew we should be heading in a generally easterly direction, but the road twisted and turned and because our progress over its corrugated surface was torturously slow, I soon began to fear that perhaps we were lost. Had we taken a wrong turn and gone off on one of Bullara's outstation tracks? Or were we past Bullara station and now on Marrilla property? Dave joked about Guy's being there to point us to the highway. Oddly enough, I had been entertaining the very same thought.

We were back on the coastal highway, but that didn't last very long. After driving less than forty miles on it, we turned off onto another dirt track, this one almost twice as long as the last. It ran northwest and led to Onslow.

On the edge of town we passed a new housing site. According to a roadside sign it was a government project for the aboriginal community, which throughout the country was almost totally dependent on social welfare for its subsistence. While most of the homes were still under construction, the few that were occupied already looked ramshackle and neglected. Young children wearing tattered clothing played in the dust of unlandscaped plots in front of the houses. A couple of mangy dogs lying in the road refused to move as we approached, and we were forced to drive around them.

We continued down the dusty, tree-lined main street, past the shire office, the post office, and the Beadon Hotel, the only pub in Onslow. As was so often the case in W.A., the pub, a two-story wide-verandaed structure, was the most impressive, as well as the most important, building in town. When the Beadon's top story blew away during a 1934 cyclone, it had been replaced almost immediately, while the pub downstairs continued to operate.

Though only a small town, Onslow is known as Cyclone City. Each year during monsoon season the W.A. coast from Carnarvon northward is battered by cyclones, which storm ashore off the Indian Ocean, bringing torrential rains, floods, and leaving paths of destruction in their wakes. But then there are times when the monsoons never arrive, and the droughts that follow sometimes last for years.

The main street of Onslow, like that in Denham, terminated at a caravan park overlooking the bay. We'd discovered early on that stopping in caravan parks was often a better way to meet Australians than camping out on our own. And the people we encountered there were open, friendly, and generous to a fault.

Margaret Millican, who ran the Ocean View Caravan Park with her husband, Fred, had asked a few of her friends over for a Saturday night barbie, and even though she'd met us only a few hours earlier, she invited us to join the company. On our arrival Margaret had offered accommodations in a small caravan she owned right on the water.

"You're really in luck," she'd informed us. "There was a young tradesman here only yesterday. But he won't be needin' it now, 'cause he's in the jail for a bit."

"What did he do?" asked Dave, as if he was considering a resumption of his aborted legal career.

"He got drunk last night an' turned 'is car over. The police arrested 'im. He seemed like such a nice chap," replied Mrs. Millican, a frown crossing her face.

"It appears we're obliged to a drunken driver," I explained to Dave, as we unloaded our gear. "If that creates a moral dilemma for you, you can sleep outside in the truck." Dave prided himself on his logical, lawyerlike thinking, and I felt it was my responsibility to keep his razor-sharp mind properly honed.

That night a group of about fifteen of us sat around the big table outside Margaret Millican's caravan. Everyone had brought something in the way of food or drink. One guest had caught a couple of snapper earlier in the day and had contributed those to the pot. Another had netted a huge basket of prawns and steamed them up in beer, and there was also a mess of crabs that had been trapped out in front of the caravan park. The table held lots of steaks, beer, potato salad, baked beans, homemade pies, and all sorts of other good things that made up standard fare at an Australian barbie. Since Dave and I had nothing to contribute, we went to the bottle shop at the Beadon Hotel for some beer and a few flagons of wine.

Robby Nesbitt sat down next to me, introducing himself to all the people at the table he hadn't met. He was a clean-cut, dark-haired fellow with a stocky build, in his late forties, and had made a good start on developing an Australian beer belly. Despite his crooked nose—it had once been broken in a punch-up—Robby had a distinguished manner, and would probably have been more at home in a dark business suit than the faded pair of navy blue shorts and T-shirt he was wearing. With a warm sense of humor he told a few Australian jokes that had everyone at the table roaring with laughter.

"What brings a Yank to W.A.?" he asked me, initiating the conversation.

"Just seein' a bit of the country," I answered. "How 'bout yourself?"

"Oh, ya know what they say, 'Don't go to Europe and Saint-Tropez, it's betta to see W.A.' I'm makin' a trip around Australia that I've been plannin' for a long time. Been here in Onslow about a fortnight now. I reckon I've had a good look around, an' I'll be movin' on soon.

"This is a friendly enough place, like most little country towns. Ya can usually get people talkin' if ya tell a joke or two. No matter where ya go, people laugh at the same thing, whether it's about Australians, the Irish, or the Polish."

During the course of the evening Robby told me that he'd been married for twenty-odd years and had two grown daughters. One day, out of the blue, his wife informed him that she wanted a divorce and then moved in with another man, a professional photographer much younger than Robby.

"Before all this happened I was an accountant," Robby continued, with obvious pride, "but I gave that away because it was drudging office humdrum. When I got married, we had a family early on. The car I had was just about shot so I got a job sellin' cars and trucks and got one free. I enjoyed that. But that's all behind me.

"I've got no time schedule now. Sometimes, what you think you want when you're younger, isn't what you want at all. Now if I want to go fishing, I go fishing. Doesn't matter if it's Sunday, Tuesday, or Friday. By the way, what are you chaps doing tomorrow?" As we had no plans, we decided to pool our resources and go fishing.

Early the next morning, Robby knocked on our caravan door and handed us a hot pot of coffee he'd brewed up across the way in his miniature motor home. A cross between a panel truck and a station wagon, the vehicle, an old Holden built by Australia's only automobile manufacturer, was a curious-looking relic. Everything Robby owned, from clothes to cooking utensils, was jam-packed inside it. Somehow, he managed to sleep there, too, crawling into the rear and wedging himself in between all his worldly possessions. Up front there was hardly room for the driver, let alone us, so we piled into our own vehicle and the three of us headed for Old Onslow.

The old town, abandoned many years earlier, had originally been founded at the mouth of the Ashburton River and named after a family that had come over from a small village in Surrey, England, during the last century. What a shock the founders must have experienced when they arrived at that barren spot! The only similarity between Surrey and the area around Onslow was that they happened to occupy a bit of space on the same planet.

Over the years silt from the Ashburton had built up in front of the original port, making it impossible for ships to get over the tidal flats and into the jetty. At the same time the low salt marshes at the rear of the town often flooded the dirt track that led into it. Since nature had decided for them, the town fathers had little choice but to move Onslow to a new location on Beadon Bay ten miles to the north. In 1925 they simply dismantled the wooden houses and loaded them on wagons, and camel teams hauled them to the new townsite. All that remained of Old Onslow were a few sandstone buildings surrounded by shifting sand dunes.

Though its roof had long since been torn off by some raging cyclone and the frame that once supported the front door had collapsed, the most prominent structure left standing was the Old Onslow Gaol. Portions of the outside walls had crumbled, and those still standing appeared on the verge of toppling over, but we stepped inside past a weathered sign that ironically read KEEP OUT and wandered through the empty cells. With the fierce tropical sun overhead heating up the building's interior, the prison must have been an unbearable place.

We drove over the red sand dunes toward the sea in the hopes of catching some fish with Robby's net. The sand was soft, and on the way up one steep dune we bogged.

"Put the four-wheel-drive in low," Robby advised. "She'll be right."

The vehicle shuddered but slowly pulled out and made the crest of the dune. In front of us lay the Indian Ocean, gently lapping on the fringe of a deserted red beach. We drove along the edge of the water until we came to a small cove, where we parked and unloaded the net from the back of the truck. We were bare-footed and had to run to the water across the fiery sand, searing our feet even at the ocean's edge. The sky was perfectly clear, and the sun had a strength far greater than any I'd ever experienced, even in the Florida Keys.

I took one end of the net and waded a few feet into the water while Robby held the other end and walked out until he was up to his chest.

"Keep yer eyes out for the bloody sharks, mates," yelled Robby, as we made our first pass along the shore. "I'm in too deep to see 'em."

"No worries," Dave hollered back.

"That's easy fer you to say, mate," Robby answered. "Yer sittin' up there on the bloody beach. They're not gonna come outta the water afta ya."

Robby wasn't joking about the sharks. We'd seen them by the thousands in the shallows off Dirk Hartog Island. Sharks infest the waters around the entire Australian coast, and in some areas even wading can be dangerous.

We dragged the net three or four times along the shore, but the incoming tide had stirred up the fine red sand, clouding the water and bringing our efforts to a halt. In the silty water, Robby warned us, sharks could come in undetected.

"Where do you go from here?" I asked Robby, as we sat on the edge of the Indian Ocean sipping a beer.

"North along the coast, I guess," he answered. "Up through Port Hedland an' then Broome. There's always cab drivin' in Broome. Ya don't make much money, but they provide accommodations an' that keeps the costs down. I'll go north into the Kimberleys after that an' take lots of Kimberley currency with me."

"What in the world is that?" I asked.

"If a chap helps ya out with a couple a' gallons of gas an' ya give him half a dozen stubbies for his trouble, that's Kimberley currency. It's Kimberley cool, too, meaning it's not chilled. Then ya sit down an' help him drink it, an' you're both back to square one."

"Don't you miss Perth and your friends?" Dave asked him.

"Not really," Robby replied. "I like to meet people, so I'm just continuin' that in a little different vein. People are the same the world over. Ya just gotta take 'em as they are. You get a chance to think when you're drivin' along by yourself. No telephones beltin' down your neck, no mortgages to worry about, no schedules, no deadlines. You really aren't out of society, but you've stepped off for a little. It's like comin' out of the ninety-k lane and goin' down to ten while you're lookin' for a parking spot. A lot of people go through this country an' see very little, but there's a lot here. Ya can't see much tearin' through it at a hundred and ten k's. You've got to have time to pull up, switch off, an' walk around."

Taking his advice, we waded along a stretch of deserted beach, picking up a few of the more exotic-looking seashells the rising tide had left glistening on the sand. By the water's edge legions of fiddler crabs darted away at our approach, scurrying for the safety of their holes, while a short distance offshore a flock of screeching frigate birds dove frantically on a school of bait driven to the surface by feeding fish below. As the sun sunk low in the sky we relinquished the beach to them, climbing into our Toyota and heading back to town.

16

Parked in front of the Beadon Hotel sat a number of battered vehicles, while inside the pub their drivers engaged in boisterous conversations. Entering the establishment to the accompaniment of Bruce

Springsteen's "Born in the U.S.A." blaring on the jukebox, we steered our way through a group of stockmen and up to the crowded bar. The pub resembled a turn-of-the-century western saloon, as many of its patrons wore cowboy hats, boots, and faded work jeans. Shouting to the barmaid over the din in the high-ceilinged, smoky room, we ordered drinks and waited for a table. As we stood at the old-fashioned bar gulping down beers, Robby pointed out our first Blair to us. Since we planned to see his father the following morning, our host thought an introduction to Ian Blair's youngest son was in order.

David Ross Blair, the baby of the Blair family, was almost too huge to be human. Standing at least six feet six inches tall, he was nearly as wide, and he had to have weighed well over three hundred pounds. But for an enormous beer belly, he might have been a National Football League lineman who had inadvertently taken the wrong flight south.

Cradling four empty pitchers in his arms, Baby Blair lumbered up to the bar and pushed them across to the barmaid. As Robby introduced us, Blair peered through the tangle of long blond hair obscuring his vision. He blinked several times and, gazing at us through opaque blue eyes, grunted an acknowledgment in our direction before shuffling back to his table. In his skin-tight T-shirt and with his matted, shoulder-length hair cascading down his back, he looked like a bleached-blond bear in drag.

A waitress with four full pitchers of beer made her way precariously over to Blair's table and set them down. The four stalwart lads sitting with him filled their hefty mugs to the brim. But young Blair, disdaining so wee a vessel, snatched up a pitcher in his massive hand as if it were a cordial glass, and quaffed most of its contents with two gargantuan gulps.

Pausing only a moment to snarl something to the chap sitting beside him, he raised the pitcher to his lips again, finishing it off with a single swallow. He now emitted a thunderous belch that reverberated throughout the pub. But Blair's feats had apparently not yet concluded, for in one swift, deft motion, he shoved the empty pitcher to the center of the table, grabbed the handle of a full one, and yanked it toward him without spilling a drop.

"That boy's got fast hands," observed the awestruck Dave, carefully nursing his own pathetic pot of beer.

After a few moments Blair heaved himself out of his chair, carrying a half-full pitcher, and lurched over to the jukebox, where he hovered. Was he deciding whether to devour it whole, or smash it into smaller, more digestible pieces? Neither, for after pushing some change into it he simply made a few selections with a finger as thick as a wrist.

"If he plays something slow, why don't you ask him to dance," I suggested to Dave.

"But if he accepts, what would we talk about?" he answered, unflappable as usual. "I'm not sure we have a great deal in common."

As we were leaving the pub after our meal, Baby Blair was standing at the bar settling his bill. Under one arm he carried a case of beer, as if it were an evening paper.

"A little nightcap for later," observed Robby.

Early the next morning we walked the short distance to Ian Blair's. A sign outside his home, a single-story wooden bungalow, announced in bold black letters that he was agent for KLEENHEAT GAS, MACKEREL ISLANDS, PAGGIS AVIATION, HONDA ENGINES, VOLVO, AND THE WESTPAC BANK. It also advertised the fact that he was a SECONDHAND DEALER, JUSTICE OF THE PEACE, MARRIAGE CELEBRANT, and last but not least, FUNERAL DIRECTOR.

"Is there anything else you do that's not on the sign?" I asked Ian, after he'd made us comfortable in the living room, where the collection comprising his SHELL AND BOTTLE MUSEUM was on display.

"Yeah, there is," he replied, his Irish face beaming. "I write for the newspapers, I'm the ABC correspondent for the area, I run a car wrecking yard, and I do a bit of veterinarian work." He stopped to catch his breath and continued, "I'm also the field service officer for the aboriginal community, the parole officer, a legal service volunteer, and Master for the Masonic Lodge."

"What do you do in your spare time?" asked Dave.

"I write a bit of poetry." Ian laughed, fumbling in a desk drawer and handing me a sheet of paper. "You can read this one on the road."

Ian Blair was a giant of a man, but unlike his youngest son, he wasn't carrying much of a belly, nor did he share Baby Blair's passion for the pub.

"I go crazy at Christmastime and have a beer. I used to drink, but I gave it away. My youngest son hasn't though," said Ian, shaking his head disapprovingly. "He drinks enough for everyone in town."

Ian first came to Onslow in 1958 as its only policeman, but he had resigned the police force in 1966 to avoid being transferred when he was promoted.

"I went to see the commissioner in Perth," he recalled, "and asked him how long I'd have to stay in the city before I got another country station. 'Could be six days, might be six years,' I was told. So I said righto, and gave notice."

After leaving the force—the department assigned four men to replace him—Ian returned to Onslow, accepting work that nobody else would do. Funeral director was the least favorite of his many occupations.

"It's a thankless job in a small town," he said. "If it's not a friend you're buryin', it's someone you've known for a long time.

"But to stay in Onslow, I had to do something. The pearling was already finished when I first came here," Ian reminisced, "but even in those days they were still shipping thousands of bales of wool out of here. Yet most of the stations closed down, or converted to cattle. This country's had the bomb for sheep; they've overgrazed it and eaten it out. But raising cattle isn't our salvation either—that's a dying industry too."

As a result of the disappearance of major industries, Onslow's population of 350 aboriginals and 250 whites depended primarily on funds allocated by the government for the aboriginal community. Most children in the public schools and patients in the hospital were aboriginal, as were the majority of people using the health and welfare services. Were it not for the money spent by aboriginals, the hotel and most other businesses in town couldn't exist.

"It makes you wonder how we got along in the old days, doesn't it?" Ian laughed aloud. "I guess we're a welfare state."

"With all the problems in Onslow, aren't you sorry you didn't stay in Perth?" asked Dave, for whom it was inconceivable that anyone would want to live anywhere but a metropolis like Manhattan.

"I wouldn't live anyplace except Onslow. I own a house in Perth, but I wouldn't want to go down there 'cause the winters would kill me. I've got enough comin' in now and I don't have to work at all if I didn't want to. But keepin' busy suits me just fine."

A policeman knocked, stuck his head in the screen door, and hollered, "You're goin' ta be late for court, Ian."

"Duty calls," Ian announced, rising briskly from his chair. "I'm hearing a case on a drunken drivin' charge in a few minutes."

"That must be the fellow who was staying in our caravan," I said.

"It's the only case on the docket, so it must be," said Ian. "You're welcome to come along if you want."

We entered the Onslow courthouse, a recently built one-story red brick structure, which was across the street from the caravan park and adjacent to the police station. It was empty except for the defendant, Paul Downey, a thin, sandy-haired young man in his early twenties. When we asked him what had happened to bring him there, Downey related that an aboriginal was driving his car when it turned over about thirty miles out of town. Luckily, the vehicle had landed right side up, but the driver had injured his arm. Being the decent chap he was, Downey had driven him to the hospital to see that he got proper medical attention. But once in town Downey was promptly arrested. He admitted that his aboriginal friend had been drinking, but said that he himself had had only "one or two beers." He didn't know why he'd been arrested and insisted that he had never been in trouble before. "I can't understan' it, I didn't do nothin'," he said, shaking his head with bafflement.

After a few stragglers wandered in from the street and took seats Ian Blair entered the courtroom dressed in a black robe. It was a remarkable transition, and I couldn't help but wonder if his honor was still wearing shorts and flip-flops under the judicial garb. Judge Blair took his seat on the bench and asked the bailiff to state the charges against the defendant. Paul Anthony Downey was accused of driving under the influence of alcohol, refusing to undergo a breath analysis test, and driving without a driver's license.

Judge Blair asked him if he "wished to press for legal advice, or deal with the three charges now." Replying that he didn't want a lawyer, Downey maintained that he had a license but had lost it. He didn't address the other charges and seemed somewhat confused by the bailiff's legalese. Sympathetic to his plight, Judge Blair called him out of the witness box and up to the bench and patiently explained his predicament.

"You say you've got a license, but you've lost it. What about the first charge of driving under the influence? How do you plead to that?" asked Ian.

"Guilty, I'm guilty," said Downey.

"How about the charge of refusing a breath test? Do you wish to plead guilty or not guilty?"

"Guilty," mumbled Downey.

"The little bastard spotted you for a bleeding heart and lied to us," I leaned over and whispered to Dave, who was somewhat taken aback by the defendant's admission of guilt.

"What caused the defendant to be arrested?" Ian asked the bailiff. The bailiff related that, according to witnesses who'd made statements to the police, Downey had driven his partially demolished vehicle up a footpath outside the news agency, smashing into the front of it. He then got out of the car carrying an open bottle of Scotch and entered the store, leaving his vehicle parked on the sidewalk. At that point the police arrived.

"He was probably looking for reading material for his friend at the hospital," Dave muttered.

"Does his record show any previous arrests?" asked Ian.

The bailiff informed the court that Downey had been convicted on two other occasions for drunken driving. And when it was revealed that Downey's license had been permanently revoked for a previous offense, Ian found him guilty on all charges, fining him only the minimum on each count. Australian frontier justice wasn't so rough, after all.

As we left the court, I looked at the piece of paper Ian had given me. It was a bit of doggerel verse he had written, with the title "The False Alarm," which I proceeded to read to Dave:

> *"It was only just yesterday when the police received a call,*
> *From a man who was an American and spoke with*
> *   a Yankee drawl.*
> *Just over from the States, I am, and have a sad tale to tell,*
> *I just ran over a pedestrian, I left him where he fell.*
>
> *Well the law in their efficiency, went out along the road,*
> *And wondered who the poor chap was that they would*
> *   have to load.*
> *But their language on return to town made the air*
> *   turn blue,*
> *The stupid Yankee so-and-so had run over a kangaroo."*

We'd already met a number of Australians of Ian's type—sharp-witted, sanguine jacks-of-all-trades. They brought a survivor's instinct to their pursuits, priding themselves on their ability to make a go of whatever they turned their hand to. Such men were not necessarily contemptuous of urban dwellers—Ian certainly wasn't—but since they lived in the "country," where life was harsh and generally more arduous, they fostered a certain bush superiority. Their success was measured in their ability to make things work and to succeed in the face of seemingly impossible situations, and under the most challenging circumstances.

17

After leaving the courtroom we continued walking along the dusty road toward Ces Piesse's residence. Earlier, Ian had strongly recommended we visit the old sea captain, who had once sailed a pearling lugger out of Onslow. We'd heard he not only could tell a good yarn but also knew the town's history better than anyone. His small caravan sat next to a stately old frame house with a veranda on two sides, and entering its front yard through the creaking gate of a weathered picket fence intertwined with purple bougainvillaea, we knocked on his door.

Captain Ces Piesse was a tall, gaunt man in his seventies, and though he was wearing only a lava-lava, he was no less dignified for it. He had a slight stoop now, but he must have cut quite a figure years earlier standing on the deck of his ship issuing commands to his Malay and Japanese crew. Weathered by a life spent at sea, his face was lined with deep furrows, which were especially pronounced around his pale blue eyes from years of squinting at the tropical sun. The old captain still had a presence about him that he imposed on his undignified surroundings.

Captain Piesse didn't follow the sea any longer, but the inside of his caravan looked uncannily like a ship's cabin and almost seemed suffused with a marine light. Having utilized every bit of space, he had painstakingly laid out his entire stock of possessions, and knew the precise location of every neatly arranged object in the room: The wall opposite a small stove and sink was lined with built-in shelves, the top one displaying a huge carved mother-of-pearl shell and the one below a sextant and other navigational instruments, along with nautical memorabilia. Beneath those shelves was his narrow bunk, which also served as a couch. Shelves on another wall contained his library, with volumes of Voltaire, Conrad, and Tolstoy.

Captain Piesse had gone to sea when he was twenty. He and two of his mates were working with the Main Roads when, during a holiday in Broome, they decided on the spur of the moment to buy a lugger with the money they had saved. They jumped into "the pearling game" and away they sailed, up the coast. It was an adventure I would have loved to have experienced, one I had dreamed of as a boy back in Boston, poring over maritime charts and reading stories of Somerset Maugham late into the night.

"Of the three, I was the closest to bein' a seafarin' man," the old captain mused, recalling the experience. "I'd been to Rottnest Island on a yacht once, so they elected me skipper. How we survived that first trip, I'll never know. I had my twenty-first birthday in Alligator Creek. We had plenty of dried turtle meat hangin' on the riggin', bottles of tomato sauce, and rice. That was the extent of our larder. The rest of our gear was borrowed 'cause we'd spent every quid we owned. There was nothing left for beer an' stuff. I always maintained I'd have a proper twenty-first birthday party the following year, but it never really developed. I'm seventy-five now, and I'm still waiting to have it.

"We were after the mother-of-pearl. The shells were our living, and any pearls we found were the cream on the top. Pearlin' used to be the most important trade in W.A., but the damn technology got too good and the bottom fell out of the market.

"It wasn't just the invention of plastic. The engine boats came along, and they didn't need the old hand pumps any longer. Earlier on, we never worked in water beyond fifteen fathoms, but with the new hard-hat gear, they could go down much deeper. And the divers were able to get a lot more shell. At the end, we were getting less for the shell than it was costing us to fish it. Oversupply is what buggered the market, not just plastic."

Captain Piesse rose stiffly and took a watercolor down from the wall to let us examine it more closely. "That was my last lugger," he said wistfully, clearly stepping back in time. "She was built in Broome with jarrah timber brought up from the south. Her frames were cadgey-bark, and I called her the *Voltaire*. Voltaire was a pretty cunning fellow, you know. Must have been a bastard of a bloke, but you had to admire him in a lot of ways. It seemed like a good name for a ship.

"I used to go out to the Montebellos for a bit of fishin' every now and then. But as I got older, I found I couldn't handle the anchors and things on my own anymore. She was moored up here in the creek for about eighteen months and didn't go out. I got to thinking it was a damn silly way to treat a fine ship like that, so I sold her and got this caravan. But it's not the same, you know." The tinge of nostalgic remorse in his voice could have been that of a lover.

Our conversation was interrupted by a knock on the door. An attractive woman in her mid-sixties, with long graying hair that fell to her shoulders, poked her head into the caravan. It was Mona, a neighbor who had come to deliver his mail. Seeing us there, she excused herself quickly, explaining she had to pick up a few items at the store.

"Life has its own way of just going along," said Captain Piesse, after she had gone. "Before he died, I knew Mona's husband very well. He was the driver on that funny little train that used to haul things back and forth from the goods shed down to the jetty and the ships. He left Mona the house and I've got the caravan, and we share meals and that sort of thing, and she's actually very good. She'd have to be or she couldn't put up with the likes of me.

"I've been married twice, but I guess it was mostly to my ship and to the sea. My first wife died, and the second one, well, we just sort of separated. Once when I was going off to sea, she said, 'I'd like to see the last of you,' and I told her, 'No worries, it won't be long now.' But when I think about it, I guess I was probably a bit hard to live with.

"I've got two sons and two grandchildren in Perth. I suppose I could have stayed with them when I retired, but I wouldn't find much pleasure down there. I suppose there are some negative aspects to living in Onslow but I'm so used to living on my own I don't really miss company. Living here is like bein' ashore on a desert island, but one you could get off if you wanted to."

The old captain stopped talking for a moment as he worked to frame a thought, letting his gaze take in the heritage assembled around him.

"I could have gone anywhere I liked after I sold the *Voltaire*. I got a good quid for her, you know. But after all these years here, and what with Mona . . . Yes, I reckon I've always had a yen for this sort of country."

It was an afternoon for farewells—not just to Captain Piesse, who had so touched us with his tales of the seafaring life, but also to Robby, who met us for a last lunch at the Beadon Hotel. He was heading east to Wittenoom, near Marble Bar, and we were moving north. When we'd finished our meal of fish and chips, Robby handed us a sheaf of letters of introduction to people he'd met during his travels.

"Beats goin' into some town and not knowin' anybody," he said. "Just a bit of reassurance, a little confidence builder. And here's an address that 'ill find me if ya write. Me mum will forward it on, wherever I am."

After we parted ways in front of the hotel and were driving up the coastal road through the desolate landscape that would take us to Port Hedland a few hundred miles away, I found myself thinking a lot about Robby and his lonely existence. He was my age and, like me, had several grown daughters. But my divorce had come when I was a lot younger, and after only a few years of marriage.

Robby had shared twenty years of his life with a woman he obviously still cared for, and it wasn't difficult to see that their divorce had shattered him. Remarkably, he didn't seem embittered by the experience, nor did he appear resentful of his ex-wife. "No use carrying around a grudge," he had joked when we discussed it late one night, "I couldn't fit it into the Holden."

Like the virulent Useless Loopers "holidaying" at Nanga, and even station owner Ted Sears himself, Robby had done what seemed to be the Australian thing to do under such circumstances. He had hit the road, heading out of the city and into the wilderness to wander around by himself in quest of who-knew-what.

18

We didn't reach Port Hedland until late the next afternoon, having made a slight detour to see Karratha, a new town recently sprung up on the flats of Nickol Bay to serve businessmen involved in the area's mining and mineral industries. Karratha boasted an international-class hotel, a shopping mall, and one or two other amenities, but we found it had little else to recommend it. A few miles farther north was Cossack, a totally uninhabited ghost town which before the turn of the century had been the center of the pearling industry—aboriginal women had worked as divers for unscrupulous traders, who paid them in worthless trinkets—and a major jumping-off point for the Pilbara goldfields.

The gold rush in this part of Western Australia began when a fifteen-year-old boy, Jimmy Withnell, found a chunk of the precious metal while looking for horses at nearby Mallina station. He had left his tucker bag near a hut and returned to find a crow nibbling at his lunch. He picked up a stone to throw at the bird and noticed the rock was speckled with yellow.

When the discovery was reported to Colonel Angelo, the Government Resident at Roebourne, the colonel rushed to his office to telegraph Surveyor-General Forrest in Perth. The find had so excited him, however, that his message neglected to state one important fact, and merely read: WITHNELL, LOOKING FOR HORSES, PICKED UP A STONE TO SHY AT A CROW. [Signed] ANGELO. The reply came back: DID HE REALLY? WHAT HAPPENED TO THE CROW? [Signed] FORREST.

But Cossack's prosperity was short-lived. Asian seamen brought smallpox to the area, and though the aboriginals were the hardest hit, many whites also died. During that time, Jimmy's mother, Emma Withnell, who had helped put a stop to the use of aboriginal women as divers, sent out word to the native population that Cossack was "bad medicine." An epidemic of typhoid fever then followed the smallpox. By the time the gold petered out and the harbor silted up in the early 1900s, Cossack itself had expired.

We wandered around its empty dirt streets and through the old courthouse in the thin light of early morning. Though the post office had been built with bricks imported as ballast, most of the buildings in Cossack, unlike those of many other ghost towns in Western Australia, had been constructed of stone (and their tin roofs secured by chains) to withstand the cyclones that so often swept through the area. Except for the red dust that coated them, they were still in remarkable condition.

Climbing to the crest of a small knoll referred to in the old town plan as Nanny Goat Hill, we looked down on the silt-filled harbor and the deserted town, which even in its heyday lacked a sufficient supply of fresh drinking water. The few wells that had been drilled turned saline almost immediately, and the water had to be barged in from the south. A Japanese "water man" delivered it door to door, and standing there on the hill we could almost envision him making his daily rounds, drawing the precious commodity from a large wooden barrel he hauled through the streets on horse and wagon. Even without people Cossack had a lot more character than Karratha.

We passed through Roebourne, eager to discover why it had once been called "the Cinderella town of the North West," but found only a settlement consisting of a few houses on either side of the road. According to a girl we met in a small shop there, it, too, was fast becoming a ghost town. The whites were leaving, she said, abandoning the place to "fringe-dwelling" aboriginals, those who had left the bush to settle on the edges of the country towns, living in government camps (or in tin humpies of their own making) and almost totally dependent on social welfare for their survival. Fifty miles beyond Roebourne was Whim Creek, once the largest copper mine in Western Australia. Except for a ramshackle pub owned by a morose man people referred to as "the Whim Creek Dreamer," who talked of converting the abandoned miners' shacks into a resort hotel, it was totally deserted.

We had seen nothing but devastation for hundreds of miles—the scattered remains of settlements that, though built on illusions of permanence, had long since passed into oblivion. If there had been no attempt at reclamation, it was because there was nothing in the land to reclaim. As Digger Dawes had observed back in Kalgoorlie, minerals weren't like seeds, something you could throw on the ground and harvest. Gold, in short, was an exhaustible resource. "When it's gone, it's gone," Digger had said. This region, like so much of Western Australia, had been totally dependent on a single economy. Lacking water, or even a viable topsoil for agriculture, it evidently could support no other.

Port Hedland, our next stop, had been extravagantly promoted by the Royal Automobile Club of W.A. as "the dynamic and growing administrative centre for the northwest and a major deep-water port for the area." But having been duped by optimistic Australian travel brochures before, we were not surprised to find that both literally and figuratively it was just a dump. To put it more precisely, it was a dumping ground for the tons of iron ore that rumbled in by rail on mile-long trains from the Pilbara, the mineral-rich region extending several hundred miles to the east and south.

Because the tidal flats on the outskirts of town were used as evaporation ponds for a solar "salt farming" industry, a ghostly white glaze filmed the surface of the mud, which made the entire area look as if it were in the throes of a dermatological blight. Closer to the center of town, mounds of blackish ore sat on a pier awaiting shipment, and the local tourist association, lacking a better attraction, advertised free conducted tours to view them.

"I can't think of anywhere I'd rather not be," read one entry in the visitors' book at the tourist center. "Horrible," said another. "Great," said a third, "but when's the next plane out?"

For one brief moment Jack showed signs of weakening. Perhaps, he suggested, we should stay the night in Port Hedland. But a spin around town, which reminded us of a smaller yet shabbier version of Bayonne, N.J., was enough to convince him to leave. Despite the hour and the fact that we'd been on the move since early morning, we'd keep on driving. We'd be able to cover half the distance to Broome that evening, spend the night at the Sandfire Roadhouse, and have only two hundred miles through the desert the following day.

We'd been warned that the road from Port Hedland to Broome ran through four hundred miles of absolute desolation. It was known as the Horror Stretch, and though it was mercifully interrupted in the middle by a solitary service station called the Sandfire Roadhouse, it passed through a wilderness whose malevolent power was legendary. Yarns were spun of people who had succumbed to the Horror Stretch after hours behind the wheel—of a man who had to be helped from his vehicle babbling incoherently; of a woman motorist found sitting alone in her car sobbing and unable to speak. Their senses had been bludgeoned, their nerves shot, it was said, by the sand and the fire of the sun.

According to the map, not a single riverbed (not even a dry one) was to be found along the route, as had been the case farther south. Nor were there hills to hold back the endless desert sands as they swept toward the coast. The area around Perth was shielded from the Nullarbor and the Great Victoria Desert by the low hills of the Darling Range, the area from Carnarvon on up insulated from the Gibson Desert by the rugged, iron-laden ranges of the Pilbara. Stony, eroded tablelands barely distinguishable from those of the desert areas themselves, they nonetheless served to catch the scarce rainfall and, at rare intervals, to channel it down their scarps into the riverbeds whose "floodways" we had crossed on the way up.

But at the De Grey River, a few miles north of Port Hedland, all that stopped. The road simply ran, almost tentatively, along the edge of the Great Sandy Desert, paralleling the coast a few miles from the shores of Eighty Mile Beach, where, because of sharks, poisonous jellyfish, and sea snakes, no one dared to swim.

It was twilight when we hit the Horror Stretch. Weary from the long day's drive through the monotonous terrain, we were expecting the worst, but except for the extraordinary number of cattle carcasses that lay alongside the road, the highway looked no different from any other we had traveled on elsewhere in W.A. Some of the carcasses were long-decayed, dried-out heaps of weathered bones and hide. Others had been killed more recently, and even with the windows tightly closed we could smell the putrefying flesh long before we reached the mangled remains.

Emaciated cattle, unrestrained by fences, grazed nearby, and it seemed only a matter of time before they, too, would succumb to the few roadtrains that passed this way, running over everything in their path as they roared down the highway without ever braking. How the cattle survived in that desert environment and what they were doing there in the first place was a mystery to me. A government official back in Perth had told us that Australia exported two hundred fifty thousand tons of meat to the U.S. each year. "Lean manufacturing beef," it was called, a reference to the fact that most of it was ground up and used by American hamburger chains like Wendy's and Burger King. Here on the Horror Stretch were, perhaps, the leanest of the lot, still on the hoof but only barely so.

About an hour outside of Port Hedland, we ran over a ten-foot python—at least we *thought* it was a python. Just after dusk we caught sight of something thick as a man's thigh slithering across the road in the faint beam of our headlights, and though we swerved to avoid it, our two left wheels went over the snake with a jolt. According to the snake book I later consulted, the desert death adder, too, was "stout," but it grew to only about half the length of the one we had just struck. In any case, neither of us really cared to go back for a positive identification.

By the time I saw the eerie light of the roadhouse way off in the distance, my senses were blurred. In the three and a half hours it had taken us to drive the two hundred miles, not a single car had passed us going in either direction. I stared at the glow on the distant horizon, distrustful of my eyes. But even though it took another fifteen minutes, we did finally reach the roadhouse, a small oblong structure set back from the highway behind some petrol "bowsers." It was about 10 P.M. when we pulled in, and the thermometer outside registered 102 degrees.

A big bearded fellow in a grease-stained undershirt and a pair of shorts took our order—four beers from the bar and two cheeseburgers from the kitchen. Even holding a skillet, and with a dirty white apron wrapped around his waist, he was unquestionably a bushman. "Cheeseburger?" he asked, with a puzzled look on his face. "Is that a hamburger with cheese on it? Don't have much call for them." There was no hesitation over the beer.

Someone had tacked a copy of a poem on the wall next to the kitchen counter. *"The Drover's Cook"* was written by an old bush balladist named Tom Quilty, and its first few stanzas read as follows:

> *The drover's cook weighed fifteen stone,*
> *He had one bloodshot eye,*
> *He had no laces on his boots,*
> *No buttons on his fly.*
> *His pants hung loosely round his hips,*
> *Hitched by a piece of wire,*
> *They concertinered round his boots,*
> *In a way that you'd admire.*

He stuck the billy on to boil,
Then emptied out his pipe,
And with his greasy shirt sleeve,
He gave his nose a wipe.
With pipe in mouth he mixed a sod,
A drip hung from his chin,
And as he mixed the damper up,
The drip kept dripping in.

"A cook," I said, "you call yourself,
You dirty slop-made lout,
You should be jailed for taking work,
You cannot carry out."

It was hard to know whether the poem had been put there as a warning to the cook or to the customers, but we felt reassured to see that the fellow who threw our cheeseburgers on the grill wasn't smoking a pipe.

We walked into the harshly lit dining room and sat at one of the Formica-top tables. Crawling on the floor were scores of albino-colored, scorpionlike creatures apparently drawn to the light and disoriented by their inability to burrow into the cement. The cook had referred to them as sandgropers, an affectionate term by which Western Australians themselves were known. Later we learned that their correct name was sandhopper, and that they were crustaceans related to water lice and sand fleas.

Like bump cars at a carnival, the sandhoppers maneuvered in a circular motion, erratic and unpredictable, stopping only long enough to nip our feet with their pincers before backing off, then moving on in a rapid burst of speed. Large blue-black moths and a number of other flying insects darted around our heads, making eating something of a catch-as-catch-can proposition.

Wearing a housedress that was a size too large for her thin frame, Barni Norton, the daughter-in-law of the so-called Desert Fox, who owned the place, brought in our beers from the bar. She called her husband, Ken, a short, well-built fellow in his early thirties, and both of them sat down at our table, chatting with us as we ate.

Ken had a number of tattoos on his muscular arms—a panther, an octopus, a snake, an Indian squaw. "I got real aggro over that one," said Barni, pointing to the squaw on his left biceps. "Almost divorced him for puttin' a bloody broad on his arm.

"When I first come here it was early in the mornin' and the bar was full," Barni related. "I was only seventeen then, lookin' for work before goin' back home. I asked Pop, and he played dead, jus' gimme a runaround. Colin's wife, Jo, went and told Ken a broad was outside lookin' for work. "But I got pretty jacked off. I was revvin' up my bike gettin' ready to go when Ken come out. And he said, hey, don't listen to Pop, I'm the barman around here and I need a barmaid. And there I was, doin' his washin' the first day, livin' with him the first month, engaged after six weeks, pregnant after three months . . . no, two months. Little old innocent me."

A large mural, which looked as if it could have been painted by a child, covered one wall of the dining room. It depicted a man lying on the sand about to expire with what appeared to be a camel standing nearby.

"What's that painting all about?" asked Jack, glancing at it over Ken's shoulder.

"That's Leichardt," said Ken. "Ludwig Leichardt."

A scientist who had emigrated from Germany, Dr. Ludwig Leichardt had become one of Australia's earliest explorers. He was also one of its greatest failures. The first man to undertake "the gigantic task of crossing the continent from east to west," he never made it. In Australia he became a hero, since Australians had a penchant for making heroes of their losers. The following account of "Dr. Leichardt's lost expedition" was provided by David Carnegie, a historian who himself was an explorer:

> Towards the end of 1847, accompanied by eight white men, two black-boys, and provisions to last two years, he started, taking with him one hundred and eighty sheep, two hundred and seventy goats, forty bullocks, fifteen horses, and thirty mules. After travelling with little or no progress for seven months, during which time the whole stock of cattle and sheep were lost, the party returned. Not discouraged by this disastrous termination to his scheme, Leichardt resolved on another expedition with the same object in view.
>
> Before many months he, with the same number of companions but with fewer animals, set out again. On the 3rd of April, 1848, he wrote from Fitzroy Downs, expressing hope and confidence as to the ultimate success of the expedition. Since that date, neither tidings nor traces have been found of the lost explorer, nor of any of his men or belongings. Several search-parties were organized and a large re-

ward offered, but all in vain—and the scene of his disaster remains undiscovered to this day.

"Dad read an article in Derby before he come down here," Ken Norton explained, "and from what he could decipher, Leichardt perished jus' out back here. The last thing he wrote in his journal was, 'the sand appeared to be on fire,' so Dad decided ta call this place the Sandfire Roadhouse."

By opening a business on the Horror Stretch, Ken's dad had become almost as legendary as Leichardt himself. "Eddie Norton's a bit of an eccentric," we had been advised by a friend in Perth. "Has to be to run a roadhouse up there. But you've got to admire him for his determination and business sense." And, indeed, we did feel some grudging admiration for the man, if only because he wasn't there. The Desert Fox had returned to Perth, leaving his son and daughter-in-law to hold the fort. (Ken's story had a hole in it, however, for if Leichardt did leave a journal, like the explorer himself it was never found.)

"How did your father manage to get you up here from Perth?" asked Jack. "Did he tell you he'd found a beautiful little spot in the desert?"

"Nope, he jus' told me ta stop when I got ta the first sandhill, two hundred miles outside of Hedland." Ken chuckled. "I was at a bit of a lost end at the time, anyway, ready to change jobs. So I flew up ta Derby, met Pop, and down we come, campin' on the way."

"We like this sort a' life," Barni added. "The business side is a lotta hard work. Maybe it don't seem that way now 'cause only five or ten cars a day come through durin' the Wet.

"But otherwise it's a normal sorta life out here. Last fortnight was no different from any other. After the travelin' tattooist left, we had the itinerant teacher out. Each kid gets one day a term, so Jan was all excited and we weren't gettin' much done except the three hours readin' and maths I was helpin' her with. The teacher left on Wednesday, and Saturday a python got in and ate my canary. I only got three canaries and Jo's got twenty budgies, and it had to pick on my canaries.

"On the Sunday Jan got fly-bite and come out in a rash and all that. Then on Tuesday the power plant blew and we had to rig up the alternate generator. On Wednesday the Main Roads blokes come. An' last Friday a death adder got into the office, another was in the tire shed, an' the very same night the new girl found a six-foot mulga snake inside the cool room. She thought it was a hose at first—good job she didn't use it ta water the garden. We shot it an' cooked it up

that night. So I'd say it's a fairly normal, regular routine kinda life."
We talked and drank beer till well past midnight. Barni had mentioned that there was plenty of room at the roadhouse motel, and
since we hadn't had a shower in days, we decided to stay there instead
of pitching our tent or simply throwing our swags on the ground. Ken
and his father had built the motel themselves by dividing two house-
trailers into small cubicles. According to Barni, it had never been in
great demand.
"What's the reason for all the snakes these past few days?" asked
Jack, looking around gingerly as Ken opened the door and the three
of us stepped out into the darkness. "Are they coming in for a conven-
tion or something?"
"Cyclone season," said Ken. "They smell rain."
The only thing I could smell was the hot desert air.
"They must be hallucinating," Jack said.
The motel room was dark, cheerless, and fetid with the stale smell
of tobacco and soiled linen, which lay in a heap on the unmade beds.
But the units had been built on cinder block footings and at least there
were no snakes crawling around. Shoving the dirty sheets off the bed
and onto the floor, I threw my swag on the mattress, and tried to sleep.
Jack, too, spent a restless night.

19

We left the roadhouse for Broome just after dawn, racing as quickly
as we could along the narrow strip of bitumen between the sea and
the Great Sandy Desert, across the Sandfire Flats. By midmorning the
sun had climbed high in the sky and the thermal winds were beginning to push out from the interior. Aside from patches of stunted gray
vegetation, the only sign of life was a few more head of cattle that
wandered dispiritedly across the sand.
Except for an abandoned car or two, its enamel bleached off by the
sun, we saw no other vehicle. One of the unwritten rules of the road
in the bush was that you waved whenever someone drove past and
stopped to offer assistance to any car that was disabled. Those rules
didn't apply, however, when it came to aboriginals—one didn't stop
for them. That could be dangerous, we had been warned, and there
was really nothing you could do to help them. Their cars were so
badly maintained, they were always breaking down, and in any case,
went the justification for not stopping, "boongs are at home in the

bush." And of course, they had no real destination. They were just doing their thing, going "walkabout," wandering about as the spirit moved them, as their ancestors had done from time immemorial. Only now they were doing it in cars.

Off to our left, an occasional sandy track led down to Eighty Mile Beach, which we couldn't see but knew was just over the horizon. We would have liked to have gone down there if only to give our eyes relief from the harsh glare of the desert and the black tar road, shimmering with heat ahead of us like a huge ribbon of melting black licorice. But Ken Norton had told us of people who had done just that and had become hopelessly mired in the soft sand. The Outback by the sea was a treacherous place.

We continued across the baked and barren flats, a dismal scene that stretched endlessly before us, an infinity of low sand ridges and a horizon as level as an ocean.

Broome burst on us with all the color and brilliance of the tropics. Nothing in the depressing country we'd just come through had prepared us for that startling change of landscape. As if we'd arrived on another planet, we were suddenly out of the desert and enveloped in lush green vegetation.

Overhead, forming a canopy for the road leading into town and shading us from the intense tropical sun, rose the great trees: glossy-leaved mangoes, flaming red poincianas, gums, palms, bauhinias, and bloated boab. Closer to the ground, bougainvillaea blazed purple and crimson, interspersed with pinks and fiery reds. The intense contrasts in light and the brilliant colors caused our frazzled spirits to soar.

Still known as the Port of Pearls, the present-day town had changed dramatically since its early days as the brawling seaport of the 1870s, the first settlement on the site. Narrow streets like John Chi Lane and Sheeba Lane, long since vanished, once teemed with Japanese divers and brown-skinned Malays, Javanese, Singhalese, Timorese, and Thursday Islanders, many of them indentured crewmen on the pearling luggers that dropped anchor in Roebuck Bay.

The din of a dozen diverse languages filled the town when the luggers laid up in port during the cyclone season, from December to March each year. There were boardinghouses operated by and for the Japanese and eating establishments run by the Chinese. And there were billiard parlors, barbers, laundries, and shops that sold practically everything. A raucous red-light district, replete with gambling dens and brothels of every description, flourished in Broome's Chinatown, which, though small, was known throughout the South Pacific. Chinatown was now a quiet place, consisting of only two or three virtually empty streets. Sun Pictures, once practically an institution in Broome, had closed, a victim of the video boom, but the facade of the outdoor theater on Carnarvon Street still stood. Old movie posters, with pictures of John Barrymore, Mary Pickford, and Douglas Fairbanks, remained displayed on the wall out front. The one sign of continuing life in the district was the annual Shinju Matsuri Festival of the Pearl. Held each August, the nine-day event combined everything from aboriginal dances to Chinese dragon floats. But since Broome's Chinese residents had long forgotten their native tongue, the language of the festival was English—spoken with a pronounced Australian twang.

Broome also held many reminders that, only fifty-odd years before, it had been the pearling capital of the world. At Streeter and Male's in Chinatown, a company that had been in business for over a century, we watched as Ken Male opened an old safe and removed a small leather pouch. He untied the pouch and with a reverence befitting the crown jewels, emptied its contents—about a dozen perfectly circular pearls—onto a piece of black velvet on the desk in front of him. "These are flawless specimens and that makes them very special," he said, as he nudged them with his finger and explained to us the subtleties of grading.

In earlier days, a number of world-renowned natural pearls had come from the waters off Broome. The Southern Cross, a cluster of pearls joined together in the shape of a crucifix, was discovered by a boy collecting shells along the beach in 1883 and was first traded in a pub at Cossack for a few dollars. After passing through a number of hands, it eventually found its way to London, where it was put on display and purchased for the Vatican collection at a price of $48,000.

But the most notable and largest pearl ever found was the infamous Star of the West, which was discovered off Broome in 1917. Valued even then at $12,000, the star-crossed roseate pearl brought disaster to its owners before it disappeared from the face of the earth. One committed suicide, another suffered a fatal heart attack. A murder was committed for it, and the crime resulted in two further deaths—on the gallows. Its last known owner drowned.

But in Australia pearling had always been a dicey business, and once again it had fallen on hard times. The Japanese, who dominated the industry, had recently closed down their Kuri Bay operation and pulled out of W.A., taking with them the closely guarded secret of culturing pearls. It actually involved the implantation of a minute particle of mussel shell from a species found in the Mississippi River, into the genitals of the pearl oyster, but no Australian knew the precise particulars of performing the operation.

Along Broome's waterfront, in back of Streeter's jetty, a few beamy sailing luggers, like the one in Ces Piesse's watercolor, lay on their sides on the mudflats of a mangrove-lined creek that flowed into Roebuck Bay. Over fifty feet long, they were squat, practical old vessels with rusting anchors and iron stays spliced around their deadeyes. In the old days, during the "lay up," or cyclone, season, the luggers were careened this way for repairs and refitting, left with the bilge cocks open so that the rising thirty-foot tides would cover the entire ship. Submersion in salt water would drown the cockroaches that had been such pests during the long months at sea.

Only a few years earlier the opening of the bitumen highway from the south made Broome accessible to conventional vehicles, at least during the dry season, which resulted in the town's being gradually inundated with gourmet restaurants, posh hotels and specialty shops catering to the well-heeled tourist, unlike older towns of W.A. that managed to retain a trace of exoticism. But reminders of Broome's colorful past were still in evidence: the old customs house with its sweeping veranda, several elegant homes masterfully crafted by the old pearling captains. A Japanese cemetery, its gravestones obscured by tall sawgrass, lay untended at the edge of town. We walked through it one afternoon, and Dave deciphered the Japanese *kanji* on the weathered tombstones. Few of the dead had perished from natural causes.

Broome proved to be so agreeable a spot that we decided to stop there for a while and enjoy it before heading off into the bush once again. After a few days of ambling around we discovered that the main topic of conversation in town was Lord Alistair McAlpine, a contractor/politician whose name was equally well-known in the U.K., where it was plastered on construction sites throughout the country. With seemingly unlimited funds, the English lord was already involved in a number of multimillion-dollar projects in Australia, including the Intercontinental Hotel in Sydney and the Parmelia Hilton in Perth. He was now engaged in buying up most of the available property in Broome: first a few of the old pearling captains' homes, then a large tract of land near Cable Beach, where he had built himself a private zoo, now property in Chinatown, including the old Sun Picture theater. Whether you drank at the elegant Continental Hotel lounge or the rough-as-guts Roebuck Bay Hotel pub (which McAlpine had also just acquired), everyone was talking about the impact His Lordship was having on Broome.

A number of townspeople were enthusiastic about his presence, especially those whose property he was buying at inflated prices, and the politicos and merchants who saw him as a social, not to mention financial, asset to the town. But he also had his detractors, one of whom was Father McMann, an outspoken and influential Catholic priest.

Father McMann had lived in Broome for over twenty years, and his love for the town had led him to decline advancement in larger parishes. To him, the interracial harmony that prevailed in Broome was a very special and unusual state of affairs, and he feared that McAlpine's plans, rumored to include huge resort hotels, casinos, and gambling, would destroy the social fabric. Like Denham, Broome did, indeed, seem to have a remarkable degree of tolerence, and consequently the town had also become a haven for people interested in living alternate life-styles.

"Everyone these days is concerned, and rightly so, when development affects the ecology," he said, when we spoke with him at the furniture co-op he ran for aboriginals. "But people don't take anywhere near the same precautions to protect our human resources."

Our stay in Broome happened to coincide with one of those infrequent occasions when, like a hawk, Lord McAlpine swooped down out of the sky in his private jet to gobble up yet more of the town. We had difficulty tracking him down, but early one evening we learned that our request for an audience with His Lordship had been granted.

20

The following afternoon we drove out to see Lord McAlpine at Cable Beach, where he had recently opened his personal zoo to the public. Walking past the unattended admissions booth to a makeshift office, we were greeted by a tall, elegant-looking gentleman whom we assumed to be Lord McAlpine, but he immediately disabused us of that notion. Identifying himself instead as the publicity director, he apologized that the zoo was still in the throes of construction, and commented on how fortunate the town's residents were to have such a wonderful facility, before leading us outside where a group of people were conferring in front of the kangaroo cage. The publicity director pointed out His Lordship to us and, waving at him, finally managing to get his attention.

A short, stout man in his late forties, Lord McAlpine was attired in a long-sleeved checkered shirt that fit him rather snugly, and the bell-bottomed trousers he wore almost concealed his magnificent brown cowboy boots. He had hawklike eyes, like Peter Eaton's, which skittered about under the wide-brimmed felt bush hat he wore to protect his fair skin from the tropical sun.

"So good to meet you," he said in a carefully modulated English accent as he approached us. Extending his hand but not looking directly at me or Dave, Lord McAlpine gave us each a limp handshake. Perhaps other considerations, such as the host of assistants jealously clamoring for his attention or the press of urgent business responsibilities, had distracted him: Someone had ordered the wrong seed for the cockatoos, but that could be sorted out later; provisions had to be made for the new emu that was arriving that afternoon; a masked dove had died in a "snake panic"; and an ass had to be put down because of some "unsuitable public display." If that wasn't enough, His Lordship's dinner had been rescheduled for eight-thirty that evening.

"I've always kept animals, and I have a zoo in England," he proudly informed us as, the more pressing affairs having been attended to, he consented to show us around the facility. "But it's really impractical keeping them over there. The climate's bad and the food's expensive, so I decided to do it here in Broome."

"Will this be a money-making operation?" asked Dave. It was a tactless question and for an uncomfortable moment I feared that His Lordship would take offense at such effrontery. But dignified chap that he was, he rose to the occasion unruffled.

"No, no, my good fellow," he replied, an indulgent smile lighting up his aristocratic features. "If it shows any danger of that, we'll spend it on something else. I didn't build this place for the public's good, you know. I did it simply for my own pleasure. I make no bones about that, really."

Lord McAlpine paused to examine the door of the emu cage. "I only have about twenty-five acres now," he remarked, satisfied the latch was secure. "But I want to expand it to fifty or more so that I can have herds of animals rather than just two or three of each. I've got all of the Australian cockatoos and nearly all of the Australian parrots. I just intend to go on expanding the place, running it as a private collection that the public can come and have a look at."

As he guided us through his zoo, Lord McAlpine related the sequence of events that had led to his becoming interested in Australia. In 1958 His Lordship was enjoying an around-the-world cruise on the maiden voyage of the luxury liner *Oriana*, a gift from his parents on his twenty-first birthday. "I went to Perth because the boat went there," related the peer, with a wave of his plump hand. "The whole of Australia was a very stuffy, staid sort of place then. No decent hotels or good restaurants to be found anywhere in the country."

We could well appreciate how disagreeable His Lordship's experience had been, forsaking the opulence of his stateroom for the rigors of Perth. But stout fellow that he was, he sallied forth nonetheless, and that initial introduction was enough to bring him back to Perth six years later to build a suitable hotel of his own.

Chance, as well, had brought Lord McAlpine to the unlikely vicinity of Broome. "I was looking for something to do at the weekend and decided to take a flight to Kalgoorlie," he related. "But that flight was canceled, so I simply got on another one and came here."

As we stood in front of the donkey cage, Lord McAlpine regaled us with a few of his titles: treasurer of the Conservative Party in England, as well as its chief fund raiser. Both he and his father were life peers in the House of Lords.

"That's rather unusual, you know," added His Lordship. "It's the first time a father and son have ever sat in the House of Lords in their own right."

"How did that happen?" asked Dave, his mouth agape, heedless of the squadron of flies about to reconnoiter it.

"It's really quite simple," replied His Lordship, obviously taken aback that the question had needed to be asked. "We were both given peerages, my father for his work in industry, and because he was an eminent industrialist. I was awarded mine as a politician. Before that, because my father was a peer, I was known as the Honourable Alistair McAlpine, but now I'm Lord McAlpine of West Green, which is my estate in England."

We were interrupted by an impending crisis in the kangaroo cage requiring a decision at the highest level. After His Lordship had dealt with the matter, I asked him whether or not he liked the Australian bush.

"Indeed I do," he replied. "I like the size and the feel of it. I get a fantastic feeling of freedom just sleeping rough on the ground." The previous year he had hired a safari guide and driven across Australia through the Simpson Desert, from Broome to Sydney. His party had traveled in two vehicles and made the trip in four days. "To anyone considering such a trip, my advice would be not to take tents," he said. And then, with the authority founded on that journey, he added: "Go to bed early and get up early. Be off at first light." Since we ourselves had to be off at first light the following morning, we took our leave of the Baron of Broome. Except for the size of his bankroll and the scope of his projects, there wasn't, we agreed, much difference between him and our friend Peter Eaton, though the latter was out to make a fortune and McAlpine seemed intent on spending one. But both men in their own ways romanticized the bush, even if it meant envisioning it as a setting for a tourist empire. Peter planned someday to replace his battered Volvo with a private jet, and indeed, stranger things have occurred in W.A., the land of unlimited opportunity, where a onetime sign painter like Alan Bond could become a multimillionaire. Were Peter to succeed in having Mt. Augustus supplant Ayers Rock as the nation's number-one tourist attraction, knighthood would undoubtedly be his reward, as well.

We stopped for dinner at the Continental Hotel. Dave, who was puzzled by Lord McAlpine's place in the polyglot community that was essentially egalitarian, brought up the subject with the bartender.

"What is he known as here in Broome? I mean, what do you call him?" asked Dave.

"A fat cat," replied the bartender.

21

The next day we left for the Kimberleys, a remote region in the northwest corner of Australia over three times the size of England. The Kimberleys took its name from a mountain range in the area, which itself had been named after the then English Secretary of State for the Colonies, Lord Kimberley, by explorer Alexander Forrest during an expedition in 1874. Forrest created one of the major stirs of the century when, on his next trip there (in 1879), he reported "25 million acres of good pastoral country capable of depasturing a million of sheep." That grossly exaggerated report spurred an influx of settlers from as far away as New Zealand, most of whom soon left in disappointment. The few that stayed on despite the hardships included the Duracks, an Irish clan led by Patrick Durack, who shortly before leaving Queensland for the Kimberleys had written prophetically: " 'Cattle kings' ye call us. Then we are kings in grass castles that may be blown away upon a puff of wind." Forrest himself invested in a pastoral company whose sheep died from drinking salty water shortly after they arrived.

In 1886, John Forrest, Alexander's brother, published an article in the journal of the Royal Geographical Society of Australasia speculating that the Kimberleys were the "centre of rich gold mines, which are likely to attract thousands towards them, and will result in the whole country being opened up by telegraphs and railways." Again people flocked to the area, and again widespread disillusionment soon led to a mass exodus. Almost a century later, in the 1970s, two young geologists discovered a large diamond deposit in the Kimberleys, stumbling upon it while out "gouging"—not seriously prospecting—in the bush. But no influx of fossickers followed on the heels of that discovery, perhaps because diamonds are De Beers' best friend, and the South African cartel, in collaboration with an Australian outfit called Ashton Joint Ventures, immediately stepped in to gain a controlling interest in the output of the mine. Though much of it was of "low-grade" (not gemstone) quality, the mine was soon generating 25 million carats a year, primarily for industrial use, making Australia far and away the largest diamond producer in the world. The frenzied activity of gold rush days was now a thing of the past—according to what we heard, most of the workers at the diamond mine were flown in from the south on ten-day shifts, then flown out again for equal intervals of rest.

Our first stop was Derby, the self-proclaimed "capital of the West Kimberley." It was about a 130-mile drive from Broome, and since the long wet season was coming to an end, the heavily wooded scrubland along the tropical coast was exceptionally green. It was easy to understand why the Forrests could have been misled into believing that the region was so full of promise.

3

Crocodile Country— the Kimberley Northwest

Boab Trees
in Crocodile Country

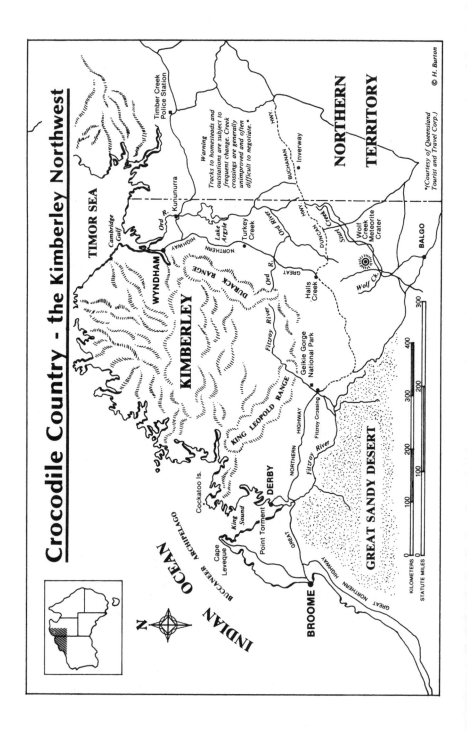

Crocodile Country – the Kimberley Northwest

TIMBER SEA

NORTHERN TERRITORY

Warning
Tracks to homesteads and
outstations are subject to
frequent change. Creek
crossings are generally
unimproved and often
difficult to negotiate.*

Timber Creek
Police Station

Inverway

BUCHANAN HWY.

Kununurra

Ord R.

Cambridge Gulf

Lake Argyle

Turkey Creek

DUNCAN

Sturt Ck.

Wolf Creek Meteorite Crater

NORTHERN HIGHWAY

DURACK RANGE

Ord R.

Ord R.

GREAT

Wolf Ck.

BALGO

WYNDHAM

KIMBERLEY

Halls Creek

Fitzroy River

Geikie Gorge National Park

KING LEOPOLD RANGE

Fitzroy Crossing

Fitzroy River

NORTHERN HIGHWAY

Cockatoo Is.

DERBY

Point Torment

King Sound

Cape Leveque

BUCCANEER ARCHIPELAGO

INDIAN OCEAN

N

BROOME

GREAT SANDY DESERT

GREAT NORTHERN HIGHWAY

KILOMETERS 0   100   200   300   400
STATUTE MILES 0   100   200   300

© H. Burton

(Courtesy of Queensland Tourist and Travel Corp.)

1

Back in 1884, on the eve of the Kimberley gold rush, when Derby was the nearest seaport to the Halls Creek mining settlement, the town had been described by a Catholic priest named Father McNab as "a hot, ugly little trading post, hurriedly thrown together in the makeshift Australian style from bush timber and galvanized iron, its inhabitants a few business people, a contingent of police, and the inevitable chain gang of native prisoners." Although over a hundred years had gone by and the chain gangs were no longer in evidence, the good father's description had withstood the test of time in almost every other respect.

"It's a real hole," a salesgirl at the local bakery told us, nonchalantly, "but people seem to like it."

Like an old barge thrown up on a muddy bank, the town sat precariously on the edge of a tidal marshland on the southwestern foot of King Sound, whose frequent thirty-five-foot tides had been menacing seafarers since Dampier's day. It looked out over nearby locations that early-nineteenth-century explorers had evidently adjudged even less attractive than the spot on which Derby was eventually founded in 1880—places like Skeleton Point, Disaster Bay, and Foul Point. Close by, too, was Point Torment, a particularly mosquito-infested area that had initially been proposed as the site for Derby and then, understandably, abandoned, though later it did become the site of a

leprosarium for aboriginals, who in that area of Australia were especially prone to the disease. With leprosy now under control, the facility near Point Torment, designed to accommodate two hundred patients, was nearly empty, its only occupants six nuns, five lepers, and
a caretaker.

The man largely responsible for conferring these disturbingly accurate names—Lieutenant George Grey, who was also the first person
to publish descriptions and drawings of aboriginal art—had arrived
in the Kimberleys in 1837, at the beginning of the wet season. According to the diary he kept, his ponies suffered terribly from exposure to
"the pitiless pelting of the storms, making a very wretched appearance
as they stood with their sterns presented to the blast, and the water
pouring from their sides in perfect streams." Grey himself nearly died
from a spear wound inflicted by a hostile aboriginal and, some
months afterward, from starvation. Yet he later had described the
area as "a most beautiful country that must be as well watered as any
region in the world." Well watered it was: one of the first consign-
ments of wool awaiting shipment out of Derby was swept away from
shore by a tidal wave, caused by the eruption of the Indonesian vol-
cano Krakatoa. Grey, noted one Australian historian, was "a senti-
mentalist."

With so little exposure to civilization, change had come slowly to
Derby. It was 1959 before a radio-telephone network had been
inaugurated, and the land-line telephone service replacing it was introduced only in 1965, finally linking the town to the outside world,
especially to Perth, fifteen hundred miles away. The road to Perth,
otherwise known as the Great Northern Highway, was completed
around that time, too, a thin red line on the map referred to by
those who traveled on its corrugated surface as "a cartographer's
confidence trick, not to be trusted farther than you could throw a
tire jack." Yet residents of Derby remained optimistic about their
progress, for, as one local historian observed, "The township continued to develop markedly throughout the remainder of the 60s: a
new caravan park began operations in June 1969, the Numbala
Nunga nursing home was opened, and the old Club Hotel changed
its name to the Spinifex Hotel."

Now that the road to Perth had been sealed, and the town's population had reached 7,000, Derby was making a modest effort to achieve
recognition as a tourist destination. But other than a new hotel large
enough to accommodate busloads of Australian pensioners, who

seemed duty-bound to spend their twilight years orbiting the periphery of their country, the town had little to offer by way of attractions. The hard-pressed tourist brochure listed only two: an enormous, hollowed-out boab tree used in the old days as an overnight jail for aboriginals, and a cattle trough "believed to be the longest in the Southern Hemisphere."

While the squat, potbellied boab was typically characterized as gourd-shaped, Aussies persisted in describing the tree as having a "Vat 69–shaped trunk" and imagined it as "a refuge for gnomes, hobgoblins, and their antipodean equivalents, bunyips." Their view of Derby's other attraction was perhaps best summed up in the judgment of one Australian we met: "If you've seen one cattle trough, you've seen 'em all."

Derby had also begun promoting itself as the "Gateway to the Gorges," a reference to a few small, nearly inaccessible river limestone gorges in the King Leopold and Napier ranges, many miles inland. But even the tourist bureau itself admitted that those "grandiose gorges," promoted as one of the best fossilized coral reef complexes in the world and the site of some as yet unvandalized aboriginal cave paintings, were of more "interest to geologists and anthropologists" than to the average traveler. In any case, the track was impassable during the Wet, so we had to confine our own excursions to the town itself.

"Life's different here ta anywhere south. We call it Kimberleyitis—if ya don't get it done today, do it tomorrow, or the day after. Unless you're talkin' ta Perth, that is. They bloody well want it done yesterday. But there's a lot less stress here, a lot less aggression."

Peter Kneebone had lived in Derby for twenty years, a decade longer than any other residents in the shire, which alone was sufficient to ensure his status as the town's unofficial spokesman. He owned several businesses in Derby and also served as its justice of the peace. Jack and I met him soon after we arrived in town when we drove into his auto repair shop to pick up an extra fan belt.

"It's the climate," he explained. "If ya push yerself here, ya wouldn't last. No way. We get into trouble with the exploration people because of it. Mostly the Americans. When they say, jump, they're used to hearin', how high, sir? Well, here, we say, go and get stuffed, we don't need yer business that bad.

"They come for five months, during the dry season, when we're tryin' to recuperate. They've had their holidays and they're all excited about lookin' for something. But we've just come through the Wet and everything's drained out of us. The Wet's called 'the mad season,' ya know." And as if to underscore the gravity of that tantalizing phrase, he pointed to the mangled remains of a badly wrecked car that had been brought in by his tow truck only that morning.

We drove down the main street, past the police station, the shire office, and a few stores, to the King Sound Motel. The word "motel" was really a misnomer, at least as much of the world understood the term, for in Australia it was often used by the better hotels to distinguish themselves from the rough-and-ready frontier variety that did little more than serve beer. The King Sound was definitely one of the former.

A carpeted stairway off to the left of the small, sparsely furnished lobby led down to an empty bar. In the courtyard outside, a group of young women—welfare workers from aboriginal communities in the Kimberleys—were enjoying a barbecue. They had come to attend a conference and were chattering away like college coeds at a reunion.

"Derby's always had a transient population," the barkeep told us, as we downed a few beers. "No old, established families, like in Broome. It's a man's town. Women hate it. There's nothing for them here but housework. A man's got his mates, and there's pig shootin' and barra fishin'. The Fitzroy's three hundred miles long and full of fish.

"But Derby was a better place when I first got here," he continued. "It was a frontier sort of place. People were friendly, had to make their own fun. Video's changed all that. People just sit around their air-conditioned house, keepin' cool and watchin' tele. Derby's just another town now."

After dinner that evening at the local Chinese restaurant, we bought some cold stubbies and went back to the hotel to do what everyone else in town was presumably doing that night—watching TV in an air-conditioned room. (Only Derby's fringe-dwelling aboriginals managed to resist those dual temptations, for they preferred to do their drinking outdoors under the boab trees.) The evening news, piped in from Perth, was almost over, and since there was nothing more I wanted to see, I decided to head back to the bar, hoping to find some company among the women welfare workers attending that conference. Jack, however, stayed in his room to watch the latest rounds in the broadcast of a dwarf-throwing contest.

2

(A Short Diversion)

When Abner Doubleday invented the American "National Pastime" over a century ago, spectators attending those first baseball games probably never imagined that the sport would one day achieve the popularity and universal acceptance it now enjoys. I can still recall the thrill of watching my first game from a seat high in the bleachers of Boston's Fenway Park. On that blustery May afternoon in 1951, the Red Sox trounced the cellar-dwelling St. Louis Browns, the same hapless team that later in the season attempted to put a little scoring punch in their lineup by sending Eddie Gaedel, a dwarf, up to bat. Unable to get the ball into Eddie's diminutive strike zone, the pitcher walked him, bringing cries of "foul" from opposing teams and demands that dwarfs be banned from professional baseball.

DWARFS UP IN AIR read the prophetic banner headline in a Boston tabloid, while the commissioner of baseball mulled matters over before reaching a decision. DWARFS NIXED, proclaimed the newspaper following his ruling, which set minimum height requirements for players and resulted in Gaedel's being barred from the game. Once again small athletes had come up short, but such narrow-mindedness may soon be a prejudice of the past, at least in Australia, where the rapidly proliferating sport of dwarf-throwing is winning fans and enthusiastic devotees.

Dwarf-throwing, once regarded as a "joke," had its beginnings in a smoke-filled Perth pub as a competition between unemployed night-club bouncers. The object was to throw a dwarf as far as possible—but ideally not beyond the pile of mattresses awaiting him. An enterprising promoter, who was quick to recognize their appeal to sportsmen and spectators alike, introduced dwarf-throwing contests in Sydney, where, before sellout crowds, they literally took off.

While the sport was in its infancy, tosses seldom exceeded a dozen feet or so, and like the sub four-minute mile, fourteen feet was considered an impossible barrier. But dwarf-throwing has grown up since then, and skilled competitors regularly exceed that distance today. The current world record holder, a psychiatrist from Adelaide, obliterated all existing marks by throwing a dwarf an incredible fifteen feet four inches on two separate occasions. Robust men usually make the best tossers, yet finesse rather than force is the key element for developing a successful throwing technique.

For ease of gripping, dwarfs are fitted with leather harnesses around their hips and shoulders, and for safety's sake they don motorcycle crash helmets as protection against concussion should they miss the mattresses. Generally, jogging suits are the traditional attire, but some of the more fashion-conscious establishments that stage throwing contests now provide dwarfs with brightly colored silk uniforms similar to those worn by jockeys.

Not surprisingly, in its initial stages, dwarf-throwing did not readily gain public acceptance. Before attaining its current popularity the sport experienced considerable resistance from dwarfs' rights groups and elicited humanitarian concerns throughout Australia. Even during our stay in Perth, Dave and I saw a number of television editorials condemning the contests as "tasteless and barbaric," and one commentator concluded his remarks by observing, "If this were aborigine throwing or paraplegic throwing people would be positively appalled."

The medical community, too, expressed some anxiety about the long-term effects of repeated throwings, and though the question of safety is still open to debate, the introduction of improved crash helmets and the development of better protective equipment and more commodious landing pads have greatly allayed such concerns. Advocates of the sport also point out that the dwarfs have chosen to enter the profession of their own volition, and are paid handsome salaries and provided with excellent retirement benefits, despite the relatively low-risk nature of their enterprise. Under Australia's National Health Plan, every dwarf who competes is assured extensive medical coverage.

Despite that early opposition, hostility has generally given way to adulation, and enthusiastic fans are now confident that dwarf-throwing is destined to become the Australian national pastime. Plans are currently being formulated to hold future tournaments in the U.S. and Europe, eventually leading to the crowning of a world champion. Carefully drafted rules and regulations governing dwarf-throwing have been standardized, and a vocabulary unique to the sport has evolved. "Trajectory trauma," for instance, describes the rigors of being tossed too frequently and traveling at high velocities; "reentry stress syndrome" is another term that may soon be as familiar to sport fans as the term "batting slump."

Initially, we found the notion of throwing people (regardless of their size) in dubious taste, until we considered some of the sports other countries enjoy. Americans entertain themselves with such exotic diversions as frog-jumping contests and chasing greased pigs, while the English, the most staid of all Western people, enjoy watching competitors shove live ferrets into their pants to see who can hold them in there the longest. After witnessing our first contest, we found ourselves caught up in the excitement and attended matches whenever we had the opportunity. For true aficionados, nothing is more gratifying than watching a brilliantly clad dwarf flung into the air by a skilled thrower, as a screaming audience pays homage to the talented athlete who dares defy the law of gravity.

Dave, in particular, came to find dwarf-throwing intriguing, and confessed his regrets that the sport didn't come along earlier. After years as a program officer at the Ford Foundation, a position providing him with many opportunities to push people around, he realized it would have been far more gratifying to have simply thrown them. "Lookit him go!" Dave would yell with delight, each time a dwarf soared through the air on a graceful flight toward the waiting mattresses. "Whatta kick!" Indeed, the spectacle of one human ceremoniously tossing another did seem to fulfill a deeply rooted, inherent urge that hitherto only those fortunate enough to be bouncers could indulge.

3

Since the hotel bar was deserted I bowed to the inevitable and headed back upstairs to join Jack in watching the dwarf-throwing contest—it was either that or the movie, *Morons in Space,* a video playing on the other channel. But in passing through the lobby I struck up a conversation with the night receptionist, an attractive twenty-two-year-old woman named Marie, and as there was no business to interrupt her, I invited her back to the bar for a drink.

"I first came up here four years ago and I love the place," she told me, adjusting the barstool so she could keep an eye on the lobby, which was deserted. "A classmate of mine and I were offered jobs at the Boab Inn. Mum wanted me to fly if I insisted on going, and Dad said, 'you be careful.' He was up here once when it was quite a wild town. He thought it still was. It is, if you go looking for it. It's there.

"When we walked into the Boab," she continued, "we were staggered because everyone knew we were the new waitresses even though we were a day early. And they made us feel welcome. Of course, there were undercurrents—interest in the new blood, particularly because we were female and they were hoping to make a pass. They were sussing us out, but it was all done in the nicest possible way."

While waitressing at the Boab, Marie had met a young Englishman who'd been living in Derby for eight years—working first at the abattoir and, when that had closed, the hotel—and after a brief courtship, they had married. "Paul really loves this town," she said, perhaps unwittingly revealing that her own infatuation with Derby was to some extent governed by her husband's enthusiasm. "It's the intimacy of it—he knows everyone at the pub and he likes to be able to wave to just about every car that goes past on the street. He hates Perth, hates the isolation of the people. He gets upset when he talks to someone and the person doesn't respond. This place itself is isolated, so the people can't be. Everybody has to make an effort to be sociable. You can't afford to be rejected in this society because it's the only one around."

When I alluded to the bartender's comment that women tended to hate Derby, she responded, "Some people don't fit in here, particularly people who aren't happy doing nothing. They get frustrated when they can't find something to do, like playing squash or having afternoon tea. But I love doing nothing, like sleeping."

She didn't impress me as someone who'd be content to sleep her life away, and when I remarked on that, Marie agreed that perhaps she had painted too lethargic a picture of herself.

"Sometimes I do get angry with Paul," she confessed. "Like when he's supposed to go to the post office and put some checks in the mail at knock-off time. But then at the pub he says, no, we'll do it later. I know he's right—there always *is* plenty of time. If we don't go out on the river this weekend, we'll go the next one, or the weekend after that. No worries, he always says, we'll get there. But I can't quite cope with that, not yet at least."

Apart from the "Kimberleyitis" of its residents, I asked, was there anything else about Derby she found hard to cope with?

"Well," replied Marie, after a moment's reflection, "we do have 'the mad season' here, when a lot of weird things happen. People get very frayed and short-tempered, and I don't like that. It seems to affect the older people more. They tend . . ." Her voice trailed off and she paused. "They tend to commit suicide."

Marie finished her drink and returned to her station behind the desk in the empty lobby. The latter part of the conversation seemed to have embarrassed her. Perhaps she thought it somehow disloyal for a resident of Derby to be divulging that sort of information to a

146

stranger. Or perhaps she didn't like acknowledging even to herself what could happen to someone who remained too long in the town she professed to love.

We had heard from Peter Kneebone that the nearby Fitzroy River was inhabited by thousands of freshwater crocodiles, a relatively small reptile harmless to man. But Peter had said nothing of the far more dangerous saltwater crocodile, which despite its name and its tolerance of high salinity was also known to nest and feed in the rivers of northern Australia. It was left to Sam Lovell, a part-aboriginal ex-stockman who had settled in Derby and now made his living as a safari guide, to fill us in on the whereabouts of that species.

From what we had heard about him, Sam, a soft-spoken, unassuming man in his mid-fifties, was a real "blacktracker." He had grown up in the bush, learning traditional aboriginal hunting skills—how to make a spear, how to throw a boomerang, how to identify a snake and even the direction it was traveling from its tracks in the sand. He was someone who could never be lost in the bush, not only because of his sense of direction and his ability to take star fixes (which his desert-dwelling forebears and the Polynesians alone had mastered), but also because, as he put it, "you learn to take notice of things."

"Plenty of salties in the Fitzroy, and in the King Sound area, too," he said. "There's a big one that used ta knock around the jetty. He's probably still there. And we see 'em near the Kalumburu Mission, up along the coast ta Wyndham. Twenty foot long, some of 'em. Wild country up that way. A lot of places nobody's ever been into.

"He's a funny creature, the old croc," continued Sam. "He won't come out and take ya straight away. He waits, watches every move ya make. He times ya—when ya come down to fish or go for a swim. He learns yer habits and then he waits. Then one time, he's there, and he's got ya."

With that image fresh in our minds, we left Derby the next morning to travel further into crocodile country, our ultimate destination being Wyndham, where several fatal croc attacks had recently occurred.

4

The heavily wooded country outside of Derby gave way to a sparser landscape of stunted trees, scrub, and singed wild grasses which, as the road approached Fitzroy Crossing, abruptly became low hills and rocky outcrops that loomed up on either side of the road.

Fitzroy Crossing itself might well have served as inspiration for an Australian version of Dante's *Inferno*—and not merely because of its stifling heat. As we drove into town late that morning, we were startled by the shadowy forms of aborigines, who emerged unexpectedly on the road and lurched drunkenly toward us. We soon noticed others languishing about in small groups, staring blankly at the ground or off into space. The dust had given their ocher skin a deathly chalkiness and in the hazy mist rising from the Fitzroy River, they seemed more spirit than flesh, condemned forever to wander the streets of this spectral town.

Among the many Englishmen who ventured to Australia in the nineteenth century and encountered aboriginals was Anthony Trollope. Like many of his contemporaries, he was imbued with notions of empire and racial superiority, and had little use for native peoples. After his 1872 visit he mocked those Europeans who saw in the aboriginals a natural dignity, and argued in a book he later wrote about Australia that their bearing represented little more than the cunning of a "sapient monkey." Far from being noble savages, they were "infinitely lower" than even the black African, who at least could be useful as a servant and plantation worker. If civilization was to advance, the aboriginals had to be exterminated. Trollope did temper his arguments with humanitarianism—the aboriginals must perish, but it should be accomplished "without unnecessary suffering."

If Trollope's notions of how to deal with the Aboriginal Problem seem extreme, they were fairly representative of the attitudes of new settlers in the country, and throughout the nineteenth and twentieth centuries Australia witnessed almost endless conflict. Launching a military operation known as the Black Line in 1830, male colonists on Tasmania (then known as Van Diemen's Land) formed a human chain across settled districts, moving south and east in a pincer movement. The openly hostile policies implemented by settlers there were devastating, and ultimately led to the eradication of the island's entire aboriginal population.

According to one noted historian, "Black men, women and children were shot down mercilessly, or bayoneted, or burned alive. Out of the several thousands who, thirty years earlier, were a laughing, happy, kindly people, only two hundred had survived by 1835." A conciliator named George Augustus Robinson traveled Tasmania in search of the survivors, whom he rounded up and removed to Flinders Island in the stormy Bass Strait for "civilizing" and "Christianizing." By 1860, disease and starvation had completely eradicated them. The last Tasmanian aboriginal, a woman named Trucanini, died on Tasmania in 1876. Fitzroy Crossing itself had a long history of conflict between whites and aborigines. In 1894 a black tracker named Pigeon, while working for the police, shot and killed a white constable in an outpost not far from town. Freeing fifteen chained aboriginal prisoners, he led them off into the bush, where they waged a guerrilla campaign against both settlers and police, eluding capture for almost three years. (Like the Apache chief, Geronimo, Pigeon was regarded by some as a murderous villain, while others considered him a valiant warrior expressing the rage of his people.) His fugitive band was slowly decimated in shoot-outs with pursuing patrols, and on April 1, 1897, Pigeon himself was finally run to ground and shot to death by another aborigine tracker named Billy.

The town today seemed as hostile as any group of run-down buildings could be. We stopped at the Fitzroy Crossing Hotel, which overlooked the Fitzroy River not far from its source in the King Leopold Range. For perhaps the only time on our trip we were hesitant about entering a drinking establishment, as the one we were now facing was notorious. Stories had circulated as far away as Perth about the drink-fueled brawls that occurred in the hotel-pub. On occasion, police from Port Hedland, nearly seven hundred miles away, had to be called in to reinforce the local constabulary and bring the conflict under control.

The shabby hotel had two bars, one of which, classified as "the lounge," had a dress code excluding people in thongs and singlets. The rule had been instituted to prevent aborigines, and certain whites, from drinking there. The second, located behind the lounge, was known as the back bar, which readily translated to "black bar." As the only licensed watering holes within hundreds of miles, both dingy dens were usually crowded to capacity. The melees generally erupted at closing time in the back bar, when patrons not yet ready to stop drinking defiantly refused to leave and tore the place to pieces.

The pub was closed when we arrived, but four slightly built Asians—three young men and a woman—were sitting on the fly-screened veranda of the old frame building, relaxing with a pot of Chinese tea and having a smoko. They were Vietnamese refugees, we learned, who'd come to Australia as boat people and were now working in the hotel's restaurant.

Speaking to Dave in Chinese so the surly publican wouldn't understand, they told him that they'd arrived in Fitzroy Crossing just before one of the worst riots and had been more afraid of being killed then than they had during the fall of Saigon. Not only did the drunken brawls in the back bar often spill over threateningly into the hotel's dusty front yard, but the four Vietnamese also lived in constant fear of the publican's wife's evil temper.

We had planned to spend the night in the town, but even on a Sunday morning with the pub closed an air of corruption pervaded the place, and we were anxious to leave it. The hapless Vietnamese had no such option, and with nowhere else to flee, they were virtual prisoners in a hopeless situation. They had risked their lives to reach Australia as boat people only to find themselves beleaguered here in Fitzroy Crossing. In planning their escape from Saigon and contemplating their new life in "the lucky country," as Australia is often called, they could hardly have imagined this.

On that particular Sunday morning I had not bargained for so disheartening an encounter. That godforsaken hotel in the middle of nowhere was the last place I wanted to be, and my thoughts wandered home to Key West. As we drove out of town heading east on the desolate track toward Halls Creek, the opening lines of Wallace Stevens's "Sunday Morning" came to mind:

> *Complacencies of the peignoir; and late*
> *Coffee and oranges in a sunny chair,*
> *And the green freedom of a cockatoo . . .*

Glad of the consolation of Stevens's alluring images, I remained mewed up within myself, concentrating on the driving, avoiding conversation, while Dave settled back to wait patiently for one of my "black moods," as he called them, to pass.

5

"Christ!" yelled Dave, as the top of his head bashed against the roof of the Toyota for the third time in ten minutes. Though I was clutching the steering wheel, my elbow slammed hard against the door handle as I came down, first shocking, then numbing my arm. The springs in the front seat and the vehicle's shock absorbers launched us several times more, but mercifully, gravity prevailed, pulling us back earthward, at least for the moment.

All along this part of the route the Main Roads Department had neglected to provide any safety warnings—just spine-jarring plummets into pits and "breakaways" alerted us to the condition of the track. But this time my eye caught a dust-covered sign on the side of the track that cautioned DIP just before we hit it. It would more accurately have read SLAM or better yet, JUMP.

Hitting the brakes hadn't helped. The pit we'd plunged into, and catapulted out of, was a gaping chasm, smack in the middle of W.A.'s vehicle-destroying "Great" Northern Highway. "Abysmal" would have been a more accurate designation for the paved goat path we were on, a dirt and boulder-strewn track that would have made an ideal trail bike or demolition derby course in the States.

After a long stretch on the winding dirt track, which twisted through low, stark ranges furrowed by ravines and weathered sawtoothed crags, we finally picked up the bitumen again a few miles south of Halls Creek. To clear our throats of the fine red dust we'd been swallowing for hours, we pulled over to the side of the road just outside of town to get our bearings and to guzzle some of Alan Bond's Emu beer out of tinnies.

The heyday of Halls Creek had been remarkably short—less than ten years. Its history had begun in 1885, when a prospector named Charlie Hall came up from Roebourne with his mate, Jack Slattery, and discovered gold on the creek that now bears his name. Within a matter of months, over three thousand diggers were scouring the area's spinifex-covered hills and rocky gullies. One of these was Russian Jack, now a minor folk hero in the Kimberleys, whose name became synonymous with "mateship" after he pushed his sick companion in a wheelbarrow from Halls Creek to the nearest doctor, over two hundred miles away.

As was inevitably the case in bush towns, the gold quickly petered out, and when word of the Coolgardie and Pilbara rushes reached the Kimberley district soon thereafter, the entire region went into decline. Unlike many other mining communities, however, Halls Creek didn't quite give up the ghost, and the shantytown of wood, stone, canvas, tin, and bark went on to survive off the cattle industry. Early in the twentieth century it served as the jumping-off point for cattle drives over the now-abandoned Canning Stock Route, a fifteen-hundred-mile trail that crossed the Great Sandy Desert but that was only passable in "exceptionally good years." In 1954 Halls Creek was relocated to a nearby site with a water supply (which the original town lacked), where it became an administrative center for a mostly aboriginal population.

151

As we pulled up to the "bowser" for fuel outside the only pumps in town, a short, thin man slowly shuffled out of the café toward us. "This seems like a nice place," I said amiably, trying one of our usual conversational gambits in a new town.

"It's a bloody rotten place," he replied in a heavy Irish brogue, as he struggled with the cap on our fuel tank.

I couldn't argue with that assessment—as far as the eye could see, crushed tinnies, Styrofoam cups, and other discarded refuse littered the road just on the other side of the gas pumps. The "new" Halls Creek consisted of a few short streets, all of which quickly gave way to scrub. Just off the main road sat a couple of stores, a butcher shop that also sold bread, a garage, and another little café, which had long since gone out of business and was boarded up.

Behind the grill in the kitchen slouched the Irishman's dour, hatchet-faced wife from whom Dave and I each ordered a hamburger. "It ain't my fault, is it?" she said, when I complained about hurting my tooth on a large chunk of bone. "I didn't buy it. If ya don't like it, don't eat it. Makes no difference ta me." I regretted that she wasn't working for the publican's wife in the kitchen at Fitzroy Crossing.

We paid our bill and left for Wyndham, about two hundred miles to the north. The map indicated bitumen all the way, so we were anticipating an easy drive, but as Digger Dawes would have put it, we were wrong again. A few miles outside of Halls Creek, heavy black clouds moved in from the northwest off the Durack Range, and I soon had to switch on the windshield wipers against the drizzle.

Suddenly, a blinding downpour enveloped us, wind-driven rain pelting the Toyota. The din of the storm rose to a crescendo with booming thunder and the crackling of jagged bolts of lightning that briefly illuminated the water-covered road ahead. I slowed the vehicle to a crawl, finally stopping when the deluge rendered the wipers useless and I couldn't distinguish the road from the shoulder on either side of it. We sat there as the sky lowered, black clouds merging with the earth, buffeted by wind and rain. After a while the downpour let up, and slowly we continued on our way, grateful for so mild a scrape with the notoriously fickle weather of the Kimberley.

6

For hundreds of miles we'd noticed yellow signs along the road that read FLOODWAY, and we now discovered precisely what they meant. A creek just south of the Ord River had flooded and was racing directly over the Great Northern Highway, forcing us to come to a stop behind a four-wheel-drive truck that had pulled up to its bank. Sprawling in the rear of the vehicle were about twenty aborigines in varying states of intoxication and repose. Their garish polyester clothing—even the children with them were dressed outlandishly—made them seem comically out of place in the monochromatic lunar landscape.

The passengers themselves looked even more battered than their partially wrecked truck. A few wore cheap rubber beach thongs, but most were barefooted. Two men and one of the gins sported dirt-blackened bandages, emblems of honor often worn by aborigines injured in drunken bouts and domestic brawls. The truck and its occupants had probably come a long way, as both were thickly caked with reddish-brown dust.

We were considering how to proceed when the driver of the vehicle tossed an empty tinny out the window, ground the clutch into gear, and nosed the vehicle into the water. Fascinated by the potential for disaster, we watched as it agonizingly sloshed toward deeper water. In midstream, with water lapping at the bottom of its doors, the truck surrendered to the force of the surging current, and its rear end began sliding toward the bed of the creek. But with the passengers' weight providing ballast, the driver was able to hold the road and reached the opposite bank.

"Let's go before the water gets higher," said Dave nonchalantly. To Aussies, he was known as "Dive" and at that moment the name seemed particularly appropriate.

"We can't make it," I replied, reminding Dave that the sum total of his experience in fording rivers was limited to hopping over gutters in New York City to avoid getting his feet wet. Even as we spoke, the current was getting stronger. A few miles back up the road we'd crossed a floodway not nearly as deep, and my heart suddenly leapt into my mouth when I felt our rear end being swept off the road. We'd barely made it across, and that stream had been meandering compared to the torrent we now faced. If the vehicle got swept into the creekbed, it would probably roll over and tumble downstream, trapping us inside. We'd heard back in Perth that a couple from Sydney had drowned that way in the Ord the year before. After thirty-odd years of driving, I knew that only an amphibious landing craft would be likely to get across.

"It'll be easy, Jack. I'll turn the hubs and put us in four-wheel-drive," declared a confident Dave.

"You can do what you like," I replied, "but I'm not going now. Let's just wait for the rain to stop and the water to drop. What's the big rush? Get out your coloring book and crayons or do some more work on your afghan."

"Don't be silly," he said calmly, as he got out to engage the hubs. "We'll make it easily. No worries." To reassure me further, Dave walked to the edge of the swift running water and stuck his Birkenstock-sandaled foot in it. "If you're concerned, I'll drive."

However genuine, that offer was less than an encouraging prospect. Dave had an arguable talent for reading road maps, but his driving experience hardly inspired confidence. Back in New York, his practice had been limited to moving his mother's car from one side of the street to the other to avoid getting parking tickets. Except for a brief period while he was in college, and before it was demolished by a moving brick wall, he himself had never owned a car in his life.

Early in the preparation for our journey we had agreed to take turns at the wheel. But when Dave stalled in the middle of a narrow road while attempting a U-turn, and, after mistaking the cigarette lighter for the throttle, he couldn't find either first or second gear, I convinced him that I would gladly take responsibility for all the driving. I would enjoy it immensely, I told him, and it would give me something to do to make the time pass. He could be the navigator. That plan had worked faultlessly till now.

"We'll get across," Dave reaffirmed, slowly withdrawing his foot from the water.

His tone reminded me of that of an old family physician removing his hand from a child's forehead and calmly pronouncing the patient fit. Some years earlier, Dave and I had owned a boat together, and as a tribute to his optimism, I christened it Candide. So positive an attitude might have been suitable for a slow day at sea when the fish weren't biting, but it hardly seemed appropriate in the Australian bush.

"Do you have any final requests or messages you'd like to leave with me?" I asked.

"What do you mean?" Dave replied, clearly surprised at the annoyance in my voice.

"Even if you survive your little drive, you won't be able to call the AAA to pull the truck out of the creek." I had discovered from past experience that when Dave made up his mind, his determination was unshakable. I could be equally as stubborn.

"What are you doing?" he asked, as I pulled my duffel bag out of the backseat.

"I don't want to lose my gear when you flip over," I answered. "You might think about leaving yours with me, too. You're not going to have any use for it. At least let me have your cash, and the Nikon, too." Our argument was interrupted by a roaring crash upstream. From the startled expression on his face, Dave looked as if he expected a saltwater crocodile in heat, but charging toward us instead came an immense melaleuca tree. Torn from its roots by the current, it tumbled downstream, flattening and knocking aside everything in its path. The huge tree slammed onto the road directly in front of the Toyota, twisting around for a moment before rolling off into the bed beyond. It continued its destructive course until it rounded a bend and we lost sight of it.

At that moment a beat-up four-wheel-drive Toyota pulled up behind us, and out jumped two men with stubbies in their hands. Both were short and stout with large pendulous beer bellies that hung suspended over their belts. They might have been twins were it not for the fact that one was an aborigine.

"You hir lung?" asked the white one, speaking in a jarring combination of Eastern European and Australian accents and slang. A dark-complexioned man in his late fifties, his bristly salt and pepper hair was cropped close to his head.

"Only a few minutes," I answered.

"Whea ya from? Ya American?"

"Yeah," I told him. "It didn't take you long to spot the accent."

"I luv American, I owe lif America. Hir, haf beer. Jack, dese fella Yanks," he shouted to his aboriginal companion. Lifting the lid off the esky on the front seat beside him, he pulled out two stubbies for us. "I Mahtin," he told us, pumping our hands vigorously. "Dis Jack. He good black vella. Dink up, dink up, plendy more is."

It was raining heavily now, and after backing our truck farther away from the bank of the steadily rising creek, I went over to join Martin and Jack in their Toyota, while Dave, who hadn't slept well the night before, took a nap.

As we drank beer companionably sheltered from the storm, Martin told me he was a Pole who'd emigrated to Australia after World War II. During most of the war he'd been prisoner in German slave labor camps in France, working first on repairing bombed railway lines and later at a submarine base on the coast. Following D-day and the German surrender, he'd been employed by the Americans on a military base outside Paris. It was there that he'd met a sergeant who'd taught him to be a mechanic.

Martin was now the head mechanic for the aboriginal community at Turkey Creek, about thirty miles up the road to the north, and Jack was his assistant. Sunday was a day off, and they had gone to Halls Creek to pick up a dozen cases of beer to see them through the week, if they didn't drink it all waiting for the river to go down.

"I haf beaut job Turkey Creek," Martin laughingly announced. "I boss. Ain't dat right, Jack?"

"Dat's right, he da boss," confirmed Jack, nodding his head. He knew exactly how to handle Martin.

"Jack good black vella," Martin assured me again.

After about two hours or so, just before dusk a car pulled up behind us. The rain had by now slackened. The two couples got out and walked over to us for a chat, in the course of which we learned they all worked in the office of the Argyle diamond mine to the north. The mine had recently come under contract to De Beers of South Africa to maintain its monopoly on the diamond market, and they were having labor problems with some of the unions. Like Martin and Jack, the two couples had gone to Halls Creek for the day. It was difficult to imagine why.

The group of us had stepped down to the creek's bank when a huge stainless steel tanker-trailer joined the line of waiting vehicles. A powerfully built truckie, well over six feet tall, jumped down out of the cab and approached us. He wore shorts and heavy boots, the sort used in the bush.

" 'Ow long's it been like this?" he asked in a heavy English accent.

"Du hours, meybe more," answered Martin.

We all introduced ourselves to Alan, who told us he was an Englishman, a "Brummy" from Birmingham, who regularly made the round-trip run from Perth to Darwin. It wasn't that he was especially fond of that particular route, he explained, but it was simply the only one that existed. In that big rig of his he covered over five thousand kilometers a week, often driving through the night, and he was no stranger to rivers blocking the road. He told us that, a couple of years earlier, he'd been held up at the Murchison, north of Geraldton, for almost a month during the Wet.

"I couldn't get across or go back, so I lef' me lorry 'n' took a helicopter to Geraldton. The water dropped three weeks later 'n' I cum back 'n' drove 'er out o' there." Stepping over to the bank of the creek he cast an appraising eye at the rushing waters. "It's a late Wet," Alan observed, "but this 'ill g'down in a few hours if it stops rhining over there," he said, pointing to the mountains off in the west. "It don't much matter what 'appens 'ere, but off there is where the water comes from."

Alan and Martin talked about the changes they'd seen in the Kimberleys since they'd come to Australia. Only recently had some stretches of the Great Northern Highway been bitumenized, making it possible for ordinary vehicles to travel it at least during the Dry. "Lotta traffic from city now," said Martin. "Last year du vella in Ford Falcon try cross hir an' drown. Young vella from city no belung in bush. Always git trouble." Martin's conception of a lot of traffic was a curious one. For over five hours now we had been stopped on the only bitumenized road in Northwest Australia and had seen only four vehicles besides our own. Not a single car waited at the bank across the creek.

Alan was anxious to move on to Darwin, and as the level of the water had noticeably dropped, despite the rain's having started again, he decided to try to cross. "Good luck, Yanks, hope ya enjoy Australia," he hollered down from the cab above the diesel's loud clattering. "See ya later, Martin, I'll catch ya on the way back."

Turning on his wipers and giving us a thumbs-up sign, he eased his big lorry into the stream. As he reached the middle, the tops of the huge tires were completely submerged, at a level that would have put the hood of our vehicle completely under. The swift current didn't budge the fully loaded tank-trailer, allowing the powerful diesel to gain the opposite shore easily. Sounding his horn as a final farewell, Alan drove off into the night toward Darwin. For a long time his headlights glowed eerily in the distance, until they finally disappeared into the darkness.

"Nuter vile ve go," announced Martin. "You vellas stop my place. Jack, you go look riber. You vellas dink up. Dink up. Haf 'nother beer."

Using a branch he snapped off a tree to maintain his balance, Jack walked down into the torrent on the muddy, slippery bitumen. When the water reached his waist he turned back and hollered, "Too deep, boss. Strong current. Lemme have more beer."

Another hour went by during which the creek receded a bit more. "Ve go now," announced Martin, having taken stock of the situation. "Put in low drive an' folla me. Don' stop for nutin'. Folla me my place."

We did as Martin instructed, proceeding in the wake of his Toyota into the stream. In the middle, the current pushed our rear end slightly, and I could hear the water slapping against the door on Dave's side. After his slumber Dave seemed to have regained his senses, for he was now sitting bolt upright, his arms extended to brace himself against the dashboard. I was glad we had diesel power as a gasoline engine would probably have gotten wet and stalled. On reaching the opposite bank I accelerated with relief to catch up to Martin's taillights ahead of us.

The road wound like a black serpent through the rainy countryside, illuminated in the hypnotic glare of our headlights. I began to wish that I could see the way I once did at night when, in my teens and twenties, I could spot reefs on the darkest nights off the New England coast.

After we had driven about forty minutes, Martin's directional signal blinked a right turn, leading us to Turkey Creek. Although it was only around nine thirty there were no lights anywhere. The town was little more than a trailer park, with a small store and fuel pumps out front and an ablution block in back, and we could have passed through it in a matter of seconds. We followed Martin off the bitumen and along a dirt track for a mile or so until he pulled up in front of a trailer.

"Park hir, park hir," Martin instructed. "I tell vife ve home."

"Boss missus plenty mad," Jack informed us, with a wide grin on his face, as Martin walked around to the other side of the trailer. "We go Halls Creek and didn' tell 'er. He catch it good."

"Where 'ave ya bean, ya barstard? Ya've bean boozin' all bloody die, an' lef' me 'ere alone. What time is this to get 'ome," a woman's shrill voice screamed from inside the trailer.

"Shad up, shad up, voman. I got Yank friends wid me. Make 'em tucker."

The yelling stopped and a sharp featured, overweight woman in a faded housedress came around to meet us. "I'm sorry," she apologized, unable to conceal her annoyance, "but this barstard Polack's bean away all day. What was I supposed ta due 'ere by meself on Sunday? Me name's Gladys. Cum round n'I'll fix youse tea."

The back side of the trailer had a lean-to canvas porch attached to it, and as we lifted a flap to enter it two large mongrel dogs jumped up at Dave and me, barking.

"Shad up! Shad up! Ged out," Martin shouted at the mangy-looking animals, which he called "bitsers"—bits a'dis and bits a'dat. In his most polite tone he invited us to, "Sidown, sidown," pointing to the canvas chairs around the folding table that served as their dining room. "Haf beer, haf beer," he said, handing cold stubbies all around while Gladys fixed a large platter of sandwiches in the kitchen.

We were starved, and ate them ravenously while Gladys told us she was from Birdsville, a small outback town in western Queensland known only for its pub and a country race meet held there once a year. Except for those few hours of excitement once every twelve months, Birdsville was, according to her, even smaller than Halls Creek, but it was where her parents had settled when they came over from England.

Stepping into the trailer, she returned with a faded photograph of a couple with a little girl standing in front of them, a child with light hair and fair skin. Except for her aquiline nose, it would have been impossible to recognize her as Gladys. The harsh outback climate and fierce Australian sun had exacted a terrible toll, for although she was only forty-eight, Gladys had the appearance of an elderly woman. Deep lines circled her eyes, and her once-fair English skin hung loose and leathery on her face.

Gladys had been married to Martin for twenty-odd years—how many exactly she'd forgotten—but would have married the devil himself to get out of Birdsville. The couple had been living in Turkey Creek for twelve years, and while Martin was off at the garage working on engines, Gladys stayed home and looked after the trailer and Cocky, their pet galah.

"I wouldna' wanna live in a city," she stated flatly, feeding a piece of uneaten sandwich to Cocky. "I couldn't live like that. This isn't such a bad life, really. We're outta the rat race, an' there's some nize people 'ere. Every once in a while some bloke comes along an' we have a nize visit an' a yarn. I'd niver 'ave met you blokes today an' 'eard all about America if I was livin' in Sydney, now would I?"

"You got me there, Gladys," I admitted.

After we had eaten, Jack said a polite round of g'nights and walked home to his trailer. We sat in companionable silence, watching the stars appear in the clearing skies, and I offered Gladys a beer. "No thanks, I'm off it. One in the family on the terps is enough."

We talked for a while longer about living in the bush until Gladys got up and started to make up the two cots on the porch for us. She and Martin excused themselves and went into their trailer for the night, but a moment later she came back to the door. "We're glad ya stopped with us," she said, shyly. "I'll fix ya brekie in the mornin'."

Gladys's generosity and kindness were touching—she proved to be not at all the gruff, embittered housewife she had seemed when we had first met. She and Martin had invited total strangers—foreigners, in fact—into their home, treating us as honored guests. Yet by this point in our journey, such a show of hospitality was no longer surprising. What initially struck us as hostility turned out in fact to be the wariness and caution that living for long periods in solitude engendered. By the same token, it was that very solitude that made Australians genuinely congenial, eager to relieve long periods of isolation with a companionable chat or meal. It was almost an "outpost mentality," and we found ourselves over and over in the course of our trip gratified by the graciousness that was inevitably extended, and, realizing that our visits meant so much to our hosts, more than a little humbled.

7

Everything was lush and green the morning after the storm, and the rolling countryside we crossed as we drove north offered a welcome contrast to the withered scrub around Halls Creek. It was a late Wet in the Kimberleys, and the monsoon season not yet over. During the summer, when the Wet occurs, the "deep north" of Australia is subject to cyclones and frequent storms that sweep in off the ocean. Farther south, where we'd been traveling, everything remained dry and dusty, as rain seldom reached the areas far inland.

We made Kununurra early in the afternoon. Like Carnarvon and Derby, it was a regional administrative center (for the East Kimberley district), but unlike them, it lacked any sort of history. The northeastern-most settlement in Western Australia, Kununurra was less than thirty miles from the Northern Territory border and had been established only in the 1960s. It also lacked any sort of character.

The post office, the shire office, and all the shops had been recently built, and the small residential area on the edge of town consisted almost entirely of prefab housing. Kununurra—the name derived from an aboriginal word meaning "big waters"—had a small newspaper, but the one issue we saw contained the following notice: "The *Echo* regrets the lack of news content in this edition caused by strikes and equipment breakdowns."

After setting up camp, I decided to head off to the tavern for a beer and to hunt up Stu Skoglund, a Yank helicopter pilot we'd heard about from Martin. Dave didn't share my enthusiasm for pubs, and even less so for grog, that early in the day, so I went off on my own, leaving him to pay a visit to the laundromat.

Although Stu Skoglund wasn't at the busy tavern, the barmaid assured me he came in every day, and gave me his phone number just in case. As I drank my beer I got into a conversation with a fellow standing beside me dressed like a ringer, a stockman, who'd been out mustering. He wore faded denim jeans and a blue cotton work shirt, with cowboy boots and a battered dust-covered hat that had seen lots of service.

Tony Oliver was thirty-two years old and made his living contracting to string wire fences on stations. He'd come to Australia as a child with his father and two sisters, having left Vancouver after his parents divorced and settled in Brisbane. But when his father remarried Tony ran away from home, and though he was only fifteen he found work on stations, first as a jackeroo and later as a head stockman.

"I earned $206 a month and most of it went on board and taxes. It was a good life, and I'd still be doing it if it paid anything at all, but cattle raising's a dying industry in this country."

I shouted Tony a beer while he talked about his mother back in Canada.

"When I ran away, I was afraid to write to her because I thought she'd tell my father where I was. After a couple of years on the stations, I wrote to my father in Brisbane, but he'd moved away and the letter came back. Then I wrote to my mother because I had our old address in Canada, but I never heard from her. I wrote to her two more times, but I never got an answer. Maybe she moved away, too. That was years ago. It's like the earth has swallowed them up."

Tony was in Kununurra killing time until he could fly out to a station and work on stringing fences somewhere in the Northern Territory.

"It's a pretty lonely life for a single bloke out on the stations," Tony admitted. "I come into town when I can and try to meet a girl and maybe take her out to dinner. There's a good Chinese restaurant down the road, but if I buy a bottle of wine to go with it, it's pretty dear, and I can't afford it very often. Anyway, I can't drive to the Territory now because it's been a late Wet. We've only had eight inches of rain this year, and we usually get thirty-two. The country around here's never known drought, so we're sure to get it. It might even rain into April."

I finished my beer and got up to leave, declining Tony's shout. I wanted to be coherent when I caught up with Stu Skoglund. "If I ever see you again, I'll buy you a drink, mate," he promised, as I shook his hand and left the bar.

Walking out into the blinding midday sun, drowsy and slightly tipsy in the stifling humidity, I felt melancholy, as Tony's story had reminded me of my own father's disappearance. When he left home my mother told us that he was dead, but twelve years later he suddenly appeared at our door, claiming that he'd been searching for us for years. I knew that couldn't have been true because we'd lived at the same address since he'd left. In any case, he didn't stay long, and I never saw him again after that. I wanted to reassure Tony that, since his parents had allowed themselves to be swallowed up by the earth, perhaps he was better off never having found them.

8

It wasn't until later in the afternoon that I finally reached Stu Skoglund, who seemed pleased at my call and gave me directions to his home. A rangy man with gray hair greeted me on the porch of his prefab bungalow, having been warned of my arrival by his dog, a small bitser I'd roused from its sleep when I banged the sagging wooden gate behind me. The animal raised its head to bark desultorily a couple of times before slumping down to resume its doze, oblivious to the flies buzzing around its face.

"That's a ferocious watchdog you've got there," I said, by way of introduction.

"Yeah, he'd make a great civil servant up here," replied Stu, with a laugh. "But he's probably too ambitious for government work. Come on in and get outta the heat."

It wasn't much cooler sitting in the living room of the house but at least a ceiling fan was stirring the humid air. Though acknowledged to be the man responsible for introducing helicopter mustering to Australia, Stu obviously hadn't gotten much in the way of financial reward. The room was inexpensively furnished with a worn green couch and two easy chairs that didn't match. A huge pair of mounted steer horns hung on one wall, the only decoration in sight.

Now in his mid-sixties, he and his wife, Ellie, rented their modest house from the government. A few miles outside town they owned a six-hundred-acre farm, which was part of the Ord River irrigation project, a disastrous government program that attempted to turn the East Kimberley into an agricultural area. According to Stu, his farm wouldn't be worth much even if he could find someone foolish enough to buy it. Only a few optimistic souls, he said, bothered to cultivate anything in the Ord Valley, and even then many of the fields quickly became overgrown with weeds. To make ends meet, Ellie worked, for Stu could no longer fly since losing his right arm.

"I escaped from Minnesota durin' World War II," Stu recalled, after he'd gotten some beers out of the fridge for us and we were seated in comfortable chairs under the whirring ceiling fan. "But maybe I'd've been better off stayin' there. I've lived in nicer places since then, like Florida and California. During the Korean War, I was a flight instructor. After that, jobs in aviation were hard to come by, so I came over here on a contract to spray crops with a helicopter.

"To get me to come over, they told me I'd earn as much as a doctor or lawyer. But when I got here, I found out that people in those professions don't make anything like the kind of money they make back in the States. That was back in 1965, and I've been here ever since."

Stu adroitly rolled himself a cigarette and sat back in his soft plush chair to examine his handiwork. Satisfied, he lit up and took a long drag on it, drawing the smoke deep into his lungs. "They didn't taste as good when I could roll 'em with two hands," he remarked.

Stu first attempted mustering cattle with a helicopter on Victoria River Downs. Before the government broke it up, VRD, as it was known throughout Australia, was the largest station in the country. The cattle there hadn't been mustered for years and had gone wild. None of the old-time stockmen had any faith in the copter as a replacement for mounted horsemen, so Stu agreed to work on a percentage for each head that was sent to the meatworks.

"The musterin' went a lot better than anyone expected, but all I got outta that one was a set of horns," he said, motioning toward the pair hanging on the wall. "The road trains didn't come to pick up the cattle, and the station manager didn't have enough brains to water 'em. We went off to muster in another paddock, and when we got back four days later, they were all piled up dead.

"The next season an English company that owned a few stations hired me by the hour and paid me for every head I drove into the yard. I did real well that year," Stu recalled, "and I thought I was on the way to makin' my fortune.

"I bought a second copter and hired an experienced pilot, but he didn't know a thing about musterin' cattle, an' he crashed the copter twice. Then, just as he was gettin' good at it, the heli utilities offered him more money and he left. So I got a Yank heli pilot who'd been in Viet Nam. But on his fifth day musterin', he crashed and killed himself."

"But I heard you had a big company and were doing pretty well," I said, remembering Martin's enthusiastic descriptions.

"The big company was me, and one helicopter. But I reckon Australia's a lot like Texas, except everything is supposed to be even bigger out here."

Stu went into the kitchen to get us another cold beer and as he took his seat, a large brown palmetto bug darted out from under his chair, scurrying across the floor.

"Ellie's been on my back to go home to the States ever since we got here," said Stu, watching the huge cockroach disappear under the bedroom door. "When we first came to Kununurra, we lived near the airstrip in an old bus I bought in Darwin. I put flywire all over the place, but that didn't keep the insects out. Every time we turned a light on, they came in by the thousands.

"One day we went shoppin' in town, and while we were in the store it rained seven inches. When we came back, the whole valley was under water, and everything in our house was floatin' around. It rained seventeen inches that day between here and Turkey Creek, washed out the roads and the fences. It ruined everything we owned. This place is the Australian version of Siberia. The government sends people up here to get them out of the way."

The front door opened, and Ellie Skoglund, an attractive woman in her mid-fifties, entered the house carrying groceries. "I see he's on his soap box again," she said, shaking her gray-blond hair out of her face. "Don't pay any attention to him."

"Martin down in Turkey Creek mentioned you were part Chero- kee Indian," I said to her, after she'd put her shopping away and joined us.

"No, not Cherokee," said Stu, answering for his wife. "Her father's Irish, her mother's English, and way back there's a bit of Apache Indian. Her mother told her that when she was a little girl, she stubbed her toe and lost all her Indian blood."

"Is your name Ellie?" she asked Stu. Her green eyes were glowering as she turned to me and remarked, "You might have noticed that Stuart likes to do all the talking."

The three of us sat around for the rest of the afternoon drinking beer and swapping yarns. The Skoglunds hadn't run into anyone from the States for a long time, and they wanted to talk about things back home. As her husband had told me, Ellie was particularly unhappy in Australia.

"I don't know about the rest of the country," she said. "But I sure don't like it here. The climate and the bugs are appalling. Even at night the humidity is so high you could swim around the place instead of walking. You wear as little clothing as possible and try not to get arrested for indecent exposure.

"The people here are terrific," she added, waving her hand emphatically. "But they have a very casual way of living, and that can get on your nerves, because they don't seem to worry about anything. I suppose that's good in a way, but if they don't get something done today, well, not to worry, they can always do it tomorrow . . . or even next year.

"Then why not go back to the States?" I asked.

"No money," replied Stu. "And if we did, at our age we'd have a hard time findin' jobs. We've lived here so long now we'd be like fish out of water. We'd be freaks. We couldn't fit in because our way of livin' is so different."

"Three of our kids live here, and they've married Australians. It'd be hard to leave them," said Ellie.

Stu clutched the empty sleeve that draped over the arm of his chair. "Things were goin' along alright until I lost this."

"How did that happen?"

"About four years ago I was drivin' my Toyota and had my arm up on the window," Stu recalled, with no apparent bitterness. "It was the beginnin' of the Wet, when no one wants to get off the bitumen onto the soft shoulders. A big roadtrain on the way to Perth came around a curve and its lights hit me straight in the eyes. I was watchin' the side of the bitumen to keep from runnin' off the road, and all I heard was breakin' glass.

"I didn't know the arm was gone and I kept on drivin'. But soon enough I saw what happened. My arm was torn off from the shoulder down. I passed out and my mate put on a tourniquet. After that the Department of Aviation pulled my ticket, and I couldn't fly anymore."

"Losing your license must have hurt as much as losing your arm," I said, commiserating with him.

"There's another way a' lookin' at it," said Stu, philosophically. "I figure that losin' my arm might a' saved my life. If I hadn't lost my license, I probably would've crashed the copter into a tree and gotten myself killed. Christ, heli musterin' ain't the safest occupation in the world, ya know."

With regrets on both sides I headed off to meet Dave at a coffee shop across the street from the "animal bar" at the Kununurra Hotel. Stu Skoglund's bitterness wasn't difficult to comprehend. He had been the first to realize and exploit the commercial potential for helicopter mustering in the wilds of Australia, yet except for a brief mention in a mimeographed pamphlet on the history of helicopter aviation in northern Australia, which he had shown me with nostalgic pride, he had absolutely nothing to show for it. He had been a pioneer, but was now a one-armed, unskilled ex-officer, living in a place that no longer had any claims on him.

Stu Skoglund had lost more than his arm in that roadtrain accident—he had lost his spirit as well. He'd just given up, in a way that we couldn't conceive any Australian we'd met, no matter how difficult the circumstances, would ever consider doing. The resilient Aussies seemed to face hardship almost as a point of pride, for in a harsh and hostile country, where nothing came easily and disasters occurred with almost predictable regularity, dogged determination was essential for survival. Stu had refused to do battle for battle's sake, and in this respect, his self-imposed isolation seemed almost philosophical, a silent protest that his life and achievements had gone unrecognized.

9

A friend of ours in Perth had suggested we meet Reg Birch, an aboriginal bird-trapper living in the East Kimberley who, when he wasn't out snaring birds for a living, was usually to be found stumping the region as a spokesman for the aboriginal cause. Equally at home on a rostrum as he was in the bush, he represented his people even at international forums, including U.N.-sponsored conferences on indigenous populations. Jack and I got together with him one afternoon in a Kununurra coffee shop.

Reg was a tall, handsome man of forty-five, with smooth, mahogany skin that made him look much younger. Though he had left school at the age of fourteen, he spoke as learnedly as a wise old professor and as eloquently as a seasoned diplomat. His voice, which hadn't the slightest trace of that harsh, twangy Australian accent known as Strine, was very much in keeping with his gentle bearing.

"Bird trapping takes a lot of preparation and a lot of patience," Reg explained, as he sipped a fruit drink. "First you've got to go out and find them. Then you've got to figure out where it's best to lay your trap.

"If the ground's level, you rake it, just to get all the sticks and stones out of the way. Otherwise you have to dig out rocks and chop off roots and cart some sand back from the creek to fill in the holes, to get it smooth enough for the trap.

"Then you've got to spread the seed. At the very beginning of each season we put out a whole bag of seed. When we retrace our tracks, we can see which birds have been there. We can tell roughly how many there were, too, just by the amount of seed they've eaten. We can tell the way they've been facing because they blow out the husks in the same direction. Then you set your spring-loaded nets.

"That's where the patience comes in. You hide yourself away in the shade of a tree and there's nothing else to do but wait for the birds to come in. That's when my mind wanders to all sorts of subjects. Sometimes I even get to wondering what makes the white person tick."

In the eyes of the white community in Kununurra/Wyndham—he lived in Wyndham but was known throughout the area—Reg was a half-caste, a term not necessarily derogatory in the Australian context. True, there were those who despised mixed bloods (or "Kimberley yella-fellas," as some people called them) as rabble-rousers within the aboriginal community, but most whites held them in relatively high regard if only because they were more "motivated," more "assimilated," more understandable than their pure aboriginal cousins still living in "the dreamtime" past or, worse yet, in a perpetual drunken stupor.

Reg was a second generation half-caste. His grandfather on his mother's side was a Norwegian, on his father's side, an Englishman. Both his grandmothers were, in his words, "full-blooded aboriginals, just out of the bush." But in the Kimberleys no one seemed to go in for such fine distinctions.

"I was very angry at white society when I was young," he told me. "Very belligerent, too. And very good with my fists. It was my wife who saved me. If not for her, I probably would have ended up spending most of my life in jail."

Instead, Reg had become a licensed bird trapper. Plenty of unlicensed ones operated in the area as well, not surprising given the fact that Western Australia was home to all sorts of wondrous birds—galahs, major mitchells, sulphur-crested cockatoos, rainbow lorikeets, and parrots and parakeets of every description. Often trapped illegally, these spectacular and in many cases endangered species were smuggled out of Australia, many of them bound for the exotic-bird market in America. First chloroformed and then stuffed into tennis ball cans, sometimes as many as three to a tin, they were delivered to boats waiting off the almost totally unguarded northern coast for transshipment to the United States via Singapore. Or they

were simply concealed in someone's luggage and slipped past surveil-
lance personnel at Darwin's international airport, where prominently
displayed signs warned that the offense was punishable by heavy fines
and jail sentences.

The birds—those still alive upon arrival—commanded huge sums
of money from exotic-bird dealers in San Francisco and Los Angeles.
So much so that even with a mortality rate as high as one-third, bird
smuggling was still an extremely lucrative business. It was conserva-
tively estimated that over two thousand birds, captured in the wild,
were brought into America each day, most of them from Australia,
Indonesia, and Papua New Guinea. Certain rare and highly desirable
species, like the eclectus parrot and the golden parakeet, were said to
be worth their weight in cocaine, which perhaps explained why the
underworld was often involved.

Reg confined his trapping to finches, of which there were eleven
different varieties in the Wyndham area. Three of these were protected; the other eight were fair game. The finch-trapping season was
only ten weeks long, but during that period, which began on September 1 and ran through mid-November, he was able to catch an average
of six thousand birds each year. These he sold to dealers in Perth at
the going rate of about six dollars per bird; $36,000 for ten weeks'
work wasn't bad. Still, Reg complained (though not too strenuously)
that with the season that short he "could never ever fill all the orders"
he had.

I asked Reg whether trapping threatened Western Australia's tropical birdlife.

"I think we're only a small part of the problem," he said, referring
to himself and the seven other licensed finch trappers in W.A., the
only state that allowed the capture of finches. " 'The march of progress' is a much bigger threat. Look at what the Ord River Project has
done to the valley. The water's stagnant and the river's choked with
weeds. This part of the Kimberleys has become a rice-paddy ecology.
We're even getting birds from Southeast Asia. There's an orange-col-
ored egret—I don't know its scientific name—living in the fields in
Kununurra and it's only been here since they built the dam. The
destruction of the habitat has been going on for thirty years. That's
where the serious problem lies."

Reg's attack on the Ord River Project was directed primarily at its
by-product, Lake Argyle. The artificially created lake, named for the
legendary cattle station that now lay beneath it, contained eleven
times as much water as Sydney Harbor and, according to the statis-

tics, was designed "to irrigate over 72,000 hectares of unproductive land." (However unproductive, in 1939 Western Australia had been prepared to set aside that general area for the large-scale settlement of Jewish refugees from Europe, a scheme that was ultimately vetoed by the Commonwealth Government in Canberra.) But with the irrigation project largely considered a failure—the insects were too destructive and the markets too distant—Lake Argyle had become little more than a place where the kids of Kununurra could race their speedboats. The Durack family, who had settled the region and founded Argyle Downs in the 1890s, and whose struggle to survive was immortalized in Mary Durack's *Kings in Grass Castles,* had good reason to be turning over in their graves.

We had hoped to spend more time with Reg, but that afternoon he was leaving for Derby to attend a conference on "Aboriginal Land Rights and Sacred Sites." Land rights was a deeply divisive political issue throughout Australia, one that had been haunting the country for years, provoking "nightmares of sudden dispossession," particularly among white station owners in the north.

As I walked Reg to his car that afternoon, I asked him if he had come to any conclusions about what made the white person tick.

"They've yet to find themselves," he said, emphasizing that he was talking only of whites in Australia. "You can watch television to see what the average Australian is like. Turn it on to a football or cricket match and all you see is a bunch of ockers—drunks in floppy shorts, a pair of thongs, and a cold stubby in their hand. If that's an Australian, well then, I'm ashamed.

"My idea of an Australian is a person who thinks clearly and expresses his feelings. Most of those others, even when you try to discuss something sensible with them, can only talk about losing to the West Indies at cricket or things like that. They have no real deep-down feeling about Australia.

"To me Australia is my mother's and father's homeland. It means something to me. It's an intense feeling. But Australia to them is a quarter-acre block and the pub down the street and their nice big car. That's their Australia. But it isn't mine."

Sadly, Reg might have been right. It *was* their Australia, and many of them didn't want it to be his, especially if that meant relinquishing their property rights to a nation of 160,000 people, all of whom called themselves aboriginals despite the fact that only a few could legitimately lay claim to being "of unmixed ancestry."

Having long since abandoned its infamous "white Australia policy," which was aimed not at its own aboriginals but at would-be Chinese immigrants (as the slogan "Two Wongs don't make a white" made clear), Australia had in recent years gradually transformed itself into a multiethnic society whose cities, especially, had become havens for Vietnamese boat people and refugees from elsewhere around the world. But Australia's long and sordid history of confrontation with the native "blackfella" had not resolved itself so peaceably, and the country was still reaping the legacy of its bitter past in the form of festering antagonism over ownership of the land. There was a particular irony in this because both sides in the controversy—the white station owners as much as the aboriginals themselves—purported to share the ancient "dreamtime" view of the land as something immutable and transcendent, something beyond possession. In the plane over Mardathuna, for instance, I had remarked to Dudley Maslen that, as ruler of all we surveyed, he must have taken great pride in overseeing such a vast expanse of property. "Not really," Dudley had replied, with obvious sincerity. "My feeling is more that *I* belong to the land, not that it belongs to me."

As Reg explained, however, the fundamental question facing aboriginals was not really land rights, but their position in contemporary Australian society. From surface appearances, Reg seemed to have found his own answer to that question through total assimilation into the modern world. He himself vehemently denied that, arguing by way of vindication that even after the bird-trapping season was over, he often went into the bush on weekends, shedding his clothes in emulation of his aboriginal ancestors, and with only a boomerang and spear for weapons, running naked through the scrub in pursuit of kangaroos, goannas, and other such game.

Many months later, back in New York, I came across an article on the Australian aborigine in an issue of *The New Republic.* Written by the late Shiva Naipaul, who on a visit to Australia had been exposed to the Land Rights debate at an aboriginal gathering in Darwin, the article posed provocative questions that perhaps I had been too timid (or slow-witted) to ask Reg directly: "How real could the connection be between these citified gentry of the cause and those dusty, stick-legged, dark-skinned ones who squatted so patiently on the flagstones? By what bonds of sympathy and desire and cultural affinity were they linked?"

Naipaul's eloquently written article concluded on a note of reproach and admonition, a plea to the aboriginal majority—mixed-bloods like Reg "whose genetic exoticism and de facto assimilation make absurd all those claims to mystical sensibilities and vulnerabilities"—not to seek regeneration through a retreat to their "imagined essences":

> It is one thing to reinterpret and rewrite the Aboriginal past, to reach a new understanding of the virtues (and vices) of a society so long ignored and denigrated: Trollopian presumption deserves to be discredited. No harm is done if the settler kingdom should experience tremors of anxiety and see its own past in a different, less than heroic light . . . But it is quite another thing, in the name of restitution to deform our vision of the present and its needs, to invoke afresh cultures and identities ravaged by time and contact and powerlessness. These attempted acts of restoration are not merely dishonest: they are cruel. Too much has happened.
>
> At best, atavism is a harmless fantasy, not sustainable with any degree of persistent realism under skies crisscrossed by satellites and jet aircraft. At worst, it must be considered a tragedy—a failure of nerve . . . an escape from the challenges of history.

I sent the article to Reg and asked for his reaction, but he never replied.

10

We'd been delaying doing anything toward the ostensible goal of this part of the trip, which was to learn as much as possible about *Crocodylus porosus*, the saltwater crocodile. But one morning we decided it was time we visited Wyndham, a nearby town on the coast known to be infested by the ferocious reptile. Apart from boasting one of the largest insect populations in the Southern Hemisphere, the tiny port had but two claims to fame: a number of its residents had been devoured by saltwater crocodiles, a state of affairs it could ill afford since it had so few inhabitants; and it was the place former crocodile hunter Hugo Austla called home.

Dave telephoned Hugo from Kununurra, arranging for us to meet him at Vagg's Liquor Store in Wyndham. For seasoned bushmen such as ourselves it wasn't a difficult trail to follow, as only one road led into town. Winding some sixty miles through hilly green countryside, the narrow strip of bitumen terminated at a slaughterhouse overlooking sediment-laden Cambridge Gulf.

Sixty miles long, the Gulf was the tortuous passageway from the Timor Sea to the port of Wyndham. Extremely narrow in places, its swift, twenty-seven-foot tides, rising and falling twice daily, created dangerous eddies and whirlpools and swept mud more than a hundred miles out to sea. The sediment got thicker closer to Wyndham and one captain, bringing a ship in to the meatworks for the first time, said that in all his voyages around the world, he'd never before seen water "with cracks in it"—referring, of course, to the fact that the mud was so thick. The water itself was the color of dried blood, and an oil spill would have gone a long way toward enhancing its appearance.

To refer to Wyndham as a dead end is to make it sound a more appealing place than it actually is. The tiny backwater hamlet is fringed by brown, mud-oozing tidal flats and silt-shrouded marshes. Spindly mangrove roots, which ring the rim of the Gulf like the slime-coated legs of gigantic spiders, form a labyrinth of winding tunnels, ideal hiding places for the large saltwater crocodile population inhabiting the area. Standing at the water's edge in that primordial setting for even a few seconds left us both apprehensive. Small wonder, since we both had read several accounts of people having been dragged into the water by crocodiles from right along that very shore.

We left the malevolent-looking Gulf and drove to the bottle shop to meet Hugo. Almost everyone in the Kimberleys seemed to know him, at least by reputation, and even residents of Perth, thousands of miles to the south, were familiar with his exploits. Hugo was personally responsible for shooting more than four thousand crocs for their hides, and as a crew member on hunting vessels that probed the far reaches of tidal rivers, he helped to kill about eleven thousand more. He was also generally acknowledged to be an expert on crocodile behavior. Whenever fatal crocodile attacks occur at the top of Australia—two or three take place each year—newspapers and government authorities usually contact him, hoping that his insights will somehow help diminish the elemental horror human beings experience when one of their own kind is devoured.

The front of Vagg's looked dismayingly like the porch of a saloon in an old western movie. To reach the entrance we had to dodge and hop our way through a group of drunken aborigines sprawled under a low tin roof that shaded them from the fierce midday sun. Most of them were in stuporous slumbers, and the few that weren't sat with their backs against the wall, staring at us with dim brown eyes.

"We're supposed to meet Hugo here," I announced to the elderly proprietor who, standing behind a counter, might have been a character out of a Dickens novel. He was almost bald, except for a few long strands of white hair that he'd carefully arranged and plastered straight back on his head. Using his beaklike nose as a sight, he peered at us through a pair of old-time wire-rimmed glasses that perched precariously on the tip of his nose.

" 'E'll be right along. 'E said ya was comin'. Yanks ain't cha? There was some Yanks 'ere durin' the war. Don't see many up this way now. Ya kin wait'n there if yez like." He motioned towards a faded pink curtain that served as a partition as well as a door. "If yez came from Kununurra, you'll be needin' a tinny or two ta wash the bugs down." Opening the battered refrigerator behind him, he handed us two cans of cold beer. " 'Ere ya go, mates," he said. "Get stuck inta these."

We entered the storeroom and took seats on some stacked cartons of beer. Holding our tinnies with one hand, we used our others to swat at the flies that were attempting to use our faces as landing fields. After we had been waiting a few minutes one of the most impressive physical specimens either of us had ever encountered brushed the flimsy curtain aside and strode into the room.

"You the blokes what's lookin' fer me?" bellowed the giant in an immediately intimidating voice. Hugo stood well over six feet three inches tall, and though he appeared to be in his mid-forties, there wasn't an ounce of fat on him. The imposing croc hunter looked as though he could tear crocodiles apart with his bare hands. He spoke with an accent that was a blend of bush Australian and Estonian.

Hugo's full mane of dark brown hair cascaded over his high Slavic cheekbones, emphasizing his square face and muscular, jutting jaw. Beneath a broad, flat nose with flaring nostrils bristled a thick mustache. There was a menacing aspect to him, and when he glared at us with his gimlet green eyes, he seemed like a large, powerful cat about to pounce.

Hugo was extremely suspicious of our motives for wanting to see him, believing, perhaps, that we were wildlife officers, who were always on the prowl for crocodile poachers. We quickly explained that we only wanted to ask him some questions about crocodiles for a magazine story.

"Ya can't hunt 'em anymore. Vut cha vant ta know about crocs fer?"

At that moment the grocer entered the storeroom with a six-pack of cold beer we'd asked for. He eyed Hugo for a moment, and when he observed that he was agitated, he soothed him by handling him like a child.

" 'Ere, 'ere, Hugo, these er good lads! Don't be gettin' yerself all worked up. They've cum from America ta see ya. Yer a famous bloke over there, too. 'Ere, they even shouted ya a beer."

His comments seemed to reassure Hugo, who took a can of beer, snapping it open with his thick thumb, while fixing us with an icy stare. The wary croc hunter made a quick assessment and concluded we were harmless. He wouldn't need a gun for us, but a fly swatter might come in handy. Hugo's eyes changed expression, dancing with amusement, and he bared his teeth in a sneer. If I'd been seven feet tall, and had Dave been carrying a submachine gun, we'd have wiped it off his insolent face. Instead, we had to settle for being secretly elated when he opened a can of beer and it sprayed him.

"Ve go my place for more drinks," he commanded, and we followed in his wake, past the aborigines on the porch who, recognizing him, moved gingerly out of his way.

There was nothing unusual about Hugo's home, a modest two-story brown frame structure with upstairs and downstairs front verandas facing Wyndham's only road. Aside from the legions of teeming insects buzzing around, and the suffocating heat and humidity, it was identical to houses found in tract subdivisions in the States. And Hugo himself seemed to lead a very conventional life, with a wife, children, and even a pet dog, and a good living operating heavy earth-moving machinery.

The only aspect about his existence that precluded Hugo from being considered just a Regular Joe was his unusual leisure time interest. Instead of seeking satisfaction in arts or crafts, or dabbling in some other suburban pursuit, Hugo was rearing two saltwater crocodiles in his backyard.

As if he were about to exhibit rare orchids Hugo led us down the path through his wife's flower beds and vegetable garden to the crocodile pens. The monsters were basking in two muddy pools at the bottom of two chain link–enclosed pits. They were well over sixteen feet long, but Hugo was confident that when they matured, they'd be much larger. Our host's preoccupation with crocodiles was not limited to his beloved *Crocodylus porosus*, upon whom he lavished so much care. He also provided a good home for a freshwater specimen, *Crocodylus johnstoni*, which he kept in a less conspicuous pen nearby.

The born-again croc shooter told us that he captured the "freshie" and the two "salties" in funnel nets before crocodile hunting was prohibited in 1970. (Since the ban went into effect, attacks on humans and livestock were on the increase, and though vehemently opposed by conservationists, some residents of the deep north were demanding an end to the prohibition so that the proliferating crocodile population could be reduced.)

As we stood beside the chain link cages staring at the lethal yellow eyes of the armor-plated beasts, each in a separate enclosure and partially submerged in a mud hole, Hugo dispensed with the usual schedule. It wasn't regular feeding time, but since the crocs enjoyed unexpected company, he'd offer his charges a small morsel so that we might observe their appreciation of good, nourishing food.

Yanking both haunches of a wild boar he'd shot and butchered the day before from a large refrigerator, Hugo heaved one into each cage. Instantly, both crocodiles exploded out of the mud holes, their jaws snapping shut on the huge slabs of meat. Beaming like a doting parent whose child had just made the honor roll, Hugo observed, "Aren't dey jus' beautiful?"

"Yes, they're really lovely," Dave agreed. "But why are they in separate cages? Do they like their privacy?"

"Cause dey keel each other," replied Hugo, flashing a toothy grin, as if that ability was a particularly endearing quality. He related that at one point he had to go into a cage to separate the crocodiles during a territorial dispute. They'd been growling and slashing at each other through the fence, when one ripped it apart. The enraged croc squirmed into the other's pen and attacked it. Had the encounter occurred in the wild, one crocodile would have abandoned the fight and withdrawn, but as the cage made retreat impossible, a fight to the death would have been inevitable.

Without hesitation Hugo joined the fray wielding a two-by-four as a weapon. By bashing and clubbing his pets repeatedly, he managed to separate the combatants, although blood was drawn, teeth lost, and hides slashed in the encounter.

Hugo led us back to the house, where we sat on the veranda drinking beer. He was undoubtedly feeling more at ease with us, because as he recalled his days as a crocodile hunter, he even grew a bit nostalgic and decided to share some of his memories.

Stalking inside the house he returned a few moments later with a worn red-leather scrapbook. Fondly, Hugo leafed through some old newspaper clippings and photographs that showed details of some of his handiwork. He turned to one page and, smiling with satisfaction, modestly revealed that he'd taken some of the pictures himself.

The half-dozen black and white photographs were neatly mounted in a sequential order. The first was a picture of a large crocodile he'd shot, which was now hanging by a rope from the branch of a tree. The next two showed his mate hacking open the reptile's belly with a long machetelike knife.

The next page of his album displayed only three photographs, but from the look of satisfaction that came over Hugo's face, he obviously relished them the most.

"Dey're from police files," he confided, slipping them out of their mounts and handing them to us so that we could see them even better. "I'm not supposed ta have 'em."

They were close-ups, taken from different angles, and they showed the grisly remains of a dead man in a crocodile's stomach. In each, the victim's tortured face was clearly recognizable.

I would have liked to believe that the awesome Hugo could still experience human emotions, but after his last display of crocodile memorabilia I wondered if something of the deadly reptile hadn't entered his soul. He was genial enough to us, but like his former prey, he seemed ever watchful—and unnaturally alert to the point of being ever ready to strike. As though taking our measure, he had showed us those photographs, gauging our reaction to detect the slightest weakness, to see if we would flinch. We managed to suppress our revulsion, but his knowing smirk made it clear that Hugo hadn't been fooled. As we left his place and headed back to Kununurra, I remembered what Sam Lovell had said about the crocodile:

"He won't come out and take ya straight away. He waits, watches every move ya make. He learns yer habits and then he waits. Then one time, he's there, and he's got ya."

4

The Desert Road South

Cue Hotel and Bandstand

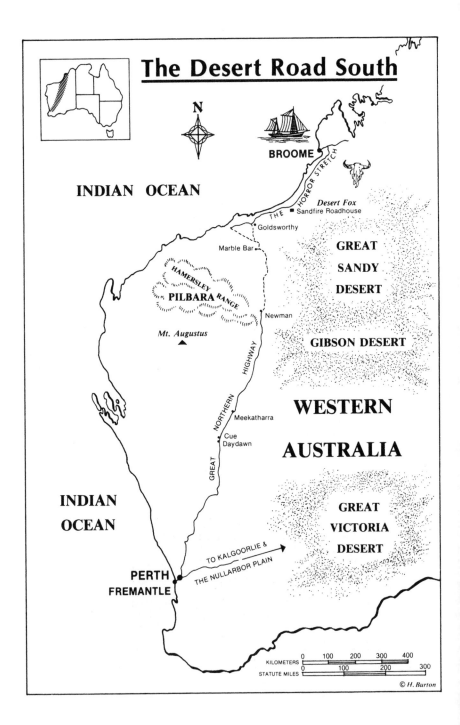

The Desert Road South

N

INDIAN OCEAN

BROOME

THE HORROR STRETCH

Desert Fox
■ Sandfire Roadhouse

Goldsworthy

Marble Bar

GREAT

SANDY

DESERT

HAMERSLEY

PILBARA RANGE

Newman

Mt. Augustus ▲

GIBSON DESERT

WESTERN

NORTHERN

HIGHWAY

Meekatharra

Cue
Daydawn

AUSTRALIA

GREAT

INDIAN
OCEAN

GREAT

VICTORIA

DESERT

TO KALGOORLIE &
THE NULLARBOR PLAIN

PERTH
FREMANTLE

	0	100	200	300	400
KILOMETERS					
	0	100	200	300
STATUTE MILES				

© H. Burton

1

We had gone about as far as we could go, or wanted to go, on this, the western leg of our trip. Twenty miles to the east, beyond the W.A. border, lay the Northern Territory, over 520,000 square miles (the combined area of France, Spain, and Italy) of near-nothinginess inhabited by only 130,000 people, half of whom, at least, cherished solitude even more than their neighbors in Western Australia. The other half of the population lived in Darwin, the capital of the Territory, which had been leveled by Cyclone Tracy on Christmas 1974. No longer a rough-and-tumble frontier town, Darwin had been rebuilt to look like any other administrative center in northern Australia, and in the process its personality was said to have suffered even more than its architecture.

Not that we intended to avoid the Northern Territory entirely. We had, in fact, already paid it a brief visit, having joined a young pilot we had met in Kununurra on his seven-hundred-mile mail run, which took us over the border to some cattle stations deep in the N.T. interior. As far as I was concerned, flying over it at 6,000 feet was the best way to see the Australian bush. Only occasionally did we have to swoop down out of the sky onto a dun-colored airstrip barely discernible from the surrounding salt pans to deliver a few welcome letters to the station's solitary inhabitants, who without fail invited us to join them in the homestead's earthen-floor kitchen for a cup of tea and a kibitz before taking off again.

Jack derided my "surgical strike mentality," but I suspect that his criticism had more to do with his own fear of flying, especially in small planes with daredevil bush pilots, than with any deep affection for the dusty track. In any case, any attempt to reach such remote places at this time of year, even in our four-wheel-drive, would have been foolish. The wet season had yet to end, and though we hadn't encountered a great deal of rain since being in the Kimberleys, the track farther east would most certainly have been washed out. The station hands we met that day, who professed to love their isolation, had been unable to get to town—the nearest being Halls Creek, about three hundred miles away—for the past four months.

It seemed more sensible to wait for the onset of the Dry before making our next foray into the Territory, and then to approach it from the east, through Queensland, as most of the early cattle drovers had. In the interim, we decided to retrace our steps as far south as Port Hedland and, at the point where the road split into two, to turn off the coastal highway, returning to Perth along the inland route, which bordered on the desert. From Perth we would fly to Cairns, in northern Queensland, where we'd make the necessary preparations for the second part of our journey into the bush.

The drizzle that began when we left Kununurra had turned into a pelting downpour by the time we reached Turkey Creek. The Ord River (where we'd met Martin) was still down, but off to the north, massive storm clouds blowing in from the Joseph Bonaparte Gulf were sweeping inland over the Durack Range, and it began to look as if the 150-mile stretch of unsealed road back to Fitzroy Crossing might be impassable. The track became increasingly soft and muddy the farther south we drove, and the Toyota began to flounder as its wheels churned up deeper and deeper furrows.

About an hour beyond Halls Creek we came to a spot where the road forked and the old track, branching slightly to the right, dropped into a flooded gully. A new extension had been built on an earthen embankment that ran parallel to the old road and ten feet above it, but a sign indicated that the road was still under construction, and its entrance was blocked by barricades.

"Crash the barrier and take the high road," I urged Jack. "We'll never make it on this one."

Jack must have wanted to rough it, though, for he continued on the old road, plowing through the huge puddles of water like a small craft in heavy seas until it became apparent even to him that it was senseless to try to go farther. Yet it was impossible to turn back, and simply to stop meant bogging right on the spot, perhaps to be stuck for days.

I pointed to a place where the embankment sloped at less of an angle than it had for the previous mile or so, and heedless of the danger of flipping over on the way up, Jack swerved to the left and headed toward it. Whining in protest, the four-wheel-drive inched its way up the incline, tearing away half the embankment before we finally made it over the top to the safety of the new road.

Slightly shaken by the experience, Jack put the Toyota in neutral, and I reached into the esky for a couple of beers. They were only "Kimberley cold" (i.e., lukewarm) but we weren't about to be fussy. The rain continued unabated as we sat there drinking, but we knew that the high road, even in its unfinished state, would be smooth—or at least smoother—sailing from here on in.

2

After our long and tortuous drive across the flats that skirted Eighty Mile Beach it was comforting to see the low, squat shape of the Sandfire Roadhouse looming ahead off to the side of the bitumen, looking like an oversized shipping crate that had fallen off a roadtrain. As if under siege, it was surrounded on all sides by the encroaching desert. Off to the left, in the deserted caravan park, a few stunted trees struggled for survival in the sterile red sand. With tortured branches drooping, their dust-blanketed leaves wilted as they sought to escape the late morning sun. Nothing seemed to have changed since we had passed through there months earlier.

But when we pulled up to the fuel pump, we soon learned that the Sandfire's notorious owner, Eddie Norton, was back in residence. The fabled Desert Fox had arrived from Perth a few days earlier to resume personal command of his bastion in the arid wastelands of the north. Jo, a waitress we'd spoken to on our first trip through, knew we were anxious to meet the daring fellow who'd become a living legend in W.A. She ran up to us as I pumped diesel distillate from the bowser.

" 'E's 'ere, 'e's 'ere, ya can talk with 'im," she announced in an excited but reverential voice. "The Desert Fox 'imself. Ya wanted ta see 'im, didn't ya?"

We certainly did. Besides having read about him, we'd heard all sorts of tales about the Desert Fox's victories over both desert and government bureaucrats. Single-handedly, Eddie Norton had vanquished those two seemingly insurmountable forces and had built a solitary roadhouse smack in the middle of one of the most desolate and forbidding stretches of country in Australia. His feat made it possible for conventional vehicles with limited fuel-carrying capacities to make the arduous four hundred-odd mile trek across the desert between Port Hedland and Broome. Besides having a refueling stop on the sun-blasted Sandfire Flats, dust-caked travelers could also get a hot meal, take a shower, or even stay overnight in the motel or caravan park.

Those amenities aside, perhaps the most important contribution provided by the Desert Fox at the Sandfire Roadhouse was a real honest-to-goodness watering hole, where wayfarers with parched throats could slake their thirsts on the "coldest beer in the north," as the sign outside boasted.

When our tank was filled, Dave headed for the bar to find Eddie Norton, while I parked our truck at the side of the roadhouse. When I entered the lair of the Desert Fox I was certain for a moment that I'd been struck blind. After the harsh desert light the pitch blackness inside had me thinking of Saint Paul on the road to Damascus. In the past I'd occasionally had difficulties exiting bars, but never entering them.

"Over here, Jack. We're over here," echoed Dave's voice above the roar of the air conditioner.

"Keep talking," I replied, "I'll follow your voice. Are you blind, too?"

"Naw, no worries. You're headed in the right direction. Keep coming, we're at the bar. It's just dark in here," observed Dave, another flash of insight from the Master of the Obvious.

As my eyes gradually became accustomed to the darkness, I made my way toward the two figures on the other side of the room.

"Jack, this is Eddie Norton, the Desert Fox," Dave proudly announced, as if he had captured him in battle.

A figure in a rumpled shirt leaned forward on his stool and extended a bony hand. Though he had often tasted victory, it would have been unrealistic to have expected the Desert Fox to be wearing a smartly tailored officer's uniform or to possess the military bearing of a General Rommel. A tourist pamphlet describing the roadhouse operation had promised that "at odd times of the year Eddie Norton could be found breasting the bar." But who would have thought the statement was intended to have been taken literally? Despite the forewarning, it was still disconcerting to discover the legendary figure now sprawled across it and well on the way to becoming intoxicated.

"Would ya like a bloody beer?" snapped the Desert Fox. He himself was flushed with triumph, having annihilated the contents of the empty bottle in front of him.

"Wouldn't mind one at all," I replied.

I noticed that Dave was holding a bottle, too, and wondered what wiles the Fox had employed to get him drinking so early in the day. I glanced around the room and noticed dozens of torn shirt sleeves hanging from the ceiling. At the roadhouse, anything passed for humor: Travelers on their way through had been obviously so thirsty they'd given their right arms for a drink at Sandfire. In the dingy grottolike space, the smoke-blackened shirt arms resembled flying foxes hanging from the roof of a cave.

It was only after much prompting that the Desert Fox agreed to relate some of the campaigns he'd fought in the effort to build his roadhouse. "Oh, shit," he grumbled, "the bloody battles I've 'ad with those politician bahstards. I started ta write a book about it, but the bloke editin' it told me I couldn' publish it or I'd be put in bloody jail. 'Ave 'nother bloody beer," he ordered, his speech becoming more slurred.

"None for me, thanks," Dave blurted out, almost before the Fox had finished issuing the command.

"Well, I'm gonna bloody 'ave one, an' so are you. The Desert Fox don't like ta drink alone. What's wrong wif 'im?" asked Eddie, looking at me and motioning toward Dave.

"I'm not sure," I replied, "but I think it's menopause. He's unfit to drink with men who've seen combat." Seeing that Eddie hadn't understood me, I added, "You know, the change of life."

"Bloody 'ell! A couple a' more 'ere," the Desert Fox shouted to the barmaid with the authority of a man accustomed to having that particular order obeyed.

Prior to opening the roadhouse, Norton had worked for the Main Roads as a laborer. "I liked it because I was out in the bush and away from people for a couple a' weeks at a go. I 'ad the time of me life 'ere, and reckoned it'd be a good place ta start a bloody roadhouse.

"When we first opened in 1970 we 'ad maybe one motor car a day through here. The Lands Department and the petroleum companies didn't think this was a viable operation. But I gut a leave of absence from the Main Roads and come down 'ere and pumped fuel out of forty-four-gallon drums for six months. The petroleum company didn't want to put bowsers in or spend a cent until they were sure the roadhouse was gonna make a go of it.

"It was remarkable 'ow word got around that ya could get supplies 'ere, and the place went mad. We 'ad our bowsers by then, and we were flat out every day. They come from everywhere, and I 'aven't been able to look back since. In the beginning we never 'ad air conditioners, and it was bloody awful. But afta we got 'em, there was even more customers."

One often told tale we'd heard about the Desert Fox involved this very ability to convert mishap into money. The country around the roadhouse was open range, and cattle would often wander onto the road. It was said that, in the early days, when the roadhouse first opened, if Eddie heard a passing trucker hit the brakes at night, he'd rush down the road, butcher knife in hand. There was no point or profit in letting freshly killed beef go to waste, leaving it to rot on the side of the road.

"I read somewhere that once you built this place, you felt you could hold your head up and be proud," said Dave. "Is that really true?"

"Well," answered the Desert Fox, barely able to raise his face from the bar, "there was ten acres of bloody red desert sand when I first come 'ere, and we were lucky ta find good water. Once ya know the right sort a' tree ta put in, they'll do alright.

"Yeah, I'm very proud," barked the Desert Fox, suddenly sitting bolt upright on his stool as if an artillery barrage had just jolted him awake. "If ya can grow a flower in the desert, you've done somethin', but we're gonna do even more. I'm up here now to talk to my boys about our plans. We're gonna extend this bar, put in a new dinin' room and more accommodation units. There's another roadhouse goin' in down the road, an' naturally, we gutta upgrade our services an' maintain our position."

As the Desert Fox revealed his grand design, he used his hands to elucidate some of the more elaborate stratagems he had devised. One thin arm of his had a bad scrape, and noticing it, Dave asked him if he'd been wounded in action since he'd come up to the roadhouse.

"Last night I was drinkin' a bit of Scotch whiskey before I went ta bed. I'm very partial ta Scotch whiskey," he confided in a hushed voice, "and I've got ta nibble at it now and then. On the way out, I ran into a bloody post and it knocked me down." Even a living legend, it seems, is sometimes vulnerable.

More vigilant today, the Desert Fox glanced swiftly from side to side to be certain there was no danger that he could be overheard. Then he leaned forward and confided in a whisper, "I'm not as fast on my feet as I used ta be."

Or as steady. Bidding us g'day, he staggered out the back and into the kitchen, shouting a booze-strangled order for a meat pie.

3

Jack and I left the Sandfire Roadhouse in the capable hands of its legendary owner, and as we drove south toward Port Hedland, I recalled a conversation we had had with Dame Mary Durack in Perth about her legendary grandfather, Patrick Durack.

In the 1870s, "droving" a huge herd of cattle before them, the Durack clan had crossed the Australian continent from Queensland to the East Kimberley, overcoming unimaginable hardships in the several years it took them to reach their destination on the Ord River. Patrick was a symbol of everything Australians valued, yet throughout his life he considered his feats insignificant compared to those of the early pioneers on the American frontier. Her grandfather, Mary Durack told us, was enthralled by the romance and excitement of America's Wild West. That he and men like him were so matter of fact about their own lives, she attributed, at least in part, to the lack of any Australian frontier literature, without which there was nothing to create myth and romance of their adventures.

In 1906 Patrick's son, Dame Mary's father, traveled to North America, where he sat around roaring campfires "out West" and thrilled to tales of "Slippery Bill from Mexico, Deadly Dick from Wyoming, and Slim from way down Montana." No doubt, said Dame Mary, these characters seemed colorful indeed to "the hard-living, hard-riding quiet men of the Kimberley cattle camps, in their strictly utilitarian stockman's garb." She doubted, however, whether "any outpost in the world could have claimed such an odd and interesting assortment of characters as the north of Australia knew at that time."

For many of them it was the last retreat from the law—and from society. They were the toughest stockriders in the world, whose adventures outdid the wildest fiction. "While their American counterparts galloped the prairies with swinging lariats, creating legends to delight the world, these men were content to ride on in obscurity, performing feats of bushmanship and triumphs of endurance." The Australian legends that did later arise extolled this very ability to survive hardships in a hostile environment, and to that extent, I suppose, the Desert Fox met the standard splendidly.

A few miles before Port Hedland we turned off the bitumen and on to the inland route to Marble Bar. The track wound through the scarred, oxidized-red ranges of the Pilbara, and its gravel surface, strewn with jagged chunks of iron that had bounced out of ore-laden trucks over decades of use, was as hard on cars and tires as the surrounding terrain was on the human spirit.

It had been worse in the old days when the track was first cut. "To top the hills," someone wrote, describing the trip in 1920, "it was necessary to push up gullies and racket over rocks and avoid hazards—a half-hidden pinnacle of stones that would stove in the sump, timber that would stake the tyres, tipped-up boulders that could smash in the differential, and a score of other threats." Perhaps things had improved since then, but the road was still considered one of the most destructive sections of mapped highway in the world.

The track followed the desert all the way south, and we covered the hundred miles in a little under three hours, with only one flat tire along the way. The road twisted its way through broken plateau country, past stunted gum trees scattered across a landscape of volcanic rock formations, thousands of millennia old. Small headstones marked solitary graves at infrequent intervals.

The starkness of the scenery reminded me of the mountainous terrain I had always associated with scenes of the Spanish Civil War, and I half-expected to see that Loyalist soldier, rifle in hand, emerge from behind the rocks to have his moment of death recorded by Robert Capa's camera. I remembered the letter Reg Durack had written to a friend when, as a young man, he had left the Kimberleys: "The north plays strange tricks with those who have dallied long with her."

But as we learned later from Stu Stubbs, an eighty-year-old metallurgist who ran the Comet Mine just outside Marble Bar, the ghost of World War II did indeed haunt those hills. Hangared in rocky revetments and concealed under spinifex-covered nets, hundreds of American bombers, B-24 Liberators, struck Surabaja and other enemy bases in Indonesia from camouflaged airstrips nearby. Squadrons of twin-engine Japanese "Betties" flew regularly over the area at high altitude, searching unsuccessfully for the airbase hidden in the hills. Residents of Marble Bar threw weekly dances for the American flyers and worked round the clock to repair the crippled planes that managed to limp home.

The sun had by now fallen low in the sky, and the rock faces of the hills and the dry gulches were ablaze with color—eerie shades of dark ocher-reds, mauves, browns, constantly changing. If the country hadn't been so desolate, it might almost have been possible to see some beauty in it.

We came over a rise, then around a bend, and there in front of us lay Marble Bar, looking as lost as Brigadoon. Its only street, a short strip of bitumen, was deserted except for a couple of aboriginals sitting idly on the grass of the median strip. Across the road from the service station was the only pub in town, the Ironclad Hotel. A dilapidated two-story wooden structure, it dwarfed the small stores that occupied the rest of the block.

The 357 people who called Marble Bar home took pride in its being considered "the hottest town in Australia," a title that may well have qualified it as the hottest town in the world. Founded in the 1880s as the center of the then productive Pilbara goldfields, it almost passed into oblivion when the gold supply dwindled a few decades later. "Pilbara gold-seekers paid dearly for their findings," wrote one historian of Western Australia. "Many died through malnutrition and epidemics, including smallpox."

Even its very name was a mistake—apparently some dazed fossicker had spotted a bar of mottled quartz, or jasper, gleaming through the water of the usually bone-dry Coongan River, at the site of where Marble Bar now stands, and he and everyone else in the vicinity wrongly assumed it to be marble.

"When we came around that corner and saw the town for the first time, we knew we were home," said Dawn Duffy, who had been living in Marble Bar for the past five years.

"That's what Al Capone thought when they took him out to Alcatraz," said Jack. I slammed the car door hard in the middle of his sentence to prevent Dawn from hearing the rest of it.

"When *we* came around that corner, we knew we had a flat tire," I said, laughing nervously.

With her husband running the service station, Dawn watched over the little office *cum* candy store out front. She also served as the self-appointed director and single staff member of the town's tourist information center, located in the store. She was a pretty woman in her early forties, and if she looked a bit haggard it couldn't have been from the demands of her work—the office/store/center she was tending was as deserted as an abandoned mine shaft.

"This is a wonderful place, and it has wonderful tourist potential," Dawn said. "It's so quiet. And it's the hottest town in Australia. We hold the record of a hundred and sixty consecutive days where the temperature went beyond one hundred degrees, and the highest so far this year was one hundred twenty-two in the shade. We make a point of publicizing that because people really like to rough it. They'll never admit it, but they brag about it when they get home. We had seven hundred tourists through here last year."

While her husband looked at our tire (it turned out to be tubeless, and a curious W.A. law prohibited him from patching it), Dawn handed us two keys and pointed toward a row of "tourist cabins" situated on a bare, pebbly knoll on the outer edge of town. It was a five-minute walk back up the hump-shaped main street to our lodgings for the night.

Marble Bar's tourist facilities consisted of an elongated rectangular wooden shack containing seven cubicles, each not much larger than a cramped outhouse. The building looked as if it had been moved to its present site from another location—some long-forsaken mine, perhaps—and dropped on top of a few carelessly positioned cinder block footings. The ramshackle shower and toilet facilities stood a few feet farther down the hill and were in better condition than the shack we'd be staying in.

I unlocked the door to Unit 3 (with a key that said Unit 5) and turned the knob to open it. It came off in my hand. The same thing had apparently happened to someone before me, because a jagged hole had been punched through the door, which allowed me to reach in and open it from the inside. Jack flipped the light switch by the door, bringing into play a single bare bulb that had been jammed into an old, shadeless floor lamp.

The dim bulb barely illuminated the dark walls and the pock-marked linoleum floor. Broken cobwebs were everywhere, hanging from the ceiling and clinging to the walls. A filthy red scatter rug covered the cramped space in the middle of what was intended as a double room, and two narrow cots, with yellow-stained mattresses that sagged like loosely strung hammocks, occupied the side-rear corners of the cubicle. Both the rug and the rest of the floor were littered with dry grass and twigs, which looked as if they had been lying there for years. A pair of torn curtains had fallen from the dirt-blackened window on the rear wall opposite the door and lay in a heap on the floor. A yellowish PATRONS PLEASE NOTE sign posted near the door asked that the room be vacated by 10 A.M., which struck me as the most superfluous request of all time.

Jack had been given the key to Unit 4, which we inspected by flashlight because by that time the fuses had blown. (Later we learned that the fusebox had been secreted away in Unit 2.) His cubicle was a perfect replica of mine except for one additional feature—a length of rope, which served no apparent function, dangled from the middle of the ceiling.

Jack studied it for a moment in silence, then turned to me and said: "You take this room. You can hang yourself when all else fails."

It was time to go for a drink.

The street was still deserted when we walked back into town at twilight. The entire population, it seemed, was crowded into the Ironclad Hotel, solemnly drinking itself into a stupor. It was just another day in Marble Bar.

The patrons at the Ironclad pub that evening eyed us distrustfully when we walked in and responded with only brusque grunts when I tried to strike up a conversation. It was as if they were acting out a tradition—the suspicious, tight-lipped gold miner had survived even though the mines themselves had not. "A gold mine is a hole in the ground with a liar sitting alongside it," said the most talkative of them, and I realized that we must have appeared to be claim jumpers.

The publican was not behind the bar, and neither was his wife. She had just suffered a miscarriage and had been taken to Perth to recuperate. Tending bar in their stead was a weathered, wasted-looking fellow, who introduced himself as Artie Boers, the boss's "offsider." In his employer's absence, he must have been confused as to which side of the bar he belonged on, because he was drinking almost as much as he was pouring.

A handwritten notice posted on the mirror behind the bar suggested that the pub was not as crowded as it might have been. *"These People Not To Be Served,"* it proclaimed, and like some hastily drawn warrant ordering a mass execution, a list of about ten names was scrawled underneath. Each was followed by a precise date, which according to Artie Boers signified the day each person's period of banishment was to end.

The list looked like a genealogical chart as most of the miscreants were members of an aboriginal family named Yuline. With one exception they had all been sentenced to varying terms of banishment—the single exception being Irene Yuline. For some unspeakable act that Artie would not reveal, the space after her name had been branded, not with a date, but with the words, *"Never to be served again, at all."* Since the Ironclad pub was the only game in town, that was the equivalent of capital punishment.

A doorway led into a large, unfurnished, cheerless room in the back, which in turn led into a smaller, brightly lit, and now empty dining room adjacent to the kitchen. We walked in and sat down at one of the tables, all of which were covered with plastic tablecloths. Ten minutes went by before a heavy, middle-aged woman with a sallow complexion came through the swinging doors from the kitchen and waddled toward us.

"I'll take yer order," she said, without much enthusiasm, "but I dunno when you'll get it."

"Will it be hours or days?" I asked, cheerily, knowing that for food, too, the Ironclad was the only game in town. She shrugged her large shoulders, handed us two grease-smudged pieces of paper that served as menus, and waited stolidly for our orders before returning to the kitchen.

Fifteen minutes later, when she came back with the silverware, she looked exhausted, and we invited her to sit down. "Take a load off your feet," was Jack's somewhat indiscreet way of putting it, and she did.

Elizabeth Elliott had lived in Marble Bar for four years. "When I first come 'ere I thought it was downright 'orrible," she said. "But after bein' 'ere awhile, it grows on ya. Now I wouldn't want ta be anyplace else."

Born in England into what she described as "a monied sort of family," Elizabeth had emigrated to Australia and become a naturalized citizen as an act of rebellion against her mother's snobbery.

"If she saw me workin' in a 'otel, she'd just about crown me, but never mind," she said. "I come ta Australia for the sake a' the children mainly. I could see more future for them 'ere than I could in England. I wanted them ta grow up with a much broader outlook than I ever 'ad, not mixin' with common people, which I think I've achieved.

"The get-togethers here are good," she continued. "Yer barbies an' yer socials. Like Jim's got a band comin' 'ere on Monday. Then we 'ave the Mrs. Australia Quest, and there's different functions goin' on fer that.

"And a' course, there's race weekend," she said, as if she had almost forgotten to mention the most important social event of the year. "A fair few people come up then. I couldn't say exactly how many but it's a fair few because we're usually flat out in the bar. That puts us on the map, it does."

It didn't take much to be on the map in Western Australia: To the east lay a vast expanse of desert, to the west more desert, then the Indian Ocean. The pronouncements of government surveyors didn't really signify very much in that part of the world, and we had learned not to put much faith in their interpretations. "A fuckin' dunny is worth a dot on the map out here," a ringer had said to us at Birrindudu, a cattle station in the Northern Territory so remote that even the mail plane had trouble finding it. Still, the cartographer's illusions served a useful purpose, for it permitted the residents of these greater nowheres to fix themselves in some comprehensible scale amidst the unrelenting emptiness of their environs.

4

The inland track we were following clearly delineated Western Australia's easternmost edge of civilization: Off to our left lay the continent's vast interior, the region early explorers had referred to as "the ghastly blank," where frightful sandstorms could blow for days at a time. Since we had only one spare tire left my heart went into my throat each time we hit an outcrop of razor-edged rocks on the track south to Nullagine. But Dave seemed unconcerned as ever, and as we bounced over the corrugated surface, trying to stay ahead of the talcumlike cloud of dust that pursued us, he pored over the RAC Touring Guide, intent on gleaning something useful from it. Despite my protestations, I had little choice but to listen while he read the blurb on Nullagine aloud:

"Nullagine. Postcode 6758. S.T.D.091 [Subscriber Trunk Dialing, though some Aussies contend the abbreviation stands for Sexually Transmitted Disease.] A pleasant small town on the Nullagine River 296 km south east of Port Hedland. The town owes its existence to the discovery of gold in the 1890s. By 1904, there were eight batteries in the area crushing gold ore. Although some gold is still being recovered, the mineral potential of the Nullagine district is just beginning to be tapped. The variety of ores in the area which have been mined or have potential is nearly unlimited and includes an almost complete alphabetical listing from asbestos to zinc.

"Points of interest for the visitor include Lookout Hill which offers an excellent view of the town and river. Beatons Rockhole and Gorge where gold is found and the gorge scenery alone is worth a visit. The old mines throughout the area are of interest and fossicking for gemstones can be most rewarding.

"The Chinese Walls located in the gully to the north side of the lookout are believed to have been built by Chinese at the turn of the century as a method of sluicing gold. These walls, built of stone and quite extensive, have not been found elsewhere in the Pilbara."

Despite the Tour Guide's promises, Nullagine was hardly pleasant. Lookout Hill was a mound of rocks, and naturally, the "river" it overlooked was dry. And while Marble Bar may have boasted of being the hottest town in Australia, Nullagine couldn't have lagged far behind.

"Too hot even for the blackfellas," said the barkeep at the Conglomerate Hotel, the only pub in town. He was right—the only aboriginals we saw were a few small groups lying prostrate under the ragged gums that lined the river's banks.

The following day we pushed on to Newman, 125 miles farther south, passing a junction with another dirt track, that ran west to the iron mining communities of Wittenoom, Tom Price, and Paraburdoo. The town of Tom Price was named after the man who accidentally found a mountain of iron ore while flying his light plane off course to avoid a thunderstorm. That occurred in the early 1960s, and presumably much remained to be discovered in that empty country. The Kimberley diamond deposits, after all, had been found only as recently as the 1980s.

Occasionally another vehicle approached from the opposite direction. Long before it appeared, we could see a cloud of dust rising in its wake—the signal to roll up our windows. We'd wave as we passed each other, just before being enveloped in the swirling cloud. I'd hit the brakes to slow down, because for a few long seconds afterwards, until some of the dust settled, we couldn't see a thing in front of us.

It was a great relief when we picked up the bitumen in the mining town of Newman, located in the Opthalmia Range at the foot of Mt. Whaleback, which "had once been a prominent landmark." Whaleback was now a source of iron ore, which was sent over a 275-mile company-owned railroad to Port Hedland on the coast. Proudly proclaiming that the mining would cease only when the mountain had been reduced to a gaping hole in the ground, the Tourist Guide, which Dave had resumed daily readings from as if it were his breviary, was at such a loss for anything else positive to say about the place that it ended with the following observation: "It is perhaps interesting to note that a phone call between these centers"—Newman and Port Hedland—"is classed and charged as a local call."

Just south of Newman we fueled up at the Capricorn Roadhouse, our next stop being Meekatharra. We passed through a town called Kumarina without even realizing it. The Great Sandy Desert had by this point become the Gibson, but it all looked the same to me. Off to the right rose the Collier Range, and we soon noticed a beat-up wooden sign with an arrow on it, indicating the direction of Mt. Augustus. Peter Eaton's monolith stood over 150 miles away, down a narrow, unused track to the west. We didn't take it.

Not much could be said about Meekatharra except for the fact that its name was thought to have derived from an old aboriginal word meaning "place of little water." In the old days, Meekatharra had been possessed of only one well with which to water its population. When Daisy Bates requested a bath when she passed through in 1904 before settling on the Nullarbor, she was met with the outraged response: "Such a thing as a bath is not known in Meekatharra."

We had planned to find a restaurant in Meekatharra for dinner that evening, but the petrol station owner advised against it. "There's nuthin' much here, mate," he said as I paid him. "You'd be better off trying the Murchison Hotel in Cue. It's only another fifty miles down the road." By now we'd come, like the locals, to regard a distance of fifty miles as insignificant.

5

In 1891, a prospector named Tom Cue scratched 140 ounces of alluvial gold out of the ground in an area called "the patch," and the town of Cue was born. Shortly afterwards, another prospector named Edward Heffernan pegged out a reef less than two miles south of Cue, which he called Daydawn. Like Kalgoorlie and Boulder, Cue and Daydawn became "sister towns," growing up side by side in the feverish burst of activity that followed. Over the next two-and-a-half decades the Murchison goldfields (named for a riverbed that started north of Cue and ended at a point on the coast about halfway between Geraldton and Useless Loop) produced over 1 million ounces of gold.

In its heyday Daydawn boasted seven hotels and even a soft-drink factory, but now nothing remained except the old mine registry, the ruins of the post office, and the empty shells of a few other buildings. Like many country towns in Australia, it had never recovered from the effects of World War I, when most of its diggers—the town had a population of 3,000—joined the army at the outbreak of hostilities. Ironically, Daydawn's gold mining enterprise was run by a German-owned company, the Great Fingall Consolidated, which closed down during the war and never resumed operation.

Cue, on the other hand, had managed to survive. Though its population had declined to a mere handful of people, many of its fine old buildings remained intact. A panoramic photograph dated 1897 hung in the shire council chambers, and it showed that the town was then much as it is today.

On the morning after our arrival at the Murchison Hotel Dave and I walked around its deserted streets. Under a vivid blue sky the town was bathed in bright sunlight. Cue was surrounded by a flat, red desert that extended in all directions as far as the eye could see. Only occasionally was the landscape broken by a few low shrubs and scrub trees.

The streets themselves were lined with wonderful houses—some frame, some red brick, some weathered granite, taken from a small quarry near Cue—most of which had been abandoned. In their varying states of disrepair they reminded me of the old Conch houses I had once restored in Key West.

The Masonic Lodge, like an austere Victorian spinster, stood alone on the edge of town, at the corner of what had once been Robinson and Dowley streets. Built in 1899, it was a two-story, box-shaped structure with a curious-looking turret over a small colonnaded balcony in front. Not far away, a low iron fence enclosed an old frame church with a steep roof of rusting corrugated iron and a row of five lancet-arched stained-glass windows.

Austin Street was the main street of Cue. Once a wide thoroughfare, it was now divided by a median strip planted with trees and well-tended grass, though not a soul or vehicle was on it. At the center of town the median held an octagonal band rotunda with a white filigree railing. Built in 1904, it marked the site of the first well in Cue with the inscription: "With waterbag and pick they conquered an inhospitable desert and carved out happy and prosperous towns."

Only a handful of Austin Street shops were still in business. Most of the establishments had corrugated-iron overhangs that extended to the curb and shaded the sidewalks, while the larger, two-story buildings, like the long shut down Cue Hotel, featured wrought iron–laced verandas that served the same purpose. The original sign over Bell's Emporium had faded, but its green lettering was still visible: MERCERY. CLOTHING. DRAPERY. BOOTS & SHOES. And a sign on the pub door of the Murchison Club Hotel read: JUNE DORSETT LICENSED TO SELL FERMENTED & SPIRITUOUS LIQUORS. There had once been fourteen hotels in town; the Murchison was the only survivor.

Further down Austin was the two-story Gentlemen's Club, of which Herbert Hoover had been president when he was a mining engineer in the Murchison goldfields. Built of a rough, reddish stone called porphyry, the impressive fortresslike structure, which was completed in the late 1890s, extended membership only to mine managers and technical experts, most of whom were Americans and Englishmen. It, too, had been closed for years.

We had dinner that night at the Murchison Club Hotel—the only game in town, but a far cry from the dingy Ironclad Hotel in Marble Bar. The Murchison had been beautifully restored by its current owner, and its dining room was elegant in a homespun, frontier way. The hardwood tables in the high-ceilinged dining room were covered with linen tablecloths and set with pewter plates, silverware, and crystal glasses. The room was filled with antique furniture, much of which, including an old oak sideboard standing against the far wall, had originally belonged to Hoover. Some fine China service was displayed on a hutch standing near the door to the kitchen. The only other guests were two young surveyors from Perth, working on the Gentlemen's Club restoration project.

June Dorsett, the Murchison's owner, joined us for coffee after dinner. Slightly past middle age, she was still a very handsome woman—a strong woman, too, if perhaps a little on the hard side in a bleached blond sort of way. She and her husband had come up from Perth and purchased the run-down Murchison twenty years earlier. "Buying a hotel in a ghost town was cheaper than buying an empty lot in Perth," she explained.

A few years after moving to Cue, she divorced her husband, who "was spending too much time on the wrong side of the bar," but June didn't seem to find sole responsibility for the business a burden. "It's quiet here," she admitted, "but I love it. When it's your own place, you want to keep it nice, like your own home. People say, 'Fancy leaving all those expensive things about in a hotel, you should put them away.' But I enjoy seeing them there and I reckon others do, too. Nothing's ever been stolen."

June invited us for a drink at the bar. The pub had its usual share of rough-looking Saturday night characters—local fossickers, aboriginals, and a few ringers from the surrounding stations—but I was struck by the fact that, unlike so many other bush pubs we'd seen, the atmosphere in the Herbert Hoover Bar was positively sedate.

"You seem to have put your stamp on this place," I commented to June.

"You noticed, did you?" She beamed proudly. "Patrons have to behave in a one-hotel town. If they don't, I just cut off their drink—for the night, or longer. And it's easier because I'm a woman. A man tends to lose his temper when he's dealing with a mob of drunks. You have to be firm, but if you scream and yell, naturally they object. I wouldn't have had a fight in here for years."

In his short story "Your Turn," D. H. Lawrence tells the tale of a collier who frequents a Welsh pub where the publican is a woman. She rules the establishment with an iron hand, admitting only those patrons who meet with her approval. Lawrence would have admired June Dorsett, as I did.

The Australian bush was "man's country," a factor that contributed potently to its myth, but to a large extent it was women who, following their men into "voluntary exile," as Dame Mary Durack once phrased it, had made the savage land habitable. Prospectors and early stockmen were content to set up rude tents near the soaks or simply throw their swags on the ground under the stars. It was only when they were joined by their women that a station became a home, a ragtag cluster of humpies became a town. By coming out to this ghost town in the middle of the desert and transforming a derelict building into a fine old hotel, June Dorsett was carrying on a time-honored tradition.

We left Cue and drove straight through to Perth, past New Norcia, where—from the outside, at least—nothing seemed to have changed. We returned the Toyota to the rental agency—caked with red dust, its original color was indiscernible—eager to begin the next part of our journey. Ahead lay Queensland, Cape York, and the remote territory around the Gulf of Carpentaria. W.A. had been billed as "wild" country—but apparently it was tame compared to the places we now intended to see, places even Aussies feared to tread.

5

To the Top of Australia

Top of Australia

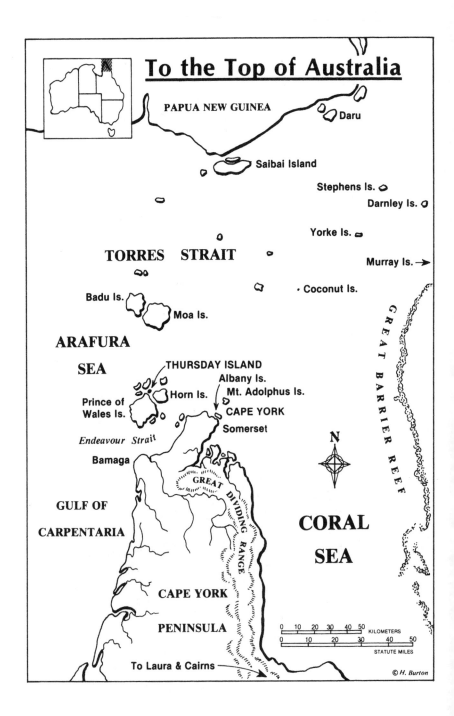

1

Early one sunny June morning, after an uneventful two-thousand-mile flight across the Great Victoria and the Simpson deserts—the cratered, utterly desolate heartland of the Australian continent—we found ourselves on the northeast coast of Queensland, in the small city of Cairns. Facing out on the Coral Sea, with the Great Barrier Reef close by, Cairns was known as the marlin fishing capital of the world, for each year from September to January schools of giant black marlin, some weighing well in excess of a thousand pounds, migrated offshore, and an international elite of big-game trophy hunters swarmed to the town in the hope of doing battle with them. For us, rather less glamorously, Cairns was merely a jump-off point for the second leg of our journey.

Most Australians regarded Queensland almost exclusively in terms of its billing as the Sunshine State, a paradise of beaches and beauty. Its populous, often crassly overbuilt eastern shore, particularly "the glittering mecca of the renowned Gold Coast" near Brisbane and the so-called Barrier Reef resorts farther to the north—many of which were in fact over fifty miles from the reef itself—attracted droves of retirees, surf bums, and honeymoon couples. But we were heading north and west, to the sparsely settled interior of tropical Queensland and the virtually unexplored coast along the Gulf of Carpentaria, extending from the swamplands at the tip of Cape York, where the

Indian and Pacific oceans met, to Arnhem Land in the Northern Territory, which was off limits to all but aborigines.

These remote parts in and around Queensland's deep north were rumored to be even wilder than the Kimberleys and, hard as it was to believe, to contain a host of even more eccentric characters. If Western Australia evoked images of the Wild West and the Dakota Badlands, Cape York and the Gulf were imbued with the mysterious, almost primeval aura one might associate with the farthest reaches of the Amazon. Indeed, with nothing but a single dirt track pushing through to the tip of the Cape and only a few stretches of bitumen connecting several small settlements in the Gulf, these areas, especially during the Wet, were often cut off from the rest of Australia for weeks, if not months, at a time.

We intended, of course, to continue our quest for *Crocodylus porosus* in Queensland with the same lackadaisical zeal that had characterized our efforts in Western Australia. But we had long since sent an apologetic postcard to our editor friend at *Audubon*, explaining that inasmuch as the people we'd been meeting were so much more appealing than the reptiles, the original point of our trip had to some extent fallen by the wayside. In short, we had shifted our primary focus from the crocodile itself to that inscrutable breed of Australian who had chosen to share its habitat. There were reputed to be plenty of those in Queensland.

Cairns itself, and its environs, had changed rapidly in the past several decades. In 1915 a newspaperman for the Cairns *Post* had written that the area was better suited to "Chinamen and coloured men . . . as it needs people with nerves, if they have any at all, like number eight fencing wire and a hide like an alligator as no white man could stand what the Chinaman has to stand and it will be a sad day for civilisation when he will stand it." Until the early 1960s, when it was "discovered" as a marlin hotspot, the town had quietly aestivated under the tropical sun, content as a sleepy little community overlooking Trinity Bay, fringed by fields of sugar cane and a range of lush green hills, which extended inland a few miles before giving way to the Atherton Tablelands.

A few of the town's old colonial "Queenslander" houses still remained. Ranging from simple cottages to stately mansions, they were wide verandaed structures, with latticed sides and cast-iron balustrading, elevated on stilts to take advantage of even the slightest breeze. The tree-shaded Esplanade had once been lined with such homes, but most of them had been torn down, bulldozed and replaced by high-rise hotels, condominiums, and fancy restaurants. What had once been cane fields were now suburbs, filled with residential homes and shopping centers for the town's burgeoning population, which was approaching 40,000.

The gracious old Hides Hotel, a rambling two-story Victorian building, had in colonial days catered to plantation owners on their way to and from New Guinea, and was something of a local landmark, standing in the center of town at the corner of Lake and Shields streets. Now it was flanked by a concrete mall, surrounded by fast-food shops and stores selling souvenirs imported from Asia and partially obscured from view by a newly constructed outdoor stage, where amateur rock musicians performed for passing tourists. Cairns had adopted some of the most garish features of American urban development, and the place was beginning to take on the appearance of a miniature Miami Beach. "You can't stand in the way of progress" was the attitude of many Cairns businessmen and politicians.

But in addition to the glittering holiday world of the big-game fisherman and tourist, there was another side to Cairns. The rough bars along Wharf Street catered to a different kind of clientele. By ten in the morning, the Australia Hotel pub and others like it were already providing refuge from the tropical sun to tattooed fishermen and deckhands off the prawn boats. Shirtless wharfies and their burnt-out, only slightly more attired sheilas, some with diapered children in tow, were swilling beer at the bar and, over the blare of the jukebox, shouting obscenities at their mates who were slouched around the pool table. No flashy brochures promoted this part of town, and as far as the local tourist board was concerned, it didn't exist.

2

A friend of ours at Qantas had put us in touch with Paul Phelan, special projects manager at Air Queensland in Cairns, who he promised would be able to show us the "Top of Australia," and some of the offshore islands as well. Paul offered to get us on a flight to some of the atolls in the Torres Strait, which I had always wanted to visit. As an enthralled boy I had pored over books like Nordhoff and Hall's *Mutiny on the Bounty,* and Joshua Slocum's *Sailing Around the World Alone,* and it had long been a dream of mine to visit some of those places whose very names seemed synonymous with adventure. Paul would then arrange to meet us at the tip of Cape York when we came in from Thursday Island and the Strait. Since the flight went out only on Wednesday, we had a day to kill, and asked Paul for advice on the area's attractions. Noticing that Dave was limping slightly from an arthritic hip, he told us about a fellow in a town south of Cairns who was on to a new arthritis remedy and suggested that we might want to meet him.

We drove south through peaceful green cane fields until we came to the dilapidated warehouse to which Paul had directed us. As we walked toward the building a door opened, and we were eagerly greeted by our host, Sam Brent, a short, stocky man with a half-smoked, unlit cigar clenched in his teeth. We followed him briskly to his office where he poured us a "cuppa" before plopping down at his desk. Sam sighed heavily, as he shook his head from side to side.

"It's hard ta believe that three months ago I couldn't get outta this chair," he began. "This is how I used ta hafta do it."

Clutching the chair's arms tightly with both hands until his fingers turned white, he slowly pushed himself up out of the seat. As he rose, Sam grimaced to demonstrate how excruciatingly painful the effort had once been, and when he finally regained his feet, he stood there frowning.

"Before I started taking Ocean-Care," Sam related, "that's how I used ta have ta do it." He paused for a few moments, allowing us time to reflect on the severity of his former condition.

"Now, watch me," Sam instructed as he sat down again. This time, he bounded up immediately, without any difficulty and without using his arms. To demonstrate that it was no fluke or trick, he repeated the performance, then struck a dramatic pose and smiled with satisfaction.

Though both Dave and I were quite impressed, we remained slightly skeptical. Sam's remarkable recovery may have been nothing short of miraculous, but we could not, after all, overlook the fact that he was the managing director of a small Queensland company that marketed the lowly sea slug, or bêche-de-mer, in large red capsules that were promoted as a remedy for arthritis, impotence, and assorted other ailments and afflictions.

"Don't just take my word for it," insisted Sam, as if he were anticipating our thoughts. "Take a look at some of these." There was a bounce in his step as he strode over to a battered file cabinet and handed us a sheaf of letters.

They were, on closer inspection, letters—testimonials from satisfied users. All were quite similar in content and most had been scrawled in barely legible handwriting. They proved to be reports from elderly people who had been cured by the product in a very short space of time. Former invalids attested to feeling years younger, and invariably, they'd thrown away their canes or crutches. One eighty-seven-year-old woman even claimed a dual benefit from using the product. In a neatly typed note she had written to say that all symptoms of her severe arthritic condition "had vanished after taking Ocean-Cure for less than a month." Gone was her walking stick, and so pleased was she with the results that she decided to share the experience with her aged German shepherd.

According to her letter, the animal suffered from a rheumatic condition and pain in its hindquarters. After administering the dog several doses she realized that "the effect of Ocean-Cure was fantastic as he lost his stiffness and became extremely active and playful."

"It sounds like the stuff can transform old dogs into puppies," said Dave, returning the letter to Sam. "You could peddle it to pet shops and call it Ocean-Dog. But is it Ocean-Cure? I thought it was Ocean-Care?"

"Oh, we had a bit of a problem with the damn government and the Department of Health," admitted Sam. "They misunderstood our intentions and thought we were claiming we could cure arthritis. They made us take the word 'cure' off the label, so we ended up calling it 'care' instead. All we had to do was change one letter and we were able to use all the old bottles," he boasted, proud of his economical use of the alphabet.

"But that's all behind us now," he added, obviously wanting to close the subject as quickly as possible. "Come on, lemme give yez a tour of the plant."

As he led us out of his office, we ran into a tall, dark-haired fellow he introduced as Malcolm Brown, the director of marketing, who according to Sam had been a very successful solicitor in Sydney before coming aboard.

"Pleased ta meet yez," shouted Malcolm. "Have yez heard about Ocean-Care?"

"Yes, we have," I replied, resigned to the fact that we were about to hear more, whether we wanted to or not.

"The Chinese have used bêche-de-mer for centuries as an aphrodisiac, and it's real good for that, if ya know what I mean," said Malcolm, with a lascivious wink. I realized the wink was a tic when it was repeated three or four more times in rapid succession. "But we're interested in promoting some of its other benefits."

"Don't knock the sex part," cautioned Sam, shaking his head from side to side and giving us a meaningful look to indicate his personal satisfaction with Ocean-Care on that score. "Lemme tell ya."

"That's just more frostin' on the cake," agreed Malcolm, with a smirk and a few winks. "But if ya've gut arthritis or rheumatism, this stuff is definitely gonna help ya. Even the Arthritis Foundation is interested in it." As Malcolm spoke, he glanced back nervously over his shoulder from time to time, as if he were expecting a bailiff or constable to come up from behind and apprehend him.

"We'll show ya the laboratory, but put these on first," ordered Sam, as he handed us soiled white paper hats he took from a rack outside the door. "Fa hygiene."

Sam unlocked the door and led us into the poorly illuminated room where, if their claims about Ocean-Care had any basis in fact, medical history had undoubtedly been made. The laboratory looked as if it had been set up by a scientist who belonged in an old B-movie. Scattered around a long counter were empty bottles and beakers, a Bunsen burner, and assorted pots and pans. An old coffee-making machine stood next to the sink, its glass pot streaked with dark brown stains. Off to one side was an inexpensive plastic microscope that might once have belonged to a child's chemistry set. The only object in the laboratory that looked as though it had been used recently was the coffee maker.

"What sort of research do you do in here?" asked Dave.

"Oh, a little bit of everythin'," answered Malcolm.

"Who's been trained as a chemist?" I asked, determined not to let him off so easily.

"Oh, Sam's been mucking about with bêche-de-mer research for years," replied Malcolm.

Over in one corner of the room sat a cot where I presumed any experiments relating to the aphrodisiacal properties of bêche-de-mer were likely to have been conducted. Sam walked past it to a large object covered with an old sheet, which he pulled back with a two-handed flourish, dramatic as a matador working his cape. At first I thought he had unveiled a work of avant-garde sculpture, for before us sat a bizarre-looking mechanical contraption whose arms gave it the appearance of a robot.

"What the hell is that?" muttered Dave, as Sam and Malcolm gazed at it in admiration.

"Our first capsule-packing machine," Sam announced solemnly, his tone implying that we would do right to regard it as we would the first telephone or the original IBM machine.

"But if ya think *that's* somethin', wait until yez see this," he said, leading us through a door into another room at the center of which stood the big brother of the machine we had just seen. Clattering loudly, it was belching large red capsules out of a spout and into a rusty barrel. The machine's operation was being monitored by a disheveled attendant. Not only was he wearing a filthy paper hat like ours, but he was dressed in a white surgeon's robe splotched with grease and a gauze surgical mask. At this stage in its manufacture the dried bêche-de-mer had been finely pulverized, and a cloud of powdery brown dust enveloped the room as the clanging machine crammed it into capsules.

"Why is he dressed like a doctor?" asked Dave.

"When ya manufacture a product like this ya want the most sanitary conditions possible," replied Malcolm, brushing the dust off his white shirt as we left the room.

The tour of the entire plant didn't take long, as the building was little more than an oversized garage. When we'd concluded it, Sam led us back toward his quarters.

"Don't forget ta put the hats back on the rack," he instructed. "We gotta maintain quality control."

On the wall of Sam's office hung a large map of the world dotted with colored pins. When I examined it more closely, I noticed that a bright red pin had been driven deep into the heart of Newark, New Jersey.

"What have you got against Newark?" I asked.

"Oh, nothin'," replied Malcolm, "we're just keepin' track of Sam Junior's round-the-world promotional sales trip. We mark every spot where he sets up a distributorship and makes a sale."

"We're international now," added Sam, beaming with corporate and paternal pride.

"The Odyssey of Young Sam," I observed. "It looks like he's been practically everywhere."

"Every continent except Antarctica," said Malcolm. "That boy's makin' a lotta sales and friends for Ocean-Care wherever he goes. Pretty soon we're even gonna come out with moisturizin' cream for the skin."

"Why don't cha give 'em a sample ta try," Sam suggested. Malcolm left the office, returning a few moments later with two small, unlabeled jars.

Dave removed the cover from his and examined its mud-brown contents. "Jesus, that's got a terrible odor," he observed, as he screwed the top back on tightly. "Who's going to put something like that on himself?"

"Yeah, bêche-de-mer really stinks," admitted Sam. He turned to Malcolm and chided him, "I told ya it was still no good. We can't even give it away like that. It's alright in the capsules cause it's dry," said Sam, directing his attention back to us, "but we're havin' a bit of trouble gettin' the cream ta smell good. It's a lot better now than it used ta be."

"We've been conductin' research on it in the laboratory. That's why we haven't marketed it yet," related Malcolm, pausing a few moments for greater emphasis. "We're a young company with a very high reputation, so we don't wanna come out with a new product until we're sure we got it just right."

3

Armed with a complimentary six-month supply of Ocean-Care, we took off the next day as guests of Sunbird Air, a small local airline servicing the remote islands in the Torres Strait. The pilot, a boyish-looking fellow of twenty-five, wearing shorts, white knee socks, and a baseball cap, told Dave he'd been flying for over six years, and he did indeed handle the craft as confidently as a seasoned veteran. The twin-engine Otter flew low over the Coral Sea and as the Great Barrier Reef edged closer to the coast in its northward thrust, the reef clusters gave way to continuous ribbons broken only by narrow tidal channels.

The Great Barrier Reef covers an enormous area, extending off the coast of Queensland from its southernmost outpost at Lady Elliot Island almost one thousand five hundred miles north to the Gulf of Papua, where fresh water and sediment from Papua New Guinea's Fly River prevent reef formation. The reef itself is composed of several thousand individual reefs, seventy of which have formed vegetated coral cays, flat islands slowly rising out of the sea, and 540 high continental islands closer inshore. Most of the tourist resorts are located on the continental islands, and visitors usually get to see only the fringing reefs nearby, rather than the more spectacular ones farther out to sea. Near Mackay in the south the reef reaches slightly more than 150 miles offshore, but from Cairns northward, where the continental shelf is narrower, it swings much closer to the mainland. Our flight to the Torres Strait took us over five hundred miles of reef and alternating emerald-green, turquoise-blue sea before our destination, Yorke Island, appeared as a green speck on the horizon. A few minutes later we landed on a narrow grass clearing in a grove of coconut palms and Australian pine. The island was 3,100 feet wide and the airstrip used every inch of it.

Yorke had been settled by "Yankee Ned" Mosby in the 1870s, and most of the island's present-day inhabitants claimed to be his descendants. Mosby was an American sailor believed to have been born in Baltimore in 1840. Making his way to Sydney on a Yankee whaler, he jumped ship and was soon master of his own lugger, working the rich reefs of the Torres Strait for mother-of-pearl, bêche-de-mer, and hawksbill turtle. He must have been a powerful man because he hunted that now nearly extinct turtle, whose only commercial value lay in its shell, with a heavy, solid iron harpoon over eight feet long. After running off with an island woman named Queenie, he settled on Yorke.

In the course of expanding his business, Yankee Ned began westernizing life on the island, even engaging the services of a European teacher for its school. In later life Yankee Ned was badly injured by a stingray. His leg became infected and had to be amputated in the hospital at Thursday Island. Hobbling around in the tropical climate on his wooden peg leg, wearing a white beard, a black cowboy hat, and a necktie, he was known to everyone on T.I., where he died in 1911.

In the week or so we spent on Yorke Island we were to meet many of Yankee Ned's descendants. For lodgings we had a two-room, kerosene-lit hut, taking our meals at the home of Mrs. Billy, a smiling, brown-skinned woman in her late forties who was Ned's great-granddaughter. There were only two dirt streets on the coral cay, and the bungalows along them stood on stilts and were painted in a variety of light pastel colors. While the houses had no lawns, the sand in their front yards was neatly raked and planted with a brilliant assortment of hibiscus, crotons, and blazing bougainvillaea.

The two hundred-odd residents of the island were devout Christians, and various religious articles ranging from crucifixes to statues were prominently displayed in every home. Before the "Coming of the Light," a euphemism for the introduction of Christianity in the Torres Strait in the early 1870s, the islanders had been headhunters and cannibals, and even a century later they still held some of the animistic beliefs of their New Guinea ancestors. The fearsome Puri-puri spirits, which were thought to roam the islands after dark and do harm, were warded off by keeping houses always brightly illuminated, and by carefully disposing of fallen strands of hair and fingernail cuttings, lest they fall into the hands of the evil ghosts. At the same time, however, the islanders reveled in "scary videos," which they watched almost exclusively, and calmly tolerated the ghost of Yankee Ned, which haunted Yorke but was considered to be a good ghost.

One evening we visited Uncle Elda Mosby, the village headman, and the only living grandson of Yankee Ned. Until a few years ago he himself had been master of his own pearling lugger, the *Maria*. A lithe, muscular man, he was bald except for a few wisps of gray hair around the temples, and though seventy, he appeared younger and carried himself like an athlete. A pair of horn-rimmed glasses sat atop a broad nose. Sporting a white mustache, he looked distinguished in his orange lava-lava, which also served as a sail if the motor failed when he was out fishing. Uncle Elda spoke in a soft voice, gesturing freely.

"De Torres Strait Islanders," he boasted, "are de highest colored race in de world. Do you know dat? I feel really sad I couldn' live in my grandfather's time. If I bin alive in dose days, I coulda helped de change ta European ways. Now we half and half—not one ting or the other. In de old days we hab our gardens and ate our island dishes. Dis social welfare bizness, when tings cum easy, people get lazy. Now we eat what dey gib us and we all got diabetes."

Uncle Elda complained that the young people on the island were on welfare, and didn't have to work. The Commonwealth Department of Aboriginal and Island Affairs had established a fish-packing plant on Yorke, but only a few of the older islanders did any fishing. He himself still fished to "show da people how ta work fer money" because "dey don't know action of de word 'work.' Dey gut no discipline."

His nephew, Joseph Mosby, the head of the Yorke Island Council, had been approached by outsiders interested in developing tourism on the island. Joseph had been lured into supporting their proposal, but Uncle Elda, who had very little use for his nephew, remained strenuously opposed.

"Yorke still place of love an' I worry tourists cum an' spoil dis island. I bin lookin' what happen ta neighbors like Tonga an' Fiji. When I need tink, I make my tent down dere on de beach. I hear dat wave cum in and go back, an' I listen ta de water's language. I listen ta dat well. De waves gut a lot ta say. Tourist pella only want money. Dere eye tell me, dey no speak me true."

Before we left Yorke we wanted to pay a visit to the disputed fish-packing plant, and a few days later arranged to meet with the young Australian couple who ran it. Like missionaries, Ross and Dale Gardner were optimistic about prospects for engaging the islanders in productive activity, but they had been on Yorke for well over a year and were still doing most of the work themselves. Of the island's entire population the Gardners had managed to persuade only six to return to their traditional livelihood, at least on a part-time basis, to provide the plant with fish to process. Even then, the cost of the fuel they used in their government-provided aluminum dinghies far exceeded the value of the catch.

The Gardners took us for a walk around the tiny atoll, pointing out sights as we made our way along the beach. I was struck by their determination to carry on toward a seemingly impossible goal. Having given up secure positions on the mainland with the Queensland government, they had left behind family and friends to come out to Yorke in search of a "challenge." At one point, on the far side of the island near an old stone church, they stopped and suggested we turn back.

"We only walk half the island on Saturdays," explained Dale. "That gives us something to look forward to on Sundays."

4

The following day at midmorning we took off for Thursday Island, which at one time was the administrative center for all of North Queensland as well as the Torres Strait Islands. The pilot had neglected to refuel from the forty-four-gallon drums sitting along the runway, and shortly after reaching altitude he noticed that both of the plane's fuel tanks were reading empty. He banked the craft in a 180-degree arc and headed back to Yorke. By the time we had set down on Yankee Ned airfield, it was clear from the fuel gauge and the beads of perspiration on the pilot's face that we had been flying on little more than fumes.

When we departed again it was with another passenger, a school-teacher on her way from Sabai, an island just off the Papua New

Guinea coast on her way to T.I. "Yorke, Sue, and Darnley are friendly places," she told Dave, as we flew over the latter, a volcanic, high land island. "Some islands aren't so congenial. There's thirty people on Stephens, all named Stephens and all related, but half of them don't speak to each other. One's even changed his name to Clouty and moved off on his own to another island." Our fellow traveler's story put me in mind of what Somerset Maugham had once written about the area: "I wish I could feel it reasonable to tell here the story of the hermit I went to see in the Torres Straits, a shipwrecked mariner who had lived there alone for thirty years."

After an alarmingly bumpy landing on Horn Island we took a ferry across the channel to Thursday Island. Like Darnley, T.I. was a volcanic island and had no room for an airstrip. Though one of the smallest of the Prince of Wales group—only two miles long and one mile wide—it figured prominently in South Seas lore. As we stepped off on the ferry dock I was eager with anticipation, for here was one of those magic places that had so fired my imagination when I was a boy.

Captain Bligh had named nearby Wednesday Island when he passed through the Torres Strait in 1789 on his voyage to Timor after the mutiny aboard the *Bounty*. Owen Stanley, captain of the *Rattlesnake*, which charted the same waters in the late 1840s, followed on the theme by christening other islands in the group Tuesday, Thursday, and Friday. (To the present Thursday Island he had actually given the name Friday, and vice versa, and who bore responsibility for later changing it remained locally a matter of talmudic debate.)

In 1877 the Queensland government established Thursday Island as the major European outpost and port of call for ships plying the route between Sydney, Asia, and Europe. At that time it was described as a "corrugated iron, goat-infested island," but it sufficed as a site "where Courts of Petty Sessions shall be holden." By the end of the nineteenth century T.I. had managed to grow into a thriving community, with a population of over 2,000, and to become a vital contributor to the Queensland economy, exporting pearl shell valued at over £100,000 sterling a year and showing handsome profits from bêche-de-mer, as well. The pearling industry attracted fortune seekers from the world over, and created a multiethnic society that seemed to represent nearly every race in existence.

During T.I.'s heyday in the early decades of the century it boasted seven two-story, wide-verandaed hotels which served pearlers from outlying islands, sea captains, and passengers off incoming and outbound ships. On his round-the-world voyage aboard the *Spray*, Joshua Slocum had dropped anchor there, and so had Zane Grey, Douglas Fairbanks, Somerset Maugham, and a host of other South Sea Islands adventurers. In the Thursday Island Hospital visitors' book, we found an entry in Maugham's own hand which read: "15/7/21, W. Somerset Maugham, [residence] London, [remarks] On record." But we were unable to locate the "record."

Perhaps the most prestigious of the island's guests, however, were the Torres Strait Pilots, a select band of master mariners licensed to guide ships through the treacherous Strait and beyond. The stretch of water the service covered constituted the longest pilotage in the world: A single pilot would guide a vessel over a route that extended more than seventeen hundred miles. (The Mississippi was in fact a longer piloting route, but it was handled in sections.) In 1901, Banjo Paterson, the author of "Waltzing Matilda" and Australia's most famous balladist, was so inspired by their feats of seamanship that he wrote an appreciation of a typical pilot:

> His appearance is not aggressively nautical, though he is a man who has served his time to that hard mistress the sea; usually he is dressed in shore-going clothes, having discarded the blue coat and brass buttons when he gave up his command and joined the Pilots' Association. And the passengers on the deep sea ships that come down our coast, not understanding why there should be a pilot on board when the vessel is at sea, often think that he is a friend of the captain, traveling for pleasure. But there is not much pleasure about his voyaging, for he is one of the hardest-worked and best paid of all men that follow the sea for a living.

The Torres Strait Pilots were still a vital force on the maritime scene one hundred years after their founding and we were fortunate enough to find lodgings with them in their shuttered residence on John Street. Like the Pilot Service itself, the house was over a century old but wore its age lightly. It was an informal place except at mealtime, when the daily "captain in charge," who was responsible for determining the menu, presided over the table with a regimental precision befitting an admiral's mess. Because there were seldom more than three or four pilots in residence at any one time, though, we were able to dine leisurely. Food was prepared and served by two Thursday Island women, Big Nora and Little Nora, and brought to us at a magnificent jarrah table under an old brass ceiling fan. The dining room itself had hardwood tongue-and-groove planking on its walls as well as on the eighteen-foot-high ceiling. A portrait of Queen Elizabeth hung surrounded by framed photos of famous ships.

The rich history of the pilots was on display in every corner of the room. A coral-encrusted cup and saucer, salvaged from a famous wreck in the Coral Sea and presented to the Pilots by the diver who recovered them, sat enclosed in a glass case under a barometer, presumably as a reminder of what happens to ships who failed to use the services of the Torres Strait Pilots. A number of copies of *Blackwood's* magazine were stacked on a table in the adjacent sitting room, where we enjoyed a glass of port after dinner each evening. The choice of reading was appropriate, for it was in *Blackwood's* that Joseph Conrad, whose ship had passed this way before running aground in Tasmania, was first published.

Like Conrad, the Torres Strait Pilots had worked their way up the naval chain of command to become masters of their own ships. But they had surrendered that privilege to join the elite Pilots Service, and in so doing may have lost more than merely the honor of a title. They had to spend long stretches at sea piloting ships belonging to other captains, and the ones we met seemed lonely and, in some cases, distant men. One reason for the pilots' dissatisfaction may have been the changing nature of their work. Some even believed that sophisticated electronics and navigational equipment had made their skills unnecessary. "These days any good second mate could bring a ship through the Torres Strait," one of them had said over beers at the Grand Hotel. "Our Pilot Service is as useless as a black stump. The only reason it's still in business is that there are no good second mates around."

Yet shortly after we left T.I., the 12,000-ton Korean freighter *Maritime Hibiscus*, which had no pilot aboard, struck a reef in the Torres Strait in the middle of the night. Loaded with grain, the ship had left the port of Newcastle just north of Sydney bound for Penang. There was great concern lest an oil spill from the ship's ruptured fuel tanks cause serious damage to the Great Barrier Reef. The incident served to reassure me that, for the moment at least, technology alone was no substitute for a master pilot.

During our stay on T.I. we often took walks around the languid town, lulled by its melancholy air. Along the empty main street a few shops struggled, selling an assortment of imported shell jewelry and cheap souvenirs, even though tourists had long ago stopped coming to the island. Most of the old hotels had burned down, though a few, like the Federal and the Grand, still survived. Both had seen better days, and at the Grand we had to walk around a section of rotting floor on the veranda to get into the musty bar.

Further along the main street was an open-air movie theater, enclosed by a faded blue wooden fence. In the past few years videos had come to T.I. and put the cinema out of business; now it, too, was slowly disintegrating. We wandered around inside, where old film containers and movie posters lay strewn around the floor of the projection room in the covered balcony section.

Walking up Douglas Street we passed a greasy take-away, a small, shabby open-stall market, a couple of boarded-up shops, and a government Labor and Welfare Office, on our way to see Gwen Maloney, a small half-Irish, half-Filipino woman who was a lifelong resident of T.I. Gwen ran the island's newspaper, the *Torres News*, and as we sipped tea with her, she recalled her childhood, and how she'd seen Douglas Fairbanks come ashore from his yacht. She now lived in a cramped apartment above a used furniture store where, with the help of a native island woman and a few Indian ladies in saris, she put together the weekly newspaper using some ancient printing machinery. She told us that the entire civilian population of T.I. had been hastily evacuated in 1942, and that when the government allowed them to return after the war, the fine home in which she had grown up was in ruins.

"The soldiers wrecked everything," Gwen said sadly. "And after we came back the big steamships didn't stop here anymore and the pearling was finished. I guess you could say time just passed us by."

The following Sunday morning, Jim Mort, a whimsical sixty-year-old Torres Strait pilot who resided in Sydney, took us to see an Australian-rules football game which, despite the oppressive tropical heat, was played with a vigor and intensity that would have thrilled even Vince Lombardi. Watching the players run and tackle each other with reckless abandon, then get up for more, I could understand why Thursday Islanders had such a reputation for endurance. In the early 1900s they had been especially sought after as workers to help build the railroad lines across the Nullarbor and through the desert to Alice Springs.

After lunch that day, Jim, who was president of the Thursday Island Historical Society, suggested we climb Green Hill to see the fort at its summit.

"We have two hours between tea and dinner," he said. "That'll allow us three times around the island."

The concrete fort had been built in 1891, at what must have been an extraordinary expense and effort, to protect the settlement from an anticipated Russian invasion, which of course never came. British Field Marshal Kitchener (of Khartoum fame) visited the installation in 1909, and recommended additional fortifications on nearby Goode Island as well. But the garrison was disbanded in the 1920s without ever having fired a shot in combat.

Clambering down a hill on the other side of the island, we stopped in a rambling cemetery crowded with tombstones. After locating the grave of Yankee Ned, Jim pointed out the headstones of others whose names and exploits were part of T.I.'s rich history. It was not so long ago that T.I. had been an extraordinary place—a far-flung outpost where adventurous souls had dropped anchor, lured by dreams of empire, riches, and who knows what. One could still picture how life must have been like then: heading for the Grand Hotel after coming ashore at the crowded jetty to drink and swap yarns with pearlers, pirates, and seamen off ships from all over the world.

But today little remains on Thursday Island, and its rickety hotels are patronized mostly by islanders on the dole or by fishermen passing through on their way to the Strait or the Gulf of Carpentaria. Few people reside there now, most having left permanently for the mainland after the government closed down everything but a few essential services. T.I., once fondly referred to by its habitants as their "beautiful island home," is slipping into oblivion.

5

The next stop in our itinerary was Cape York—the Top of Australia— by way of Bamaga, where Paul Phelan, a giant of a man with a bantering wit, was already waiting for us on the tarmac. Before leaving Cairns we didn't have the opportunity to thank Paul properly for putting us in touch with Sam and Malcolm, and to show our appreciation Dave planned to share his supply of Ocean-Care with him. Air Queensland had leased the Cape, the northernmost point on the continent, and since Paul was the airline's special projects manager, he had invited us along to show us the site where he planned to develop a wilderness lodge.

Our flight to Bamaga should have been a quick shuttle across the Endeavour Strait, but we were delayed for hours when the airstrip there flooded during a torrential downpour. The Wet was supposed to be over, but since the Dry hadn't yet commenced, more rain was expected: The deep north should by all rights have had a third season called the Damp. When we were finally able to step aboard the plane, it was like taking a trip back in time. The aircraft was one of the ancient DC-3 "Gooney Birds" Air Queensland still had in service. Bamaga airfield had been hacked out of the jungle by the Americans during World War II. A base for bombers, the field was once the jump-off point for the short run across the Torres Strait for strikes against the Japanese in New Guinea. Before the airstrip was built, the area contained nothing but virgin bush. Bamaga itself dated only from 1946, when Sabai Islanders were moved to the mainland from their overcrowded home off the Papuan coast.

The sweltering midday heat struck us as we stepped off the DC-3, and a hazy sun struggled to emerge through the mist that rose from the sodden earth and the dense tangle of forest surrounding us. The morning's rain lingered in the torpid air, and our light garments were immediately drenched with perspiration as we walked the short distance to Paul's vehicle. We threw our gear into his four-wheel-drive and began the trip up the Cape.

The country around Bamaga was hilly, and after the Wet, its vegetation was lush and green. The track we were driving wound through stands of tropical rain forest and tall bamboo thickets. Overhead, satanic-looking flying foxes clutched the lofty branches of towering trees, hanging upside down until twilight, when they'd wing off into the night. Occasionally, wallabies foraging along the edge of the track darted off into the bush, startled by our approaching vehicle. As we neared the tip of the Cape, Paul turned off on a trail that led to Somerset, which at one time was a government outpost.

Cape York, Paul told us as he negotiated the increasingly narrow road, was a haunted place. Ever since Europeans first set foot there in 1623, it had been the scene of killing and violence. First the Dutch and then Captain Cook were attacked by the local aboriginal tribes, and except for the land directly on the coast, the region remained largely unexplored.

In 1848, however, a determined explorer named Edmund Kennedy decided to lead an expedition up the peninsula to Albany Island, through country Europeans had never seen before. As the Kennedy expedition struggled northward, it was ambushed repeatedly by aboriginal tribesmen, to the point that most of the party grew so weak they could go no farther. Eight men had to be left behind at one of the camps, where they quickly perished.

The other five trudged on toward the Cape, but soon only Kennedy and Jacky Jacky, his black tracker, had the strength to continue. Within fifty miles of Albany Island, where a ship was waiting, the aborigines launched their final attack. Kennedy was fatally wounded when he was speared in the back. Jacky Jacky was also injured, but managed to hide Kennedy's journal and make his way to safety, the only survivor of the disastrous expedition. Kennedy's mortal remains were never recovered. "I've little doubt that he was eaten by the aborigines," one local historian maintained.

The Kennedy debacle, dramatic as it was, only set the stage for the Jardine expedition, one of the most remarkable episodes in the history of pioneering, but, curiously, one with which few Australians are familiar. The story seems to have been swallowed up by the Cape York wilderness, as if the events had never occurred:

In the years following Kennedy's death, a Marine garrison had eventually been established on the mainland opposite Albany Island. The post was named Somerset, and John Jardine, the son of a Scottish baronet, was appointed magistrate there by the Queensland government.

Heedless of the fate that had befallen Kennedy, Jardine's twenty-two-year-old son, Frank, decided to drive a herd of cattle up to Somerset from Rockhampton, about twelve hundred miles to the south on the Queensland coast. In 1864 he headed north with his younger brother, Alex, a band of four aboriginal stockmen, and four Europeans, all armed with breech-loading rifles. The group planned to follow a route farther west than Kennedy's to avoid the rough country he had encountered. They set out with forty-one horses and 250 head of cattle.

The ten men were soon attacked by more than eighty aborigines in a pitched battle on the banks of the Mitchell River. Using their superior firepower and aided by the speed of their horses, the Jardines were able to drive the aborigines back into a swamp and cut them to ribbons. Not a single member of the Jardine party was wounded.

As the band made its way up the peninsula through the trackless forest, the aborigines abandoned direct frontal assaults and resorted to guerrilla tactics. But Jardine and his men were skilled bushmen and made of sterner stuff than the indecisive explorers who had gone before them. With the aborigines in pursuit, they fought their way across crocodile-infested rivers and mosquito-ridden swamps until, finally, in March 1865, they limped into Somerset without having suffered a single fatality. With all of their horses dead, they were forced to walk the last three hundred miles on foot. They had lost only fifty head of cattle.

Later the same year Frank Jardine led a punitive expedition against the fierce headhunters of Badu Island in the Torres Strait. The tribe was ruled by a mad white man—Wini, "the wild man of Badu"—who incited them to murder the survivors of shipwrecks. Only a few Badu Islanders escaped Jardine's wrath, and Frank himself personally killed Wini with a single shot from his Terry carbine.

From that moment on, Frank Jardine's name struck terror into the hearts of Torres Strait Islanders and mainland aborigines alike. In fact, some historians claimed that the "Coming of the Light" was due more to the natives' dread of Jardine than it was to the work of the missionaries.

When his father retired, Frank Jardine assumed the post of magistrate and spent a great deal of time fighting the Yardigans, an aboriginal tribe so large it could field over three thousand warriors. To deal with them, Jardine replaced the Marines, who had ineffectually clumped around in the bush wearing red uniforms, with his own Queensland Native Mounted Police. On one occasion, when two of these troopers deserted to the local aborigines, Frank arranged to have them betrayed and captured, and then rode out to where they were being held and personally shot them both in the head.

Jardine envisioned Somerset as a "New Singapore." Cape York was, after all, much closer to Asia and Europe than was Melbourne, Sydney, or even Brisbane, and he hoped to see his father's settlement grow into a major trading port. But because the waters around the outpost were constantly buffeted by the prevailing southeast trade winds, the place proved to be unsuited for a port. It eventually degenerated into a collection of ramshackle hovels and wild policemen, and in 1877 the magistrate's office was moved to Thursday Island.

Still, Frank Jardine was "sung to the land" and could not bring himself to leave. He was thirty-seven years old and no longer working for the government. He purchased the Residency, which rested on top of the hill overlooking Albany Pass, and there established a copra plantation and a pearling fleet.

Old photographs show the Residency as an imposing mansion, surrounded by a sweeping veranda. Dignitaries off passing ships, pirates, and "blackbirders" (traders who brought indentured labor from the South Sea Islands down to the cane fields of Queensland) all came ashore as Jardine's guests, mixing freely in the estate's huge ballroom and dining like royalty on heavy silver plates.

Jardine married a Samoan girl he claimed was a princess. If you're going to sleep with a gin, went an old Australian saying, she'd best have royal blood; Frank evidently believed that the adage applied to islanders, as well. He died at Somerset in 1919, and his Samoan princess followed him four years later. They were buried side by side in now-vandalized graves overlooking the sea.

Standing on a windswept hill beside those graves, we found it difficult to believe that Somerset had ever existed. White ants had long since obliterated the last vestiges of settlement, and the land had reverted to a desolate wilderness. Each day the encroaching bush reclaimed more of the clearing where Somerset once stood, obliterating the last vestiges of Frank Jardine's empire.

6

As we left Somerset and continued on toward the top of Cape York, a few scrub cattle on the track ahead of us bolted into the forest at our approach. They could well have been the wild descendants of the herd brought up by Frank Jardine.

"I haven't been up here for a while, and I'm not sure what we're gonna find," said Paul, just before we arrived at the end of the track, where he told us a wilderness camp had been established on the site at which the lodge would eventually be built.

"What do you mean?" said Dave. "That's not the way you were talking back in Cairns. I thought you had everything organized?"

"No worries, I do. But I can't vouch for the bloke up here. Besides, I wanted company. No one from the office is foolish enough to come up here, so I invited you two.

"I really don't know what ta expect. I thought the last caretaker I left up here was doin' a great job 'cause I talked ta him on the radio every day. 'No worries,' he'd tell me, 'everything's fine.' They probably were, 'cause there's nothin' ta do there. I guess things were goin' along so good that he had a bit of time on his hands, and he decided to take a little drive over ta Thursday Island."

"You can't drive across to T.I.," interrupted Dave, wondering if he had heard right.

"You know that, and so do I." Paul laughed. "But he was a bloody Kiwi, ya know, from New Zealand. They don't see things the way other people do. They think they can do anything. They're gonna take the Russians on with sticks and rocks, aren't they?

"The Kiwi drove the truck on the beach at low tide and got stuck in the sand. No worries, he was a resourceful bloke or he wouldn't be workin' for Air Queenie. So he went up to get the backhoe and pull it out. Of course, that gets stuck down there too. In comes the tide an' that was the end of 'em. He must 'ave been in the grip of the grape. Pity there was nothin' else ta drive, 'cause he could have taken that down there too.

"I'm hopin' the chap I got ta replace the Kiwi isn't as imaginative as his predecessor. He used ta be a London bobby. There's nobody ta arrest up here, so he's probably finding things a bit slow. Of course, he has ta be a little crazy ta spend the Wet up here in the first place, but he's probably alright 'cause he's got his wife with him if he needs someone ta talk ta."

Ernie Pullen evidently wasn't satisfied with just his wife as an audience, because after we arrived in camp, he talked almost constantly. An emaciated-looking man in his late forties, he preferred monologues to conversation. Even had she wanted to, his wife, Joan, a frail, harried woman, couldn't have gotten a word in edgewise, but she didn't appear to be interested in talking at all, or, for that matter, in listening to Ernie. After years of married life she had devised an ingenious way of ignoring him: Whenever he spoke to her, she would continually nod her head in agreement, and every so often mumble, "Yes, dear."

Ernie and Joan had come over from England only a few months earlier. Paul had met them in a Cairns pub, and when he discovered they were looking for a job "out of the rat race," he pounced on them, and the following day the Pullens were shipped off to Cape York. "I can't say ya won't see any rats up there," Paul had told them, "but if ya do, I can promise ya they won't be racin'." When they finished up as caretakers for the Air Queenie project, which could conceivably take years to complete, the couple planned to buy a caravan and travel around Australia.

The entire camp consisted of four tents—three for sleeping, and the fourth serving as kitchen and storeroom. Life in a caravan would have to be a lot more comfortable than in the small tent in which they were currently sheltered. A rude outhouse, or dunny, stood close by. Paul and Ernie had constructed a primitive dam in the rocks on a hill, and water was pumped up to it from a well they'd drilled down below. A length of black plastic pipe ran down from the dam, supplying the camp, but if the Pullens needed hot water for bathing or washing dishes, it had to be heated on the wood-burning stove. Except for the few hours at night when it was shut down, a diesel housed in a tin shed a couple of hundred yards away clattered incessantly.

Paul and Ernie led us up a steep hill past the dam, onto a large outcrop of sandstone rock high above the sea and overlooking Cape York. Directly below us, the Coral and the Arafura seas collided like two titans locked in a colossal, ceaseless struggle for supremacy. The powerful surge of their currents created whirlpools as they clashed, which went spinning off to dissipate in eddies.

The Australian continent and Papua New Guinea had once been linked by a landmass that had gradually sunk into the sea. The resulting expanse of water became the Torres Strait, and all that remained of the original land bridge was the chain of tropical islands we had just visited. Far off, almost imperceptible in the distance, was Thursday Island.

A few hundred yards to the right, rising abruptly out of the water and buffeted by the wind, were the craggy Mt. Adolphus Islands. An unmanned beacon sat high atop the crest of the largest. In 1890, a terrible shipwreck occurred in the waters directly below us when the steamship *Quetta* struck a submerged rock in the Adolphus Channel and sank with the loss of 133 lives.

In 1770, Captain Cook sailed through the same channel aboard the *Endeavour.* Captain Bligh followed in 1789, sailing the longboat in which he was set adrift after Fletcher Christian had seized the *Bounty.* Bligh managed to pilot his overloaded vessel across the Arafura and Timor seas in an epic feat of seamanship and navigation. He later became governor of New South Wales, ending his tenure as an object of derision when he was found hiding under his bed during an insurrection.

We made our way back down the steep hill toward the white sand beach on the Gulf of Carpentaria, which stretched to the southwest as far as the eye could see. Paul cautioned us to keep a wary eye for amethyst pythons, which lived in holes around the rocks and often reached lengths of twenty feet and more. Snarled vegetation crept beyond the edge of the dank forest down onto the beach, burying roots deep in the sand. Tall mangrove trees with delicate white blossoms and dark green, waxy leaves swayed gracefully in the wind. All along the shore wafted the sickly sweet odor of decaying sea grapes, which had dropped from their branches high above and littered the sand. Closer to the water, legions of fiddler crabs darted in and out of holes as we passed.

A mile or so down the beach was a tidal river that ran into the Gulf.

We followed it into the canopied forest until we came to a crocodile slide on a muddy bank between two spiderlike mangrove roots. The sight convinced us we had explored far enough, at least in that direction.

"Any barramundi here?" asked Dave hopefully. I'd anticipated the question even before he knew he was going to ask it. An ardent fisherman, Dave was determined to catch at least one of the elusive gamefish, which inhabited the waters of northern Australia as well as those of Papua New Guinea. Accomplishing that feat would lend some credibility to a magazine piece he planned to write.

"Oh, yeah," came the predictable reply from Paul, lapsing momentarily into his role as tourist promoter. "They're all over the place."

As we retraced our steps along the Gulf I stepped up beside Ernie, and asked him what he did to occupy himself when Paul wasn't around. A frown came to his brow as he pondered the question, and then he replied, "I watch this."

"Watch what?" I asked, confused by his answer.

"This," he repeated, and made a sweeping motion with his arm that encompassed all of the vast wilderness. He spoke with the same air of proprietorship and heavy responsibility that he would have used were he back in his London precinct.

It was early evening, and the sun was slowly sinking into the Gulf. The tide was out, exposing a wide expanse of beach. The mirrorlike surface of the water—flat calm, because it was the lee shore—was broken only by the occasional feeding fish. On the way back to camp we startled some wild boars foraging at the water's edge, sending them crashing into the bush.

Ernie decided on chicken stew for dinner, and we sat around in the kitchen tent while he and Joan prepared it. Paul unpacked a bottle of Scotch, pouring a large quantity into each of the four tin mugs he set on the table. Joan had declined a drink.

"Help yourselves," Paul urged us. "There's plenty more where that came from." It had begun raining outside, as well as turning chilly, and we didn't need much persuasion. The whiskey warmed me and left me a bit light-headed, since we hadn't eaten anything in hours.

The stew was delicious, and it seemed to taste even better in the setting. Rain was pelting hard against the tent's canvas, accompanied by a gusting wind that moaned as it swept through the trees, lashing branches and leaves. During the meal Paul told us jokes in Pidgin English, including one about a fisherman. At that point Dave tried once again to raise the subject of barramundi, but I managed to forestall that conversation by bribing him with my dessert. After pouring himself another drink, Ernie related that a few days earlier he had killed a large python, which had taken up permanent residence in the dunny.

"Any poisonous snakes on the Cape?" asked Dave, cramming the last of my canned peaches into his mouth.

"There's five species of snakes up here that are deadly," Paul informed him. "And three of 'em will strike if ya shine a flashlight on them. They like ta come in out of the rain and sleep under cots—especially the death adder. Common as flies they are, we see quite a few of 'em. Wear boots if ya get up or have ta leave the tent at night."

Our bush dinner party continued far into the night, and later, Paul broke out another bottle of Scotch. Both Dave and I were far too courageous and experienced bushmen to be worried about something as trivial as a snake. No doubt Dave took further comfort in my assurances that if we encountered one, I'd pick the reptile up and toss it into the bush. Curiously though, after we'd turned in that evening, neither of us left the safety of our tent again until morning, a remarkable display of self-control considering the quantity of beer and whiskey we'd drunk.

The morning we left Cape York to catch the return flight from Bamaga, heavy rain squalls moved in from off the Strait. The track was still muddy from the previous rains, and we sloughed through it splashing red muck in all directions. About two miles out of camp we approached a dip in the road that was flooded with standing water. Paul pulled off the track, veering sharply to the left, and drove into the scrub to avoid it. But the Toyota suddenly struck a patch of deep mud that dragged it slowly to a stop even as Paul floored the accelerator. He shifted into four-wheel-drive and tried to pull out, but we only bogged deeper.

Ernie took the wheel and the three of us got out to push. We immediately sank into mud up over our ankles, and could hardly move. The suction of the muck clinging to our boots retarded every step and made pushing the vehicle impossible. Paul sloshed around to the front of the Toyota and unwound braided steel cable from a winch attached to the bumper. He secured it to a melaleuca tree, but as he engaged the winch to haul us out, a pin in the clutch snapped, rendering it useless.

With the driving rain stinging our faces, we tried digging out with the shovel kept in the rear for such emergencies, but the soft mud gushed into the holes made by the shovel as fast as it was removed. Paul must have noticed the worried expressions on Dave's face and mine, for he assured us that this sort of bogging was a commonplace in the bush, and easily enough remedied. Calmly, he chopped some branches from a tree with a machete, and placed them under the wheels for traction, but the tires spun them out as soon as the wheels began to turn. Our drenched clothing was by now steaming, and a mist rose from the ground as if it were a primeval swamp. We scurried back into the Toyota to give some thought to our predicament. Our breathing fogged the glass, obscuring our vision, but it hardly mattered because the rain was coming down in sheets, hammering on the metal roof and beating a tattoo against the windows. Paul decided the only solution was to make his way back to camp and get the backhoe to haul us out.

During the hour or so he was away, Ernie regaled us with stories about his days as a bobby. To our relief he was finally interrupted by Paul's noisy return. The backhoe headed directly toward us, and we watched with disbelief as it, too, got bogged in the mud, sinking in deeper as its huge tires spun around, throwing out streams of mud behind them. Paul shut off the engine, and jumped down, joining us again in the Toyota.

"That bloody Kiwi should see me now," he said. "He'd get a real hee-haw out of this."

If we missed our flight out of Bamaga, there wouldn't be another one for two days. Even though we still had plenty of time to make the plane—we'd left camp early because we had planned to stop and have a look around Lockerbie, an abandoned cattle station once owned by Frank Jardine—Dave and I couldn't help but be anxious. Paul himself had to get back to Cairns that day, as he was flying to Sydney the following morning. Being an executive of a small airline had certain advantages, and he considered walking back to camp again and arranging to delay the flight. He thought better of the idea, though, when it occurred to him he could call in a helicopter from Thursday Island to pick us up. It was just as well he didn't have to, for, as we discovered later, that very afternoon the helicopter crashed into the sea.

Just as Paul was preparing for another hike back it stopped raining, and in a few short minutes the spongy earth soaked up much of the water. We dug holes around all four wheels and stuffed branches in front and behind the tires. With Ernie driving, and with the three of us pushing, the Toyota jerked, roared, and finally with a great heave climbed out of the pit and slogged back on the track.

Ernie stayed behind to attend to the backhoe, and we raced on to Bamaga. We just made the flight, boarding the otherwise empty plane in wet, mud-splattered clothing. As the DC-3 climbed into the sky and headed away from Cape York toward Cairns, Paul leaned across the aisle.

"Maybe that Kiwi wasn't mad after all," he muttered, wiping the dirt off his face with a towel. "After I fired 'im, he told me ta shove my bloody wilderness camp. He couldn't wait ta get back ta the rat race."

6

The Gulf of Carpentaria

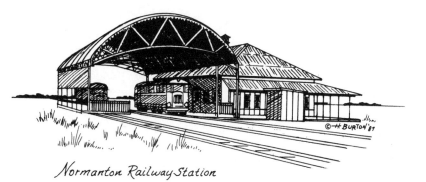

Normanton Railway Station

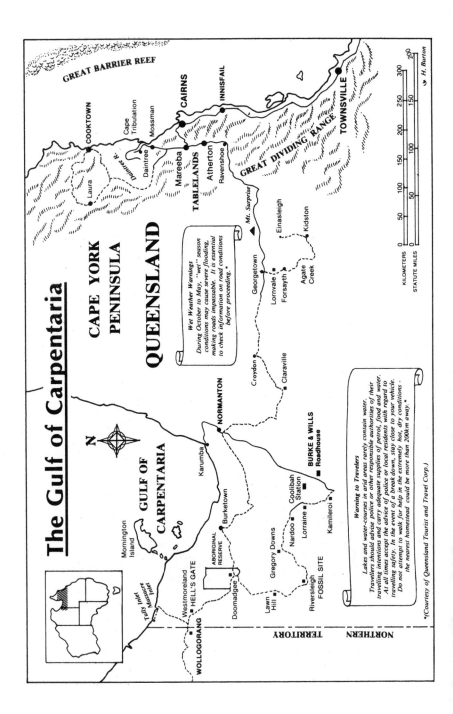

The Gulf of Carpentaria

GULF OF CARPENTARIA

CAPE YORK PENINSULA

QUEENSLAND

GREAT BARRIER REEF

Wet Weather Warnings
During October to May, "wet" season conditions may cause severe flooding, making roads impassable. It is essential to check information on road conditions before proceeding.

Warning to Travelers
Lakes and water-courses in arid areas rarely contain water. Travellers should advise police or other responsible authorities of their travelling intentions and carry adequate supplies of petrol, food and water. At all times accept the advice of police or local residents with regard to travelling safety. In the event of a break-down, stay close to your vehicle. Do not attempt to walk for help in the extremely hot, dry conditions - the nearest homestead could be more than 200km away.

(Courtesy of Queensland Tourist and Travel Corp.)

COOKTOWN
Cape Tribulation
Daintree
Mossman
CAIRNS
INNISFAIL
Mareeba
TABLELANDS
Atherton
Ravenshoe
GREAT DIVIDING RANGE
TOWNSVILLE
Laura
Daintree R.
Mt. Surprise
Einasleigh
Kidston
Georgetown
Lornvale
Forsayth
Agate Creek
Croydon
Claraville
NORMANTON
Karumba
Burketown
Kamileroi
BURKE & WILLS Roadhouse
Coolibah Station
Nardoo
Lorraine
Gregory Downs
Lawn Hill
Riversleigh FOSSIL SITE
Doomadgee
ABORIGINAL RESERVE
Westmoreland
HELL'S GATE
WOLLOGORANG
Mornington Island
Tully Inlet
Massacre Inlet

N

NORTHERN TERRITORY

KILOMETERS 0 50 100 150 200 250 300
STATUTE MILES 0 50 100 150 200

H. Burton

1

After Thursday Island and Cape York, Cairns no longer seemed so laid-back a town. The women on the streets wore fashionable tropical clothes, the stores were full of merchandise, and the weekends were enlivened by a Saturday morning flea market. There were even laundromats, where ersatz bushmen like us could wash our clothes, and coffee shops that served croissants.

We hadn't come back to enjoy the amenities of the city, however, but to meet a friend who was flying in from the States to join us. Before we had left Cairns for the Torres Strait Islands, Jack had called his buddy Phil Caputo in Key West. Jack's boat was still in the water—he hadn't expected to be in Australia this long, nor had I—and he wanted Phil to take it out.

One would have thought that a Pulitzer Prize–winning journalist and author of two best-selling books had better things to do with his time than scratch around in "the back of beyond" with two fishing mates. But Phil had just finished a novel that had taken over four years to complete, and was in the mood for a bit of a holiday. He had been planning a trip out west, but his phone conversation with Jack fired his imagination about Australia.

"Thursday Island, boy—pearlers, blackbirders, Somerset Maugham!" Jack enthused. "Too much for you to handle. I'll tell you all about it if I ever come back."

Phil was quickly hooked, but Jack, who couldn't resist having a little sport with Phil any more than he could with me, had only begun to play him. "The Outback's too rugged for you, boy," he insisted. "Dave and I are heading out through Queensland to the Northern Territory. Out to the Gulf of Carpentaria, one of the wildest places in the world. Man-eating crocodiles and the deadliest snakes on earth. Some pretty tough blokes, as well. *Real* men. You're better off in Montana, Phil. Stick to playing cowboy with McGuane on that dude ranch of his."

That did it. Phil promised to call the next day to tell us when he'd be arriving in Cairns.

"Good," said Jack, before putting down the phone. "We'll take you to see some dwarf throwing."

There was a pause.

"No, no, don't worry," said Jack to the new recruit. "You're fifty pounds overweight and at least two inches too tall."

There were four of us now—Phil, Jack, me, and John Barlow, the Bushranger.

Jack and I had met the Bushranger at the Blue Marlin pub in Innisfail, a quiet coastal town south of Cairns, on our way back from what Jack had taken to calling "the Ocean-Scam factory." Nothing much could be said about Innisfail except that it was in the heart of sugarcane country and had the highest rainfall in Australia—over 400 inches a year.

John had recently returned from a long stint managing a copra plantation in Papua New Guinea, and though he was trained as an accountant, he was hoping to get into something that would keep him out of an office. He loved the bush and had spent a lot of time in northern Queensland, particularly in an area known as the Gulf Country, collecting freshwater tropical fish from creeks that flowed into the Gulf of Carpentaria. (A vast tract of wasteland stretching, roughly speaking, from the western slopes of the Great Dividing Range all the way to the N.T. border, the Gulf Country was now somewhat predictably being billed by the Queensland Tourist Office as the state's "newest holiday star.") Before that he had worked as a stockman on the Tablelands, where his thick, reddish-blond beard had earned him the nickname Bushranger, a term that in Australia's early days was applied to outlaws like Ned Kelly. John was no outlaw, but he certainly was a free spirit, and we left promising one another to link up again sometime in the future.

The Gulf of Carpentaria

After Phil arrived in Cairns and we had mapped out a tentative itinerary, we decided to drive back to Innisfail and discuss our plans with John. As it happened, the Bushranger himself was at loose ends for the next few months, and when he heard where we were heading, he asked to throw in with us. But why bother hiring a four-wheel-drive in Cairns, he asked, when his own was gassed and ready to go. More to the point, it was equipped with an extra fuel tank, an emergency radio, and an electric icebox to keep the beers cold. That settled it— we'd be glad to have him along. With his Irish wit, his passion for everything Australian, and especially his icebox, John would be welcome company on the dusty track to Carpentaria—"Australia's Outback by the sea."

2

The southeasternmost corner of the Gulf of Carpentaria lies about three hundred miles from Innisfail as the crow flies, a route just slightly shorter than the so-called Gulf Development Road, a sinuous, only intermittently sealed highway. Running across the foot of the Cape York Peninsula, the Development Road affords the most direct route to the Gulf Country. Still, we chose not to take it, for with the rainy season over, there was no need to stick to the beaten path, as we had had to do through much of the Kimberleys.

We decided instead to zigzag our way toward the Gulf of Carpentaria and the Northern Territory, ranging first north, then south on a generally westward drift, a bit aimlessly, perhaps, but with the intention of spending the last few months of our journey seeking out the most isolated human haunts we could find. They were there to be found, but not without a certain degree of determination. Still infused with the lessons he had learned as a young marine lieutenant in jungle-warfare school, Caputo had brought along his compass, and as soon as he arrived in Cairns he had plundered a large bookstore of all its relevant maps and charts. Printed on each of the maps in bold red letters were the following *"Warnings"* (interspersed with a number of others that were equally ominous but applicable only during the Wet):

Tracks to homesteads and outstations are subject to frequent change.
Creek crossings are generally unimproved and often difficult to negotiate.

Lakes and water-courses in arid areas rarely contain water. Travellers should advise police or other responsible authorities of their travelling intentions and carry adequate supplies of petrol, food and water. At all times accept the advice of police or local residents with regard to travelling safety. In the event of break down, stay close to your vehicle. Do not attempt to walk for help in the extremely hot, dry conditions—the nearest homestead could be more than 200km away.

As a "fair dinkum" Aussie, the Bushranger was reluctant to miss his favorite race meet, which was held on the same weekend each year in Laura, a town 150 miles northwest of Cairns, so we agreed to make it our first destination.

"No country in the world worshipped the horse with the same fierce veneration as Australia in the nineteenth century," wrote historian Geoffrey Blainey. "In many towns the day of an important race meeting was declared a public holiday. Vast crowds assembled at racecourses and racing results had a news value which often exceeded that of national calamities or international wars." The same was equally true of the twentieth century, if the daily tabloids were any indication. Even the most respectable and sober of newspapers devoted pages to racing, and the most popular exhibit in Melbourne's Museum of Victoria was not its wonderful collection of dinosaur relics but the stuffed skin of a champion Thoroughbred named Phar Lap. Laura's own race was one of the area's most popular, and from what the Bushranger told us about the characters who gathered there, we were eager to go.

The road from Innisfail to Cooktown, a small settlement eighty miles east of Laura, ran along one of the most scenic coastlines in the world. Banana and coffee plantations and endless fields of sugarcane lined both sides of the highway. The area had once consisted of rich, lowland rain forest very similar to the jungle of Papua New Guinea, but much of it had been cleared long ago to grow sugar. Now there was a glut of sugar on the world market, and the rain forest was irretrievably destroyed.

It was late June, and all along the road cane fields were being burned in preparation for harvesting. A hazy, sulphur-colored smoke hung over the horizon and muted the scenery, but far from being acrid, the smell that permeated the air was pleasantly sweet and candied, reminiscent of roasted marshmallows.

A range of cloud-covered mountains rose in the distance off to our left, and their steep, verdant slopes, reaching a height of a thousand feet or so, faced out on a vista of coconut palms and white sand beaches, emerald-green lagoons, and a stretch of dark-blue sea dotted with the coral islands of the Great Barrier Reef. As the sun broke through the clouds, its rays penetrated to the valley floor in luminous columns, like slanted shafts of light falling through the stained-glass windows of a Gothic cathedral. All that was missing was organ music, but the only station on the car radio was playing country-and-western instead.

A few miles beyond the sleepy sugar town of Mossman, we came to the broad mouth of the crocodile-infested Daintree River, where a cable-operated barge ferried us and our four-wheel-drive across to Cape Tribulation. The track on the other side had only recently been opened. It was perilously narrow, climbing along the edge of a precipice to a height of about 4,000 feet and winding through a spectacular rain forest. A lush expanse of tropical growth extended from the mountain tops right down to the coast, ending only where it met the mangrove swamps and fringing coral reefs.

The environmentalists, or "greenies," as they were often contemptuously called, were worried about the effect the new road would have on Cape Tribulation, the only place in Australia where upland and lowland rain forests, each with its own peculiar flora, merged in a single locale. On one hand, over half of the state's rain forests had already been destroyed, and Queensland's timber interests saw no reason why they shouldn't be allowed to log out the rest. The newly opened track would provide easy access to the rain forest interior should the state's notoriously business-oriented politicians decide to give the lumbermen a free hand to do it.

But at a more fundamental level even the very cutting of the track had taken its toll. The edges of the road had already been "colonized" by a dense, almost impenetrable thicket of stinging shrubs, brambles, sarsaparilla bushes, and lantana, all of which had taken root in the open areas so rapidly that nothing else in the immediate vicinity had a chance to germinate and grow. Where the track reached its highest elevation, we pulled off on the shoulder and got out for a walk, fighting our way through the roadside vegetation to get into the forest.

Despite the depredation of road clearing, the fragile interior of the Cape Tribulation rain forest remained in a near pristine state. Cool and damp, it was also surprisingly spacious; a horse and rider could have traveled through it as if on an open trail, and indeed, the early pioneers had done just that. The entire area was alive with the enchanting sounds of unseen birds: the whipcrack call of the whipbird, the wail of the jungle fowl, the "walk-to-work" whistle of the pitta, and others even the Bushranger couldn't identify.

Soft rays of sunlight filtered through the forest canopy, a blurred, interwoven mass of green in which the individual leaves, vines, orchids, and giant ferns looked like brushstrokes of Cézanne. A little lower was the forest understory, which consisted of luxuriant large-leaved plants, strangler figs snaking around host trees, and thick, ropelike lianas. Phil was reminded of Viet Nam, and though he seemed to be enjoying himself as he walked through the forest, I detected a certain wariness, as if he half-expected a booby trap to go off at any moment.

The forest floor was carpeted with decomposing leaves, branches, and fungi of every description. Leaf-tailed geckos and other camouflaged lizards clung to the tree trunks, and we saw an occasional chlorophyll-green tree snake coiled around a branch. Creeks and cataracts shimmered in the dappled light, and Jack and I waded through almost every pool we came to, unable to resist, even at our advanced age, one of the greatest of boyhood pleasures. What a difference from W.A.! I thought, momentarily forgetting that less than an hour's drive away the same arid landscape, the same bushless bush, awaited us.

"By and large, Australia's a very peaceful country," a government zoologist based in Townsville had told us. "I spend a lot of time in the bush and never run into trouble. Still . . . ," he mused, reconsidering what he had just said, "western Queensland has some awfully bad characters, a few real rednecks. When I head out that way I carry a weapon myself."

He was the second person to have given us such a warning. Chris O'Hanlon, a writer friend in Sydney, had put it more colorfully: "I always pack a piece up there. It's a huge, unguarded coast with a lot of drug dealers running around. And they carry some pretty heavy artillery. Lot of weirdos up there, too. *Deliverance* types, and that sort of thing."

As it turned out, the Bushranger was also one of those Australians who never ventured into the Queensland bush without his rifle, a Winchester lever-action 30-30 that fit snuggly into a short, suede saddle holster. "Just somethin' to shoot pigs with when we want a little sport," he explained, as he packed it away with the rest of the stuff in the four-wheel-drive. When he went fishing in the upper reaches of Cape York, he told us, he kept the rifle close at hand, primarily as a precaution against crocodiles and king brown snakes. (The latter became so aggressive during the mating season they sometimes chased intruders hundreds of yards before giving up the attack.) Against people, the Bushranger had never yet had occasion to use his rifle. His fists had sufficed for that, and if all else failed there was always the "Redfern uppercut," a quick knee-to-the-groin technique he had mastered while growing up in the tough Sydney district of Redfern.

It was in the rain forest, a few miles beyond the Daintree ferry, that we encountered our first "weirdo." He didn't look particularly dangerous, except maybe to himself. Parked at a shaded river crossing called Isabella Falls, he was standing beside an old olive-green pickup truck with an even older and more beat-up trailer in tow. The trailer was full of trash, and from the devious look on his face and the hang-dog slouch in his posture, we knew what he was about to do: dump his garbage at the campsite adjacent to the Falls just as soon as we left. Nodding a "g'day," we pulled off the road, got out of the Toyota, and walked over to the campsite to boil the billy.

"Dem toureests shoots our horse an' cattle," he bellowed rather defensively, his accent a peculiar mixture of Australian and French. "Eet's brought us bushies into a reign of terreur." It was clear that he didn't like outsiders, though there were few enough around, and trashing the campsite was apparently his way of keeping them out.

Michael Budd (which he pronounced "Bewd") had a long Gallic nose that dominated his gaunt face. He was wearing a paint-streaked pair of jeans and an unbuttoned army shirt with a corporal's emblem on each arm. A dusty-brown cowboy hat shaded his weather-beaten face as he leaned against the side of his pickup truck, spinning yarns. He told us he owned a property nearby, a station he had named Louisiana when he took possession of it on the 150th anniversary of the Louisiana Purchase. As a boy he had fought with the Maquis during World War II, later joined the French Marines, and—here it was hard to follow him—then either served in Viet Nam and came to Australia on R & R, or jumped ship in Sydney Harbor on the way to Viet Nam and faded into the bush. He claimed to have stolen some horses and cattle and then "deed what my ancesteurs 'af been doing for four tousand years—I drove cattle. I drove bloody cattle up to bloody Queensland and I settled 'ere."

He prattled on about his ancestors, Moors from Morocco who settled in the Loire Valley after being driven out of Spain. Now he, the last in his long line, had established himself in northern Queensland, the recipient, so he said, of a land grant from King George VI (bestowed on him for his services during World War II): "De certificate says, 'I, King George of England, Defendeur of de Faith, Empereur of India, and all dat bloody bullshit, do hereby grant to Michael Budd, and so forth.' "

The Bushranger didn't believe a word he said, though he kept his doubts to himself until we climbed back into our four-wheel-drive, forded the river, and continued on our way to Laura, leaving Budd free to dump his load unobserved. But we did learn later, from a woman we met in Laura whose property bordered on his, that though he was "as mad as a meat-ax," he was indeed the owner of Louisiana Station and lived there with his wife and several daughters.

A more menacing experience awaited us a few miles farther along the road, where we spotted two heavily bearded men hunched over a car that had skidded off the track into a small gully. The car was lying on its side amidst a tangle of vegetation, and seemed to be undergoing an attack by wrecking bars and axes. Thinking that an accident had just occurred, we slowed down to see if we could help, whereupon the two men looked up and, without so much as a glance passing between them, clambered up the bank toward us. We had caught them in the act of ransacking an abandoned vehicle, and they clearly didn't like it.

Jack edged the Toyota ahead slowly. Another two road warriors emerged from the woods onto the track in front of us and moved in our direction. They were carrying broad axes on their shoulders and they had mayhem in their eyes.

Jack and I looked at each other. We had studied karate together for many years back in Boston, and each of us knew what the other was thinking: This was the time to toss Phil out. And if need be, we could always throw in the Bushranger to sweeten the deal.

Wielding their tools as weapons, the four "dirtbags," as Jack called them, were getting closer. Phil wanted to reach for the rifle. Jack, more moderate, suggested simply running them over. The Bushranger and I urged a more pacifistic approach and, fortunately, our counsel prevailed, though I wasn't certain what Jack had in mind when he accelerated toward them. In any case, at the last moment they leapt aside. One took a swipe at us with his ax as we passed, but the blow merely glanced off the fender as we sped away, kicking up a smokescreen of dust in our wake.

Many months before, when we were starting out on our journey in Western Australia along its own coastal road, we had stopped outside of Geraldton to get our bearings before proceeding into the vast expanse of bush that lay before us. I had been apprehensive then about the hostility we anticipated from the natural environment, but I had never taken seriously any of the tales we'd heard about the dangers from people in the bush.

Though the continent had been settled by felons and convicts, not to mention their often more villainous overseers, Australia took pride in the fact that throughout its history the country had for the most part been spared the kind of Wild West violence that had accompanied the development of America. Despite its brutal slaughter of aboriginals (which could indeed be likened to America's extermination of the Indian), there had been no tradition of gunslingers and lynch mobs on the Australian goldfields, and generally the worst thing that happened to a claim jumper was that he was run out of town. Even today, Australia was considered a safe place, relatively free from crime.

But perhaps things were changing, at least in the deep north. In Cairns we'd heard rumors about travelers to Cape York who had mysteriously disappeared without trace, and reports of private armies employed by drug dealers to protect the large marijuana plantations said to exist deep in the sparsely settled peninsula. Since these troops were heavily armed, the limited police force in the area (many of whom were reputed to be tainted by drug money) were unwilling to move against them, though occasionally vague stories did circulate about pitched battles between the law and the drug minions.

The Bushranger insisted that the foursome we had just encountered were aberrations, and maybe that was so. But if pockets of violence did exist in Australia's otherwise tranquil society, this remote area along the coast of Cape York would certainly have been the place to look for them.

3

Laura sat off to one side of the dirt track running from the truck stop at Butchers Hill to Coen, another settlement further up the Cape York Peninsula. Consisting of a general store and a pub, it was a shantytown sheltered from the sweltering sun by a few bush mangoes. A dust bowl in the Dry and an inaccessible mud hole in the Wet, it was not the kind of place that attracted visitors. Few people ever went to Laura except for that single weekend in early July when the "township" held its annual race meet.

Like other such events around Australia, the Laura meet was the one occasion a year when ringers from anywhere within a several-hundred-mile radius could gather at the local hotel "to drink piss" for the weekend and, only incidentally, to display their skills of horsemanship at the competition on Saturday.

The rodeo was held in a sunbaked corral just outside of town, and by the time we reached it the event had already begun. Some of the spectators were resting their arms on the top rail of the weathered bush-timber fence or sitting on it to get even closer to the action. Others had brought along folding chairs or were perched on the tailgate of their four-wheel-drive pickups. Parked nearby in a sparsely wooded grove were the caravans and horse trailers of the rodeo participants. As we pulled our vehicle into a patch of shade under a stunted eucalyptus tree, I noticed one young ringer, in jeans and a western-style shirt, saddling a black mare as his girl stroked the horse's neck. It was a scene reminiscent of *The Sundowners*, one of the best-known novels of the Outback, which told the story of a family who took its horse around the country to compete at the various local race meets.

The first event was bronco riding, and watching each contestant as he tried to last the required eight seconds brought back memories of when I myself, an eighteen-year-old college student, had wrangled horses one summer on a ranch in Colorado. The rodeo we were watching could well have been taking place anywhere in the American West—were it not for the voice shouting over the loudspeaker. Every time a rider ended up in a heap on the ground, the announcer would shout in his inimitable bush-Australian accent: "Hold yer hand up if yer alright," and an arm would rise feebly out of the dust. The two horsemen serving as pick-up team galloped over to the fallen rider and snatched him out of harm's way, before he was trampled or kicked by a flailing hoof.

Occasionally a bronco didn't want to perform, and its rider would try to spur the animal into action before being disqualified. In one awful instance, though, a horse performed too well. A bone-white stallion bucked so violently that in just a few convulsive seconds it broke its own neck, and as the rider jumped free, it fell to the ground in one last spasm and died on the spot. The rider and pick-up men knelt at its side, tugging and lifting its head as if unwilling to believe the stallion was dead, while the spectators groaned and then grew silent. But as soon as the truck came out and dragged the carcass away, the crowd grew cheerful and the action began again.

Now it was the kids' turn—small ones, eight, ten, twelve years old.

They, too, wanted to prove themselves, and their parents were eager to let them do so. Too young for the challenge of riding full-fledged bulls and broncos, they came hurtling out of the chutes astride smaller bullocks. Even though the older competitors had farther to fall, the younger riders hit the ground just as hard. "Hold yer hand up if yer alright," said the announcer, and the father of one boy, kneeling in the dust over his dazed son, lifted the child's limp arm in the air before picking him up and carrying him away.

An Aboriginal Dance Festival had also been scheduled that weekend to coincide with the race meet. We had never seen a corroboree before, and though we were doubtful that we'd be experiencing the real thing, we decided it was worth a visit.

The festival was held a few miles outside Laura, down an almost impassable track that cut deep into the bush, and a number of people who tried to get there in conventional vehicles had already been forced to turn back. The track ended in a small circular clearing that was part of the Quinkan Reserve, quinkans being mischievous demon-spirits that featured prominently in the aborigine's totemistic belief system. To the natives the clearing might have been a sacred site, but the uninitiated saw only a large expanse of dust surrounded by stands of withered eucalyptus trees that looked more like a refugee camp than the setting for a dance festival.

The event had drawn nearly two hundred body-painted aboriginal performers, none of whom showed much enthusiasm at being there, and about a hundred white spectators. The performers belonged to different tribes, each of which had its own particular dances. In some cases the men were dressed in traditional grass skirts; in others they wore a strangely variegated assortment of bathing trunks and boxer shorts, in striking contrast to the chalky-white and ocher-red patterns they had daubed on their upper torsos. A few of the older women were bare-breasted, but the majority of them wore tank tops or T-shirts.

Most of the spectators had been recruited from the ranks of the Department of Aboriginal Affairs, which had conceived the idea of the festival. The remainder had come up from Cairns and other coastal communities out of a liberal commitment to the aboriginal cause. Sitting cross-legged on the ground and politely applauding at the conclusion of each uninspired performance, they looked like middle-aged holdovers from a Beatles concert.

Both sides were going through the motions, but the whole affair was as spontaneous as a Soviet press conference and slightly less festive.

"No bush whites are interested in a bloody mob of abos," observed one cynical spectator. "All they want to do this weekend is get pissed." As for the aboriginals, this was no impromptu corroboree of their own making, which in the old days had been known to go on for three days and nights running. In the words of the same cynic, this get-together had been "planned by white folks to encourage black folks to get closer to their cultural heritage, and to show other white folks that black folks could do something other than drink."

But whatever the goals of its organizers, the festival could hardly have been counted a success. Sitting at opposite ends of the field, the aboriginal performers and the white spectators had stared at each other as if across an abyss, and it must have been clear to all but the most idealistic observer that their two such vastly different worlds were as irreconcilable now as they had been at their first confrontation in Botany Bay, two centuries before.

4

Most of the visitors to Laura that weekend had set up their tents on a campsite directly across the road from the Laura Hotel. This spot was basically a large tract of dust, but it did have an ablution block, and it was within easy reach of the pub, the site of impromptu head-butting contests throughout the weekend, which we were never fortunate enough to witness.

Our own campsite had neither of those amenities but, tucked away on a still pool of the Laura River among a stand of well-watered paperbark trees, it was peaceful and even picturesque. We shared it with a group of three other campers, an older woman and two teenage girls who had pitched their tents on a nearby clearing overlooking the lagoon.

Phil was rapidly becoming as acclimated as we were to the Australian bush. A thunderstorm came up during our second night in Laura, and as we were unprepared for rain during the "dry season," everything got soaking wet in the downpour. Earlier that evening he had slipped and plunged feet first into the lagoon, falling into water well over his head. Before his unscheduled dip, he had stepped on a large snake, which slithered into the bush without biting him. Phil himself had jumped aside with a startled yell.

"Scared of snakes, sweetheart?" Jack had asked, with his usual sympathetic smile.

The next morning, while in the course of fixing breakfast, we met our fellow campers. Iris was a round-faced, red-headed lady in her late fifties, a cheerful, grandmotherly sort with a stout, knockwurst-like figure and the strong, veined hands of a manual laborer. As for the two young girls, they were sisters, and Iris was a friend of their family. They had come along for the ride, and to help the older woman set up camp and cook meals.

Now a nurse in Mareeba, a small town outside Cairns in the Atherton Tablelands, Iris always came to Laura for the race meet. To her it was a bittersweet homecoming. For almost twenty years she had struggled to make a life for herself and her family on a nearby cattle station. But Iris had never adjusted to station life, and once her children had grown up, she "gave it away," divorcing her husband and leaving the bush for Mareeba.

It was Sunday, and Iris agreed to take us to the races, which began later that morning. When we arrived at the track it soon became clear that she knew practically everyone there.

"That's Myles Costello," she said, pointing to a lean, bleary-eyed, bearded fellow who had just staggered out of the toilet. Fumbling with his still unzipped fly, he was trying to find his way back to the Fosters beer stand, which served as a makeshift pub. I didn't think he was going to make it.

"No worries," Iris assured me. "He's got a lot of sway left in him yet. He's never the first one down. They look forward to this weekend all year, and then they never leave the bar."

For the most part it was a young crowd. The girls, many of whom were governesses on neighboring stations, were wearing their prettiest dresses. The ringers had on the customary western shirts, jeans, and cowboy hats they always wore, but since it was a festive occasion, they wore rubber thongs on their feet instead of the usual work boots. Far more numerous than the girls, they huddled around the Fosters stand, drinking incessantly and keeping pretty much to themselves.

"Around here the only place a woman is welcome is in the maternity ward," said Iris, "and even that's debatable." She spoke without bitterness; it was just a matter of fact.

Iris herself had married in the mid-1950s, not long after which she moved out to the station. Though the property had been in her husband's family for some time, she arrived to find that the homestead consisted of a poorly furnished one-room, corrugated-iron shack. It had no kitchen and, of course, no toilet. "It was such a shock," she said. "And to make matters worse there were no other women around."

The first thing the couple did was to build an outhouse, but a few weeks later Iris encountered a big brown snake while using it. "I screamed and ran out," she related, smiling as she recalled the incident. "My father-in-law grabbed his shotgun and took careful aim. He didn't get the snake but he sprayed himself somethin' awful. Came out completely covered. All he said was, 'Shit.' Then he poured petrol down the hole and threw in a match. Got the snake alright but burned the entire dunny down as well. We had to go bush again until we built a new one."

She placed twenty dollars on the first race, and stepped up to the rail to watch it. The starting line was on the far side of the track and it was a minute or two before six horses galloped by in a cloud of dust, with six proper little jockeys standing in the stirrups, clinging to their necks. (Having come from Brisbane, the jockeys were outfitted in satiny red shirts, red caps, and white jodhpurs.) Another couple of minutes went by before they rounded the turn, coming into the home stretch toward the finish line. Iris watched stoically. Her horse came in last.

"No wuckin' forries," she muttered, ever the lady.

We walked back to our chairs to await the second race, as Iris continued to reminisce. "This is bandicoot country," she said. "Not fit for human beings. I remember lookin' for firewood when we made camp once durin' a severe Wet. There were huge gray scorpions under each piece of wood, keepin' dry. We put up tarps and shoveled out channels all around us for water gutters. The centipedes came out by the thousands. We were occupyin' the one dry spot around and all those little bits of wildlife wanted to join us there.

"One time I got lost all night. We were musterin' and I was followin' a bunch of bullocks. Then all of a sudden I couldn't hear 'em. They say if you're lost, give your horse the reins and he'll find home. Well, my horse was a brumby"—a wild horse, the equivalent of the American mustang—"and he headed for the ranges. Howl!—I cried so loud that night the dingoes didn't have a chance to be heard.

"I was pregnant with my first child that year and we got cut off by the Wet. Couldn't get to a hospital. Fortunately, the midwife got stranded, too, several miles away. So my husband took the jeep and drove overland to get her. If he hadn't made it, I would have died. With that first one everythin' that could go wrong did go wrong.

"The aboriginals were tougher," she continued. "I remember one old gin named Lora. She was doin' my ironin' and I went out to take somethin' off the line. When I got back she was gone, but the iron was still on. She came back forty-five minutes later and started ironin' again. When I asked her where she'd been, she said: 'Jus' 'ave picka-ninny.'

"But a white woman never saw another white woman for six months at a time. There was no one to talk to. So when she went into town, she just started talkin' and she wouldn't stop. She couldn't stop. If anyone had interrupted her, he probably would have been mauled. But the people in town didn't interrupt; they understood."

"What about your husband?" I asked.

She shook her head. "He didn't understand. Not many of 'em do. He was out in the bush for weeks on end. They don't care. Around here, if a sheep dog barks too much in the night, they shoot it."

Iris herself was a jovial sort of person, yet somehow her reminisc-ing left me feeling rather sorry for her, that she had wasted so many years in a place she hated for a man she didn't love. But I reminded myself that it was unusual for a bushman's wife to take such steps toward independence as she had, and that now at least she seemed to be enjoying her life. Perhaps I was feeling sorry not so much for Iris, but for all the women who hadn't had the courage to do what she had done. However unpleasant the years in the bush, the thought of mov-ing to town and beginning a new life on their own must have been a terrifying prospect.

Even in Sydney I'd heard Aussie women lament the fact that Aus-tralia was "a man's country." It had earned that reputation early in its history, when six out of every seven convict-settlers were men, and the female convicts, handed over to a mob of "randy colonists" on arrival, became (in Robert Hughes's words) the "prisoners of prisoners," vic-tims of the vilest sorts of physical and sexual abuse.

Although women of Iris's age, of course, had been born into a more enlightened era, those who followed their husbands into the bush were still, to some extent, prisoners, locked into their role as keepers of hearth and home and confined by the isolation that way of life imposed. Some had chosen men who at least were understanding and sympathetic to their needs ("It's just as well I loved the *man*," Reg Durack's wife, speaking of her life in the Kimberleys, had confided to us back in Perth many months before, "for I despised the place he lived in"), but not all of them were so fortunate. At a roadhouse in Western Australia, we had encountered firsthand the attitude Iris described. The owner had been a roadtrain truckie, who had "jacked it in" to buy the dismal bit of property where he was now living. "Missed your wife, did you?" asked Jack, who was homesick for his. "Fuck the wife," he replied. "You can get a wife anywhere. I wanted a place of my own."

5

After breaking camp the following morning we loaded the Toyota, an involved and time-consuming procedure. Dave scrambled up on the big roof rack atop the vehicle, while we passed tables, tents, swags, emergency fresh water, cases of beer, and other such articles up to him. The pots and pans went on the roof as well, stowed in a large wooden ammunition box we kept between several spare tires.

Each item had its designated spot, and when everything was in place and secured, we covered the load with a heavy tarpaulin and tied it down on all sides. Though the tarp didn't keep much dust out, it did hold everything down when we bounced along rough tracks and forded rocky rivers. In the rear of the Toyota was a battery-operated freezer for perishable foods, a large cooler, and a fresh water container, on the top of which we piled all our personal gear to shield them from the sun.

On the way back from Laura we stopped in Cooktown, named after Captain Cook, who had beached the *Endeavour* on the site of the present town to repair her hull, which was severely damaged when she struck a reef. A boomtown during the 1870s, Cooktown was the entry port for countless shiploads of prospectors heading to the gold-fields on the Palmer and Bloomfield rivers. As records were not kept then, no one knows what the town's peak population was, though one estimate places the figure as high as 30,000 Europeans and 50,000 Chinese. Today only a few hundred people reside there. Leaving Cooktown and heading south along the coastal road, we recrossed the Daintree River, and after climbing over the Tablelands, eventually reached the Gulf Development Road, which ran west toward the Gulf of Carpentaria. About sixty-five miles farther on, a dirt track turnoff led us toward a tiny dot on the map called Einasleigh.

We had now crossed over to the other side of the Great Divide, a mountain chain separating the coastal plains from the arid interior. West of those ranges, the timbered hills quickly gave way to flat grassy plains and finally to the same kind of desolate scrubland with which we had become so familiar during our many months in Western Australia.

"Gulf Country"—so called because of its proximity to the Gulf of Carpentaria—began the second major leg of our trip, which would eventually take us into the Northern Territory. We'd planned an extensive and difficult route through the bush, one that would take us to remote stations and isolated settlements, many of which seldom saw visitors. Except for one or two short stretches on the bitumen, we would be following rough dirt tracks almost exclusively, since there were only two sealed roads in the entire region.

As the landscape became bleaker, so did my mood. We were a long way from the lush rain forests and the turquoise waters of the Queensland coast. After all those months in Western Australia, I thought I'd become inured to that sense of sadness the bush seemed to evoke in me. I couldn't tell what was on Dave's mind, but I suspected his spirits were sinking, too. The change the landscape wrought in Phil, though, was immediately apparent. Usually jocular, he had grown silent, almost morose, and when I commented on it, he admitted that the "somberness of the land" made him feel "uneasy."

Yet Phil was no stranger to desolate terrain. As a correspondent for the Chicago *Tribune*, he had visited some of the most inhospitable places on the face of the earth. His assignments had taken him as far as Siberia, and though he had even crossed the Sahara Desert in the company of a ragged group of Bedouins, he muttered, "This is worse than the Sahara," as he shook his head in disbelief at the stark brown terrain.

Oblivious to Phil's invidious comparison, the Bushranger seemed delighted to be back in familiar surroundings. He grew even more animated than usual, chatting away and joking about the pleasures awaiting us in the bush.

"There's only four things you really need out here," he said. "Five, if you count stubby-holders to keep your beer cold. A snake-bite kit, a bottle of olive oil, a winch, and a Bible. The olive oil's for drowning insects that get stuck in your ear, not for cooking. The winch is for when the car turns over. And the Bible," he added, smiling at Phil, "is for administering last rites."

At the Bushranger's suggestion we spent the night on a dry riverbed near a grove of stunted droop-leafed acacias and ragged paperbark trees, a place he had camped once before. Although there was no danger of being caught in a flood at that time of year, the site wasn't a particularly inviting one. Dried cattle dung littered the red sand

243

around us, and as soon as we began setting up camp, the flies descended in hordes.

"Nice spot," I remarked to the Bushranger, waving my hand in front of my face to keep the insects from landing.

"It'll look a lot better when the sun goes down," he replied. "Any camp's a good one after dark."

The sun went down, and with it the temperature. I put on a heavy sweat shirt and, later, as it grew even colder, added a jacket. As night descended, a cold wind from the south soughed through the trees, and we ate our meal hovered around the fire.

A yellow moon rose over the crest of some distant ridges, casting a pearly haze over our encampment, and the rustle of the drooping paperbark's leaves reminded me of willow trees back home. Sitting companionably around the fire eating a hot meal, we were inclined to find the bush at night to be an almost congenial place.

6

The Central Hotel in Einasleigh, North Queensland, stood resolutely in the middle of a rock-strewn plain. It was the only hotel in town, and if it weren't for the abandoned frame structure that tottered beside it, defying the law of gravity, it would also have qualified as the only building. Off in the distance lay the shriveled bed of the Goldfield River, its rough contours delineated by lunarlike black lava basalt. The river had dried up long months ago, leaving no indication that anything other than lava had ever flowed in it.

To enter the hotel's front door we had to maneuver through a herd of cattle as they vainly nuzzled the arid ground for a sprig of anything to graze on. They roamed dispiritedly about in front of the hotel, their hooves stirring up small puffs of red dust that drifted up and blanketed their hides.

It was a Saturday afternoon, but only three patrons sat at the bar in the Blue Lagoon Pub. As we entered, a large black dog snarled at us, but Dave shot him a fierce glare, and the animal slunk out the side door with his tail between his legs. The barkeep and the patrons were far more amicable, and when they discovered that we were Americans, a stockman named George informed us that a Yank was currently living in town.

"This is the time he generally comes in to buy his case of beer for the week," he stated firmly. After chatting with George, a huge man who had biceps like truck-tire inner tubes, it was clear that nothing much happened in Einasleigh; but whatever did happen, George knew about it.

The grotty pub smelled of musty beer and sweaty cattlemen, but its drab interior provided refuge from the furnacelike heat outside. On the wall hung an old lithograph of a racehorse, but my eye was drawn to a well-executed pen-and-ink sketch of the hotel, which actually succeeded in making the rickety frame structure look attractive.

We waited awhile, downing more brew than we should have at that time of the day, and when the Yank failed to make his appearance, decided to move on. But halfway to the dusty Toyota, we heard someone shout and looked back to see a short, stocky figure emerge from the hotel. Having got our attention, he ran toward us, cradling a case of beer with both arms.

"Are you the Yanks they told me about at the pub?" asked the beer bearer, in an unmistakable American accent. "Boy, am I glad to see you. It's been a long time since I talked to anyone from back home."

Joe Gelati had a friendly grin and a manner as open as the land he now called home. He was obviously delighted to see some of his countrymen, and he admitted that he hadn't spoken to an American in over a year. "It was at the Mareeba Rodeo last summer. I met a Yank that owns a store there. Gee, it's good to see you guys!" he exclaimed. "Where are you from?"

"We were practically next door neighbors," he declared, when he discovered that Dave was originally from Rhode Island and I was from Boston.

Joe and his wife Cathy were born and raised in Danbury, Connecticut. They had been childhood sweethearts, and after they were married, they'd left New England and moved first to New Mexico, and then West Texas. But the Gelatis found those areas were developing too rapidly for them, and in 1982, after reading about life in the Outback, they emigrated to Australia.

"How in the world did you end up in Einasleigh?" asked Dave, looking around at the desiccated terrain.

"I went to work for the Queensland Railway. I was only temporary at first," said Joe, smiling as he recalled the experience. "But the farther out you were willin' to go, the easier it was to get a permanent station. Einasleigh was the end of the line, and when I asked about comin' here, they told me to pack my bags."

Joe laughed aloud, and so infectiously that he had us all giggling with him. The railway knew that Einasleigh was a miserable posting, but that fact didn't trouble Joe at all. He was happy to be there and working permanently.

"I'm a gandy dancer," Joe related, "on a section gang that repairs the tracks. I pound spikes into the rails with a sledge hammer. Back when we lived in Connecticut, I thought only John Henry could do it. But it's a lotta fun."

"Do you really like it?" asked Dave. He was now visibly wincing at the thought of living in Einasleigh, and of the physical exertion involved in wielding a sledgehammer.

"Oh, we really love it here," answered Joe. "You can look out there at the country around us and swear you're in West Texas. We bought a Shetland pony, and we're raising a baby kangaroo whose mother died. We live in a little caravan behind the railroad quarters, and the wife's just happier than hell. She's over there with our daughter in the car. She followed me halfway around the world," said Joe, who couldn't contain his pride. "Would you like to meet her? That 'id be great. She'd really be glad to see some Americans."

Cathy Gelati and their seven-year-old daughter, Sarah, got out of an old Holden as we approached them. Cathy was a small, attractive woman about thirty years old, whose long, blond hair had been bleached by the sun. After asking us about things back in the States, Cathy spoke about her life in Australia.

"It takes a long time to make friends here, and I'm not as outgoing as Joe. Gosh, when we first came to Australia we stuck out like outsiders from Mars. We didn't know about things like celebrating the Queen's Birthday, and when we talked about Thanksgiving, they thought we were crazy.

"But now we're sort of accepted, at least here in Einasleigh, and some of the people are real nice. There's only about twenty people in town, and most of them work for the railway. But you meet new friends as you go along. I guess you can't worry about the old ones you used to have, just the new ones you're going to meet tomorrow. But I'd still be happy even if we didn't have any friends. I've got Joe and Sarah, and we've got the caravan, our little home on wheels." Like Joe, she smiled as she spoke.

"That's our seventh heaven," added Joe proudly. "We got a real good deal on it in Cairns. It only cost us a thousand dollars. My job only called for a single man's accommodations. We could've stayed at the pub, but that's no good for the little one."

I envied Joe's great enthusiasm, remembering that I had felt that way when I was younger. I asked him how old he was.

"I was thirty-five two weeks ago today," he replied. "I came down to the pub for a couple of drinks to celebrate, and then I walked home."

"Do you miss the States?" Dave asked.

"Not really," replied Joe. "I guess the army did that. We were over in Germany for two years, and we were always going from one place to another. We never had a real home until we came here."

"There's no TV here, and the only radio station is hard to get unless you have a really good receiver," observed Cathy. "But you get used to it, and it's not too bad."

Joe mentioned that he was Italian, and I asked him how he managed to get his pasta.

"You either stock up when you go shopping or drive five hours to get it," he answered, with a laugh. "Every six weeks, after payday, we drive to Atherton. We have to leave at three in the mornin' to get there at eight thirty, when the stores open. There's not much time 'cause they close on Saturdays at noon."

"You probably can't believe it," said Cathy, in mock imitation of her excitement, "but our biggest thrill is sitting up in bed all night making up a shopping list before we go to town. You plan for weeks ahead. Oh boy, what do we need? What'll we see? The night before we go, I can't sleep, and that's just a trip into Atherton. If we went to Cairns, the excitement would be too much. I'd probably have a heart attack."

"It sounds like you'd be a lot happier in Atherton or Cairns," observed Dave.

"No, not really," replied Joe. "On the way back we'll stop in a little town for a bite to eat, and Cathy 'ill say, 'I can't wait ta get home to Einasleigh.'"

"We'll be here for three or four years," said Cathy, "until Joe has enough seniority to transfer to a post closer to town."

"Sometimes you can get one faster if you tell 'em your wife is going crazy and your children need to be in school," Joe added. "There's no school here, so Cathy has to teach Sarah through a correspondence course."

It was still early in the afternoon, but we wanted to start on our way to Forsayth and set up camp before dark. "We'd better think about moving on," Dave suggested.

"You could stay the night at our place if you liked," offered Joe. "We'd love to have you. You go by a clump of houses on the road to Forsayth and just beyond them you'll see our little caravan sittin' all alone in a paddock. That's ours. Even if you can't stay, you're sure welcome to come out and have a beer."

We discussed his proposal for a few minutes. Phil and the Bush-ranger were inclined to stay, but Dave and I urged that we move on. A lot of empty miles stretched ahead of us, and we didn't know what lay beyond. We said reluctant good-byes to the Gelatis, and followed them out of town, until they reached the paddock, where they waved and then turned off. I shifted around in my seat to watch them step into their trailer, and I couldn't help wishing that we had stopped.

As we continued down the track toward Forsayth I found I couldn't get Joe Gelati out of my mind. We were as far from home as it was possible to be, while still being on the planet, and we'd bumped into a guy who was practically from our own home town. He had been desperate to talk to us, inviting us home for a meal and a bed—but we had been intent on moving on. What was happening to us that we could easily forgo the hospitality of so amiable a family?

While Joe seemed to have acclimated himself to the bush, its oppressive emptiness had left him eager for conversation, eager for company. The bleak country we found ourselves in had affected us, as visitors, differently: To cope with it, we had turned inward, insulating our emotions. We had all sensed a terrible vulnerability in Joe; we had actually been afraid to pause, even for a moment, lest we be forced to confront his loneliness, and behind it, perhaps, our own.

7

Forsayth, a two-street, one-pub town, stood on the bank of a river that was dry except for a mudhole in the middle. The one pub, the Goldfields Tavern, looked more like a cinder block storage shed than a pub. It sat in a dusty lot by the side of the road, curing in the midday sun. Off to its right struggled a solitary coconut palm, whose drooping brown fronds did little to shade the dunny beneath it. The dunny had two cubicles. The door on one read, DRIP DRY, on the other, SHAKE DRY.

"Yeah, this is a quiet country town, so lunchtime around here is usually pretty slow," observed John Smith, the Goldfields Tavern's publican. "We'll only get a couple of customers between now and late this afternoon."

"In this dry climate it must be hard for you to just sit there and not drink between now and then," I remarked.

"Not fer me," replied John. "I only allow meself two beers a day. Ya can practice self-discipline wherever ya are."

As he set four stubbies before us three cowboys on horseback rode up Forsayth's main street toward the tavern. John looked up from his comfortable perch behind the bar. He took a long swallow of beer that emptied his second can of the day and added, "I might a' spoken too soon. That's Barry Petrocini an' his bunch."

Since the tavern's front door was wide open, the three horsemen decided to save both time and energy. Instead of dismounting and hitching up, they tried to ride straight indoors for faster service. The lead rider's horse, however, didn't welcome the opportunity to visit the bar and get out of the midday sun, and it began to buck wildly in protest. In a matter of seconds he threw his rider out of the saddle and onto the ground. The other two horses also started to buck, perhaps as a gesture of equine solidarity, but their riders managed to remain in the saddle and soon settled the animals down.

"Hold yer hand up if yer alright," the Bushranger yelled at the prostrate cowboy rider. From his prone position he immediately shot up his hand; it was not the first time he'd been thrown, nor was it likely to be the last. Luckily, the grog he'd been drinking served to cushion his fall, and he hadn't sustained any obvious injuries.

Since their horses couldn't be persuaded to join them inside, the fallen rider's companions unsteadily dismounted and hitched their reluctant mounts. Leaving their comrade sprawled on the ground to catch up on his sleep, they staggered inside.

"Lads, I'd like yez ta meet Barry Petrocini, the Italian cowboy," said John Smith. "He owns Lonvale Station here a few miles outta town."

"Can't cha say it right," protested Barry, miffed by the publican's pronunciation. "I'm the Eye-talian cowboy."

Having weaved his way toward the bar, he now leaned against it for support. Barry shook our hands and politely introduced us to his ringer sidekick, Kenny Ryan, who, though a thousand miles away from surf, was wearing a Seaworld Surfers T-shirt.

"That's Bob Priestley takin' a nap outside if yez wanna go out an' say g'day ta 'im. I dunno what's the matter with them damn horses. They must be bloody wowsers."

Convincing animals to share beer with them seemed to be a major preoccupation for many Australians, who were prepared to go to any lengths to cultivate new drinking companions. We met a number of imbibing kangaroos and an assortment of other beasts who, having acquired the habit, were on the grog. The prize attraction at one roadhouse was a pony who guzzled beer out of a bottle. Not to be outdone, the owners of a nearby station practically idolized a huge bull they patiently assisted to develop the same talent.

The Eye-talian cowboy told us that his crew had spent the morning rounding up horses for the Mareeba Rodeo, and with that accomplished, he planned to spend the rest of the day at the much easier task of mustering. When I suggested that the tavern seemed an unlikely place to find any cattle, or horses, for that matter, he explained that they had dropped into the tavern only to get a few cold beers to see them through the hot afternoon. Barry was short and stocky, and his pendulous beer belly made him appear top-heavy. He had difficulty focusing his bloodshot brown eyes, and apart from them, I wasn't able to pick out any other feature that pegged him as a son of Italy.

"What's an Eye-talian doing up here in the Gulf Country?" I asked him.

"There's Eye-talians everywhere if ya wanna look fer 'em. Me grandfather immigrated ta here frum Italy, an' ran a pub called the Australian Hotel in Georgetown. Couldn' speak a word a' English. But he wouldn't let me father learn no Eye-talian 'cause he wanted 'im ta be Australian. I can't talk no Eye-talian either, but I'm still an Eye-talian cowboy, even if me mother's Irish." He went on to tell me that his station was a small one, with only five thousand head of cattle grazing on 185 square miles of property. He lived with his wife and two kids.

"Lemme have three tinnies a' beer ta go an' I'll shout these blokes too," Barry interrupted his biography with a yell down the bar at Grace Smith, the publican's wife.

"Ya want lights ta go?" Grace shouted back.

"Naw, make 'em heavies," he replied. "It's time ta hit the track, Jack."

Once he was served, however, the Eye-talian cowboy didn't seem in a particular hurry to go, and soon had Phil and Dave engaged in a long conversation off to one side of the bar.

After a couple of more beers, Barry took a last swig and wrapped the tinnies in newspaper. We followed him outside, where he stuffed them in his saddlebags, and prepared to mount up. Bob Priestley had apparently had sufficient rest, for he was now back on the teetotaling horse.

Because of his size and the extent of his intoxication, the Eye-talian cowboy had considerable difficulty with his animal. He attempted to put his foot in the stirrup a number of times, but couldn't quite reach it. When he finally did, his horse moved off to the side, leaving Barry to fall backward onto the ground and onto his well-cushioned backside.

Undaunted, he rose, brushed the fine red dust off the seat of his pants, and retrieved his hat. We thought he had given up when we saw him stride away from the horse in a huff and back into the tavern. But we didn't appreciate the resolve and determination of the Eye-talian cowboy. Barry emerged only seconds later with an automobile battery he kept inside the tavern for just such emergencies. Placing it beside his horse, he stood on it and again attempted to mount the animal, but once again the uncooperative mare stepped sideways. He twice moved his mounting battery, but both times the horse executed the same subtle maneuver.

"Fer Chrissake, don't just stand there watchin' me, Kenny. Get the hell over on the other side an' hold 'er," shouted the exasperated Eye-talian cowboy.

Kenny walked around to the other side of the recalcitrant animal and braced his shoulder against its flank. Once again Barry moved his mounting battery into position. He quickly stepped up on it, put his foot in the stirrup, and with a less than graceful motion, swung himself up on the animal's back.

"Back in the saddle again," announced the Eye-talian cowboy with satisfaction. "Stick the battery back inside fer me, John. I might need it again." He took off his hat and waved to us as he and his crew rode off in a cloud of dust.

We watched them until they disappeared over a rise, and then returned to the tavern, where John had resumed his familiar perch, with another stubby in front of him. Though still early afternoon, the excitement had apparently caused him to rescind, at least for the moment, his rigid code of self-discipline. His ruddy cheeks, criss-crossed by a network of tiny red and blue capillaries, looked like an RAC road map, and if the condition of his bulbous nose was any indication, it was likely that his two beers a day would end up closer to forty.

"What does the Eye-talian cowboy do if he gets off his horse out in the bush?" I asked, as we joined him at the bar. "There aren't any batteries to stand on out there."

"No worries," replied John, opening us, as well as himself, fresh stubbies. "There's millions a' ant hills out there ta stand on. When he's out in the bush, he can get on an' off that mare like she was a pony."

8

Leaving Forsayth and picking up the main Gulf Development Road at Georgetown, we made our way west on alternating stretches of bitumen and rutted dirt track. After camping for a couple of days at a cattle station called Claraville, we pulled into Normanton to pick up supplies. With a population of under 200, it hadn't quite attained ghost town status, but its huddle of iron-roofed houses amidst broad red streets and bare building allotments was hardly bustling with activity. A few cars and four-wheel-drive vehicles, caked in dust, stood along the wide main thoroughfare, parked at right angles to old wrought-iron street lamps. Outside the post office a lanky young ringer, his face puffed from drink, was pounding the side of a public telephone trying to get coins to drop. I couldn't tell whether he had been unsuccessful with a phone call or was hoping to get change for a few middies.

Although it was midmorning, there was no one else on the street but for a few aborigines (also referred to as "murrays" in this area), who were sitting on the porch of the Purple Cow waiting patiently for the swinging doors to be opened and business to begin. The town looked as if it had recently been under siege—the glass of the public telephone booth and the windows of the post office and many of the stores were shielded by heavy iron grilles, presumably to protect them from getting smashed by patrons during drunken brawls.

Things had been different during the gold rush days, before the turn of the century. Normanton had been a boomtown then, a port and supply center for the Croydon goldfields and, later, for the rich copper mines around Cloncurry, to the south. But mineral ores weren't the only reason for the area's economic upswing. The exaggerated reports of a Melbourne syndicate described the so-called Plains of Promise— the long stretch of flatland running from Normanton to Burketown— as "the most fertile country in this continent ready for the plough." The first plough, however, had yet to arrive.

As in Coolgardie and elsewhere, the gold in Croydon, once the third most populous town in north Queensland, soon petered out. Shortly afterwards, an outbreak of cattle tick destroyed the cattle market, the region's only other significant industry. Then the area was struck by Gulf fever, a typhoidlike disease that decimated the population. After the turn of the century the Gulf Country, and Normanton with it, went into an economic tailspin from which it never recovered. A shire that once supported more than 20,000 people now had a population of fewer than 1,500.

Dave, a railroad buff, insisted we see the old train station, which still stood on the edge of town as a vestige of Normanton's better days. A corrugated-iron building at the end of a dirt track, it was surrounded by an open plain of scorched, dun-colored grass extending off into the distance as far as the eye could see. Inside the station a corridor led past a polished hardwood ticket counter and through to the platform, where a huge, dome-roofed, hangarlike structure covered the entire interior of the terminal.

The station now served as a museum containing a few rusting railroad relics. During the boom years of the 1890s, the railway between Normanton and Croydon, a distance of ninety-four miles, boasted five passenger cars, sixty-odd freight cars, and two guard vans. A few of the rolling stock had been preserved and were on display, sitting alongside the Gulflander, a single-car railmotor that had been in service since 1922.

On the day we visited, the "officer in charge," old Charlie Honey, his stationmaster's hat cocked back on his head, sat behind a rolltop oak desk rummaging through drawers and shuffling papers. But on Wednesday and Thursday of every week Charlie was able to lock up his office, put on his conductor's cap, and become the trainman, making the run to Croydon on one day and returning to Normanton the next. Sadly, the train had little freight to carry, and only a few diehard tourists and train enthusiasts ever bothered to make the trip.

We picked up our supplies and left Normanton with no small relief, making our way north toward Karumba over a road that sliced through a long stretch of salt pans and desiccated spear grass known as the Plains of Karumba. Small groups of cattle grazed on the few brown clumps of grass that somehow struggled up between the cracks in the sun-baked mud. Some of the animals were skittish and moved away from our vehicle, raising red dust with their hooves as they went.

9

Some historians consider Karumba "the place that never was." Officially proclaimed as a town when the Croydon gold rush began, it failed to materialize beyond a detailed plan on a draft map, a "crosshatching of streets," all of them named, that was eventually filed away in Brisbane and forgotten. Someone had even been sent up by steamer, a voyage of over two thousand miles by sea, to drive in the survey pegs, but the projected town (which was to be called Kimberley) remained nothing more than claypans and sand interspersed with a few scrubby trees.

As the years went by, however, sea captains, camel teamsters, and prospectors on their way to the Croydon goldfields needed a name to identify the "flimsy settlement" that had eventually arisen at the mouth of the Norman River. They asked the local aboriginals their name for it, and were told "Karumba." In the early 1900s Karumba was a collection of about fifty bark humpies and shacks scattered throughout the claypans. A decline set in shortly before the First World War, when the Croydon mines shut down and the majority of the town's few inhabitants pulled up stakes and left the area.

Something of a revival resurrected Karumba in 1935, when two brothers from Brisbane built a meatworks at the mouth of the river, hoping to exploit the huge herds of second-grade cattle that grazed on rank pastures around the Gulf of Carpentaria. Studies they had commissioned had indicated that a large potential market existed in the South Pacific, particularly in nearby New Guinea. Defeated by shipping problems, however, the meatworks lasted only two seasons.

The Gulf of Carpentaria, it so happened, was an unusual body of water. It had only one tide each day, not two, as in most other parts of the world. Vessels found it virtually impossible to maintain schedules, for they were often held up for days, waiting for a high tide to carry them across the sandbar. To make matters worse, when strong winds blew in from the southeast (the prevailing direction in the Dry) they pushed water to the far side of the Gulf, preventing ships from docking until the water returned. As one observer reported: "Sea captains did not find that amusing, especially in waters that had never been properly charted."

The town got another chance in the 1930s when Qantas—Queensland and Northern Territory Air Services—began international flights to compete with the slower ocean-shipping services to England, and Karumba was chosen as one of the many intermediate stops for the Catalina flying boats Qantas was using in those early days. With the advent of World War II, the Catalinas were taken over by the Australian Air Force and were soon destroyed by Japanese Zeros. (American flyers were also stationed in Karumba, as they had been in Bamaga and other bases in the north of Australia; in fact, Lyndon Johnson was aboard a bomber that, lost over the desert and low on fuel, made a forced landing near Winton, farther inland.) By the 1950s, the Qantas base was turned into a lodge catering to wealthy businessmen who came to Karumba to hunt crocodiles for sport. When that became illegal, the building was used as the offices of a fish-processing company, and was subsequently destroyed by fire.

Though Normanton and Karumba were separated by a mere forty-odd miles, a negligible distance by outback standards, the two settlements were as "different as chalk and cheese." Solid and conservative for the most part, Normanton residents were at least peripherally involved in the cattle industry.

Karumba, on the other hand, was a rowdy fishing town, most of whose inhabitants were transients who had formerly lived in cities to the south, which inclined them to regard country people, particularly their neighbors in nearby Normanton, as yokels and hicks. Little love was lost between the two communities, nor did they have much contact, apart from an occasional pub brawl that might erupt between deckies off the Karumba prawn boats and ringers up from stations around Normanton looking for sheilas. On our first night in Karumba, Phil and the Bushranger, both of whom wore their cowboy hats to the bar, almost got into "blue," a fight, when a few deckies mistook them for ringers.

Still, Normanton residents were at times accorded a degree of welcome. These occurred when its bank sent personnel to staff its branch in Karumba, which opened its doors for business only twice a week. Both customers and bank employees, we were told, displayed exemplary behavior on those occasions.

Karumba was known throughout Australia as a haven for people who for one reason or another wanted to escape. A Sydney publication had run a story about Karumba's populace entitled "Drunks, Defectos and Dogs." It might just as accurately have included defrocked priests, disbarred lawyers, doctors whose licenses had been revoked, drug smugglers, and other assorted deadbeats and "drongos"—an Aussie catch-all term for fools, simpletons, and no-hopers. At one time or another, just about every type of character imaginable had left his past behind and fled to Karumba.

In the Gulf, the phrase "He must be from Karumba" was used to describe a despicable person whose behavior was so boorish it didn't even meet bush standards. The Bushranger's attitude was typical of his countrymen. "If I was a kid growing up in this town," he said, pointing to the Air Queenie office, "that's the first place I'd head for." He'd have had a hard time getting out, in any case, since the office always seemed to be closed.

Because of the nearby prawn beds and its protected harbor, Karumba was the major port for the prawn fleet, attracting boats from around the entire Australian coast. Closemouthed captains paid crew members in cash, asked few questions, and were far more interested in a deckie's strong back than in his background. Karumba was so remote that its few policemen were concerned almost exclusively with keeping the peace within its confines. They had little interest in trying to apprehend fugitives or in solving crimes that had occurred elsewhere.

Some unlikely characters had made their way to Karumba over the years—an Eskimo from Baffin Bay known only as Esky, who worked as a deckhand; a German named Fritz, who reportedly was once a Panzer tank commander; and even an American who'd brought his shrimp boat over from Louisiana through the Panama Canal and across the Pacific. Many had, in fact, come to Karumba to escape the law, having changed their names along the way. Shortly before we arrived in town, a deckie known only as Corned Beef Freddy had committed suicide. The police had been unable to identify him, and his suicide note had been of little use to them, either, since it simply read: "Fuck off."

While Karumba promised anonymity, good money, and hard cash, its residents had to acknowledge the hazards of living there, not the least of which was the prospect of contracting Karumba rot, a fungal infection brought about by a combination of the heat, perspiration, and the torpid salt air. The rot caused boillike lesions to erupt on the skin, and persons with particularly severe infections had to be flown back to Cairns and hospitalized for treatment.

Regular bathing and medicated soaps were usually effective in controlling the problem, but the town had no potable water—its supply had to be brought in by freighter from the south. Fresh drinking water was at a premium, and few of the prawn or fishing boats had shower facilities. In fact, Karumba's town fathers were concerned that the industry would soon be forced to move elsewhere, and a few local promoters were already beginning to tout the place as a tourist destination.

The Karumba Lodge was, as ever, the only game in town, and sooner or later everyone made his way to its outdoor bar—so called because its front did, in fact, stand wide open. Hot and humid air wafted in unchecked, but it did, to some extent, dissipate the smells of stale beer and fried food inside. Overhead, whirring continuously, rusty three-bladed fans were suspended from a nicotine-darkened ceiling, and on every Formica table sat an empty tuna fish tin that served as ashtray. Galvanized metal garbage cans were placed in strategic locations throughout the room in the hopes that patrons wouldn't throw refuse on the floor.

To one side of the room was the kitchen area, which sold fish and chips and other hot meals pushed across the counter on Styrofoam plates. The food wasn't very good, but that didn't seem to bother any of the patrons. As Jim Lynch, a gray-bearded old sea dog with a plastic nose (his real one had been surgically removed because of cancer caused by long exposure to the sun), said: "When I get hungry, I could eat a Chinaman's arse through a wicker chair."

One evening Dave and I were sitting in the bar having a drink when a gentleman by the name of Johnny Indonesia dropped by to pick up his lady. A few days earlier I'd gone up with Johnny in a spotter plane, searching for banana prawns over the Gulf. He had been hired by one of Karumba's prawn-packing companies to look for "prawn boils"— schools of shrimp spawning on the surface. We'd found only a single boil that morning, and after Johnny called in its position, we circled over the turbulent patch of water waiting for the trawlers. Created by millions of prawns in a mating frenzy, the boil was over a mile wide and almost as long. Johnny told me that some boils were three or four times as large, and that a single pass through one of them would fill the hold of a trawler.

Johnny was said to be a very successful fisherman, but his life ashore had been full of romantic complications. He'd even crossed swords with the local constabulary when, in response to a policeman who was paying too much attention to a lady friend of his, he picked up the officer bodily and stuffed him, in full uniform, head first into a garbage pail.

There was something enigmatic about Johnny, and he had a certain presence. In his late thirties and of average height, he wore his long brown hair in a ponytail and had bulging biceps covered with tattoos. I'd heard that he'd originally come to Australia from Dutch Indonesia, from which he'd taken his name. He didn't talk much, and he wasn't the sort of fellow you'd be encouraged to ask about himself. One of the barmaids described him as a "lovable rogue," and I would have liked to have gotten to know him better. But the evening he dropped by the outdoor bar we didn't even have the opportunity to say "g'day" to him, for he seemed to be in a bit of a rush.

So pressed was Johnny for time, in fact, that he didn't bother to park his pickup truck outside, but drove straight through the eight-foot-high wooden fence surrounding the bar's entrance and careened right into the middle of the outdoor pub, sending splintered fragments of wood flying in all directions. The truck's bull bar—which in Australia was often called the 'roo bar, but in Karumba was sadistically re-ferred to as the "boong bar"—bashed aside a few empty tables and chairs before it slammed into one of the garbage cans, strewing its contents all over the concrete floor.

The truck screeched to a stop at a table where Johnny's lady, a well-endowed young sheila who sported a striking red-and-blue tattoo of a butterfly on her right shoulder, sat drinking with three deckies. Johnny jumped out of the cab, lifted his lady out of her chair with her arms pinned to her sides, and deposited her cursing and kicking into the truck.

"You can't do this ta me, ya fuckin' sonofabitch," the sheila screamed. But Johnny ignored the hail of obscenities she directed at him, and none of the deckies interfered because Johnny had a reputation for knowing how to use his fists. He slammed his truck into reverse, backing out of the pub through the hole in the fence he'd made a few moments earlier, successfully spiriting his lady away from the evils of drink, bad companions, and the stunned patrons of the Karumba bar. We were all impressed, and remained so even when we learned that Johnny had been less successful in a previous encounter with another lady, who when she discovered he was seeing someone else on the sly, had bitten off his right earlobe.

10

If Johnny Indonesia represented one typical aspect of Karumba, it was not the only side. Civility did still exist in the town, as we discovered one evening when the four of us were eating dinner at the pub; the manager invited us over to her table and introduced us to Jenny Lott, a former British airline stewardess. For the past five years Jenny had been skippering her own thirty-foot barramundi boat, fishing the shark- and crocodile-infested rivers that ran into the Gulf of Carpentaria. Except for her dog, G.P. Slug (it had the face of a guinea pig, which explained the initials), she fished without a crew, alone on those virtually uncharted waters for as long as eight weeks at a time.

Jenny didn't look at all like the wind-wrinkled, leathery old sea dog I would have expected. Though in her late forties, she was a striking woman with perfect white teeth and a dark complexion that had grown ever richer from exposure to the tropical sun. Only a few becoming streaks of gray coursed through her thick brunette hair, and when she smiled, her dark eyes sparkled with lively wit. She referred to herself as a fisherman—she laughed when I called her a "fisherwoman"—and until I shook her hand, cut and scarred from years of hauling and picking nets, I didn't believe she was one.

"I used to strum my guitar a lot, but my hands got so stiff I gave that away. You get terrible hands with this fishing and I couldn't get around the chords anymore."

She'd grown up on the Isle of Wight, daughter of a vice air marshal in the RAF. Like him, Jenny had wanted to be a commercial pilot, but that was "unthinkable twenty years ago, so I became a stewardess instead." Jenny was still working for the airline when she took a long holiday, driving overland with a Canadian girl friend to Ceylon and from there taking a ship to Perth. Unlike Lord McAlpine, however, by the time she came ashore in Perth, she was out of money as well as work. She took a position teaching in a girls' boarding school.

"I kept a couple of horses there, and it was lovely," she said. "But I knew teaching wasn't for me. I liked the horses more than the children."

She resigned at the end of school term and set off to see the rest of Australia, driving a friend's car across the Nullarbor—there was no road then, only a track—and then north to Brisbane. From there she hitchhiked to the Great Barrier Reef and got a job as a waitress in a pub near Townsville.

"It terrified me at first because it was so much rougher than an English pub," Jenny recalled. "But then I met a couple of brothers who had a fifty-foot schooner and caught mackerel, and I started fishing with them. We caught heaps of fish and filled the freezer up. It was magnificent. I didn't get paid at first, but I said straight away, 'Well, that'll do me, I like this way of living.' "

The following year Jenny borrowed £600 from her father back in England to buy a share in the brothers' boat. She worked with them for three years before selling out and buying a run-down boat of her own. By that time she had obtained her coastal master's ticket, the certificate that qualified her to run vessels of up to a hundred tons. She made her first solo voyage at the age of twenty-six, making an eight-hundred-mile run from Townsville to fish the Torres Strait.

"The other fishermen told me I was crazy, that I couldn't run the boat on my own. I thought they were probably right, but I was going to have a go anyway. I was stuck with the wretched thing so I took her out, and I did alright. She wasn't a bad little boat after all, and in a few years I was accepted as just another fisherman. Thinking back on it now, I wouldn't do it again, but then I was young, keen, and crazy."

By the mid-1970s the prawning boom was on in the Gulf, and Jenny worked those waters for banana prawns. She ended up buying her own prawn boat, the *Tony Christine*, fishing the Gulf with a crew of four. Except for one male deckie, they were all women. When the season was over, she decided to "have a go at barramundi," a highly prized and sought-after fish for which restaurants in southern cities would pay top dollar.

"I knew absolutely nothing about setting nets in rivers, or even how to get up the rivers, because I only knew the sea. There were very few barra fishermen in those days, but there were so many fish around you couldn't miss. I quite liked it, sneaking in where there were no buoys and over sandbars at the mouths of rivers. You had to go in at high tide and map out a channel to get out. It was a bit dicey in a fifty-six-foot boat.

"But I loved it. There was no skill or adventure in prawning. They're not really boats, just mechanized platforms that go out there and drag along the bottom. I still kept a crew then, one guy and a little girl cook. She was reliable and I kept her on for years. Finding good deckhands was always a problem. You got those twits that expected to earn a million dollars."

The next morning Dave and I stopped by the pier where she kept her boat. It was moored out back, where Jenny was fiberglassing a big stainless-steel water-cooled muffler she'd removed from it.

"It's full of holes," she explained. "It was spraying water all over the engine room. The welder couldn't fix it so I have to do it myself." She stood up and wiped her hands on her overalls. "You have to be able to do most everything yourself. When you're out there and something stuffs up, you learn very quickly. A diesel's pretty reliable as long as it has oil. But you can run into trouble with things like alternators, pumps, drives, and bearings. You carry all those spares and after a while you get pretty cluey."

Dave asked her about the dangers she encountered from saltwater crocodiles.

"I'm always seeing their evil-looking red eyes in my spotlight when I'm up those rivers in a dinghy running around at night," Jenny admitted. "Always hanging about to have a go at the fish in my nets. They're cunning devils but sometimes they get fouled in them.

"Last year I got a monster. The net had sunk to the bottom, and I went out to it thinking it was snagged on a rock. I started heaving it in when suddenly I brought up this great thing with its mouth gaping and all those terrible teeth. I hadn't even known he was out there, but he was longer than my sixteen-foot dinghy. I let go in a hurry, and he sank. In the morning I hauled the net ashore and cleared it after he'd drowned.

"But crocodiles aren't the real problem for barra fishermen. It's those saw-toothed sharks always getting caught in the nets. They don't drown, and I usually have to shoot them."

As I was helping Jenny apply fiberglass resin, I asked if she ever got lonely out there on those distant rivers.

"Sometimes it's a lonely life, but I still love it. At first I found myself looking around for another boat or somebody to talk to. I was pretty unsure of myself in those days. After four weeks of not seeing anybody, it's smashing when another boat pulls into the cove and I go over and have a yack.

"But after a while I found that I needed time to myself and to be on my own. It's grown into me now. Away from all the bills, all the garbage that happens in town. Anchored in a creek at sunset, watching a couple of wallabies scratching around on the white sand beach and the pelicans hanging around the back of the boat waiting for a handout. I've gotten so used to that peace that as soon as I come back to civilization I want to be off again."

When Jenny finished applying the resin to the muffler, discarding the empty container and brush, she walked to the edge of the pier to wave to a prawn boat captain heading out toward the gulf. Even in old work clothes she was a very attractive woman, and I suspect Dave's thoughts ran along similar lines, because he asked if she had ever been married.

"No, and a lot of people think that's strange," she replied, pausing to reflect for a moment or two. "But I reckon I'm married to boats. They've owned me. I once thought I owned them but it was always the other way around.

"And then there were the Australian men, who wanted you to cook and look after the kids, while they went off to their football matches or out on the reef fishing. At the parties you'd have all the women lined up along one wall and the guys clustered around the keg. That seemed wrong to me and I could never understand it. I'm just another fisherman now, and I don't have to trouble about that sort of thing anymore."

As we bade her farewell and made our way back along the decrepit waterfront I couldn't help but admire Jenny Lott—even in her refusal to conform, and by her daring to live the way most people only dream about, she had managed to become a truly fulfilled person. Instead of taking her place in the secure, predictable existence that some women from her background might be inclined to prefer, Jenny had dropped out, and in the great tradition of the Australian pioneers, she had carved out a place for herself in one of the toughest towns in the world. A gentle and thoughtful woman, she had successfully competed in a man's world, mastering skills like diesel mechanics and navigation that were generally considered to be an exclusively male province. She had learned, in short, to be totally self-sufficient, a goal I had always longed to attain, but had begun to realize I never would. Jenny had dismissively considered herself as only "a fisherman," yet how remarkable a one she had become.

11

Leaving Karumba, we headed southwest on the Burke Developmental Road, and after a refueling stop at the Burke and Wills Roadhouse, turned northwest toward Burketown. On either side of the bitumen stretched interminable expanses of claypans and the parched, colorless plain dotted with sparse patches of saltbush and spinifex. My weary eyes resisted the dismal scene, and for fleeting intervals I dozed off, lulled by the drone of the engine and the languorous heat. It was midmorning, and the thermal wind was increasing, stirring up spiraling dust devils that occasionally darted across the road.

It was an unlikely place to encounter anything, other than the infrequent automobile going in the other direction. But suddenly Phil pointed ahead, where a dim chrome shimmer was slowly making its way toward us. As the distance closed we were able to make out a solitary figure pedaling along on a bicycle. The four of us were so astonished that no one uttered a word as the bike whizzed by. A full minute or so elapsed before I recovered the presence of mind to yell at Phil, "God Almighty! Turn around."

"To chase a silly cyclist through the desert?" objected Dave, forever the pragmatist.

Phil, however, was as intrigued as I was, and spun the Toyota around. We quickly overtook the bicyclist, and Phil pulled off the road a few hundred yards ahead of him.

"What in the world are you doing out here in the middle of nowhere?" I asked, after we had jumped out and waved him down.

"I might ask you the same question," replied the cyclist, with a bright smile and an American accent. A well-built young fellow in his early twenties, whose glasses gave him a scholarly appearance, Andrew Graham came from Seattle, Washington, where he worked as a carpenter and was a graduate student in anthropology. He was bicycling around the Australian continent, a feat he hoped to accomplish in six months. He'd already cycled around the entire United States and

North Africa, and he'd been on the road in Queensland for two weeks. "I enjoy seeing new places and meeting people," Andrew told us, removing his cycling gloves and helmet. "And I like the pace of doing it on a bicycle. I'd walk if I could, but I'm too lazy. I'll average a hundred twenty to a hundred fifty kilometers a day, depending on how much there is to see, and how hot it is." Andrew explained that his touring bicycle, an extremely lightweight but rugged ten-speed, had been especially designed and built for this particular trip.

"I do most of my traveling very early in the morning and early in the evening and I siesta during the heat of the day. Under a moon and the bright stars in this hemisphere, I can cycle until nine or ten at night. That's when the weather is cool, the wind is light, and there aren't so many bugs out."

"I camp whenever I get tired. I carry a sleeping bag and there's certainly no shortage of places to set up my tent," he added, laughing and gesturing toward the desolate plains that surrounded us.

"You probably think it's strange for me to be doing this by myself, and I would have preferred to have done it with somebody. But I couldn't find anyone foolish enough to join me, and being alone gives me an opportunity to do a lot of reading, and to keep up with my journal. You can be by yourself and not be lonely."

"I'm glad you're not twenty anymore," Dave muttered to me. "At least we're out here in a four-wheel-drive." And then he turned on Andrew. "What do your friends and family say about this trip? They must think you're crazy."

"My brother would certainly agree with you." Andrew laughed. "And he's a cyclist, too. I guess the two of us have just taken different directions on the same vehicle.

"Traveling on a bicycle through Australia is far less difficult than the States. When I cycled through New York I had to go through Manhattan or make a two-hundred-mile detour. That was a terrible experience. Boston's another city that's not very kind to cyclists either. But Australia's far more open and there's much less traffic, so it's easier to get around.

"So far, this has been a great trip. The Australians I've encountered have been extraordinarily generous and kind. My first three days on the road, I received six invitations to stay at people's homes. Cars are always stopping when I'm on long stretches of road, and offering me a drink or something to eat."

Andrew was well equipped for his trip; in addition to a sleeping bag and tent, he was carrying cooking utensils, food, and water, but he didn't have a billy to boil tea. He planned to buy one in the next town, he told us, because Australians expected him to have one.

"It's very important when you're traveling in another country to blend in and not be eccentric. I even stop outside a town and take off my helmet and cyclist's gloves so that I don't call attention to myself." It was sage advice that unfortunately was lost on Dave, who attracted a great deal of attention wherever he went. None of the Australians we came across roaming around the bush were accustomed to seeing anyone wearing a surgical mask and Birkenstock sandals.

As the sun was climbing higher in the sky Andrew was eager to move on, so we gave him the names of some people we knew in W.A., and wished him luck. "Would you like a cold drink before you go?" asked Phil, as Andrew was adjusting his helmet.

"No thanks," he replied, "I'm doin' just fine."

Shifting into gear, Andrew headed off with a wave toward the Burke and Wills Roadhouse, almost fifty miles away. I watched him fade from sight and disappear into the undulating desert heat.

I volunteered to take the wheel when we got back in the Toyota, for I always felt more positive about driving through the featureless landscape when I had something to occupy my thoughts. As I drove along the empty road I found myself ruminating wistfully on what Andrew had said about his taking a different direction than his brother. When I had been his age I had gone so far as to apply for "assisted passage" to Australia—those were days when the government was trying to attract new immigrants. Just a few short weeks away from emigrating with my family, my wife and I split up, and I settled for a job in a shoe factory instead.

I confessed to Phil that the roads not taken had left me feeling a little regretful, a little nostalgic for endless possibilities. Wisely, he reminded me that while I might have been leading a life as adventurous as Andrew's, I could well have become an émigré, as uprooted as Joe Gelati, never quite at home and unable to come to terms with the unwelcoming Australian bush.

12

One of the most cherished characters in Australian fiction is Jean Harman, the heroine of Nevil Shute's novel *A Town Like Alice*. Jean, an Englishwoman, meets an Aussie bloke, Joe Harman, when both are prisoners of the Japanese in Malaya. Separated by the brutalities of war, they are reunited in Australia in a primitive settlement called Willstown, where he's a station manager. She sets about to make Willstown another Alice Springs, and at first Joe doesn't want the place to change. But because she was the stuff of fiction, reality proved no obstacle to Jean Harman. The once moribund town, consisting of not much more than a pub and a small store when she first arrived, grew under her inspiration into a thriving community. By story's end, Willstown boasted an ice cream parlor, a swimming pool, a beauty salon, and an open-air cinema.

Willstown wasn't on our map—there was no such place—but Burketown, which had served as model for it, lay some hundred miles from the Burke and Wills Roadhouse, where we'd camped the night before. Willstown (prior to Jean's renovation) was characterized by Shute as a "derelict little place" with a population, "not counting boongs," of no more than 120. Except for the fact that today it had even fewer people, Burketown fit that description to a tee.

"Where's the ice cream parlor?" asked Jack, as we stood at the lonely intersection of Burketown's two dusty roads. Except for a young aboriginal in a cowboy hat who staggered through the swinging doors of the corner pub and out into the blazing sunlit street, the place was deserted. It could have been *High Noon*, just before the gunfight. The glaze-eyed aboriginal stopped short at the sight of us, blinked several times, and then, as if he were merely a groundhog out for a quick look around, turned and reeled back into the familiar darkness of the pub.

In 1841 an English captain, J. L. Stokes, had passed this way in his explorations of the Gulf of Carpentaria. Coming up the Albert River for the first time, he chose the site of what was later to become Burketown at the western edge of the Plains of Promise, just above high water mark. So enthralled was he with the barren marshland extending before him that he conceived a vision of the future, which he described quixotically in his journal: "I breathed a prayer that ere long the now level horizon would be broken by a succession of tapering spires rising from Christian hamlets that must ultimately stud this country."

Stokes's vision, of course, never materialized. The Burketown that broke the level horizon had never been much more than a rough bush settlement, beginning as a single "grog shanty" in the wilderness and expanding only slowly to include first a shop or two, then a few wooden shacks. And if the short-lived gold boom at the turn of the century had had much impact on the town, momentarily swelling the population into the tens of thousands, its effects were no longer discernible. With its dirt-track streets and now vacant lots long overgrown with scrub, Burketown today looked much as it did at the time it was founded. By nightfall, in fact, it was possible to forget that we were in a town at all. No lights shone except those that glimmered dully through the swinging doors of the pub or through the occasional uncurtained window of the few remaining houses. The sense of isolation continued at daybreak, when sulphur-hued fog banks known as "morning glories" often rolled in off the Gulf of Carpentaria and hovered over the humid town until the tropical sun burnt them off.

For once, even the unflappable Queensland tourist bureau was hard-pressed to paint a rosy picture. "Since being settled in the mid-1800s," began a brochure promoting the Gulf as a tourist destination, "Burke Shire has experienced devastation from cyclones, tidal waves, floods, Gulf fever, and isolation. The environment is hostile and cruel. The roads are bad and during the wet season, totally unusable. Burke Shire is not a home away from home. But the true adventurer will love this forgotten land that still reverberates with the sound of loneliness, the didjeridoo, and the drover's stock whip."

"Aren't you glad I dragged you along?" Jack twitted Phil. It was up to me to remind them both that the last time an Irishman dragged his mate into this part of the country, the two of them had ended up dead. The Irishman's name was Burke, his mate was Wills, and the pair were inextricably linked in the annals of Australian history.

In 1861 Burke and Wills had been the first European explorers to conquer the interior of Australia, crossing the continent from Melbourne in the south to the Gulf of Carpentaria in the north. But if their names were linked in the glory of this accomplishment, so was their ultimate fate: ill-provisioned for the journey and stubbornly resistant to help from the aborigines, both men starved to death on the return leg of the expedition. "There is something about the Irish temperament," wrote one Australian historian, "that is not ideal for exploration; it is too quick, too mercurial, too imaginative, too headstrong and, paradoxically, too brave."

Ironically, it was their dying that brought Burke and Wills fame. While "the dead explorers were dressed and buried as heroes," the only surviving member of the expedition, a man named King, was quickly shunted aside and all but forgotten by history. And to add to the irony, the heroes succumbed to starvation while camped by a creek where food was plentiful. From the outset, it seems, life in the Gulf was synonymous with frustration and failure.

Forsayth, Georgetown, Croydon, Normanton, and now Burketown—we had passed through them all. Like saprophytic spores themselves in the throes of decay, these sad little settlements scattered throughout the Carpentaria region were so much alike it was hard to distinguish one from the other. The dilapidated pub in Georgetown was a little bigger than the one in Burketown, or was the one in Burketown the larger of the two? There was an "abo-owned" supermarket in Normanton called Mai (the aboriginal word for food), or was it in Croydon? It didn't matter, because all these towns were fundamentally the same. They had all been built on dreams, of gold and prosperity, and when the lodes dried up, the dreams did, too.

"Welcome to Croydon, mate," an old man at the garage had said when we pulled up to the petrol bowser there. "Twenty-three hotels, nine brothels, twenty thousand Chinese. That was in 1910, son. Things have changed a bit since then."

They sure had. Now, like every other settlement in the Gulf, Croydon was almost a ghost town. "Even the termites have deserted the place," admitted the man at the garage. Where once had been streets of wooden houses, now remained nothing but a few long-abandoned roads, tracks etched like a grid into the reddish-brown surface of the earth, and a few odd buildings.

One of the structures that had survived was the old corrugated-iron courthouse; its wood-plank prisoner's box and witness stand were still there, as were the original gas lamps out front. On a wall inside hung a faded photograph of an aboriginal prisoner in neck chains, identified by a small sign as Gumjam, a notorious killer convicted in the early 1900s. The district hospital had also withstood the elements. Elevated on stiltlike blocks and encircled by an open veranda, it was a large, rambling structure built when John Angus MacDonald, who had made his fortune in gold, bequeathed his entire estate (£10,000) for that purpose. MacDonald, who died in 1892, also left one shilling to his wife "so she can buy a rope and hang herself with it."

Even the Australophile Nevil Shute never seemed able to get much beyond the word "derelict" when writing about the Gulf. And I was beginning to understand why: a more nuanced description was impossible. Once you got beyond the Woop-Woop or the Black Stump, those mythical places celebrated in Australian folklore as the gateways to the Outback, you entered a world of almost undifferentiated desolation—over 2 million square miles of desert or desertlike plains, scrub, salt lakes, and worn-down mountain ranges, totally uninhabitable, or if habitable, only marginally so.

"Dry as a dead dingo's donger," quipped an aboriginal horseman we had met in Georgetown. We had looked up the shire clerk there and found him in the town's only pub. There wasn't much point in his being anywhere else. The shire consisted of 15,280 square miles, about twice the size of Massachusetts, but it had a population of only 1,100 people.

The shire clerk handed us a glossy sheet of paper that looked like a "Wanted" poster, and in a way, it was. Printed at the top, above the photo of a large, warty, pale-brown amphibian, were the words: "Help halt the cane toad." *Bufo marinus*, it warned, was a serious pest, which had been introduced from the Americas and which "poisons, kills, pollutes, erodes soil, and disperses the eggs of human parasites." According to the poster, it had taken less than five years for it to infest the Queensland part of the Gulf of Carpentaria, and it had recently crossed the border into the Northern Territory. Sometimes "hitching lifts in cars and trucks," but more commonly "hopping at 27 km per year," it was moving relentlessly westward, toward Darwin.

"When you get transferred to a place like this," muttered the shire clerk, as he lifted another stubby to his lips, "your first wretched thought is, what the hell have I done wrong?"

Of course, not everyone felt that way. A number of Australian writers, poets mostly, had romanticized the bush in verse that only thinly concealed their annoyance at the abuse heaped upon their country by their uncomprehending and arrogant English cousins. ("Those Pommy barstads give me the irts," was the average Aussie's way of expressing his irritation.) Often, as we sat around the campfire in the evening, the Bushranger would read some of that verse aloud, perhaps sensing from the wistful way I was staring into the fire that, after almost eight months on the road, I was longing for home. Dorothea Mackellar's "My Country," which Australian schoolchildren recited in unison almost like the Lord's Prayer, was one of those poems he knew by heart:

> *The love of field and coppice*
> *Of green and shaded lanes,*
> *Of ordered woods and gardens,*
> *Is running in your veins,*
> *Strong love of grey-blue distance,*
> *Brown streams and soft dim skies,*

I know but cannot share it,
My love is otherwise.

I love a sunburnt country,
A land of sweeping plains,
Of ragged mountain ranges,
Of droughts and flooding rains;
I love her far horizons,
I love her jewel-sea,
Her beauty and her terror—
The wide brown land for me!

Nice stuff. And in the evening, under the stars, lulled by the cadence of the verse and the feeling the Bushranger was able to impart to the lines, my eyes grew moist, and I almost imagined that what those poets said was true. But the harsh light of morning always brought me back to reality. The moistness in my eyes the night before must have been caused by smoke—smoke or dust.

7

The Gang
from Wollogorang

Wollogorang Crocodile

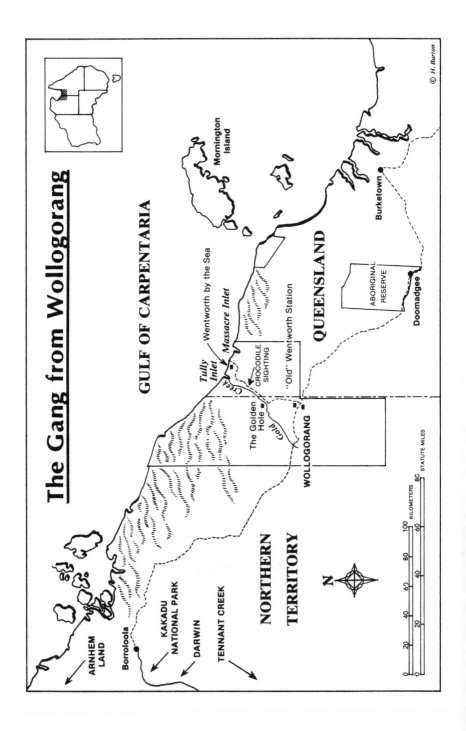

The Gang from Wollogorang

© H. Burton

1

For most of the fifty-odd mile journey southwest between Burketown and the Doomadgee Aboriginal Reserve, we encountered nothing but a flat, desolate plain of dun-colored spear grass. Innumerable anthills, eerily reminiscent of grave markers, extended to the horizon, giving the landscape the aspect of a vast cemetery. Only occasionally was the monotony of the terrain broken by a stunted acacia tree or the carcass of an abandoned automobile. Like the husks of enormous locusts, cars lay along the side of the dusty track, stripped of wheels, transmissions, and anything else that could be removed from them.

As we jolted along, our tires stirred up an immense cloud of bulldust that enveloped the Toyota and moved along with us like a crimson fog. A diminutive dust storm raged inside the vehicle, and we were completely blanketed by a fine red-brown powder. It caked in our nostrils, and I could feel the tiny grains accumulating in my mouth and throat. Dave tried wearing his surgical mask, but it clogged after only a few minutes of use. But there was nothing to be done about it: We wanted to get to Wollogorang and the Northern Territory, and the only way to do it was to keep driving and swallow the dust.

Every two or three hours we'd pull up for a smoko and a cuppa, and one of us would boil the billy. Since Dave and I didn't smoke, we'd walk away from the Bushranger and Phil, who were busy flushing out their lungs with nicotine, to drink our tea and breathe fresh air. But after only a few minutes the four of us would escape the flies and be off and back in the storm again. Our destination, the Wollogorang homestead, was located just over the border in the Northern Territory, the most sparsely settled region of Australia—more than half a million square miles with a mere 130,000 inhabitants.

After Doomadgee the track veered to the northwest, and the flat country gradually became more hilly. Nothing along the road detained us until we reached Hell's Gate, a jagged outcrop of sandstone overlooking the surrounding countryside that served as the jump-off point for pioneers heading west at the end of the nineteenth century. Queensland police accompanied them to Hell's Gate, where they were left on their own to face the perils of the bush—including attacks by hostile aborigines—until they reached the safety of Darwin.

We stopped to chat with Bill and Lee Olive, another couple who spoke to us about their desire to get out of the rat race. Recalling the unhappy experience of the Birches at Wooramel back in W.A., I wondered what had led them to flirt with financial disaster by building a roadhouse in such an isolated spot. During construction they were living in a caravan next to a gaping pit in the ground, where they eventually planned to locate their fuel tanks.

It was the second marriage for both Bill and Olive, whose first husband had been killed by a saltwater crocodile. They were a middle-aged couple with a five-year plan to work hard, earn a lot of money, and eventually retire. From what I could see, if traffic on the road was any indication, and this was the busy season, they could have started their retirement immediately.

We continued on until we reached the Northern Territory late in the afternoon. Just across the border was a gate that led onto Wollogorang, the Bushranger's promised land. A few more miles of rough track brought us to the homestead, where we set up camp in a paddock nearby. Dave and I threw our swags under a sandpaper tree, aptly named because its leaves scraped the skin off his arm when he brushed against it, and Phil and the Bushranger found another one nearby.

Almost everything in that inhospitable country seemed to have evolved with the sole purpose of discouraging the presence of human beings. If it wasn't snakes or double-gee's, a needlelike thorn that could penetrate feet through thick, leather soles, it was wattles, spiny acacia, or some other prickly scrub that could puncture or poison. Earlier, Phil had even required treatment by the Flying Doctor Service, so severely infected were his insect bites. The Bushranger jokingly diagnosed the condition as Karumba rot, and suggested Phil might have to be evacuated. It hadn't been necessary for the doctor to fly out on that occasion, for most stations had medical kits and he simply prescribed some antibiotics over the radio.

We were reaching the last stage of our trip, and I wondered what we would find here at Wollogorang. I'd had my fill of pounding over rough tracks, of eating bulldust, of painstakingly setting up camp only to break it next day. I would have given almost anything for a hot shower, a change of *clean* clothes, a meal in a good restaurant. I'd listened to enough of the deluded, harebrained schemes of incubating entrepreneurs who fantasized about becoming millionaires and building tourist empires out in the middle of nowhere. One fellow back in Karumba had even talked about the windfall he expected when his Hovercraft arrived, and he could zip hordes of tourists around on sightseeing tours of the harbor. Striking it rich—the bush gospel according to Peter Eaton—no longer seemed, even remotely, a heroic pursuit.

2

"It's the most tumbledown property in the world. Shockin', really. It's a large station . . . in the Gulf area, on the border between Queensland and the Northern Territory. But they're just scratchin' out a livin'. Even the road into the place is the worst I've ever seen."

The first we ever heard of Wollogorang was at a pub in Cairns where Jack, Phil, and I were enjoying our last few draft beers before heading out on the second leg of our trip. We were "havin' a yarn" with a sun-ravaged fisherman, who couldn't have been more than thirty-five years old but who looked pretty tumbledown himself. Having hung around the north most of his life, he was familiar with the area around the Gulf of Carpentaria, and especially with Wollogorang.

"I can't remember the name of the bloke who owns it," he continued. "Paul somethin'-or-other. There's an interestin' story there somewhere, fair dinkum. He's old and grotty. Not the best-lookin' bloke in the world. But he's got this young English wife. Name's Sue. She's pretty . . . bit overweight but pretty. They live in a little shack. Got this photo hangin' on the wall. He's all spruced up, lookin' swish. Probably went off to England one time, met this upper-class sheila, and told her he's got the largest cattle station in Australia. She didn't know what she was gettin' into." He chuckled, perhaps a little maliciously.

Everyone we met in far north Queensland seemed to talk about

Wollogorang, but few had anything good to say about it. Even to the hardened people of the Gulf, the station just over the N.T. border was somewhat of an embarrassment, a pariah. "I can't understand anybody living like that," huffed the wife of one station manager, whose homestead on the Leichardt River was three hundred miles southeast of Wollogorang.

But the Bushranger understood. He had been out to the station before, and he actually liked Wollogorang. Perhaps it made him nostalgic for the years he had spent as a plantation manager in Papua New Guinea, where he would sit around his bungalow before going to bed each night shooting the rats that scampered through the living room.

"It's just a matter of priorities," he explained, as we were breaking camp near Burketown. "They like bush livin'. Fixin' up the place isn't so important to them."

Yet Wollogorang was a lot worse than anything I'd ever seen in Papua New Guinea. It reminded me more of some isolated part of Bangladesh that had been devastated by a tidal wave and never again resettled.

"This looks worse than Marble Bar," I had said to Jack when we first pulled in, speaking in a whisper so as not to hurt the Bushranger's feelings.

"Take another nap," he had replied, with his customary sardonic sneer, "and try to sleep for a month."

Our campsite at Wollogorang was only a few hundred yards from the homestead, and the following morning, after a night under the stars (with only the sounds of a brumby's distant whinnying and galloping hoofbeats to disturb the silence), we walked over to the house to meet the celebrated couple who ran the station. They were seated comfortably on a bench on their front stoop, enjoying a cup of tea, and if they seemed a bit wary of us, they were obviously pleased to see the Bushranger.

The fisherman had been wrong in several respects. For one thing, Paul Zlotskowski wasn't a bad-looking bloke at all. At fifty-two (though like most longtime bushmen he could have passed for sixty-two) he had character in his gnarled, mellow face. Had he been living in the city, he might well have been considered a "new Australian," a phrase used to describe recent immigrants with foreign-sounding names. But Paul was a fifth-generation resident—his great-great-grandfather had left Poland for England and from there had migrated to Australia in 1835—and despite his Slavic origins he was very much "a dinki-di Aussie" in both appearance and speech. No place seemed to assimilate immigrants more thoroughly than the Australian bush. If the harsh, lonely life didn't kill the first-generation pioneers outright, it somehow managed to eliminate every trace of lineage in their offspring.

Sue was his second wife, and the mother of his two youngest children, a fragile-looking four-year-old girl and a spindly-legged boy of six. If Sue could be considered attractive, it was in a rough-textured, Glenda Jackson sort of way. At twenty-nine, she had curly brown hair and a light, unwrinkled complexion, but she looked, or perhaps acted, more like a seasoned mother of forty. Rawboned and stocky, she was carelessly dressed, and on the surface, at least, she and Paul didn't seem like such an unlikely pair after all. Gulf gossip to the contrary, she *had* known what she was getting into with Wollogorang, and now that she was there, she seemed to relish every minute of it.

"My mum was brought up by Zulus," she said, by way of explanation, "so I think she's rather pleased I'm out here. The pioneering blood has come back out in me, sort of thing." Sue had brought me to the "kitchen," where she mixed batter as she talked to me, one arm cradling an earthenware bowl against her large, shapeless bosom while the other hand stirred with a long wooden spoon. I had the image of her mother's being found wild in the South African veldt and brought up as a warrior woman by Zulu tribesmen, but it hadn't been quite so dramatic. She had been raised on a sugarcane farm in South Africa by parents who had emigrated from Scotland; their servants had been Zulus.

But how had Sue herself, a former employee of a London firm that served as jeweler to the Queen and the daughter of a professor at the Royal School of Mines, found her way out to this idyllic little spot? "I inherited some money from a wealthy aunt," she explained. "And since my friend Polly and I always wanted to see Australia, we came out here for a few months. We spent two or three weeks in Sydney looking around, and then we decided to get a job. But we couldn't get one. We weren't long-legged or brown enough . . . we were just two rather undistinguished girls. Making inquiries over the phone, though, we did have some extraordinary offers: 'Do you mind looking after tourists?' 'Oh no, we don't mind.' 'And do you mind, uh, sort of wearing next to nothing?' 'Well, not too keen, thanks.'

"We left Sydney and headed for the Great Barrier Reef. And one day, on Brampton Island, we were having a cup of coffee overlooking the sea and I said to Polly, 'Wouldn't it be wonderful just to go sailing off somewhere.' And a fellow at the next table said, 'Well, have you looked in the paper this morning? There's a guy wants two girls to go crewing on a yacht.'

"The advert said contact Mr. Paul at the pub, so we did."

For the seven years that Sue had lived with Paul at Wollogorang, home to her had been a dark, dingy, corrugated-iron hovel that had doorways but no doors, windows without panes, and an A-frame roof collapsed on one side, allowing what little rain there was to fall unimpeded on the dirt floor.

"It was originally built in 1926, and it's an awful place to keep tidy," she explained. Speaking with a very proper English accent and in a hearty, almost bellowing voice, she sounded like a guide giving a tour through one of Great Britain's historic monuments. "In the old days the Chinese cook used to live in the end room there," she said, pointing to the opposite side of the shack. Now it was just a space, divided (if that word was at all applicable) by a few seemingly misplaced ironwood beams, all hand-cut with an adz, and marked by a small step where the floor descended an inch or two. "It's the dining room now," she continued, "though I haven't used it as that for a couple of years. We eat here in the kitchen instead."

The floor of the kitchen was made out of river stone, a smooth, flat rock which, according to Sue, people in the cities paid thousands of dollars to get for their patios. It had been laid in "higgledly-piggledly" fashion, meaning that the stone didn't extend all the way to the walls. Nor had it been laid beneath the dirt-encrusted table and worn benches at which I was now sitting, sampling some fresh scones Sue had just pulled out of her wood-burning stove, a huge cast-iron thing that sat against one wall and occupied at least one-third of that side of the shack.

The dining-room floor, in contrast, was made of antbed. "That's white ants' nest," she explained, a little surprised at my ignorance of bush building material. "You knock it down, pummel it into a powder, add water to it, and mix it up like a paste. After a couple of days it dries into a very hard surface, hard as cement. There are different types of antnest. Red looks nice but it makes a very bad floor. The gray has a bucket of clay in it and that's the best. I've asked a few old-timers and they say always use the gray."

"Did you ever think about using linoleum?" I asked timidly, almost ashamed to utter the word in front of her.

"If you're living out here, you're living on a shoestring," she replied, with conviction. "It costs a lot to run the place—to keep the generator going, to pay the men. You use whatever's available."

But I didn't buy her justification, because she and Paul were simply not that broke. They had money enough to go on holiday to Europe and rent a house on the Gold Coast, near Brisbane. And behind their shack they were in the process of building a new home with all the modern facilities, even toilets. Although it was less than half finished, they already were sleeping in the new place—where they had slept before remained a mystery.

No, the real reason for the almost cozy dilapidation of the station was as the Bushranger had suggested: Sue just liked it that way. She was proud of being primitive even though there was no need to be, even though others might find her life of self-imposed privation to be anachronistic. "The fridge isn't electric, it's kerosene," she said, continuing her tour of the premises. "It's about eighty years old. Found a huge king brown under there the other day. And before someone fixed up that copper water heater for me last year, I always had to keep a big bucket atop the stove to heat my water." She wasn't complaining; she was being self-congratulatory. "I have no hot running water at all. I've lived without it for seven years. You just learn to cope . . . you adapt. I enjoy it that way."

A psychiatrist probably would have said that she was proving something to herself. My mother would have said that she was just a schlump. It was probably a little bit of both.

3

Wollogorang was by no means the largest station in Australia. Victoria River Downs, which at one time consisted of as many as 3.3 million acres, held that distinction. Wollogorang's only claim to fame was that it was the largest station in the Northern Territory whose boundaries had remained unchanged throughout its 105-year history.

One morning, when Jack and the Bushranger were out in the "bullcatcher" with Paul, I again found myself in the kitchen and asked Sue to tell me about the old homestead, a boarded-up corrugated-iron hut that still stood near the creek close by. It was called Settlement Creek because drovers once settled their Queensland bills there before moving into the Northern Territory, where the law, and even the wage structure, were totally different. In those days it took pioneer families like the Duracks and the MacDonalds up to three years to run their cattle up from New South Wales to the Kimberleys. Some never made it, including the man who built the old Wollogorang homestead. His cattle contracted ticks further south, and before he reached the border, most had died from a disease called red water. In 1886 he stopped where he was and built the two-room hut.

"At the turn of the century," Sue went on enthusiastically, as if she had read the documents only yesterday, "a chap named Anning bought the lease to Wollogorang. He wrote to his nineteen-year-old son and said: 'Dear Harry, I've bought Wollogorang, out on the rim'— he meant the rim of civilization—'now go and take delivery of it and walk the two thousand bullocks on the property to the meatworks in Burketown. Good luck. Love, Dad. P.S. Be careful. Some of the blacks are bad.' "

As Anning had foreseen, aboriginals did attack the homestead on a number of occasions and, in fact, the holes where their spears had punctured the corrugated-iron walls were still visible. But native troubles were the least of the problems.

"Harry came up here and walked the bullocks into Burketown. They were bad bullocks—Wollogorang bullocks had a reputation for being bad—and Harry had a rough time of it. Every night they'd rush the fences and scatter. It took him months to get them into Burketown, and by the time he did the price had plummeted. He wired his father: 'What do I do now?' To which his father replied: 'Not enough money, walk them back.' But Harry said no way, and he bushed the whole lot of them. He just opened the gates and off they went. Everyone around Burketown lived on Wollogorang bullocks for years thereafter. Whenever they needed food, they'd just go out and shoot one."

By any standards, however, the property was a huge one. Wollogorang encompassed 2,700 square miles (or 1.73 million acres), making it almost one-third larger than the state of Delaware. It was so vast that even Paul, who had held title to the property and worked it for almost twenty years, admitted that there were parts of it he'd never seen.

And it was wild, almost lawless country. Cattle rustling was still rife there, as it was on much of the Australian frontier. The Aussies called it poddy-dodging, and though it was no laughing matter when your neighbors did it, they managed to smile at their own occasional indulgences. It was a bit like income tax evasion.

"The police established a station here in the early sixties," Paul told us later that evening, when Jack, Phil, and I joined him for a few beers after dinner. "Shut it up in 1980, but it's still known as the Police Paddock.

"There was a property up the end a' this valley owned by Arthur

Wallace and Reg Finckley, two crafty old characters. They used to get George Butcher that owned Wollogorang then to do their drovin', and while he was out doin' it, they'd be in here pinchin' weaners.

"One day, though, George found some a' his cows sucklin' their calves, which was pretty good indication they'd been pinched from Wollogorang. So the stock squad came out and held those cattle as evidence. But in the dead a' night Finckley and Wallace snuck in and took 'em over to a mining camp.

"Well, they shot those cows and calves and shoved 'em down a mine shaft and then chucked in a lump of gelignite and blew the whole thing up. Still, they got convicted and did a stretch in Darwin. After that the police decided to establish a station here."

Finckley and Wallace had only been following precedent. In earlier days a notorious Queensland poddy-dodger had blown up a town courthouse and police residence to destroy the evidence against him, and had gotten off scot-free.

Paul said he loved Wollogorang, but from our brief acquaintance with the place it certainly didn't look that way. The cattle in the nearby paddocks, as well as the wild ones off in the bush where Paul could never hope to muster, seemed nervous and skittish, as if they hadn't been worked in years. Several old cars and trucks in various states of disrepair littered the area around the work shed, giving it the appearance of an automobile junkyard. The vehicles had been dismantled and cannibalized, their parts transplanted to the bull-catcher, apparently one of the few vehicles on the property that was running. Even the road grader was out of service, "buggered," according to one of the ringers, when Paul poured diesel fuel instead of hydraulic fluid into its transmission.

The work shed itself was even worse. Tools, tires, old generator and fan belts, and odds and ends of every description lay around in total disarray. Despite the rural setting, it was a scene curiously reminiscent of urban blight. And it was self-imposed. Like Sue, Paul must have enjoyed swimming against the tide in a sea of disorder. Theirs was a match made in heaven.

Paul's first wife had refused to live at Wollogorang. "I don't think she liked it up here at all," said Sue. "In fact, before I moved in, there hadn't been a woman here for over twenty years." Until he married Sue, Paul had worked Wollogorang alone (helped only by a band of itinerant ringers), dividing his time between the station and a family property closer to civilization, where his wife stayed with their three children.

Then a water tank fell on him. "My right leg was shattered, and it was all covered in cow dung," he related. "They took me to hospital and whacked me into plaster of paris. When it came off three months later they found that infection had got in. I was in hospital for a year. Almost kicked the bucket." Reluctantly, Paul sold the lease on Wollogorang.

Not long afterwards his wife walked out, leaving him with the three kids to fend for himself. Paul rose to the occasion: He bought a fifty-foot sailboat, piled the kids aboard, and set sail. He loved station life, but he loved the sea as well. By the time he dropped anchor at Brampton Island, he (or the kids) felt the need for a governess, which explained the advertisement that Sue and her friend Polly had answered.

Meanwhile, the people who bought Wollogorang were a lot more realistic than Paul was, for instead of continuing to waste money by trying to raise cattle in that desolate wilderness, they decided to *make* money—by growing marijuana there. With the stunning self-confidence of first-time entrepreneurs, they reckoned they would never be discovered, notwithstanding the police station next door.

For a time everything went along smoothly for the new owners. They had agreed that if the partner in Darwin learned that a raid was imminent, he would radio a warning to Wollogorang in the coded message, "Your mother is dying." But when that signal was actually sent, the partner who received it, overwrought by the news, assumed it to be true. When the narcotics squad swooped down, they found him in deep mourning, the incriminating evidence still intact. When the property reverted to Paul, he yielded to fate, and leaving the boat at its mooring, happily returned to Wollogorang. Sue went with him as governess, and eighteen months later they were married.

"I'd be content anywhere so long as I'm with Paul," Sue told me. Imagining the possibilities that lay ahead after Wollogorang had led me to ask her where they planned to settle when Paul retired, and the answer was more evasive than expected.

"People tend to forget," she said, "that the person they married is the person they're going to end up with when the kids have gone away. I notice that when you have a photograph of a young couple holding a newborn baby, they're both beaming at the baby, because that's where their feelings are centered at that time. But I'd love to see a photograph where they're holding the baby and beaming at each other, because in a way I think that's even more important. Don't you?"

I was spared having to answer when James and Helen, Sue's two little kids, came running in to the kitchen. They had been playing outside, and their frail-looking, sweat-soaked bodies were covered in dust, which only accentuated their pale-white complexions. While Sue mixed them each a glass of powdered milk, they hopped around as inquisitively as two little wallabies.

"Calm down," she said. "And as soon as smoko's over, we'll start your lessons."

"Do you like Wollogorang?" I asked them, as they drank their milk and ate their piklettes, a kind of small, silver-dollar pancake. Helen was shy and responded by burying her little chin in her chest and looking away. But six-year-old James, who had already been twice to visit his grandparents in England, was more outspoken.

"Nope," he said, in a childish squeak. "I hate it. I hate the snakes, I hate the 'squitoes, I hate the flies, and I hate the hot."

Then James turned to his mother. "Aw, Mum," he pleaded, as if repeating a pathetic request for the umpteenth time, "can't we jes go live with Granny in coldenland?"

After several generations of struggling against a perhaps more dominant trait, the desire for stability seemed to be reasserting itself in Sue's family at last.

4

A few days after we arrived Alf Brien pulled into the Wollogorang homestead. Alf was the mailman, whose delivery route ran all the way from Burketown to the eastern edge of the Northern Territory. He made the two-day run weekly, and the rest of the time he ferried alcohol in his taxicab to thirsty residents of the Doomadgee Reserve, ostensibly a dry community.

Years before, Alf had come up from Sydney to give living in Burketown a try. "It was goin' from chalk to cheese, but I liked it," he said. When he decided to settle there permanently, he called his wife and convinced her to join him.

"She flew inta Mt. Isa from Sydney," Alf related, "an' I picked 'er up at the airport an' drove 'er ta Burketown. But when we gut there, she wouldn't get outta the car. I hadda turn around an' drive 'er all the way back ta Mt. Isa, 500 kilometers away."

"I guess your wife found chalk more to her liking," I said.

"Me ex-wife," Alf corrected. "Couldn' understand 'er not likin' it.

That was back in 1966, an' Burketown was even better then."

"Sounds like a very foolish woman," Dave assured Alf. "You're well rid of her."

Throughout our stay at Wollogorang we'd continued to camp in a paddock not far from an old barn housing the station's heavy machinery. Though our site had nothing in the way of facilities, it was comfortable and within easy walking distance of the homestead. During the days Paul would show us around the property, driving us over rough tracks or leading forays through scrub, and each night we'd return to camp completely exhausted. One evening, after a day spent chasing down unbranded cattle, we had a satisfying dinner of grilled sausages or "snags," as the Aussies called them. Dave and the Bushranger bedded down for the night, but Phil and I decided to sit around the campfire a while longer, sipping a whiskey before turning in. As we watched the dancing flames, lost in our own thoughts and the soughing of the wind through the trees, we heard the crunch of gravel and realized someone was approaching. A tall figure emerged from the shadows and stood just outside the light of the fire, silhouetted against the night sky, watching us intently.

"What can we do for ya, mate?" I asked firmly but apprehensively, unable to imagine what someone was doing wandering around the bush at that time of the night.

"Oh, I just wanted ta talk ta youse guys, an' see what yez was up ta," replied a boyish voice. The speaker had a pronounced stutter, and obvious difficulty forming his sentences.

Stepping out of the shadows, our visitor walked toward us, and in the flickering fire we saw that he was wearing jeans, a denim jacket, and a cowboy hat. The tall, lanky youth squatted down by the fire, rubbing his hands over it and nodding to us with a shy smile. Hundreds of stars shone overhead, and with the boy's young face illuminated by the fire, we could have been a tableau from a Remington painting of the American West.

"I'm camped out too. We're over there," he stammered, pointing in the direction of a barn in the distance. "Everybody's asleep an' I jus' cum over ta talk ta someone."

His name was Paul VanderPlast, and he was only seventeen years old. As a youngster he'd run away from home in Brisbane because his mother had beaten him whenever she was drunk. He'd gotten himself into some trouble and was sent away to reform school, where he learned to ride horses. Paul's touching story reminded me that my own mother had died when I was seventeen, and though I never learned to ride horses, I came close to being sent to reform school myself.

After Paul's release, he went to work for the government in the Northern Territory, a job he abandoned to become a cowboy, which seemed a lot more exciting. After drifting about for a few months one day in Cloncurry he ran into John Nicholson, the head stockman at Wollogorang, who'd hired him on as a ringer to work the muster.

"John's been like a father to me," Paul related. "An' he's taught me a lot about ridin' horses and runnin' cattle. John told me I could be one of the best horsemen in the business if I keep tryin' an' workin' hard at it."

Although physically a grown man, Paul was in many respects still a boy. He was completely open to and unsuspecting of strangers, and he hardly realized the extent of his loneliness. In a couple of weeks he was going south to look after another property, where he'd work alone for over a year, and I couldn't imagine he understood what that would entail.

"I've got a girl friend, an' she's a real nice girl. I met her when she visited our school. They picked me ta show 'er around the place. She comes from Tasmania, and we write each other every week. I'm goin' down there for a visit when I save up enough money."

We chatted with Paul for a couple of hours, until just before turning in Phil picked up the whiskey bottle to pour himself a last drink.

"Oh, Johnny Walker," Paul exclaimed. "Really good stuff."

"Here, I'm only gonna let you have one shot," said Phil, handing him the bottle after he'd taken a long swig of it himself. "I don't want John Nicholson to think I'm taking a seventeen-year-old stockhand and making a drunk out of him."

Tipping the bottle to his lips, Paul took a good guzzle of it, just as Phil had. But unlike Phil, he started to choke and gag just like a kid in the movies taking his first drink. Obviously embarrassed, stifling a cough, he regained his composure, and wiping his eyes, looked up to observe our reactions. Though Phil and I found it humorous, rather than risk hurting his feelings, we remained straight-faced, but we both broke into laughter when a big, sheepish grin spread over Paul's boyish face.

5

The following morning, a Sunday, dawned hot and sultry, and since the evening before Paul had invited us for coffee, Phil and I walked over to the ringers' camp. Aside from two swags on the ground that hadn't been rolled up yet, and the unwashed plates from breakfast, the site hardly looked like a camp at all. Some stations provided ringers with rude sleeping quarters and a kitchen area, but as Wollogorang employed no permanent hands and hired only for the muster, its crew lived outdoors, sleeping on the ground, under the stars. Paul stepped forward with an enthusiastic greeting, while his three companions rose slowly to their feet, and I began to wonder if we had made a wise decision in walking into their territory unannounced.

Besides John Nicholson and Paul, there were two other men in the crew. Sam, an Englishman in his early twenties, was the son of a friend of Sue's family, and had come out to Australia on a working holiday. Despite being dressed in dusty jeans and a blue work shirt, his clean, well-groomed appearance placed him in sharp contrast to the others, and he looked as though he would have been far more comfortable in a classroom or an office. The Aussie ringers referred to him as "the useless Pom"—Pom being a derogatory term applied to the English—an epithet that Stan Stone, one of the ringers and the camp cook, applied to him with particular venom. A tanned, rangy man in his mid-forties, Stan had a wizened face that made him appear considerably older—deep furrows extended out fanlike from around his cat-green eyes as if cleft by a miniature plow. Stan wore his battered brown felt cowboy hat constantly, and I suspected it remained on his head even when he rolled up in his swag for the night. The cutting wit with which he mercilessly rode Sam also found a secondary target in Paul.

John Nicholson, the grizzled head stockman and foreman of the crew, was a balding, thin man in his early sixties, who'd been fighting a losing battle with alcohol for years. A couple of weeks before we arrived, he'd gone on a tear after drinking a bottle of Bundaburg Rum and had to be locked in a storeroom until he'd slept it off. His sad blue eyes peered out from a kind face that had seen more than its share of sun, and he had an open manner that made me feel at ease when he offered us coffee, which he poured from a large black pot that hung over an open fire. As the leader of the muster, John owned most of the twenty-odd horses we had seen in the paddock nearest the homestead. In a couple of weeks his contract with Paul would be completed and he'd be moving on, "droving" his horses almost eight hundred miles overland to the next muster.

"Someone was saying that you're pretty good with taking on these young fellas and teaching them the ropes," Phil said to him, after we'd been chatting for a while.

"Good at it? I don't know about that," John replied, as he rolled himself a cigarette. "Stan thinks I make 'em useless, I'm too soft with 'em."

"He's too easy with the bloody bastards," Stan yelled over at us from his "kitchen" on the other side of the camp. "Ya gutta jump on 'em every mornin' an' kick 'em inta bed every evenin'."

"Who's gut the energy ta do all that jumpin' an' kickin'?" said John, shaking his head. Having been mates for years, the question of how to deal with the boys was apparently a long-standing issue between them.

"So ya spoil 'em instead, an' we end up doin' everythin' for 'em. Ya ought ta take a whip ta their backsides."

Stan had been carrying on his part of the argument while kneading some dough for bread, or damper, on a large rough-hewn table that stood under a lean-to with a fly tent over it. I walked over to watch him, and noticed he had brought along a tin of Capstan tobacco. He'd scratched out the "Cap" on the tin, leaving only the "stan."

"Ya gutta knock it down before it's ready," said Stan, shaping the flattened dough into a ball. "Ya know it's right when it starts ta squeak." He might have been talking about young ringers, as well, as he kneaded it with his callused hands, adding more yeast to the mixture, until the dough did indeed begin to make a squeaking sound.

Stan winked at me and roughly threw the dough into a round camp oven, a heavy covered pot. Placing the oven in a hole in the ground he shoveled hot coals over it, arranging them in an even pile. A camp stove had been fashioned out of the top of an old fuel drum that stood about a foot off the ground. A rectangular piece of metal had been cut out of its side so a fire could be built beneath it. I looked around at the rest of the makeshift kitchen equipment, and couldn't help but be impressed by the ringer's ingenuity.

"You'd think ya could teach these young fellas to do that, wouldn' ya?" said Stan, rubbing bits of dough from his hands. " 'Ave a look at this." He opened the bread box and pulled out something that looked like a baked frisbee. "That's supposed ta be damper. That useless Pom over there made it," he said disgustedly, nodding his head in Sam's direction. "A donkey wouldn't eat it. I wouldn' let 'im eat it 'cause it'd bind 'im up."

"The first one turned out O.K.," protested Sam, in a futile effort at self-defense. "Why don't ya show 'em that?"

"Yeah, but John made the dough fer that one," said Stan, ignoring

287

Sam and speaking directly to Phil and me. "That Pom rubbish made a third one, but it was so bad we had ta toss it out."

"That's not the way it's supposed to work," said Phil, goading Stan on, as if his performance was entertaining everyone, including Sam. "It should have been the best of the lot."

"Yeah, it's supposed ta get better," replied Stan, taking the bait, "but that's not how these fellas work. They get worse as they go along. That bloody Pom couldn't even light a fire an' put the billy on."

"Of course I could," protested Sam, indignantly.

"Yeah, maybe ya could," Stan acknowledged, "but ya'd ferget ta put water in it. Ya gutta start 'em young, that's the trouble. They keep 'em in school too long, an' overeducate 'em."

"We've got a fellow like that traveling with us," I said, referring to Dave. "He's probably still in the sack or over in the kitchen talking with women and stuffing himself with scones. Could you do anything with him?"

"Naw, I seen 'im. He's too old an' he's spoiled," answered Stan. "We gut enough rubbish 'ere now without takin' any more on. Besides, trouble is, he's got no interest. Ya couldn't learn 'im if ya belted 'im with a sledgehammer."

"That's an approach we hadn't thought of," I admitted. "We've tried just about everything else."

We spent another couple of hours chatting companionably with the ringers, and even sampled some of Stan's delicious hot damper, which he sliced and smeared with butter before handing us each a thick slab. But as the time came to head back to our own camp, Phil, who had once considered living in Montana and running a ranch, must have been thinking about his young sons back home. "You reckon this is still a good life for a young fellow?" he asked John. Not unexpectedly it was Stan who answered the question.

"Oh yeah, it sure is as long as he's gut some brains, but if ya can't learn 'im nothin', what's the good in havin' 'im? Try musterin' with this bunch some time an' you'll see what I mean."

When I complained about Stan's resentment of the boys to Phil on our way back to camp it occurred to me that both Stan and John had spent much of their lives on the backs of horses, and now that the cattle industry was dying, they faced an uncertain future. Even on profitable stations, skilled horsemen were being replaced by helicopters and motor bikes, and freshly made damper was giving way to store-bought bread. The new breed of station managers and stockmen knew a great deal more about computers and calculators than they did about horses or cattle, and old-timers, like Stan and John, found themselves in a plight not too unlike that of the Torres Strait Pilots, craftsmen whose skills had outlived both their time and usefulness.

6

Taking up Stan's suggestion, Phil and I asked Paul Zlotskowski whether we might accompany him when he went out mustering the next day in his bull-catcher. We'd been intrigued by the open, beat-up Toyota, girded on three sides by bull bars, that was used to knock down unmanageable wild bulls, "cleanskins" (referring to their un-branded hides) so aggressive they would often stampede a herd or charge a horseman. After a bull went down a cowboy would quickly tie its legs together, rendering the animal helpless, and it would be picked up later in a stock truck. It was a risky job—John Nicholson rode a horse that had a large lump on its side from having once been gored by a wild bull. John had stuffed the injured animal's intestines back inside him, stitched up the wound, and given the animal some antibiotics.

Paul had looked at us somewhat askance when we made our request, warning us that in addition to being dangerous it was also dirty and tedious work. But we persisted until, reluctantly, he finally agreed, telling us to meet him in front of the barn at 7 A.M. the following day.

We awoke to a pleasant morning and, after a hurried breakfast, made our way across the paddock to the agreed-upon meeting place, where we were waiting when Paul arrived. We jumped into the jeep and headed off down the track in a cloud of dust, slowing down only an hour or so later when we came upon the crew and the mob of cattle they were moving along the trail. It was a resplendent scene: Sunlight filtered through the scrub trees and dappled off the cattle's backs as the ringers drove the mob along, occasionally darting out to pick up odd strays and chasing them into the herd, and as it was the dry season, the animals' hooves kicked up small clouds of dust with every step.

"They're breakin' these cattle in a bit so they can walk 'em along that fence over there to the paddock," explained Paul. "We're teachin' them to be a herd. They used to run separately, but they have to learn they can't go where they want to anymore. They'll give ya all the trouble under the sun for the first hour or two, but by evenin' they're so quiet, you've got ta push 'em along.

"See that big bull over there lookin' at Sam?" he said, pointing at an animal that stood on the bank of a dry creek bed. It was dark gray, almost black, and must have weighed nearly a ton. "He made a run at him a few minutes ago and needs to be taught a lesson. If you chaps weren't with me, I'd civilize 'im."

"Don't let us stop you," I said.

"Righto," yelled Paul, accelerating toward the bull. "Hang on."

When the huge animal heard the vehicle approaching, he turned and glared at us. He pawed the ground a couple of times, and Phil and I were certain he was going to charge. Instead, he turned and started running in the opposite direction. The Toyota bounced fiercely over the rocky terrain, until Paul came up behind the bull and bumped him hard in the rear. Our quarry simply bounced off the bar and with an enraged look over his shoulder, started to run faster.

The chase was on—tearing through the scrub in determined pursuit, knocking down small trees in our paths as we went. We had to keep our heads low to avoid the branches smashing against the windshield and shearing across the open top. Each time we'd catch up to him, Paul would bump the bull a bit harder, but the animal had great strength and balance and just kept on running. Only after he'd been hit five or six times did he finally stumble and go down, and even then he was on his feet almost immediately.

Finally, after a chase of two or three miles, the bull began to tire, his dark gray hide whitening with lather. The jeep caught up with him again and crashed hard into his rear. The bull went down heavily, and this time rose more slowly. We turned back toward him, but now he stood firmly in a cloud of dust, watching us intently.

"He's mad as hell, and he's done runnin'. Hold on tight," yelled Paul, as he turned to face his target, "he's gonna charge."

Pawing the ground, the bull lowered his head, and after a few seconds hesitation, eighteen hundred pounds of fury charged us. Paul stopped the vehicle to lessen the impact, and the furious bull slammed into us head on, jolting us backwards. Paul quickly accelerated, bringing the animal's forward momentum to a halt. He was no match for the powerful engine and began to give ground. As the bull was pushed steadily back, he lost his footing and went down in a heap. Paul slowly drove the Toyota right up on top of him, where we stopped. The front of the vehicle was over three feet off the ground.

The Gang from Wollogorang

"Put your foot on the brake," Paul shouted to me, "and whatever you do, don't take it off." My foot replaced his on the pedal and I jammed it down as hard as I could. Paul leapt out of the Toyota with two pieces of line in his hand, and neatly tied the bull's front legs together, then the rear ones. The Toyota rocked jerkily, and for a moment, Phil and I thought we might topple over. Finally, Paul hoisted himself into the truck, and we backed off the hog-tied bull, crashing heavily to the ground as we dropped.

The infuriated animal bawled and repeatedly tried to rise, falling back in the dust each time. Finally, too exhausted to resist any further, he lay there still breathing heavily, his eyes glazed with fright. Paul put a rope around his horns and, hitching him to the Toyota, dragged him to a large gum tree, to which he tied the beast. From the back of the vehicle Paul took a device that looked like a large tree-pruning tool, which he used to snip off the sharp tips of the bull's horns. Blood squirted out in a fine stream, as if it were being shot from a water pistol, but it quickly abated.

"He doesn't feel a thing," Paul assured us. "It's like cutting toenails. But it'll take the starch out of 'im for a while. We'll come back with the truck and pick 'im up later."

We drove back to find the mob of cattle moving along easily toward a fenced paddock a little farther down the trail, and as Paul had predicted, they had already become docile. No longer did calves and skittish animals bolt from the herd, and the ringers, too, had settled back in their saddles, riding slowly beside them. John Nicholson, bringing up the rear, held his reins in his teeth, while rolling a cigarette, fumbling with his tin of tobacco, and droving the herd all at the same time. It was a memorable sight, and as I watched it, I couldn't help but admire the old stockman, who had spent all of his life learning what had once been an estimable trade. Banjo Paterson must have had men like John in mind when he wrote "Clancy of the Overflow":

> *In my wild erratic fancy*
> *visions come to me of Clancy*
> *Gone a-droving 'down the Cooper'*
> *where the Western drovers go;*
> *As the stock are slowly stringing,*
> *Clancy rides behind them singing,*
> *For the drover's life has pleasures*
> *that the townsfolk never know.*

And I somehow rather fancy
that I'd like to change with Clancy,
Like to take a turn at droving
where the seasons come and go,
While he faced the round eternal
of the cash-book and the journal—
But I doubt he'd suit the office,
Clancy, of The Overflow.

7

The route from Wollogorang to Borroloola took us west over yet another dusty track. This time our route was a "side trip" deep into the Northern Territory in pursuit of what the Bushranger was determined to show us was his nomination for the "worst place in Australia" award. Karumba might have its share of drongos and deadbeats, he told us, but where we were heading now, the Loo, was truly a place "where no one bothered to pull the chain." At midday, we stopped for a smoko on the Robinson River, about halfway to our destination, and refreshed ourselves in the cool spring-fed stream that flowed down from the Barkly Tableland. Its banks were shaded by paperbark and pandanus trees, and after traveling so long through such dry scrub country, it was exhilarating to come upon such a pleasant oasis. Unfortunately, the flies were quite fond of it, too, and since they had staked their claim first, we relinquished the spot to them and pushed on.

The town of Borroloola, situated on a vast marsh near the Gulf of Carpentaria, had a population of 300 aboriginals and fewer than 100 whites. Convincing people to live in "the Loo," as the town was contemptuously referred to throughout the Gulf region, and, for that matter the entire Northern Territory, had always been a difficult proposition—at one time the N.T. government offered free passage from Japan or India for anyone willing to become a settler. No one from either country accepted the invitation.

Most of the dilapidated houses in Borroloola's aboriginal district, as well as some of those in the white area, appeared to be on the verge of collapse. Weed-overgrown "yards" were littered with empty stubbies and discarded clothing, while a few mangy dogs wandered dejectedly about, sniffing at the contents of plastic trash bags they had torn apart and strewn on the ground. A thick blanket of red dust covered everything, including a few stunted trees and the battered automobiles that sat parked helter-skelter. To make matters worse, the steamy town was fringed by the MacArthur, a mud-brown tidal river famous for the size and ferocity of its saltwater crocodiles. Camped on either side of the river were two aboriginal tribes that had been waging a long-term battle against each other, with hostilities arising whenever they could muster the energy. These would generally occur every two weeks, when the public assistance checks arrived and the combatants could fortify themselves with grog. According to Mal Jensen, one of Borroloola's two policemen, the skirmishes were simply drunken brawls that would "last for a couple of days until their money ran out." Then everything returned to normal, and Borroloola fell back into its customary languid torpor.

The town had just marked its first centenary, but how the event had been celebrated no one seemed certain. A souvenir booklet printed for the occasion boasted of the charm of Borroloola's isolation, proudly proclaiming it to be "the place where the road turns back." If that wasn't a sufficient inducement to tourists, the pamphlet also included photographs of the destruction wreaked by a cyclone that had recently torn through the town.

For decades, Borroloola had been known around the Territory as the "refuge of hermits and misogynists." Though we had only been in town for a few hours—and had no intention of staying much longer— we all agreed with the Bushranger's assessment: "I can't say with absolute certainty that the Loo's the worst town in Australia, only because I haven't been in all of them. But it's the worst bloody one I've ever seen—and that's fair dinkum," he remarked scornfully.

Strangely enough, though, a large library had once graced the town. Old-timers remembered a plaque outside the door crediting the collection to a policeman named Power. The story goes that Corporal Power, finding himself bored in his lonely outpost, had written to the Carnegie Trust in New York, asking for something to read, and that the officers of the foundation, probably without having consulted a map of Australia, had made a sizable grant. The books eventually arrived "in an old tub of a coastal steamer," but no trace of them now remained. They had long ago been devoured by termites, which had also eaten away most of the town.

"It was a bird that brought me to Borroloola," related John Whitaker, a displaced good ol' boy from Chattanooga, who now called that Northern Territory town home. As he paused for dramatic emphasis,

I envisioned some giant prehistoric pterodactyl swooping down out of the Tennessee sky to snatch him up and carry him halfway around the world to deposit him in the middle of the Northern Territory. "The Carpentarian grass wren is very rare, and few bird-watchers have ever seen it," he continued, an explanation that brought my image crashing to earth with a thud.

We had stopped at the Whitaker home at the invitation of John's wife, Judith, whom Dave and Phil had met at the Old Gaol, where we had all ducked in to get out of the 114-degree heat. As a guide for the Historical Society, Judith gave tours of the only structure in town besides the pub that was over twenty-five years old, and she had invited us to meet her husband when she discovered we were Yanks. Located in a small subdivision of identical houses, the Whitakers' frame bungalow had been built by the N.T. government to provide state employees with low-cost housing.

Judith, a diminutive and light-complexioned Tasmanian, had first come to Borroloola as an elementary-school teacher, but after marrying John she'd abandoned her career to raise their children. John had lived in Borroloola for the past five years, and with his hawker's license he supported his family by peddling out of their home. When we first arrived, the rather overweight John had been sitting on a freezer in the carport, absorbed in poring over the classified ads in a week-old newspaper from Darwin, surrounded by racks of used clothing, a stack of secondhand books, magazines, and other assorted items. After an enthusiastic welcome, he offered us seats and handed us each a cold stubby.

A Viet Nam veteran, he was anything but a Borroloola booster. We had hardly sat down in the shade of the carport, which doubled as a store, before he began referring to the Loo as "a rat bag little place" and complaining that it was one of the most isolated towns in Australia. "If ya wanna buy a TV set or anythin' else, yew hafta drive a thousand kilometers ta get it," he said. "We only gut electricity here a year ago."

"How does a town do without electricity?" asked Dave, obviously trying to imagine his New York apartment without lights, air conditioning, and a refrigerator stocked with imported beers and delicacies.

"We had a big esky to keep our stuff cool, and kerosene lamps when we needed light," replied John. "It wasn't too bad, though. We'd go to bed when it got dark and got up at first light. But even before the sun came up, sweat would be pourin' down our faces when we was sittin' around the kitchen table havin' breakfast. It gets so hot, ya can't bear ta do any work."

John was at his most miserable during the Wet, when temperatures soared to 125 degrees. "Bein' here then is like goin' aroun' in a wet plastic bag all the time. It's like that for six months of the year. For the other six, the wind whips dust through the streets like those droughts they talk about in the Old Testament."

It was difficult to imagine how it could get any more uncomfortable—the thermometer on the wall read 112 degrees, and we'd long since given up hope that our perspiration-soaked shirts would dry. Most of the crotons the Whitakers had painstakingly hauled from Darwin and recently planted around their house had given up the ghost, and their withered leaves lay on the ground beneath them. Judith had stood up to get us some more stubbies, when two little barefoot aboriginal girls in tattered dresses came into the carport, went over to John, and shyly whispered something in his ear. He took their money and went into the house, and moments later, emerged with two chocolate-covered ice cream sticks. The girls giggled as they took them, then ran off.

"Seein' the grass wren wasn't the only reason I came ta Australia," admitted the birdman of Borroloola, when he'd sat down again on top of the big freezer, where he kept packaged vegetables and meats.

"When I went back to the States from Viet Nam, that Love Canal business was goin' on, an' I was fed up with all the pollution I saw. I was tired of eatin' synthetic foods. So I came over here an' worked as a roustabout in New South Wales because I thought Australia was the place of the future. But the government screwed this place up, and I don't mean just Borroloola. If we could take over down here, with our American know-how, we could turn Australia into a great country."

"We'll take care of our own, thank you very much," said Judy, who was changing her daughter's nappy. "It's fine as it is." The Bushranger glared at John, but said nothing.

Just down the road from the Whitakers' house rose a jumble of twisted wreckage that had once been homes and caravans. When we had driven into town, we'd noticed similar devastation in other areas. It looked as if the Australian Air Force had targeted certain sections of Borroloola for bombing runs.

"A cyclone did that when it came through here a few years ago," John explained. "It destroyed the whole town. They still haven't cleaned it up, an' they probably never will. Ya might a' noticed that nobody's very motivated aroun' here." We had indeed noticed. While most of the bush towns we'd visited suffered from some degree of blight, the Loo was almost awesome in its squalor.

"You're from Tasmania, one of the most beautiful spots on earth," Dave said to Judith. "What brought a Tazzie up here?"

"Beauty doesn't have to be green," she replied defensively, obviously a convert to the Peter Eaton theory of aesthetics. "That's a European prejudice. There's no reason we can't find it in browns, yellows, and reds. In this part of the country you can see wonderful contrasts. The land can be so dry for months and months, and suddenly it's wet and there are billabongs and wild flowers all over the place. There are so many untouched areas here that no one's ever seen."

"We're thinkin' about goin' back ta the States," John interrupted his wife's rhapsodizing. "But I'm awful worried about takin' the wife an' kids there."

"Why's that?" asked Phil. "You can watch birds there, too."

"It's not that," he replied, "but here in Australia women are different. Take my wife. She's carved out a life for herself here, comin' to a place like this on her own an' buyin' a house. An' then there's those women on the stations. They're independent, too. An' they don't care anythin' about that damn women's lib. Back in the States that's all they talk about, an' I don't want my wife ta be exposed ta it."

"*I'm* not too worried about it," snapped Judith with obvious annoyance. "It's not necessarily a communicable disease."

How, after traveling halfway around the world to escape the negative aspects of American society, did John Whitaker end up living in Borroloola? Even he had trouble explaining that. He may, as Phil had suggested, been just another casualty of post–Viet Nam disenchantment, a fugitive of sorts in search of some vague alternative—though he obviously hadn't found whatever he was looking for. But then again, many of his attitudes were not unlike our own, a contradictory blend of romanticism and, I suppose, a kind of pragmatism about surviving in the world of the 1980s. We, too, had come out to the Australian bush to see if things were any different in that great raw country on the other side of the earth, any less complicated, any richer in experiences, but we, too, had been known to complain about the lack of creature comforts beyond the Black Stump. It may have been that the quest for adventure, or freedom in the widest sense, in an overly complicated world, could no longer be sought without compromises.

*   *   *

It was late in the afternoon when we left the Whitakers' and stopped at a roadside take-away stand on the edge of town. The shadows were lengthening and a long night journey back to Wollogorang lay ahead; to fortify ourselves we bought two roasted chickens and ate them outside in front of the shop.

At the table next to us sat a truckie working on a hamburger, glancing every so often at his dusty rig, parked on the shoulder a short distance up the road. His attention was really fixed, however, on the portable television set in front of him. Though we couldn't see the screen, the volume was loud enough for us to follow the antics of a cartoon character named Danger Mouse, beamed in by satellite from Darwin, over five hundred miles away.

Diagonally across the road stood the Borroloola Inn. The high corrugated-iron fence that enclosed it seemed to have no other purpose than preventing patrons from looking out or passersby from looking in. A couple of aborigines sat on the ground outside with their backs against the fence, smoking cigarettes and sharing a bottle of wine.

The molten disk of sun vanished into the distant scrub, and blaring loudly from the pub came the mournful voice of Paul McCartney, welcoming the descending dusk to Borroloola with his plaintive "No More Lonely Nights."

8

After more than three weeks at Wollogorang we'd had all we wanted of station life, though our stay had certainly been memorable. It was also, we realized, time that Dave and I be heading home. We'd been on the road now for many long months, visiting places in Australia that even most Aussies never see. I found myself becoming accustomed to all the dust, growing comfortable with the isolation, as did Dave, and we were both a little alarmed. I was beginning to appreciate what it meant to be "sung to the land," and wasn't at all sure I wanted to surrender to it.

Back in Perth many months earlier, Dame Mary Durack had used that aboriginal expression to describe the irresistible attraction the bush held for her brother Reg, who having sold his station in the Kimberley, had "retired" with his wife, Enid, to a Fremantle suburb, where the former stockman spent his days translating Greek verse. Dame Mary had arranged for us to meet the dignified elderly couple, who had graciously invited us to their comfortable home, and as we sat sipping tea with them in their drawing room overlooking the Swan River, they recalled the many years they had spent in the Kimberley. I couldn't help but notice how distracted and restless Reg appeared, and when I later expressed my observation to Dame Mary, she had proceeded to relate an aboriginal legend that held that once a man's spirit was stolen and sung to the country, he could never escape. "That country plays strange tricks on those who dally too long. Reg can't help it, he wants to die in the Kimberleys," she had remarked resignedly. According to Dame Mary, Reg was always in the bush, at least in spirit, roaming over the country he loved and knew so well. "That poor woman," she declared, shaking her head in obvious sympathy for her sister-in-law. "She lives haunted by the constant fear he'll return." Both Dave and I had been deeply moved when we'd first heard the story, but as we had not as yet spent much time in the bush, it had been impossible to comprehend fully its implications.

It was with some relief that the next morning, after downing one of Sue's gargantuan breakfasts, we bade farewell to the Zlotskowskis and the ringers, and headed down to the Gulf, where we planned a last few days camping and relaxing on the beach before heading back to Cairns. As usual, the track was rough and dusty, and to his credit the Bushranger valiantly opted to join Phil in the backseat. Like children on holiday with indulgent parents, Phil and I had argued for weeks about whether the front or rear seat made for a filthier ride, but the consensus had finally been that the rear was less desirable.

Late in the morning we reached the homestead at what was once Wentworth Station. Some years earlier, Paul had bought the property and had incorporated it into Wollogorang. Mustering crews occasionally stayed there, using it as a place to throw their swags when it was too late in the day to return to their permanent camp, but other than that, it had been abandoned. A bungalow with a fly-screened veranda and badly peeling paint sat on the crest of a low rise, and as we pulled up in front of it we saw that a horse had gotten caught on a wire fence. The animal was a brumby, a wild horse, and had apparently been trapped there for quite some time, his rear legs tangled between two strands of wire. It was clearly frightened by our approach, but too tired and hungry to act up. We tried to free him by undoing the wires, but finally had to cut the fence. Shaking the wires from his legs he snorted heavily and galloped off into the scrub.

Like mustangs in the American West, large herds of brumbies roamed throughout the Gulf, progeny of horses released many years earlier as a result of yet another failed business venture. Horses were brought to the territory to breed remounts for the British Army in India, but on the trek inland from Darwin fever broke out, killing many of the drovers. The sick and dispirited survivors abandoned the project, and turned the horses loose. The feral animals proliferated rapidly and soon became a nuisance to stockmen, who sometimes shot them as vermin as they did the kangaroo and dingo.

We wandered around the land surrounding the homestead until we came to a pond some hundred yards away that, according to the Bushranger, was known as the Golden Hole. Why it had been given that name puzzled us, for, deep and forbidding, it was black rather than golden, and stretched about a half mile in length and 200 yards in width. The brushland sloped gradually down to meet its banks, and except for the huge, tattered paperbark trees growing around its rim, it reminded me of the abandoned granite quarries we used to swim in when I was a boy in Boston.

"Let's go for a swim," suggested the Bushranger. "Isn't this a beautiful spot?"

"Just magic," replied Phil, who had already stripped off his clothes and was clambering down the hole's steep banks. The water level was some five or six feet below the edge of the hole, and the bottom wasn't visible.

After hearing so many horror stories about crocodiles, Dave and I had no interest in testing the ominous-looking water, so we watched anxiously as the Bushranger stepped down into it, followed closely by a large snake that I had noticed slithering over the bank, rustling the leaves before it disappeared beneath the surface.

"I just saw a snake," I announced. "I think I'll wash up back at the cistern."

"What did he look like?" hollered Phil, who was frolicking as carefree as if he were in a backyard swimming pool.

"Long, thin and mean," I replied, "and he doesn't like Eye-talians ruining the neighborhood." The Bushranger laughed while Phil continued romping, obviously not believing my warning about the snake.

Leaving the deluded swimmers to their folly, Dave and I rinsed the dust from our faces, and walked over to explore the homestead. Though the exterior of the rude one-story structure was slowly deteriorating, its interior was in shambles: rusting bed frames and broken furniture lay strewn everywhere, and in what had once served as a dining area, the ceiling had collapsed. The Bushranger had mentioned that he thought the crumbling building had great potential as a tourist attraction, and he was even talking to Paul about leasing it. When he and Phil came up from the black hole and joined us, I offered to put him in touch with Peter Eaton back in Perth for some advice on development.

The swims and washups proved to be exercises in futility. As we continued on toward the Gulf, gaping potholes made it necessary to leave the track and "bush bash" to get around them. In no time, my pants and shirt were caked with red powder, which soon even sifted through the fabric of my clothes.

At another water hole we spotted some wild boars feeding in the mud along its shallow edge. As we pulled up, Phil grabbed the rifle from the back of the Toyota and leapt out. Not content to let future generations marvel at his exploits as a fisherman, he was determined to let history record his prowess as a hunter.

But the pigs declined the honor Phil was about to bestow on them, and as he was attempting to creep up for a shot at close range, they bolted into the scrub. Flocks of birds suddenly alighted, startled by the fleeing boars. Sulphur-crested cockatoos, magpie geese, and ducks soared into the sky and hovered over us. A pair of less cautious brolgas, Australian cranes, merely walked away rapidly on long spindly legs.

As we pushed on through the dense scrub and hilly country, the scraggly coolibahs and drooping paperbark trees grew taller and their foliage thicker. This part of the Northern Territory contained an unusual number of dry creek beds, as well as some enormous termite mounds that, higher and wider than the Toyota, were over a thousand years old. After climbing up an embankment so steep it was difficult to get over, even in four-wheel-drive, we ran along a sharp rise until we came to Gold Creek.

"There's plenty of salties in there," said the Bushranger as we got out of the vehicle. This time Phil grabbed his camera, and the two of us headed for the bluff overlooking the river while Dave and the Bushranger lit a fire to boil the billy. The winter sun was low in the sky, and glittered off the wavelets in the slow-moving current. Except for the deep holes in center stream, the river's rocky bed was clearly visible through the shallow water.

I walked along the rise for half a mile or so, leaving Phil a considerable distance behind, and only after making my way through a thicket of dense scrub to a sandstone promontory overlooking the river did I see the saltwater crocodile—my first glimpse of the creature in the wild. The huge animal's scaly body blended so well with the green rocks in the river at first I thought it was a large log, but the form of *Crocodylus porosus* was unmistakable: about fifteen feet long with a four-foot girth, it lay sunning itself on the bank of a small island a short distance from shore. I waved my arms to attract Phil's attention, and put a finger to my lips to indicate silence. He crept up stealthily, ever the photo-journalist in combat.

After taking a few shots with the telephoto, Phil decided to move in closer, making his way down the fifty-foot rise toward the river. But as he was scrambling down the bank he dislodged some rocks, alerting the crocodile, who with two swipes of its powerful tail slipped into the water and vanished. Except for a swirl of muddy water slowly drifting downstream, all traces of the phantom creature had disappeared.

Many months earlier, when we set out on our long journey, one of our primary goals had been to learn as much as we could about the mysterious reptile, and to accomplish that, we had been prepared to pursue our quest halfway around the Australian continent. Somehow, we had been sidetracked, discovering, I suppose, that meeting people was a great deal more rewarding than pursuing reptiles—Hugo Austla, we'd realized, had interested us in a way the "pets" in his backyard could not. Our ardor for pursuing the crocs had given way to indifference, and back in Kununurra when Dave had proposed a trip to Kakadu National Park in the N.T. to observe salties, I suggested he might just as well go to a zoo. My argument had convinced him, yet seeing *Crocodylus porosus* in its natural habitat, even if only fleetingly, still had the power of a privileged moment.

As for Phil, he returned to the Toyota feeling triumphant, carrying tales of the animal's size and speed, but his elation was short-lived. While rewinding his film he discovered that it had jammed and torn in the camera's sprocket, and tearing it out he angrily discarded it. Since Dave himself hadn't observed the crocodile, he appeared bewildered at our excitement, and sat calmly on a rock munching a sandwich.

Climbing back into the Toyota, we headed toward the coast, and once again the terrain began to flatten out, presenting us familiar vistas of termite colonies and low scrub. The wind had now shifted, bringing a cool breeze from the direction of the Gulf of Carpentaria, carrying with it the invigorating scent of the sea. For once, the bush flies were conspicuous by their absence, due, no doubt, to its benign presence.

Just before reaching the shore we came to Wentworth by the Sea, an outpost on the Queensland side of Wollogorang station, where Roy Savage, the caretaker, lived with his twenty-three-year-old wife, Julie, in an old bungalow surrounded by tall palm trees a few hundred yards from the Gulf of Carpentaria. Hearing us pull up, he came out the front door to greet us, and invited us in to join him for smoko. The floors inside the two-room structure were a hardened mixture of ant-hill mud with a few old bullock and kangaroo hides serving as rugs; the furnishings, a few odd pieces the couple had picked up on infrequent shopping trips to Mt. Isa or Normanton. Against one wall stood a bookcase fashioned out of driftwood, full of paperbacks and old magazines.

Roy himself was my age, forty-nine, heavyset, with an easygoing manner, and was living a life many people would envy. He was a specimen of that dying breed, a man of leisure, spending his days crabbing and fishing, with breaks for occasional strolls along the deserted beach. During the wet season, when he spent considerable time indoors, Roy took the opportunity to catch up on his reading. "Anything I can get me hands on, but I like westerns the best," he said.

For all practical purposes Roy had retired: He'd never again have to work for a living unless he wanted to, a desire that by his own account, he was highly unlikely to experience. For a while he had driven a bus in Sydney and roadtrains across Queensland and the Northern Territory, but those days were now behind him. Roy's good fortune had begun when he was a barramundi fisherman. While camping on the beach nearby he met Paul Zlotskowski, who, since he needed someone to look after Wentworth by the Sea, invited Roy to stay there. After he'd been down at Wentworth for a few months, it occurred to Roy that he needed some looking after himself. Shortly thereafter, Julie, who was governess at the Wollogorang homestead, left her position and joined him at the outpost.

For the past several years they'd lived at Wentworth, leasing the property from Paul for a dollar annually. Roy paid that, and any other expenses, out of the welfare money mailed to him by the government every two weeks. He had no qualms about accepting public assistance, for as he was quick to point out, all the aborigines and Torres Strait Islanders were on the dole, too.

" 'Ave some mud crabs. I caught 'em fresh this mornin'," said Roy, taking a big pot full of the huge crustaceans out of the refrigerator and placing it on the table in front of the four of us. "I always 'ave one with me smoko."

"Do you ever catch barramundi here?" asked Dave, tearing a claw off his crab and cracking it with his teeth.

"Once in a while," replied Roy. "But I like me steak an' crabs a lot better."

"What do you do besides crabbing and eating?" asked Dave, as diligently as if he were interviewing for a job as our host's assistant.

"There's always somthin'," Roy assured him. "Ya just don't sit around an' do nothin'. The windmill might need fixin' or the generator's out, or I'm workin' on me Toyota. When I'm not doin' that, there's always a bit a' gardenin'."

"Life ever get boring for you out here?" Dave persisted, while launching an all-out attack on the crab's soft underbelly.

"Borin' is livin' in a city where ya walk ta work. After work it's walk ta the pub, an' then ya gutta walk home again. Ya don't hafta do all that walkin' out here."

"You could get a car and save all that walking," the Bushranger suggested.

"But how would I get around the workin'?" asked Roy, who explained that although his nearest neighbor was Paul, over sixty miles away, he didn't feel isolated. Wentworth's airstrip was only half a mile from the homestead, and when they'd needed a doctor for the baby a few months back, he'd arrived in less than three hours.

"It gets bloody hot up at the main homestead," said Roy, commenting on the cool breeze blowing in from the Gulf, as we stepped out onto the veranda for coffee. "Wouldn' live up there for anythin'. Dusty an' dirty an' the bloody flies 'id drive ya mad. But it's like this all the time down here. I've never seen a day since I've been 'ere, when we don't have the breeze off the Gulf.

"I'll never leave 'ere. Never. Where else could I live like this? Never 'ave to work. Paul told me I can stay for the rest a' me life, an' that suits me just fine."

By the time we had finished our coffee it was almost midafternoon, and time to move on if we hoped to find a good campsite. As we were saying good-bye Roy asked, "Would ya happen ta have any Louis L'Amour books with ya? I'm just about finished with *The Man from Skibbereen*, an' I don' know when the new ones 'ill get here from Cairns."

We didn't have any, but Phil, who offered to send Roy some of his own works, wanted to know why a beachcomber was reading the formula westerns of someone like L'Amour.

"Oh, I'm crazy about his heroes," said Roy. "Country people with good old-fashioned values. Ya just can't find that anymore."

10

When we reached the beach Dave stopped the Toyota, and while he and the Bushranger let air out of the tires to facilitate traveling through the sand, Phil and I walked out toward the water. After long weeks of passing through so much desiccated country, I couldn't resist the urge to walk barefoot in the sea. The tide was out, exposing a wide stretch of seemingly endless white beach, along which only a few shore birds raced, stopping occasionally to probe the sand. We walked toward them, picking up small cone shells as we went. I had expected to come across the dense barrier of mangroves that had prevented Burke and Wills from reaching the Gulf, but recalled that the explorers had been much farther east—the only vegetation at the head of the dunes was a few stands of sea oats and the tall, slender casuarinas.

A few hundred yards down the beach Dave and the Bushranger picked us up in the Toyota, and we drove west along the hard-packed sand at the water's edge until we came to the mouth of a dry creek, which looked like an ideal place to pitch camp. The creek had carved through a dune to reach the Gulf, and both sides of the cut were shaded by tall Australian pines.

Shaded by the trees and cooled by gentle sea breezes, it seemed an ideal spot, but Dave insisted on moving on. Determined to catch barramundi, he wanted to find a river that flowed into the Gulf. Now that our journey was nearing its end, barramundi had become an obsession with him, and whenever the opportunity presented itself, he would jump out of the Toyota and rush to the bank of some muddy creek to make cast after futile cast.

About ten miles farther along the shore we came to Tully Inlet, where Camel and Settlement creeks joined and emptied into the Gulf. The juncture formed only a narrow inlet, and it was possible to walk across its mouth at low tide. The moment the Toyota stopped Dave reached for his rod and hand gaff, and, racing down to the water to begin casting, left us to set up camp.

"He's at it again," observed Phil, amusedly.

"He should be pitied rather than scorned," I said. "He's invented a new form of masochism."

"It's nothing serious," protested the Bushranger. "I've seen this before. He's just gone troppo. But if he doesn't catch a barra, there's no magazine story, is there?"

"No worries," I replied. "He's going to write about crocodiles, too, without ever having seen one, so a minor detail like catching a fish isn't going to trouble him."

A few hundred yards up the inlet we came to a grove shaded by sea hibiscus, referred to by the Bushranger as Leichardt trees. It was late afternoon, and the flowers, which bloomed a brilliant yellow in the morning, had already turned blood red and were dropping from their branches onto the white sand. The grove had been used in the past as a camp by a commercial fisherman, and traces of his presence were still there: torn monofilament net, a few empty forty-four-gallon fuel drums, and even a low stone fireplace with a pile of driftwood beside it.

While Dave continued working his way up the inlet, we pitched our tents on the sand under the sea hibiscus trees and after building a fire, boiled the billy. As we were drinking a "cuppa," the Bushranger noticed some wild boar tracks on the camp's perimeter, and Phil set out to follow them.

"Phil's a famous tracker back in the States," I said to the Bushranger, as Phil disappeared in the bush. "He developed that skill as a kid growing up in Chicago."

"Let's add a bit of excitement to his life," suggested the Bushranger. Fetching his rifle from the Toyota, he aimed it in the air and squeezed off four or five shots.

Dave appeared at the campsite first, hoping, perhaps, that we were shooting at barramundi prowling in the bush, since there clearly weren't any in the water. Moments later Phil, the great white hunter, dashed back into the clearing.

"What's goin' on?" he asked, prepared, if necessary, to take command of the situation.

"Pigs," replied the Bushranger, with a grave look on his face. "Four of 'em came right inta camp."

"Yeah, they'll come out of the thicket around dusk for a look around," said Phil, who was as knowledgeable about wild boars as Dave was about crocodiles. "Did you get any of 'em?"

"I'm not sure, my eyesight isn't what it used to be," replied the Bushranger. "But you'd have gotten them for sure."

"I'll get another chance later," predicted Phil, obviously pleased by the Bushranger's confidence in his marksmanship.

During a meal of steaks and beans we watched a full moon ascend, bright and luminous; it appeared to have surfaced from the depths of the Gulf. Glittering off the dark water, it bathed the graceful casuarinas along shore and the white sand in a silvery light. After dinner, the three of us surrendered to the inevitable and joined Dave in casting for barramundi. The inlet was alive with fish, and we could hear them slapping on the water's surface. But they were too small to be barra, and none of them was taking the bait.

After a while we gave it up, and when Phil and the Bushranger returned to camp, I remained on the beach, while Dave fished his way down along the shore, stopping every few yards to make another cast. As I sat there on the sand watching a vagrant cloud slip across the face of the moon, I felt a contentment such as this strange country had never before given me. Perhaps we had, after all, on our last night in the bush, allowed ourselves to be sung to the land, to its splendid purity, to its uncompromising wildness; to its sheer and ineffable size and expanse. For all the dust we endured, for all the endless miles of monotony, we'd been left with a respect for this unforgiving and exacting wilderness. No, we might never share the Bushranger's unqualified love for those forbidding red distances and day upon day of withering sunlight, but we'd come to find in Australia, and especially in its people, something like the last gasp of the spirit of tenacity, and of adventure. If the outback was intimidating, it was also exhilarating; if it tried our patience and frayed our nerves, confronting its challenge had proven to be worth the effort.

Dave's
Epilogue

In perfect silence the journey through the bush is made,—
fifteen miles to some water-hole, where breakfast is eaten;
fifteen on to another water-hole, where brandy and water is
consumed; fifteen again to more water, and dinner; and then
again fifteen, till the place is reached at which the night-fire is
made and the blankets are stretched upon the ground. In such
a journey, everything depends on one's companion.

—Anthony Trollope (1873)

When we returned to Cairns, Jack booked a seat on the first Qantas
flight bound for San Francisco and went back to the States, stopping
barely long enough for a hot shower and a good dinner at the Trade-
winds Hotel, a favorite hangout of the international marlin fishing
fraternity that would be descending on the town in a few weeks' time.
Enough of this Joshua Slocum adventure nonsense for him; after all
those months away from Elaine, he just wanted to get home. "It's time
to hit the track, Jack," he quipped, echoing the bush wisdom of the
Eye-talian cowboy. But his cavalier manner failed to conceal what I
sensed was a certain wistfulness, a reluctance to see the trip end. He
had developed a strong feeling of kinship with many of the wonderful
characters we had met in Australia, not least of all Peter Eaton, and
in quitting the country, he'd be leaving all that behind.

Caputo also threw in the towel. Phil had been toying with the idea of heading up to Papua New Guinea on his own after his two-month stint with us was over, but when the time came for the farewells, he decided to go back on the same plane with Jack instead. "I guess I've swallowed enough dust for a while," he said by way of explanation, as I saw the two of them off at the airport on the afternoon of their departure. But I suspect that the real reason behind his change of plans had less to do with bulldust than with Trollope's above-quoted observation that especially in the bush, companionship is everything.

In a way, I was just as eager to get back to the States as they were, but I chose to stay on in Australia for a few weeks more. Although I had never overcome my profound aversion to the bush—a reaction I first experienced in Kalgoorlie when Jack and I stood on the eastern edge of town, as if on the brink of some precipice, staring out over the empty Nullarbor—I felt very much at home among Australians, and I couldn't bring myself to leave the country quite so abruptly. If the trip had to end, it was better to let it wind down slowly, and so I flew back to Sydney, where the journey had begun many months before.

It was the end of August and the weather was damp and wintry. Cold, sullen clouds, heavy with precipitation, swept in off the ocean. Back in January, when Jack and I had first arrived in Sydney, the harbor had been a summer playground, alive with small pleasure craft; now it was deserted by all but a few intrepid sailboats and the regular fleet of tugs and double-decker ferries, which went about their business with a sort of grim determination. Intermittent squalls soaked the city in a chilly rain and churned up whitecaps on the dark, suddenly uninviting water of the harbor. It must have been this kind of weather that induced D. H. Lawrence to describe Sydney as the "London of the Southern Hemisphere . . . a [poor] substitute for the real thing."

But to me, Sydney remained a welcome port in any kind of weather. Having spent the better part of a year beyond the Black Stump, I was glad to be back amidst the hubbub of a real city. Australia was, after all, a nation of city dwellers whose opinion of the bush, if their life-style was any indication, seemed to correspond with mine. (Hadn't even Crocodile Dundee ultimately abandoned the place for New York? And he'd been sharing a swag with Linda Kozlowski!)

I spent most of my time in Sydney rummaging through the shelves of the secondhand bookstores on Bathurst Street or at the Mitchell Library, reading as much as I could on how others had reacted to the Australian bush. I guess I needed some sort of confirmation for my own negative feelings, which in all my travels I had never before experienced.

"The grim monotony of the landscape was a recurrent source of demoralization," observed the author of one abstruse land-use study of Australia's semiarid regions. "Whereas the artists could by skilful use of their imagination, conjure up a mythical landscape possessed of beauty by European standards, the writers had a more difficult task. They were supposedly dealing with the facts, and were thus forced back on description by analogy."

But the Australian bush was analogous to nothing these writers had ever known. Though flooded with sunshine, it remained stern and funereal, a "visual wilderness" destitute of life, a "ghostly blank" as silent as any place on earth. The bush towns inspired (in Trollope's words) "a feeling of melancholy sadness in the mind of a stranger."

Daisy Bates, the prim little society lady who lived most of her adult years in the bush (forsaking her husband and young son for a life among her "aboriginal friends"), purported to find the landscape beautiful. "One must love solitude for its own sake," she wrote in her diary, "to taste in its fullness the perfect happiness that these beautiful open spaces give." But in her darker moods even she described the bush as having the "fascination of ugliness . . . as there is in certain types of manhood," and she admitted that her attraction to it stemmed from a peculiar "vein of mysticism in the Celtic character." Jack might understand that sort of thing, but I was looking for a more objective assessment.

The literature confirmed that I was not alone in my reaction, that others, too, had perceived in the bush a sense of overwhelming desolation found nowhere else in the world. Curiously, though, the books said little of the people who chose to live there, and it was precisely the people that made the bush so memorable. I found myself thinking of Binnie Priestley, a little kid we met in a remote part of Queensland, who most poignantly symbolized those two aspects of the bush— unforgettable people in an unforgiving land.

"Your chili looks like shit and shampoo," little Binnie had quipped as he and his older brother helped us set up camp one evening near the homestead at Claraville, their father's run-down cattle station, where just a few months earlier Binnie had lost his baby sister—the family's only daughter—in a tragic gunshot accident. Though only eight years old, Binnie was already as self-sufficient as any adult. But despite his obvious toughness, he bubbled over with warmth and kindness.

"You wouldn't speak like that to your mother, would you?" the Bushranger chided. Though the Bushranger himself professed to love the bush, he admitted that one had to be a bit of a masochist to live there.

"Sure I would," Binnie replied. "Everybody takes a kiddin' out here."

What was so striking about the folks who lived in the Australian bush was not simply that they perservered under such pitiless conditions, which a cynic might dismiss as pure lunacy, but that they approached their lives with such resilience and good cheer. If they were not necessarily the world's most rugged individualists, as we Americans, nostalgic for our own lost pioneering past, have come to believe, they represented something even more appealing, and maybe even more important—mateship and humor. That, perhaps, was the most valuable lesson the bush could teach.

Jack's
Epilogue

Phil and I had planned to spend some time lounging around Cairns before leaving Australia, but on our return to town we happened to pass the airport. The sight of a jet beginning its ascent out toward the Coral Sea was simply too alluring, and prompted us to book the soonest flight back to the States. Seeing tropical Cairns again, with its tall palm trees and old Queenslander houses, had reminded us both of Key West, and we realized how eager we were to go home. The following evening we flew to San Francisco by way of Honolulu, and the next day we were back in Florida.

It didn't take long to reacclimate to Key West, though I had almost forgotten what it was like to sleep in a bed, and my first week home I awoke one night completely disoriented, believing I was still in the bush, afraid to get up to boil the billy lest I step on a snake. Back in his own familiar surroundings, Dave had little difficulty in readjusting to life in New York, though, even now, he continues to pore through volumes of books in his attempt to discover rational explanations that will help him understand his intense aversion for the bush. He has managed to take some comfort in the fact that he is not the first person to have felt such antipathy, and he can count among that company the likes of D. H. Lawrence.

I realized as soon as the Qantas 747 first set us down in Sydney and men in white uniforms and gas masks came through the plane spraying for insects that Australia would bear little resemblance to the idyllic land I'd imagined as a fanciful boy. Nor, it turned out, was it the place to recapture my youth. That ephemeral interval had slipped away from me back in Boston, many years earlier. I've succeeded in preserving a few illusions from that span of my life and I hope to continue to do so, taking my own comfort from what Joseph Conrad wrote in *Youth:* "Our weary eyes looking still, looking always, looking anxiously for something out of life, that while it is expected is already gone—has passed unseen, in a sigh, in a flash—together with the youth, with the strength, with the romance of illusions."

Many of my illusions were, however, betrayed by the bush, that endlessly daunting proving ground, which, I reminded myself, has through the course of history shattered more than a few romantic notions. Yet even after only a few weeks on the road it became clear to us that geography wasn't really the point. Our trip, we realized, had proved to be less a navigation of maps of the country than of maps of the spirit. Whether they infuriated or charmed us, whether they inspired us with their courage or annoyed us with their obstinacy, the Australians we met in the bush were people of character, and almost extravagantly so. Their motives for choosing to live in so antagonistic an environment may have ranged from entrepreneurial schemes that could only be described as fantastic, to a genuine desire for an extreme sort of solitude, but whatever had led them there, they all seemed to arrive in the wilderness with adventurous determination— a stick-to-itiveness that I, with my New England soul still intact, couldn't help but admire. Before we had set out on our journey a well-known wildlife conservationist back in the States, who had himself visited Australia, had assured us that the country's pioneering spirit had long since died, and that new frontiers no longer existed. Happily, he was mistaken on both counts.

It was September and sultry when I returned home to Key West, the middle of the hurricane season. In the late afternoon heavy black clouds swollen with rain would move in across Florida Bay from the Everglades, and from a terrace overlooking the sea, I'd listen to the shrill cacophony of the cicadas until crashing thunder and pelting rain silenced them. Those violent summer squalls brought back memories of Cape York, Somerset, and Frank Jardine.

But the season passed, and blustery blue northers pushed down from Canada sweeping across the continent, their cold winter winds churning up Florida Bay and turning it chalky-white. The air had a penetrating chill to it just as it had back in the bush on those nights when we'd boiled the billy and hovered around our campfire trying to get warm.

It's when I recall those times that I get to feeling restless, that the vagabond in me longs to be back on open road. I often find myself thinking about Guy Teede, Tom Wardle, Ces Piesse, Joe and Cathy Gelati, Jenny Lott, and some of the others we'd come to know. From my comfortable porch overlooking the Atlantic some twelve thousand miles away, their lives began to take on some of that romance I'd so longed for in our travels. More than the satisfaction of having roughed it, more than the accomplishment of having made a trip by jeep that, as I look at a map now, seems foolhardy, to say the least, I'd been blessed with the acquaintance of those exceptional individuals who'd stepped so far out of the ordinary.

Early in the spring I got a long letter from the Bushranger. He'd just returned to Innisfail after making another trip to the Gulf of Carpentaria and had passed through some of the country we'd traveled through together. He wrote wistfully about our journey and the time he'd spent with us. We'd been mates, the four of us, who shared much in common, and he said he'd never forget that.

Neither will I, Bushranger.